Values and Perceptions
of the Islamic and
Middle Eastern Publics

Values and Perceptions of the Islamic and Middle Eastern Publics

Edited by
Mansoor Moaddel

palgrave
macmillan

First published in hardcover in 2007 by PALGRAVE MACMILLAN® in the United States—a division of St. Martin's Press LLC, 175 Fifth Avenue, New York, NY 10010.

Where this book is distributed in the UK, Europe and the rest of the world, this is by Palgrave Macmillan, a division of Macmillan Publishers Limited, registered in England, company number 785998, of Houndmills, Basingstoke, Hampshire RG21 6XS.

Palgrave Macmillan is the global academic imprint of the above companies and has companies and representatives throughout the world.

Palgrave® and Macmillan® are registered trademarks in the United States, the United Kingdom, Europe and other countries.

ISBN: 978–0–230–62198–5

Library of Congress Cataloging-in-Publication Data

Values and perceptions of the Islamic and Middle Eastern publics / edited by Mansoor Moaddel.
    p. cm.
Includes bibliographical references and index.
ISBN 1–4039–7527–2 (alk. paper)
    1. Arab countries—Social conditions—20th century. 2. Arab countries—Social conditions—21st century. 3. Social values—Arab countries. I. Moaddel, Mansoor.

HN766.Z9M683 2007
06.0917_67—dc23   2006049325

A catalogue record of the book is available from the British Library.

Design by Newgen Imaging Systems (P) Ltd., Chennai, India.

First PALGRAVE MACMILLAN paperback edition: January 2010

10 9 8 7 6 5 4 3 2 1

Printed in the United States of America.

Transferred to Digital Printing in 2009.

For Armin, Marjan, Nilufar, and Payvand

CONTENTS

LIST OF FIGURES

x

List of Figures

LIST OF TABLES

PREFACE

The creation, organization, and production of the materials brought together in this edited volume have been a collective endeavor. An international network of researchers collaborated in coordinating the collection of a set of data that are comparable across societies. I would like to thank all of them, particularly those who led the field work in Islamic/Middle Eastern countries, including, in alphabetical order, Abdel-Hamid Abdel-Latif (Egypt); Mohamed Abidi, (Algeria); Q.K. Ahmad (Bangladesh); Kaka Akacem (Algeria); Fares al Braizat (Jordan); Taqhi Azadarmaki (Iran); Abdellah Bedaida (Algeria); Munqeth Daghir (Iraq); Mohamed Dahami (Societe D'etudes De Realisations De Consultants, Morocco); Yilmaz Esmer (Turkey); Mustafa Hamarneh (Jordan); Nadra Muhammed Hosen (Indonesia); Ahmed Houiti (Algeria); Temirlan Tilekovich Moldogaziev (Kyrgyz Republic); Tony Proudian (Pan Arab Research Center, Saudi Arabia); Tony Sabbagh (Jordan); Rahmat Sedigh (Iran); and Farooq Tanweer (Pakistan).

The data collection would not have been possible without the generous financial support from foundations and institutions. Specially, I would like to thank the National Science Foundation, the Ford Foundation, Rockefeller Foundation, Bank of Sweden Tercentenary Foundation, the World Values Survey Association, the University of Michigan, and Eastern Michigan University.

Many thanks also to the publishers who gave us permission to reprint some of the chapters that first appeared in their journals; *American Sociological Review* (for Davis and Robinson's chapter, April 2006), *Interdisciplinary Journal for Research on Religion* (for Moaddel and Latif's chapter, 2006), *International Journal of Comparative Sociology* (for Tessler's chapter, Spring 2003), *International Journal of Middle East Studies* (for Moaddel's chapter, February 2005), and *Perspectives on Politics* (for Inglehart, Moaddel, and Tessler's chapter, September 2006).

I would also like to thank the staff of the Family and Demography Program at the Center for Population Studies and Center Director Arland Thornton for all their support to create an environment that is friendly, collegial, and conducive to research. Many thanks also to the people at Palgrave who worked so diligently on this volume, in particular to Joanna Mericle, Editorial Assistant; Elizabeth Sabo, Production Associate; Sumathi Ellappan, Copy Editor; and to Farideh Koohi-Kamali, for generously sharing her nice picture of the Sheikh Lotfallah Mosque in Meidan-e-Shah, Isfahan, Iran for the cover page.

My greatest owe of gratitude goes to Julie de Jong for her hard and diligent work on many detailed and tiresome procedures involved in organizing the chapters, tables, and figures; contacting the contributors; and responding to queries. Her professional assistance not only ensured the timely completion of this volume but enhanced the quality of the final product as well.

I would like to dedicate this book to my wife, Marjan, and our three children, Armin, Nilufar, and Payvand.

LIST OF CONTRIBUTORS

Abdul-Latif, Abdul-Hamid is Affiliate Professor of Sociology at American University in Cairo, Egypt. He received his Ph.D. in Sociology from the Ohio State University in 1970, and then received a postdoctoral training in Population Sciences at Harvard University in 1974. He has held academic posts at several Universities since 1970 in the United States, Canada, and Egypt. His research interests include intergenerational value shifts, gender inequality, and philanthropic behavior. He has several publications in the fields of demography, comparative urban ecology, research methodology, and computer applications in the Social Sciences. Abdul-Latif is also collaborating with Mansoor Moaddel, Stuart Karabenick, and Arland Thornton on a comparative project on "Youth, Emotional Energy, and Political Violence: The Cases of Egypt and Saudi Arabia."

Ajrouch, Kristine is Associate Professor of Sociology at Eastern Michigan University. She earned a Ph.D. in Sociology from Wayne State University in 1997, and then received postdoctoral training in the field of aging through the School of Social Work at the University of Michigan. Recently awarded a grant from the National Institute of Aging, Ajrouch conducted a pilot study on the topic of social relations and health among aging Arab Americans. Her research interests include health, cross-cultural comparisons, social relations, immigration, gender, and identity.

Davis, Nancy J. is Professor of Sociology and Chair of the Department of Sociology and Anthropology at DePauw University. She is continuing work with Robert Robinson on the connections between moral cosmology and social action in the Muslim Brotherhood, Comunione e Liberazione, Shas and the Salvation Army, as well as on the effect of moral cosmology on political activism among Muslims in Muslim-majority nations. She recently published an article on teaching about sexuality, culture, and power for *Teaching Sociology*, where she is also on the editorial board.

Díez-Nicolás, Juan is Professor of Sociology, Complutense University of Madrid, and President of *Analisis Sociológicos Económicos y Políticos* (ASEP). He is also a member of the European Academy of Sciences and Letters, of the Executive Committee of the World Values Survey Association, of the Planning Committee of *Comparative Study of Electoral Systems* (CSES), and a member of other research groups such as the *International Social Survey Programme* (ISSP), *Comparative Survey Design and Implementation* (CSDI), *Network of Economic and Social Science Infrastructures in Europe* (NESSIE) and others. His latest publications are El Dilema de la Supervivencia (*The Survival Dilemma*, Madrid: Obra Social Caja Madrid, 2004); Las Dos Caras de la Inmigración (*The Two Faces of Immigration*, Madrid: Ministerio de Trabajo y Asuntos Sociales, 2005); Two Contradictory Hypotheses on Globalization: Societal Convergence or Civilization Differentiation and Clash," in R. Inglehart (ed.), *Human Values and Social Change* (Leiden: Brill, 2003); and "Spaniards' Long March towards Europe," in S. Royo and P. Ch. Manuel (eds.), *Spain and Portugal in the European Union: The First Fifteen Years* (London: Frank Cass & Co.Ltd., 2003).

Heeringa, Steven G. is a Research Scientist in the Survey Methodology Program, the Director of the Statistical and Research Design Group in the Survey Research Center, and the Director of the Summer Institute in Survey Research Techniques at the Institute for Social Research. He has over 25 years of statistical sampling experience directing the development of the SRC National Sample design, as well as sample designs for SRC's major longitudinal and cross-sectional survey programs. During this period he has been actively involved in research and publication on sample design methods and procedures such as weighting, variance estimation, and the imputation of missing data that are required in the analysis of sample survey data. He has been a teacher of survey sampling methods to United States and international students and has served as a sample design consultant to a wide variety of international research programs based in countries such as Russia, the Ukraine, Uzbekistan, Kazakhstan, India, Nepal, China, Egypt, Iran, and Chile.

Inglehart, Ronald is Professor of Political Science and Program Director at the Institute for Social Research at the University of Michigan. He helped found the Euro-Barometer surveys and directs the World Values Surveys. His research deals with changing belief systems and their impact on social and political change. His most recent books are *Modernization and Postmodernization: Cultural, Economic and Political Change in 43 Societies* (Princeton: Princeton University Press, 1997); and (with Pippa Norris) *Rising Tide: Gender Equality in Global Perspective* (Cambridge: Cambridge University Press, 2003); and (with Pippa Norris) *Sacred and Secular: the Secularization Thesis Revisited* (Cambridge: Cambridge University Press, 2004); and (with Christian Welzel) *Modernization, Cultural Change and Democracy: The Human Development Sequence* (Cambridge: Cambridge University Press, 2005). He also edited *Mass Values and Social Change: Findings from the Values Surveys* (Leiden: Brill Publishers, 2003) and *Human Beliefs and Values: A Cross-Cultural Sourcebook Based on the 1999–2001 Values Surveys* (Mexico City: Siglo XXI, 2004). Author of almost 200 publications, he has been a Visiting Professor or visiting scholar in France, Germany, the Netherlands, Switzerland, Japan, South Korea, Taiwan, Brazil, and Nigeria and has served as a consultant to the U.S. State Department and the European Union.

Moaddel, Mansoor is Professor of Sociology at Eastern Michigan University and Research Affiliate at Population Studies Center, Institute for Social Research, the University of Michigan. Moaddel has pursued two lines of research. One is on the determinants of ideological production in the Islamic world, where he has analyzed Islamic modernism in India, Egypt, and Iran in the late nineteenth and early twentieth centuries; liberal nationalism in Egypt and Iran and Arabism and Arab nationalism in Syria in the first half of the twentieth century; and Islamic fundamentalism in Algeria, Egypt, Iran, Jordan, and Syria in the second half of the twentieth century. A major outcome of this study is *Islamic Modernism, Nationalism, and Fundamentalism: Episode and Discourse* (Chicago: University of Chicago Press, 2005). The other is on comparative values surveys in Islamic countries. He has carried out values surveys in Egypt, Iran, Iraq, Jordan, Morocco, and Saudi Arabia. Moaddel has made presentations on Capitol Hill, organized workshops/conferences on the study of values in Jordan, Iran, and Egypt, and served on the advisory panel for the NSF-sociology program and the United States Institute of Peace. Currently, he is working on a project on "Youth, Emotional Energy, and Political Violence: the Cases of Egypt and Saudi Arabia," surveying the value orientation of youth in these countries. Moaddel is the recipient of the 2002 Best Article Award from the Sociology of Religion Section of the American Sociological Association for "Conditions for Ideological Production: The Origins of Islamic Modernism in India, Egypt, and Iran," *Theory and Society* 30(5) (2001): 669–731.

Pettersson, Thorleif is Professor of Sociology at Uppsala University. He has been involved in the European Values Study (EVS) and the WVS, and he is member of the Executive Committee of the latter. He is also a member of the area group for research in Culture, Security, and Social Sustainability at the Bank of Sweden Tercentenary Foundation, and he is Chair at the Centre for Multiethnic Research, Uppsala University. He has previously been Researcher at the Stockholm Institute for the Sociology of Religion, the Institute for Future Studies, Stockholm, Sweden, the Swedish Council for Research in Humanities and Social Sciences (HSFR), and research fellow at the Swedish Collegium for Advanced Study in the Social Sciences (SCASSS), Uppsala, Sweden. His research has focused on cultural change and secularization, and also on comparative studies on the role of religious organizations in contemporary society. He has authored several studies in international publications on these topics.

Puranen, Bi is Secretary General of the WVS and Research Director at the Swedish survey and Research Institute Bikupan. She is a doctor in economic history, Professor of communication strategies in Sophia Antipolis, France and Associate Professor at the University of Stockholm Sweden. Her main field is to conduct change-oriented research on authorities and organizations, for further information, see: www.bikupan.se and bi@bikupan.se.

Robinson, Robert V. is Chancellor's Professor and Chair of the Department of Sociology at Indiana University. He recently completed studies of the effect of moral cosmology on Americans' sense of community (coauthored with Robyn Ryle in *City & Community* 5(1) (2006): 53–69) and values for children (coauthored with Brian Starks in *Social Forces* 84(1) (2005): 343–59). He is continuing work with Nancy Davis on religiously orthodox communitarian movements in Egypt, Italy, Israel, and the United States, and on moral cosmology and political activism among Muslims.

Tessler, Mark is Samuel J. Eldersveld Collegiate Professor in the Department of Political Science at the University of Michigan, where he is also Vice Provost for International Affairs and Director of the International Institute. He is former director of the Center for Political Studies of the Institute for Social Research. Professor Tessler has collaborated extensively with researchers in the Arab world, directing or participating in surveys in Algeria, Tunisia, Egypt, Palestine, Jordan, Kuwait, Oman, and the United Arab Emirates. He directed the WVS in Algeria in 2002. His publications analyzing survey data from the Middle

East, including Israel, have appeared in World Politics, Comparative Politics, Journal of Conflict Resolution, International Studies Quarterly, and Public Opinion Quarterly, among others. He is also the senior author of *The Evaluation and Application of Survey Research in the Arab World* (Boulder: Westview Press, 1987). In addition, Professor Tessler has directed survey research training and capacity building programs or consulted on survey research in nine different Arab countries, organizing and directing workshops both in the Middle East and at the University of Michigan. He has also served as a consultant for U.S. and international agencies and a number of universities and research centers in the Arab world.

Widenfalk, Olof is a statistical analyst at Bikupan. He is a doctor in environments and has a master in environments and statistics.

CHAPTER 1

Introduction: Theoretical and Methodological Issues in the Study of Values

MANSOOR MOADDEL

Introduction

The chapters in this volume are studies based on the findings from the values surveys that were carried out, many for the first time, in Islamic countries between 2000 and 2004, as part of the fourth wave of the World Values Survey (WVS). One of the objectives of these surveys was to furnish the requisite infrastructure for the advancement of the social-scientific knowledge of the causes and consequences of mass-level belief systems, value orientations, and attitudes of the Islamic publics.

These surveys began as a National Science Foundation (NSF)-sponsored collaborative pilot project between investigators from the United States, Egypt, Iran, and Jordan. In the pilot project, the investigators collectively developed and tested a questionnaire, trying to capture the features of values and attitudes that were thought to be specific to the publics from Islamic countries. The questionnaire also replicated key batteries from the WVS questionnaire in order to permit comparisons between these countries and the data available from more than 80 societies covered by the WVS. In order to reach consensus on a common pilot survey questionnaire for all three countries, a workshop was held at the Center for Strategic Studies at the University of Jordan in July 1999. In an intensive three-day workshop, the participants in the study carefully evaluated every item of the preliminary questionnaire in terms of its relationship to the conceptual framework of the study, the effectiveness in capturing the fundamental values of the publics in each of these countries, and the clarity of question wording.

The pilot project was completed in 1999, providing a three-nation sample of 633 respondents. A grant from the Rockefeller Foundation made a second meeting possible, this time at the University of Tehran, Iran, in July 2000. In Tehran, the group evaluated all items of the questionnaire in light of the pilot survey findings and the field experiences in each country. The result was a shortened questionnaire and a sampling frame for each of the countries. Through financial support from the NSF, the Ford Foundation, and Bank of Sweden Tercentenary Foundation, and in collaboration with overseas colleagues, full-scale surveys of nationally representative samples of 3,000 Egyptians, 1,200 Jordanians, and 2,500 Iranians were carried out in 2000–01. Using a similar questionnaire and supported by a grant from Spain's Telefónica Foundation in Morocco (MEDITEL), Juan Díez-Nicolás at Complutense University, Madrid, Spain, carried out a survey in Morocco in summer in 2001.

Since the surveys in Egypt, Iran, and Jordon were completed before the terrorist event of September 11, 2001, the NSF, through its Small Grants for Exploratory Research Program, provided financial support to explore the impact of this horrific event on the worldviews of the Islamic publics in these countries. The NSF also provided financial support for the values survey in Algeria and Pakistan in 2001, for a similar survey in Saudi Arabia in 2003, and for two surveys in Iraq in 2004 and 2006.

Currently, the following Islamic countries are included in the WVS: Albania, Algeria, Azerbaijan, Bangladesh, Egypt, Indonesia, Iraq, Iran, Jordan, Kyrgyzstan, Morocco, Pakistan, Saudi Arabia, and Turkey.

The Study of Islamic Societies and

Contributions to the Social Sciences

There has been, historically, a disturbing disconnect between the disciplines focusing on Islamic societies and the mainstream disciplines of Western social sciences. On the one hand, the study of Islamic culture has been dominated by reductive and text-based approaches of Islamicists or by single-country studies. On the other hand, the social sciences, and American sociology in particular, have been primarily preoccupied with

INTRODUCTION 3

the study of Western European and North American societies. When less developed countries, including Islamic countries, became the subject of analysis, they were often treated in a derivative manner, either as an instance of a traditional society in transition, whose future was the development of the modern social institutions speculated to be similar in nature to those of the West, or as part of the peripharalized zone of the world capitalist economy whose dominant economic, political, and cultural institutions were reorganized according to the external dictates emanating from the core economies that make up the advanced industrial countries. There has been very little effort to study these societies for their own sake in order to draw the general insights necessary for building better and more effective social institutions that meet the needs of their growing population.

The parochialism of Western academic scholarship notwithstanding, the development of the social sciences in Islamic countries was further hampered by the persistence and resourcefulness of political authoritarianism. The rise of secular ideological states in these countries where the ruling elites derived their policies from certain ideological blueprints—Europe-centered secularism, Arab nationalism, Arab socialism, territorial nationalism, or Islamic fundamentalism—placed little emphasis on the significance of the social sciences for the construction of a modern society. Where ideology became the governing principle of state action, the necessity and the need for verifiable knowledge of human social relationships upon which to base policies were naturally never understood. As a result, the civil society of the Islamic Middle East never developed social institutions that were both modern and autonomous to empower its public, nor was there adequate scientific knowledge to construct such institutions effectively.

In the past several years, however, there has been a growing realization of the need to understand the specificity of Islamic culture and the social dynamics underpinning such diverse processes as the Islamic publics' growing support for democracy as an ideal form of government, on the one hand, and the rise of religious extremism and political violence, on the other. The NSF and the WVS Association have been among the major scientific institutions that are spearheading the move to expand social-scientific studies of Islamic countries. In addition to its generous support for the values surveys of Islamic countries, the NSF also funded a conference on the Muslims' worldviews in Cairo in 2003 and another conference on globalization and global tensions that focused on Islamic countries, in Istanbul in 2004. These welcome developments have provided the necessary data and a forum for social scientists to discuss and debate pertinent theoretical and methodological issues in the study of Islamic societies, and at one remove, human societies in general. Fortunately, the focus of these debates is not just whether Islamic and Middle Eastern societies are traditional or on the extent of their cultural distance from modernity. It is rather to explain how people from Islamic countries understand and address the significant religious, gender, economic, and political issues they face, how they process information, and the causes and consequences of their fundamental beliefs. This knowledge is not only important for the development of the social sciences, but for the construction of a prosperous, democratic, and free society as well.

Conceptual and Methodological

Issues in the Study of Values

What is the nature of the values and beliefs of the citizens of Islamic countries? To what extent are these values organized in their minds? Are these citizens aware of the inconsistencies or conflicts among their values? How do we conceptualize the connections between core values and people's attitudes toward significant issues? Do ordinary people understand the meaning of such concepts as democracy, liberalism, fundamentalism, and conservatism as well as the differences between secular laws and the shari 'a? How do they gain understanding and knowledge about important sociopolitical and cultural issues facing their society? How does such knowledge shape their sociopolitical choices? What is their conception of a developed society and to what extent has developmental thinking shaped this conception?

To answer these questions, we need both survey data and adequate conceptual and theoretical frameworks that give us some idea about the organization of values, the relationship between values and attitudes, and the mechanism (e.g., framing) that makes this relationship possible, the knowledgeability of the public, and the kind of pathways people use in order to make themselves knowledgeable about the issues they face.

Fundamental Values and Attitudes

The Parsonian perspective considers that a cybernetic hierarchy characterizes the structure of belief system, where abstract and universal values of the cultural system shape the norms—the dos and don'ts of the social system—and the norms in turn govern the behavior of the occupants of social roles within a collectivity. These values are not static, however. Cultural change and the production of meaning in Parsons's view are portrayed as a diffusing process in which autonomous development in any or all of the subsystems of society produces social differentiation. The latter in turn leads to the emergence of a new set of problems that the old cultural pattern cannot address or resolve. A more general, rational, and systematic value pattern is thus necessary to provide the basis of social stability by cementing the emergent cleavages in society (See Parsons 1949: 563–78, 1951: 496–535, 1966: 20–27, 1969: 55–57, and 1971: 26–28. See also Sahlins and Service 1960: 28; and Service 1971: 25).

Except for some notable exceptions (e.g., Binder 1962; Safran 1961), there has been little application and assessment of the Parsonian model in the context of Islamic societies. There is, however, a remarkable consistency between this model and the view of the Islamicists (the so-called Orientalists), who have long dominated the field of Islamic studies. The Islamicists commonly hold that the sociopolitical institutions and the attitudes of the Islamic publics are principally shaped by the core teachings of the Islamic tradition on the individual, gender relations, and politics. From this view, it thus flows that economic underdevelopment, authoritarianism, and the persistence of patrimonial values are the consequences of this tradition (Lambton 1963; Lapidus 1992; Lewis 1968, 1993a, 1993b; Moaddel 2002). To some extent, there is support for both the general Parsonian perspective and the more particular and regional view of the Islamicists. There are values that are universally cherished by the citizens of Islamic countries. For example, an over-whelming majority of the Islamic publics (more than 95 percent) believes in God, heaven and hell, the existence of the soul, and life after death. They also strongly support family values and adherence to certain codes of conduct governing sexual relationships between men and women, although there are notable variations cross-nationally. Violations of these values certainly generate serious societal reactions.

However, the Islamicists' reading of Islam has been widely criticized for being overly text-based, reductive, and ahistorical. Furthermore, the traditional-modern dichotomy proposed by modernization theory fails to capture some of the key features of cultural change in Islamic countries. Generally, contrary to both Parsons and to the views of value change the flows from the legacy of the classical tradition in sociology reflected in the work of the trinity of social theory—Durkheim, Marx, and Weber—it may not be possible to establish a direct correspondence between the changes in values and the structural transformations of Islamic societies brought about as a result of economic development, dramatic demographic transitions, changes in class relations, group formation, and the development of various forms of modern state. Despite the impressive depth and breadth of such transformations in the modern period, no lasting consensus among the Islamic publics has been realized about the most fundamental principles of social organizations: the status of rational reasoning in rule-making, the relationship between religion and politics, the form of government, the relationship with the outside world, and the social status of women. Instead, since the nineteenth century, Islamic countries have experienced a succession of diverse cultural episodes, each characterized by the dominance of different ideological movements such as Islamic modernism, anticlerical secularism, liberal nationalism, Arab nationalism, Arab socialism, monarchy-centered nationalism, and Islamic fundamentalism (Moaddel 2005).

Framing and Attitude Formation

No major survey data are available for the period before the 1990s—and thus we are unable to assess how citizens of Islamic countries felt about major issues facing their societies during the cultural episodes when ideologies other than Islamic fundamentalism were the dominant (oppositional) discourses. Nonetheless, if we base our judgment on the expressions of the political leaders of the period, the demands of the sociopolitical movements flowing from these ideologies, and the kind of policies formulated and the social and political institutions that emerged, we may reasonably argue that, while citizens were probably as religious then as they are today, considerations (e.g., liberalism, secularism, nationalism, etc.) other than the traditional religious values had shaped their political discourses, attitudes, and choices.

These considerations, in the social-scientific jargon currently en vogue among social researchers, are called framing. We may propose that semantic description of the problems and issues, as well as the stereotypical image of an ideal social order, that is, framing, provided by these ideologies might have shaped the citizens' attitudes. While we do not know quite yet how framing shapes public attitudes in Islamic countries, empirical evidence in other contexts indicated that attitudes seem "to depend in a systematic and intelligible way on how issues are framed" (Kinder 1998: 172). And it is reasonable to expect that public opinion in Islamic countries is shaped not by the fundamental religious or cultural values, but by the kind of framing that is dominant in society, and that people's attitudes may change when framing is altered. Thus, the decline of different secular ideologies and the rise of Islamic fundamentalism affected the way in which people form attitudes toward significant issues.

To be sure, the fundamental values of the Muslim publics—for example, belief in God, the Prophecy of Muhammad, and the Quran as the word of God—are undeniably important in constraining sociopolitical attitudes and choices. Atheist politicians are not going to get elected to public office. A woman who is even being accused of having premarital sex will face often insurmountable obstacles in finding her soul mate. Nonetheless, on many other issues, like attitudes toward the role of women in society, parent-child expectations, the role of religion in social life, the place of ethnic minorities, the relationship between religion and politics, and the extent of the government's intervention in the economy, there are considerable variations among the Islamic publics. The manner in which these issues are framed affects people's orientations toward them. This relationship may also be structured by respondents' social attributes and demographic characteristics.

Economic Development and Value Change

To be effective in shaping people's attitudes, framing must be embedded in the specific national context. For example, we may argue that the relationship between such general values as loyalty to the nation or to Islam and attitudes toward making laws according to the people's wishes or to the shari 'a are mediated by the semantic description of the role of religion in politics, the significance of the nation, and the stereotypical image of an ideal social order provided by the kind of secular ideology or religious fundamentalism that is dominant in society. There are, however, other conceptualizations of values that are both general and analytical, while at the same time shape attitudes toward alternative issues and affect people's choices. These values are said to be tied to levels of economic development.

One such conceptualization is Inglehart's materialist versus postmaterialist values dimension. He argues that economic development causes a gradual change in people's value priorities. Development brings about increasing survival security. This in turn diminishes a "materialist" emphasis on economic and physical security, but enhances people's desire for "postmaterialist" goals, such as freedom, self-expression, and the

8 *Mansoor Moaddel*

quality of life. Aggregated responses as the first and second choices to the following question provide the location of a country in the materialist—postmaterialist scale: (1) maintaining order in the nation, (2) giving the people more say in important government decisions, (3) fighting rising prices, and (4) protecting freedom of expression. Inglehart suggests that developed countries tend to give priority to items 2 and 4, while less developed countries to items 1 and 3. In later work, Inglehart finds that materialist/postmaterialist values tap a much broader dimension encompassing interpersonal trust, tolerance toward outgroups, political activism, and a number of other attitudes termed "survival/self-expression values." This is one of two main dimensions of cross-cultural variation in values, the other one being "traditional/secular-rational values" (Inglehart and Abramson 1999; Inglehart and Baker 2000; Inglehart and Welzel 2005).

Thornton (2005) also considers the connection between economic development and value change, but he does not attempt to establish causality between development and values. Rather, he focuses on the influence of developmental thinking or what he calls "developmental idealism"—a set of interrelated ideas that are presumed to be the cultural features of a modern society, models, and methods—on academic scholarship, policymakers of family planning, and everyday people. While the roots of developmental thinking go as far back in human history as to ancient Greece, the modern version of developmental idealism has been formulated into an evolutionary model of human progress toward a civilized order at the pinnacle of which resides Western societies. Thornton exposes the fatal flaws of this perspective as it is based on misreading European history and insufficient data. He also argues that the overgeneralization of presumed European experience to the rest of the world has been made possible by imputing a historical succession to cross-national data—reading history sideways—where less developed countries were ranked below Western countries in an evolutionary ladder of human progress. Supported by faulty historical data, backed by Western governments, or simply promoted through civilizational osmoses, policymakers from less developed countries sought the progress of their nations in the emulation of Western culture.

Thornton argues that developmental idealism penetrated not only the thinking of policymakers but also the view of ordinary public about distinctive features of a developed society—for example, secular, democratic, predominance of monogamy and the nuclear family, and equality between sexes. Although developmental idealism may have nothing to do with economic development, as a cultural force it created the conditions for its reproduction and validity. To demonstrate the permeation of developmental thinking among the ordinary public, a sample of adult respondents from Nepal and youths from Egypt and Saudi Arabia were asked to rank several countries from Europe and North America, Asia, and Africa in terms of the level of economic development and individual freedom. Their aggregate rankings of development displayed a remarkable consistency with similar rankings provided by the UN experts (Thornton et al. 2005).

Knowledgeability and the Organization of Values

One of the most interesting findings of Thornton's research is that the ordinary public on the aggregate level appeared to be much more knowledgeable about some of the key (stereotypical as well as historically accurate) characteristics of developed and less developed countries than one might have thought. Nonetheless, there are still concerns about the degree to which citizens of Islamic countries are knowledgeable about more abstract political and cultural concepts. It has been argued that the Islamic publics are muddle-headed about the issues and political choices they face, a charge that was explicitly made against Egyptians by British General Counsel Cromer (1908: 151), or empty-headed, as is claimed by the detractors of survey research in Islamic countries. What is their understanding of democracy as the ideal form of government? How do they distinguish between an Islamic government and a democratic government? What factors shape their knowledge about the role of the state in economic development or about the desirability of privatization?

Concerns about the knowledgeability of citizens and level of attention they pay to pertinent issues are not confined to the Islamic publics, who live under unresponsive authoritarian regimes. Public opinion researchers in a democratic country like the United States have also raised similar questions about Americans, and their answers were for a long time guided by a minimalism paradigm. As Sniderman (1993: 219) has aptly summarized,

One fundamental paradigm—minimalism as it has been called— dominated by the work of two decades [i.e., the 1960s and 1970s]. Mass publics, it was contended, were distinguished by (1) minimal levels of political attention and information; (2) minimal mastery of abstract political concepts such as liberalism-conservatism; (3) minimal stability of political preferences; (4) and quintessentially, minimal levels of attitude constraint.

In the past quarter century, however, students of politics have uncovered that public opinion is tied to political process and that this process yields the necessary information for citizens to develop attitudes and figure out their political choices. If the public lacks sufficient knowledge and understanding of the pertinent issues, it has been argued, they nonetheless rely on a series of short-cuts to develop knowledge about these issues. Analogic reasoning, where people try to understand unfamiliar events in terms of events they know (Holyoak and Thagard 1995), is one such short-cut. For example, Schuman and Reiger (1992) discovered that different generational experiences determine people's acceptance of different historical analogies in developing attitudes toward current events—that is, whether Persian Gulf War was analogous to World War II or to the Vietnam War was a function of which wars the respondents experienced during their impressionable years (i.e., ages 12–25).

Furthermore, opinion leaders, experts, and interest groups provide citizens the reasoning about their political choices (Brody 1994; Katz and Lazarsfeld 1955; Kinder 1998; Lupia 1994). An example of the situations in which the public uses short-cut to knowledge is the case of California voters, who were initially impressively ignorant about the content of the referenda to reform their state's automobile insurance industry. However, when they learned that the insurance industry and associations representing trial lawyers supported the proposal, they knew enough. They voted against it (cited in Kinder 1998: 175; see also Lupia 1994). Finally, citizens can make up for their wanting of knowledge about politics by taking advantage of judgmental shortcuts, or heuristics (Ferejohn and Kuklinski 1990; Popkin 1991; Sniderman 1993; Sniderman et al. 1991). That is, substantial numbers of ordinary citizens can make sense of what constitutes liberal and conservative positions on major issues by taking advantage of the "likeability" heuristics by learning how the known conservatives or liberals feel about the issues (Brady and Sniderman 1985; Sniderman 1993).

Likewise, our survey data have provided ample evidence indicating that the attitudes of the Islamic publics are not derivatives of abstract religious or cultural values, but rather connected to the existing sociopolitical processes and conflict. For example, Iranians and Saudis attend mosques significantly less often than Egyptians or Jordanians. This does not mean that Iranian and Saudi citizens have lower attachments to the fundamental religious values than Egyptian or Jordanian citizens. Rather, it indicates the negative effect of the religiosity of the state on the overall religiosity of the public, as measured by mosque attendance. Because religious institutions in Iran and Saudi Arabia are closely tied to the unpopular authoritarian regime, these institutions have become less likeable than their counterparts in Egypt and Jordan, where secular regime are in power. The variations in the nature of religion-state alliance have thus contributed to cross-national variations in mosque attendance among these countries (Moaddel and Azadarmaki 2002). This argument is also consistent with Finke and Stark's (1989) theory of the relationship between aggregate religiosity and religious pluralism. Moreover, comparative analysis of the determinants of democracy among Iranian and Saudi citizens has revealed that the relationship between attitudes toward Western cultural invasion and attitudes toward democracy depends on the national context. That is, in Iran, where the state is avowedly anti-West, attitudes toward Western cultural invasion have a negative effect on attitudes toward democracy, while in Saudi Arabia, it is the opposite; those who are critical of the West tend to be more supportive of democracy.

Another important issue in the study of values involves a lack of organization and consistency in people's belief system. The traditional perspective presumes that a belief system is a hierarchically organized set of values and normative rules of behavior. In reality, citizens adhere to contradictory values. Public opinion researchers in the United States and other Western countries have uncovered that "people, manifestly, care about more than one thing—indeed, are, simultaneously and sincerely attached to values that clash" (Sniderman 1993: 224). This is also true among citizens of Islamic countries. For example, a large percentage of respondents expressed that a good government is the one that makes law according to the people's wishes, while at the same time they agreed that a good government implements only the shari 'a laws. In the 2004 Iraqi values survey, the majority of the respondents believed that democracy was the best form of government, while at the same time a smaller but significant section of the respondents preferred a political system in which religious leaders had absolute power. It should be noted that, however, it is not at all clear if all cases of contradictory value systems are in fact real. For example, the value of having law according to people's wishes and the desirability of the shari 'a law are not necessarily contradictory, if one believes that the latter is not immutable. While for social scientists and commentators the two are in opposition (e.g., Safran 1961)—a view that is supported by conservative theologians and fundamentalists as well—in people's mind this may not necessary be the case. For them, Islam may provide cues to a good legislation and check the excesses of secularist law makers. And vice versa; appeal to the people's wishes may be a way to check the excesses of religious zealots among the legislatures.

It may also be the case that competing values are, in fact, negatively correlated: the more importance a person attaches to the value of freedom of speech, for example, the less he or she attaches to the value of order, and vice versa (Sniderman 1993: 228). Likewise, we may argue that attitudes toward an Islamic government may be negatively related to attitudes toward a democratic political system; the more people consider making laws according to the people's wishes as the characteristic of a good government, the less they consider the implementation of the shari 'a as the characteristic of a good government; the more the respondents are in favor of making laws according to the people's wishes, the more they favor democracy; and the more the respondents are in favor of the shari 'a, the less they are in favor of democracy. Specifying the nature of the linkages among values may thus resolve the problem of value clash and value inconsistency in people's attitudes.

From another angle, one may even question the desirability of living in a society where people adhere to a highly organized and consistent belief system. Authoritarian ideological states like to impose a uniformed and consistent set of values on people, and thus create a conformist and intolerant culture (Moaddel 2002). A uniformed culture that attaches a high priority to only one value or to one consistent set of values may promote a monistic belief system. Heterogeneous cultural environments and value pluralism, on the other hand, necessarily entail clashes of values. And as Tetlock (1986a, 1986b) suggested, by virtue of having to adjudicate among competing values, the followers of pluralistic ideologies are more likely than the proponents of monistic ideologies to consider other viewpoints and the complexity of their interconnections. Insofar as Islamic countries are concerned, moderate and tolerant Islamic discourses are produced, historically, in a pluralistic cultural environment, while Islamic fundamentalism is a product of a monolithic cultural environment imposed from above by the secular authoritarian ideological state (Moaddel 2005).

This is not to argue that value heterogeneity always promotes tolerance, and value homogeneity supports intolerance and cultural conformism. It may be argued that under certain conditions the former may contribute to ethnic strife and civil war (e.g., the Balkans in the 1990s and Iraq today), while value homogeneity increases the likelihood of the formation of national consensus that is necessary for building the modern state. However, value heterogeneity may constitute a potentially more favorable context for cultural innovation and the development of transcendental discourses that resolve the cultural

differences underpinning ethnic conflict. The rise of transcendental
discourse may in turn depend on a degree of intellectual sophistication
on the part of the intellectual elite, as the producers, and the public, as
the consumer of high culture. That is, to be able to understand, adjudicate,
and, to a degree, reconcile conflicting values, requires awareness of multiple
considerations, intellectual sophistication, and information about alternative
values system—all promoting complexity of reasoning and moderation of
position (Sniderman 1993: 228). Naturally, the well-informed are more
likely to express opinions, to use ideological terminology correctly, to possess stable opinions, to make use of facts in political discussion, to take an
active part in politics, and to pick up new information easily and retain it
readily (Kinder 1998: 176). One of the key determinants of political
awareness and knowledge of politics is formal education, as "higher education clearly promotes political engagement and learning about politics"
(Delli et al. 1989: 278). Education is also an indicator of cognitive ability
(Stimson 1975), which strengthens the information processing efficiency
of citizens and encourages certain values among individuals, including
"openness of mind, a respect for science and empirical knowledge, an
awareness of complexity and possibilities for change, and tolerance, not
only of people but of points of view" (Sniderman et al. 1991: 9). Thus,
value pluralism combined with a highly educated public tends to produce
a tolerant and innovative culture.

Other Scientific Issues in the Study of Values in Islamic Countries

The extant theoretical models and methods advanced in Western social
sciences are certainly useful in guiding public opinion research in Islamic
countries. Nonetheless, several points of caution must be raised to guard
against uncritical replication of these models and methods. *First*, there is
the question of the directionality in people's value orientations in Islamic
countries and the degree of their consistency with Western categories.
While acknowledging that there are no geographic boundaries for the
social sciences, it may be argued that certain concepts in social theory
have civilizational boundaries. Does, for example, the dichotomy of
liberalism versus conservatism in economic, political, and social issues
have the same meaning in the Islamic context as in Western societies?
Should we consider as conservative someone who is strongly against state
intervention in the economy under a socialist-oriented Arab regime?
Can we argue that the major dimension of the difference between the

Western and Islamic cultural traditions is the predominance of religion and ideological factors over other considerations in Islamic societies? Likewise, the term social tolerance may require different conceptualizations and operationalizations in Islamic contexts. Can one consider the disapproval of homosexuality in Islamic countries to be indicative of a low level of social tolerance? Does homosexuality convey the same imagery, feeling, and rationale in Islamic countries as it does in Western democracies? Researchers in the field have often expressed unease about asking respondents about their sexual preference and homosexuality. On the issue of gender and sex, how can we explain the Islamic fundamentalists' obsessions with women's bodies? Are such obsessions reflections of religion or culture? Or, alternatively, are they related to Muslim male sexual anxiety sublimated into the field of religion?

Does religious tolerance or social tolerance convey the same meaning in the Islamic context as it does in Western societies? How useful is the dichotomy of monolithic versus pluralistic intolerance in explaining the similarities and differences in the level of tolerance among Islamic societies and between these societies and the West? Social scientists have coined the concept of "pluralistic intolerance" to indicate the situation in which different groups within a society are intolerant of different outgroups. A monolithic intolerance, then, implies a situation in which different segments of a population are commonly intolerant of religious minorities or other groups who are ethnically different from the rest of the society.

Second, there is the issue of the effect of national-historical and cultural context in shaping the worldviews of the respondents in a manner that may convey a meaning different from what one may interpret in Western societies. Does the support for a strong military and/or a strong leader imply support for authoritarianism? How can one assess women's religiosity despite their lower level of participation in public religious activities compared to men? Does a(n) (educated) woman's action of wearing the veil have the same meaning across Islamic countries? To what extent is veiling indicative of social or religious conservatism and to what extent does it signify political opposition?

Third, and of particular significance is the issue of the relationship between Islam and democracy. Given the persistence of authoritarianism in almost all Islamic countries in the twenty-first century, there has been a strong tendency to establish a causal connection between Islam and authoritarianism. Alternative explanations may render this connection spurious. For example, the rentier-state model advocates a compelling explanation of authoritarianism. Far from being an outcome of Islamic culture or legacy of historical Islam, this model focuses on the effect of the availability of enormous petrodollars on the structure and functions of the state in Islamic countries. Rentier economy has far-reaching political, social, and cultural consequences. First, only a small fraction of the population is directly involved in the creation of wealth. As a result, modern social organizations associated with productive activities have been developed only to a limited extent. Second, the work-reward nexus is no longer the central feature of an economic transaction where wealth is the end result of the individual's involvement in a long, risky, and organized production process. Rather, wealth is accidental, a windfall gain, or situational, where citizenship becomes a source of economic benefit. To acquire wealth requires different types of subjective orientation, which researchers called "rentier mentality" and "rentier ethics." Noneconomic criteria, such as proximity to the ruling elite and citizenship, become the key determinants of income. Rentierism thus reinforces the state's tribal origins, as it regenerates the tribal hierarchy consisting of varying layers of beneficiaries with the ruling elite on top, in an effective position of buying loyalty through their redistributive power. As the state is not dependent on taxation, there is far less demand for political participation—that is, "no taxation, no representation" is no longer relevant. How do we measure rentier mentality? What are the appropriate indicators of rentier ethics? These conceptual issues need to be addressed before meaningful comparisons are made among Islamic societies and between these societies and the West.

Finally, there is the problem of preference falsification. People living under authoritarian regimes often prefer to conceal their true preferences (Kuran 1995). They may be unwilling to express their opposition to their regime's policies and give their opinions about issues they consider politically or culturally sensitive. As Bainbridge (2003: 635) has aptly stated, "unavailability of correct information about people's preferences makes it difficult for social scientists to measure public opinion, but it also gives great uncertainty to the political actors in the society itself. A situation of pluralistic ignorance may arise, in which each person is unaware of the true feelings of everybody else. Essentially random events may unexpectedly reveal to some of these actors how weak support for the regime actually is, and a revolutionary bandwagon effect may sweep it away to everyone's surprise." Indicative of preference falsification is the high percentage of the public under communism who said that they were atheists and the considerable drop in this percentage after the fall of antireligious communist regimes.

However, to overcome the preference falsification problem, in our surveys we have tried to formulate alternative measures of people's preferences concerning politically and culturally sensitive issues.

Chapters in this Volume

The chapters in this book attempt to answer some of the questions discussed so far. The common denominator of these chapters is that all are based on the findings of the values surveys. They collectively provide a range of examples of the different ways in which this scientific-infrastructural data set can be used to arrive at an objective verifiable/falsifiable understanding of some of the key aspects of the cultures of Islamic societies. At the same time, the theoretical issues addressed in these works are to demonstrate to students of the social sciences the utility of this understanding for advancing a more general and abstract knowledge of some of the most fundamental social structures and processes that are the causes or consequences of mass-level belief systems.

Three chapters in the first section analyze the value orientations of the Islamic public within a regional and global context. Ronald Inglehart in "The Worldviews of Islamic Publics in Global Perspective" explores the distinctiveness of the value system of Islamic societies. He divides these societies into mainstream Islamic societies and those that have experienced communist rule. Using his analytical dichotomies of (1) polarization between traditional and secular-rational orientation toward authority and (2) survival and self-expression values, Inglehart concludes that traditional religious values are strong in mainstream Islamic societies, while those having communist experience have more secular-rational values. He also points out that although there is strong support for democracy, self-expression values, which are strongly linked with stable democracy, are weak in these societies. The following two chapters focus on the nature of the convergence and divergence in value orientations between the European and Islamic publics. Juan Díez-Nicolás brings in "Value Systems of Elites and Publics in the Mediterranean: Convergence or Divergence" two broad levels of comparisons; one is between the developed and less developed countries, and the other between European and Islamic societies of the Mediterranean. On each level, he advances inter- and intrasocietal comparisons of the elites and the public. He observes that on post-materialism and political orientations, there is a convergence of values among the elites of both developed and less developed countries as well as the European and Muslim societies. In terms of moral, religious, family, and gender values, there is a divergence of value orientations among the elites from developed and less developed countries. Comparing European and Islamic societies of the Mediterranean, he finds similar relationships. The European elites and publics are significantly less religious, more tolerant, less socially exclusive, less traditional, and more in favor of gender equality than their counterparts in Islamic countries. In terms of postmaterialist values, the European elite displayed the greatest adherence to such values, followed by Islamic elites, then European publics, and finally Islamic publics. The findings of Thorleif Pettersson's research in "Muslim Immigrants in Western Europe: Persisting Value Differences or Value Adaptation?" are remarkably similar to these conclusions, although Pettersson compares the values of Muslim immigrants to Europe with European values. His analysis supports the hypothesis that the value orientation that immigrants had acquired as a result of primary socialization would remain unaffected by the migration processes, while the values that were acquired by secondary socialization would be more likely to change.

The next three chapters focus on the interactions between politics, culture, and economics. What are the political and economic consequences of the Islamic belief system and practices? Or alternatively, to what extent do the dominant economic institutions and the sources of state revenues have political and cultural outcomes? In "Do Islamic Orientations Influence Attitudes toward Democracy in the Arab World: Evidence from the World Values Survey in Egypt, Jordan, Morocco, and Algeria" Mark Tessler engages in a rigorous analysis of data from Algeria, Egypt, Jordan, and Morocco in order to explore the effect of Islamic orientations on attitudes toward democracy. Tessler considers the respondents' assessment of democracy as an ideal system of government and in terms of the efficiency of this system. He also uses different measures of Islamic orientations, including mosque attendance, attitudes toward the involvement of the mosques in societal affairs, the role of religious leaders in politics, and religiosity as a desirable quality for politicians. Based on his analysis of the data, he concludes that Islamic orientations and attachment have at most a very limited impact on views about democracy. Likewise, religiosity has little influence on attitudes toward democracy. Thus, on the broader question of the compatibility of democracy and Islam, his findings suggest that strong Islamic attachments do not discourage or otherwise influence support for democracy to any significant extent. These findings lead Tessler to conclude that the failure of democracy in the Arab world may be rooted in its economic institutions, unfavorable location in the international economic and political hierarchy, or the determination of the ruling elite to resist democratic change in their country.

The chapter by Nancy J. Davis and Robert V. Robinson, "The Egalitarian Face of Islamic Orthodoxy: Support for Islamic Law and Economic Justice in Seven Muslim-Majority Nations," also addresses the consequences of Islamic belief system; here the impact of religious beliefs on one's adherence to economic justice. Using a comprehensive and meticulous analysis of data from Algeria, Bangladesh, Egypt, Indonesia, Jordan, Pakistan, and Saudi Arabia, these authors develop and test hypotheses on the relationship between theology and economic orientation. That is, they assess whether the theological communitarianism of Islamic orthodoxy has the outcome of economic communitarianism, and whether the theological individualism of Islamic modernism is linked to laissez-faire economic individualism. They use support for the shari 'a as the key explanatory variable specifying the difference between orthodoxy and modernism. Their analysis of the data supports the thesis that in fact Islamic orthodoxy, as measured in terms of support for the shari 'a, is linked to economic egalitarianism for every one of the seven countries they studied.

The chapter "The Rentier State: Does Rentierism Hinder Democracy? The Rentier Mentality Hypothesis Tested In Seven Middle Eastern Countries" by Bi Puranen and Olof Widenfalk evaluates the effect of rentier economy that checks the development of modern political institutions, democracy, and work ethics in seven Middle Eastern countries. Their analysis shows that people from nonoil states show a higher approval for democratic ideals than people in rentier states, but when they are asked about democratic performance, people in nonoil state are more negative. Their analysis also shows that people in rentier states actually place more emphasis on work and money and less on friends and leisure than do people in their neighboring nonoil countries. Generally, they found that high oil income decreases people's demand for political participation. Rentierism, however, does not significantly affect work-related issues.

The third section contains two chapters; one addresses the determinants of self-rated health in four countries, and the other analyzes the value orientations of Saudi citizens. In the first chapter "Social Structure versus Perception: A Cross-National Comparison of Self-Rated Health in Egypt, Iran, Jordan, and the United States," Kristine Ajrouch and Mansoor Moaddel present a cross-national analysis of the determinants of self-rated health in Egypt, Iran, Jordan, and the United States. Building on recent sociological studies of health that emphasize the significance of perceived control in mediating the association between structurally patterned individual attributes and health, their chapter introduces other ritualistic and perceptual variables in the study of health. They assess the effects of structural indicators, ritualistic behavior, and perceptual indicators on self-rated health. While patterns between structural variables, ritualistic behavior and self-rated health vary by country, a consistent link emerges between perceptual variables and self-rated health in all four countries; that is, people who have higher perceived control and are happier also tend to be healthier. In the second chapter "The Saudi Public Speaks: Religion, Gender, and Politics," Moaddel analyzes the value orientation of the Saudi public toward religion, gender, and politics. Based on the values survey data, this chapter shows that while according to Western standards Saudi Arabia is a conservative society, compared with other Islamic countries like Egypt and Jordan, Saudi citizens are not as conservative as one might expect. In fact, these citizens are less religious than either Egyptians or Jordanians. In terms of their attitudes toward such social institutions as marriage, almost half of Saudi citizens believed that love, rather than parental approval, should be the basis for marriage. A larger percentage of Saudis over either Egyptians or Jordanians consider marriage to be an outdated institution. On religiosity and attitudes toward marriage, Saudis are closer to Iranians than to Egyptian or Jordanian Arabs, supporting the view that the religiosity of the Iranian and Saudi states has made the publics of these societies less religious instead of making them more so. Findings also indicated that gender is the most important nonattitudinal variable that divides the public and private side of religious activities, and the most significant variable shaping attitudes toward women. Finally, these results showed that Saudis' attitudes toward democracy are affected positively by concerns with Western cultural invasion, favorable attitudes toward privatization, critical attitudes toward public-sector performance, rational rule-making, tolerance, and class, but negatively by attitudes toward the shari 'a and by religiosity, and by income. Education neither promotes nor hinders religiosity, egalitarian attitudes toward gender relations, and attitudes toward democracy.

The fourth section addresses the issue of event-induced changes in people's perceptions, attitudes, and values. In the chapter "Events and Value Change: The Impact of September 11, 2001 on the Worldviews of Egyptians and Moroccans," Moaddel and Latif assess the impact of the terrorist events of September 11, 2001 on the value orientations of

Egyptians and Moroccans. Using the results of two nearly identical values surveys carried out in these two countries, one before 9/11 and another about six months later, they argue that the gruesome act carried out by al-Qaeda to rally the Muslim publics behind its banner had just the opposite effect. The Egyptian and Moroccan publics turned away from the ideology of religious extremism and toward Western values of democracy, gender equality, and secularism. The second chapter "Xenophobia and In-Group Solidarity in Iraq: A Natural Experiment on the Impact of Insecurity" by Inglehart, Moaddel, and Tessler analyzes the Iraqi values survey data to assess the effects of the current conditions of political instability and economic hardships on in-group solidarity among the Kurdish, the Shi 'i, and the Sunni sections of the Iraqi population and out-group intolerance and xenophobia. In Iraq currently, ethnic solidarity is extremely high and matched by an equally high level of xenophobia and intolerance of outsiders. Within the context of the WVS data, Inglehart et al. argue that the intolerance of outsiders among Iraqis is highest in the world.

The final chapter "Probability Sampling and the Scientific Survey Method for Population Studies: Application to Survey Research in Islamic Countries" by Steven Heeringa discusses the role of probability sampling design in the surveys of populations. After giving a brief overview of the development of survey research methodology in Islamic countries, Heeringa focuses on important aspects of probability sampling and provides a guide to judging the precision and accuracy of survey data. He also addresses the sources of variance and bias in survey data collection.

References

Bainbridge, William Sim. 2003. "The Future in the Social Sciences." *Futures* 35(6): 633–50.
Binder, Leonard. 1962. *Iran: Political Order in a Changing Society*. Berkeley: University of California Press.
Brady, Henry E. and Paul M. Sniderman. 1985. "Attitude Attribution: A Group Basis for Political Reasoning." *American Political Science Review* 79(4): 1061–78.
Brody, Richard A. 1994. "Crisis, War, and Public Opinion." In *Taken by Storm*, edited by W. Lance Bennett and David L. Paletz, pp. 210–27. Chicago: University of Chicago Press.
Cromer, Evelyn Baring. 1908. *Modern Egypt*. New York: Macmillan Co.
Delli Carpini, Michael X. and Scott Keeter. 1989. *What Americans Know about Politics and Why It Matters*. New Haven: Yale University Press.
Ferejohn, John A. and James H. Kuklinski (eds.). 1990. *Information and Democratic Processes*. Urbana and Chicago: University of Illinois Press.
Finke, Roger and Rodney Stark. 1989. "Evaluating the Evidence: Religious Economies and Sacred Canopies." *American Sociological Review* 54(6): 1054–56.

Holyoak, Keith J. and Paul Thagard. 1995. *Mental Leaps: Analogy in Creative Thought*. Cambridge, MA: MIT Press.

Inglehart, Ronald and Paul R. Abramson. 1999. "Measuring Postmaterialism." *American Political Science Review* 93(3): 665–77.

Inglehart, Ronald and Wayne Baker. 2000. "Modernization, Cultural Change and the Persistence of Traditional Values." *American Sociological Review* 65(1): 19–51.

Inglehart, Ronald and Christian Welzel. 2005. *Modernization, Cultural Change and Democracy*. New York and Cambridge: Cambridge University Press.

Katz, Elihu and Paul F. Lazarsfeld. 1955. *Personal Influence: The Part Played by People in the Flow of Mass Communication*. New York: Free Press.

Kinder, Donald R. 1998. "Communication and Opinion." *Annual Review of Political Science* 1: 167–97.

Kuran, Timur. 1995. "The Inevitability of Future Revolutionary Surprises." *American Journal of Sociology* 100(6): 1528–51.

Lambton, Ann K.S. 1963. "Justice in the Medieval Persian Theory of Kingship." *Studia Islamica* 17: 91–119.

Lapidus, Ira M. 1992. "The Golden Age: The Political Concepts of Islam." *The Annals of the American Academy of Political and Social Sciences* 524(1): 13–25.

Lewis, Bernard. 1968. *The Emergence of Modern Turkey*. Oxford: Oxford University Press.

———. 1993a. *Islam in History*. Chicago: Open Court.

———. 1993b. *Islam and the West*. Oxford: Oxford University Press.

Lupia, Arthur. 1994. "Shortcuts versus Encyclopedias: Information and Voting Behavior in California Insurance Reform Elections." *American Political Science Review* 88(1): 63–76.

Moaddel, Mansoor. 2002. "The Study of Islamic Culture and Politics: An Overview and Assessment." *Annual Review of Sociology* 28: 359–86.

———. 2005. *Islamic Modernism, Nationalism, and Fundamentalism: Episode and Discourse*. Chicago: University of Chicago Press.

Moaddel, Mansoor and Taqhi Azadarmaki. 2002. "The World Views of Islamic Publics: The Cases of Egypt, Iran, and Jordan." *Comparative Sociology* 1(3–4):299–319.

Parsons, Talcott. 1949. *The Structure of Social Action: A Study in Social Theory with Special Reference to a Group of Recent European Writers*. Glencoe, IL: Free Press.

———. 1951. *The Social System*. Toronto: Collier-Macmillan.

———. 1966. *Societies: Evolutionary and Comparative Perspective*. Englewood Cliffs, NJ: Prentice-Hall.

———. 1969. *Politics and Social Structure*. New York: Free Press.

———. 1971. *The System of Modern Societies*. Englewood Cliffs, NJ: Prentice-Hall.

Popkin, Samuel, 1991. *The Reasoning Voter*. Chicago: The University of Chicago Press.

Safran, Nadav. 1961. *Egypt in Search of Political Community*. Cambridge, MA: Harvard University Press.

Sahlins, Marshall D. and Elman R. Service. 1960. *Evolution and Culture*. Ann Arbor, MI: University of Michigan Press.

Schuman, Howard and Cheryl Reiger. 1992. "Historical Analogies, Generational Effects, and Attitudes toward War." *American Sociology Review* 57(3): 315–26.

Service, Elman R. 1971. *Cultural Evolutionism: Theory in Practice*. New York: Holt, Rinehart & Winston.

Sniderman, Paul M. 1993. "The New Look in Public Opinion Research." In *Political Science: The State of the Discipline II*, edited by Ada W. Finifter. Washington, DC: The American Political Science Association, pp. 219–45.

Sniderman, Paul M., Richard A. Brody, and Philip E. Tetlock. 1991. *Reasoning and Choice: Exploration in Political Psychology*. Cambridge: Cambridge University Press.

Stimson, James A. 1975. "Belief Systems: Constraint, Complexity, and the 1972 Election." In *Controversies in American Voting Behavior*, edited by Richard D. Niemi and Herbert F. F. Weisberg, pp. 138–59. San Francisco: Freeman.

Tetlock, Philip E. 1986a. "A Value Pluralism Model of Ideological Reasoning." *Journal of Personality and Social Psychology* 50(4): 819–27.

———. 1986b. "Structure and Function in Political Belief Systems." In *Attitude Structure and Function*, edited by Anthony Pratkanis, Steven Buckler, and Anthony Greenwarld. Hillsdale, NJ: Lawrence Erlbaum, pp. 129–51.

Thornton, Arland. 2005. *Reading History Sideways: The Fallacy and Enduring Impact of the Developmental Paradigm on Family Life*. Chicago: University of Chicago Press.

Thornton, Arland, Dirgha J. Ghimire, and Colter Mitchell. 2005. "The Measurement and Prevalence of Developmental Thinking about the Family: Evidence from Nepal." Paper presented at the annual meeting of the Population Association of American, March 31–April 2, Philadelphia, Pennsylvania.

PART 1

Islam in a Global Perspective

CHAPTER 2

The Worldviews of Islamic Publics in Global Perspective

RONALD F. INGLEHART[1]

Introduction

To what extent does a common value system exist among the publics of Islamic societies? And to what extent are their values compatible with democratic institutions?

As this chapter demonstrates, using massive body of recent survey evidence, the publics of Islamic countries have distinctive and relatively similar basic values, as compared with the values that prevail in most other societies. To a considerable extent, these differences between Islamic and non-Islamic societies reflect differences in levels of economic development. Modernization theorists from Karl Marx to Max Weber to Daniel Bell have argued that economic development brings pervasive cultural changes, and we find strong empirical support for this thesis: the worldviews of rich societies show striking and systematic differences from the worldviews prevailing among the publics of poorer societies.

But the cultural heritage of given societies also seems to play a significant role: Large differences exist between value systems of the historically Islamic societies and those of other societies, even when we control for levels of economic development. Although basic values are changing over time, the impact of a society's historical heritage remains clearly visible in the value systems of its public today.

For the first time in human history, the WVS have measured the values of people throughout the entire world (covering 85 percent of its population). These surveys provide unprecedented insight into how human values vary and how and why they are changing.

They give empirical answers to such questions as: Do Islamic countries have distinctive value systems? And if so, how do they differ from those of other cultures? We can also probe into such questions as: Are certain values linked with the emergence and survival of democracy?

Everyone knows that the world is increasingly being penetrated by global mass media. U.S.-made television and Hollywood films are everywhere; the internet provides instantaneous communication between Cairo and Chicago; and young people from Beijing to Buenos Aires are wearing blue jeans and drinking Coke. Even cuisine is being Mc Donaldized. Globalization seems pervasive. So, one might think, the various cultures must be converging into one homogenized global value system.

But they are not. Evidence from the WVS indicates that the value systems of rich societies are moving in a common direction—but they are not converging (at least, not during the past 20 years, the period for which we have data).[2] Religious differences and other historical differences continue to shape human values today, making historically Islamic societies distinct from historically Catholic, Protestant, Orthodox, Buddhist, or Confucian societies. We not only find no evidence of convergence—we actually find that the gap between the value systems of rich and poor countries has been growing, not shrinking, during the past 20 years (Inglehart and Welzel 2005).

Does a coherent "Islamic society" exist? Cultures vary across scores of dimensions. Cultures are complex and each society has a unique history. Furthermore, Islamic societies range half way around the world, from Morocco to Indonesia. Their wealth, geography, population density, and climate vary enormously. They speak a variety of languages, and interpret Islam in various ways. Obviously, there is no such thing as one uniform "Islamic culture."

But analysis of survey data from scores of societies reveals that cross-cultural variation is surprisingly orderly (Inglehart and Baker 2000). Most of the variation across a wide range of important variables—from religious values to economic priorities, to gender norms to political values—can be captured by just two dimensions. One can plot every society in the world on a two-dimensional cross-cultural map. This map could not possibly capture all the countless ways in which societies vary, but it does account for more than 75 percent of the cross-cultural variation in scores of important beliefs and values, ranging from religious beliefs to political goals, to work motivations, child-rearing norms, sexual norms, and tolerance of outgroups. On these two dimensions, the ten Islamic societies for which we have data, show relatively similar values, in comparison with most other societies.

The worldviews of the people of rich societies differ systematically from those of low income societies across a wide range of political, social, and religious norms and beliefs. In order to focus our comparisons on some crucial dimensions of cross-cultural variation, we performed a factor analysis based on each society's mean level on given variables, replicating the analysis in Inglehart and Baker (2000).[3] The two most significant dimensions that emerged reflected: (1) polarization between *traditional* and *secular-rational* orientations toward authority and (2) polarization between *survival* and *self-expression* values.

By *traditional* we refer to orientations that emphasize religion, family and child-bearing, national pride and respect for authority, and rejection of abortion and divorce. These values are most widespread in agricultural societies. Industrialized societies tend to emphasize *secular-rational* values, which have the opposite characteristics. Table 2.1 sums up the orientations linked with this dimension.

But modernization, is not linear—when a society has become completely industrialized and starts becoming a knowledge society, it moves in a new direction, giving rise to a second major dimension of cross-cultural variation. The transition from industrial society to postindustrial societies brings a polarization between survival and self-expression values. Table 2.2 gives an overview of this cluster of values. A central component of this dimension involves the polarization between materialist

Table 2.1   Traditional versus secular-rational values

Traditional values emphasize:
- Religion is very important
- One should teach a child to obey
- A strong sense of national pride
- A main goal in life is to make parents proud
- Divorce is never justifiable
- Abortion is never justifiable
- We need stricter limits on selling foreign goods
- We need more respect for authority

Secular-rational values emphasize the opposite

Note: Scores of other attitudes are also linked with this dimension; for a more complete list, see Inglehart and Baker 2000.

Table 2.2   Survival versus self-expression values

Survival values emphasize:
- Economic security over self-expression
  (materialist over postmaterialist values)
- Men make better political leaders than women;
  men have more right to a job than women
- Good income and safe job over a sense of accomplishment
- Homosexuality is never justifiable
- Reject foreigners
- Are unhappy, dissatisfied with life
- Noninvolvement in politics, environmental protection

Self-expression values emphasize the opposite

Note: Scores of other attitudes are also linked with this dimension; for a more complete list, see Inglehart and Baker 2000.

and postmaterialist values, reflecting a cultural shift that is emerging among generations that have grown up taking survival for granted. Self-expression values give high priority to environmental protection, tolerance of diversity, and rising demands for participation in decision making in economic and political life. These values reflect mass polarization over whether "When jobs are scarce, men have more right to a job than women"; or whether "A university education is more important for a boy than a girl," and whether "Men make better political leaders than women." This emphasis on gender equality is part of a broader syndrome of tolerance of outgroups, including foreigners, gays, and lesbians. The shift from survival values to self-expression values also includes a shift in child-rearing values, from emphasis on hard work toward emphasis on imagination and tolerance as important values to teach a child. And it goes with a rising sense of subjective well-being that is conducive to an atmosphere of tolerance, trust, and political moderation. Finally, societies that rank high on self-expression values also tend to rank high on interpersonal trust. This produces a culture of trust and tolerance, in which people place a relatively high value on individual freedom and self-expression, and have activist political orientations. These are precisely the attributes that the political culture literature defines as crucial to democracy.

The unprecedented wealth that has accumulated in advanced societies during the past generation means that an increasing share of the population has grown up taking survival for granted. Thus, priorities have shifted from an overwhelming emphasis on economic and physical security toward an increasing emphasis on subjective well-being, self-expression, and quality of life. Mass values have shifted from traditional toward secular-rational values, and from survival values toward self-expression values in almost all advanced industrial societies that have experienced economic growth.

Figure 2.1 shows a two-dimensional cultural map on which the value systems of more than 80 societies are depicted. The vertical dimension represents the traditional/secular-rational dimension, and the horizontal dimension reflects the survival/self-expression values dimension. Both dimensions are strongly linked with economic development. This reflects a finding of fundamental importance: the value systems of rich countries

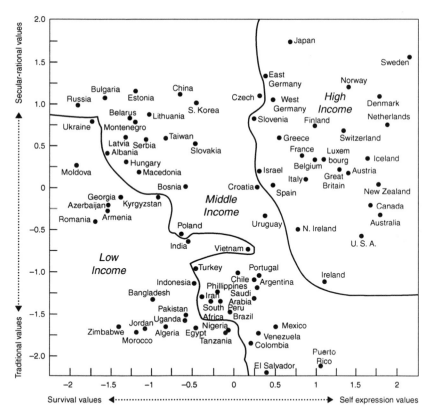

Figure 2.1   Cultural map of 82 societies, with economic zones superimposed. Cultural locations reflect each society's factor scores on two major dimensions of cross-cultural variation. Economy zones are from World Bank, *World Development Indicators, 2002*

differ systematically from those of poor countries. Germany, France, Britain, Italy, Japan, Sweden, the United States, and all of the other societies in our sample that the World Bank classifies as "high income" societies rank relatively high on both dimensions. Without a single exception, all of the high income societies fall in the upper right-hand corner of our global cultural map.

Conversely, every one of the countries that the World Bank classifies as "low income" societies fall into a cluster at the lower left of the map; India, Bangladesh, Pakistan, Nigeria, Ghana and Peru all fall into this economic zone that cuts across the African, South Asian, ex-communist, and Orthodox cultural zones. The remaining societies fall into an intermediate cultural-economic zone. One rarely finds such a clearly structured pattern in social science research. As modernization theory implies, economic development seems to propel societies in a predictable direction, regardless of their cultural heritage.

Economic Development Interacts with a Society's

Cultural Heritage

Nevertheless, distinctive cultural zones persist. Cultural change is path dependent. That is, different societies follow different trajectories when they experience economic development, because each society's historical and cultural heritage also shapes its culture. Huntington (1996) emphasized the role of religion in shaping the world's eight major civilizations or "cultural zones": Western Christianity, Orthodox, Islam, Confucian, Japanese, Hindu, African, and Latin American. Our analysis reveals consistent differences between historically Protestant and historically Roman Catholic societies within Western Christianity. These nine cultural zones were shaped by religious traditions that are still powerful today, despite the forces of modernization.

As figure 2.2 demonstrates, all four of the Confucian-influenced societies (China, Taiwan, South Korea, and Japan) have relatively secular values, constituting a Confucian cultural zone, despite substantial differences in wealth. The Orthodox societies constitute another distinct cultural zone, and the eleven Latin American societies show relatively similar values as Huntington argued. And despite their wide geographic dispersion, the English-speaking countries constitute a relatively compact cultural zone. Similarly, the historically Roman Catholic societies (e.g., Italy, Portugal, Spain, France, Belgium, and Austria) display

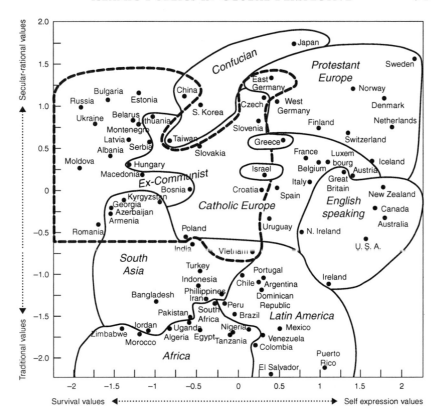

Figure 2.2   Cultural zones of 82 societies

relatively traditional values when compared with Confucian or ex-communist societies with similar levels of development. And virtually all of the historically Protestant societies (e.g., West Germany, Denmark, Norway, Sweden, Finland, and Iceland) rank higher on both the traditional-secular rational dimension and the survival/self-expression dimension than do the historically Roman Catholic societies.

Religious traditions have had an enduring impact on the contemporary value systems of the 80 societies. But basic values do not reflect religion alone. A society's culture reflects its entire historical heritage. A central historical event of the twentieth century was the rise and fall of a communist empire that once ruled one-third of the world's population.

Communism left a clear imprint on the value systems of those who lived under it. All of the ex-communist societies fall into the upper left-hand quadrant of our cultural map, ranking high on the traditional/secular-rational dimension (toward the secular pole), but low on the survival/self-expression dimension (falling near the survival-oriented pole). A broken line encircles all of the societies that have experienced communist rule, and they form a reasonably coherent group. Not surprisingly, communist rule seems conducive to the emergence of a relatively secular-rational culture. And, although they are by no means the poorest countries in the world, these societies have recently experienced the collapse of communism, shattering their economic, political, and social systems—and bringing a pervasive sense of insecurity. People who have experienced stable poverty throughout their lives tend to emphasize survival values; but the collapse of one's social system produces a sense of unpredictability and insecurity that leads people to emphasize survival values even more heavily than those who are accustomed to an even lower standard of living.

There is considerable diversity within the former communist zone. The basic values prevailing in the Czech Republic, Slovenia, Croatia, and East Germany are close to those of the West European societies on both major dimensions. These societies have experienced relatively successful transitions from communism to market economies—and they were historically shaped by the Protestant or Roman Catholic religious traditions, rather than by the Orthodox tradition.

Decades of communist rule had a significant impact on the values and beliefs of those who experienced it, but a given cultural heritage can partially offset or reinforce its impact. Thus, as Inglehart and Baker (2000) demonstrate with multiple regression analysis, even when we control for level of economic development and other factors, a history of communist rule still accounts for a significant share of the cross-cultural variance in basic values (with seven decades of communist rule having more impact than four decades). But an Orthodox tradition seems to reduce emphasis on self-expression values, by comparison with societies historically shaped by a Roman Catholic or Protestant cultural tradition.

The Islamic Societies in Global Perspective

As of 2002, the WVS included 14 predominantly Islamic societies, and their locations on the global cultural map are depicted on figure 2.3.

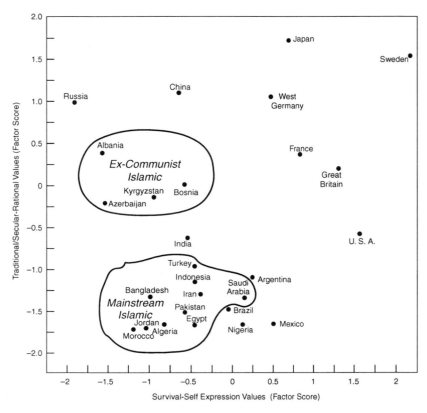

Figure 2.3   The values of Islamic societies in global perspective

Most of them are "low income" societies, as classified by the World Bank, and accordingly they tend to emphasize traditional and survival values—but there are two distinct clusters, reflecting distinctive historical experiences. Ten societies—Morocco, Algeria, Egypt, Jordan, Bangladesh, Pakistan, Indonesia, Iran, Turkey, and Saudi Arabia—fall into a "mainstream Islamic" cluster, in the lower left-hand quadrant of the map. The publics of these societies tend to emphasize traditional values and survival values, but the publics of the three wealthiest of these countries—Saudi Arabia, Turkey, and Iran—place more emphasis on secular-rational and self-expression values than most other members of this group. Although Saudi Arabia is the original center of Islam and is governed by an absolute monarchy, its public does *not* have the most traditional value system of any Islamic country—quite the contrary, the Saudi public emphasizes self-expression values more strongly than any other Islamic public. Since these values are closely linked with mass support for democracy, it would be a serious mistake to assume that the Saudi public is uninterested in democratization. The mainstream Islamic societies are concentrated in the lower left-hand quadrant of the global cultural map, but they are not unique in emphasizing preindustrial values—the public of Zimbabwe falls closer to the lower left hand corner than the public of any other society, and the publics of Puerto Rico, Colombia, and El Salvador emphasize traditional values more strongly than any Islamic public. Although the mainstream Islamic societies do have distinctive values, forming a reasonably compact cluster, this largely reflects their level of economic development.

Even more striking evidence of the fact that value systems are conditioned by a society's historical experience emerges when we examine the values of four predominantly Islamic societies that have experienced communist rule—Albania, Azerbaijan, Kyrgyzstan, and Bosnia. These societies form a separate cluster, distinguished from the mainstream Islamic cluster by the fact that the publics of the ex-communist Islamic societies place are much more likely to emphasize secular-rational values than the publics of any of the mainstream Islamic societies. The communist regimes made massive efforts to eradicate traditional religious values and replace them with the communist ideology, and the four–seven decades under communist rule experienced by these societies has left a manifest impact. Thus, we find not one but two clusters of Islamic societies, differentiated by their experience under communist rule.

We have compared the belief systems of the people of Islamic societies with those of other regions on two major dimensions of cross-cultural variation. This provides a useful overview, but it is operating at a high level of generalization. Now let us examine how these societies differ on some of the specific variables linked with each of the two main dimensions.

Table 2.3 shows cross-cultural variation in five of the most important variables that are closely linked with the traditional/secular-rational dimension. As we have noted, dozens of other variables are also strongly correlated with this dimension, but these five illustrate the general pattern. This table shows the percentage emphasizing the position linked with the *traditional* pole, so high scores indicate traditional values. On all five variables, the publics of the ex-communist countries are much less

Table 2.3 Differences across major cultural zones in the components of traditional/secular-rational values

Region	% Saying "God is very important in my life"	% Very proud of nationality	% Favoring more respect for authority	% Low on autonomy index	% Saying abortion is never justifiable	Mean score on traditional/ secular-rational values
Protestant Europe (11)	12	38	43	37	18	1.018
Confucian (4)	9	23	28	36	31	.937
Orthodox (13)	30	42	57	55	29	.571
Catholic Europe (14)	27	47	59	55	31	.210
English-speaking (7)	33	59	68	59	32	−.259
South Asia (3)	64	79	64	66	55	−.816
Islamic (14)	78	73	68	74	59	−1.031
Latin America (11)	78	79	79	75	69	−1.322
Africa (6)	74	75	65	78	72	−1.499
Overall mean	44	56	61	60	43	−.164

likely to have traditional values than the publics of societies that did not experience communist rule: for example, the publics of the Soviet successor states are less than half as likely to say that "God is very important in my life" than are the publics of noncommunist societies; they also rank much lower on national pride, are less likely to say the "more respect for authority would be a good thing," are more likely to emphasize independence and determination as important things for a child to learn (autonomy versus obedience), and are less likely to believe that abortion is never justifiable. The largest gap is between communist and noncommunist societies, but the publics of the Soviet successor states tend to be even more secular than the publics of the other ex-communist societies.

When we examine the results from each of the nine cultural regions, we find a more complex picture. Overall, Protestant Europe has the most secular public, but the ranking varies on given variables. The Confucian publics actually show more secular orientations than the Protestants on most of these variables, but rank slightly behind them on the index as a whole. The publics of the Orthodox countries consistently rank about third, ranging from as high as second to as low as fourth on these variables. The publics of Catholic Europe are slightly *less* likely to say that "God is very important in my life" than are the publics of the Orthodox societies, but they are slightly more traditional on the other variables. Overall, the rankings of given cultural zones are remarkably consistent across all five variables: if you know a region's ranking on one of them, you can predict where it will fall on the other four with considerable accuracy. On every variable, the Protestant and Confucian cultural zones *always* fall among the three lowest-ranking regions, and at the opposite extreme, sub-Saharan Africa and Latin America *always* fall among the three highest-ranking regions. And although the mainstream Islamic publics tend to emphasize very traditional values, the 14 Islamic societies as a whole have somewhat less traditional values than the Latin American publics and the sub-Saharan African publics.

Table 2.4 provides details concerning six variables closely linked with the survival/self-expression dimension. High scores indicate that a given region emphasizes self-expression values relatively strongly. Thus, the noncommunist countries as a whole have a score on the materialist/postmaterialist values index of −11, indicating that the materialists outweigh the postmaterialists by 11 percent. The preponderance of materialists is much stronger in societies that have experienced communist rule: materialists outnumber postmaterialists by 43 percent in the Soviet successor states and by 31 percent in the other ex-communist societies.

Table 2.4 Differences across major cultural zones in the components of survival/self-expression values

	Postmat minus materialist	% Very happy	Some tolerance, homosexuality	Have signed petition	Trust people	Disagree, men make better politicians	Mean score, survival/self-expression values
English speaking (7)	10	40	68	66	38	79	1.553
Protestant Europe (11)	−9	29	73	53	46	84	1.007
Latin America (11)	−5	40	46	23	16	64	.428
Catholic Europe (14)	−14	21	57	42	24	57	.323
South Asia (3)	−29	38	35	15	29	43	−.113
Confucian (4)	−36	21	40	35	42	53	−.268
Africa (6)	−25	39	19	15	14	42	−.288
Islamic (14)	−32	23	10	16	28	35	−.814
Orthodox (13)	−39	10	31	18	23	43	−1.161
Overall mean	−19	26	43	33	28	51	.050

Similarly, happiness levels and tolerance of homosexuality are much
lower in the Soviet successor states than in the societies that have not
experienced communist rule, with the other ex-communist societies
falling between these two extremes: in the never-communist zone,
33 percent of the public describes themselves as "very happy," as compared
with only 7 percent in the ex-Soviet societies, and 16 percent in the
other former communist societies.

Attitudes toward homosexuality are negative throughout the world.
Respondents were asked to rate the acceptability of homosexuality on a
10-point scale ranging from 1 = never justifiable, to 10 = always justifiable. Over half the number of the respondents in the world as a whole
chose point 1, indicating total rejection; the remaining respondents were
distributed over points 2 through 10. Thus, this table differentiates between
those who indicated "some" tolerance of homosexuality (choosing points
2 through 10) versus those who indicated that it was completely unaccept-
able. In the non-Islamic world, 51 percent express "some" tolerance—but
in the Islamic societies, only 10 percent do so. The percentage that reports
having signed a petition in the past five years also varies greatly, with
36 percent of the public in non-Islamic societies reporting that it has done
so, as compared with only 16 percent in the Islamic societies.

These large differences in tolerance of outgroups such as gays and women
have political implications—for tolerance of outgroups among the public is
closely correlated with stable democracy at the institutional level. Though
overwhelming majorities of the publics of Islamic societies endorse democracy as a general goal, they show much lower levels on such underlying
qualities as tolerance and the postmaterialist valuation of freedom of speech
and political participation as goods in themselves. These attributes seem to
play a crucial role in the emergence and survival of liberal democracy.

The right-hand column of table 2.4 shows how each of these orientations breaks down across the eight cultural zones. Again, the rankings
on one variable are generally consistent with the rankings on the other
variables. Overall, the Orthodox cultural zone ranks the lowest of any
region in emphasis on self-expression values—with the Islamic cultural
zone ranking second. Given the remarkably strong linkage that has been
found between self-expression values and stable democracy (Inglehart
2003), this finding may have significant implications.

Gender Inequality and Democracy

Fish (2002) notes that only a few of the 47 predominantly Islamic
societies (and none of the Arabic-speaking Islamic societies) qualify as

democracies, even by the most minimal standards. He argues that their marked lack of gender equality is a crucial reason for this finding. As evidence of greater gender inequality in Islamic societies than in other societies, Fish points to the large gap between the educational levels of men and women in Islamic societies; and the substantial difference in sex ratios between Muslim and non-Muslim countries: "A deficit of females relative to males often stems from various forms of lifelong discrimination against girls and women," including sex-selective infanticide (Fish 2002: 27). Fish suggests that the unquestioned superiority of the male creates a culture of domination, intolerance, and dependency in social and political life.

Similarly, analyzing cumulative results from the Values Surveys, Inglehart and Norris (2003), find that Muslims and their Western counterparts are worlds apart when it comes to their attitudes about sexual liberalization and gender equality. For example, 53 percent of those surveyed in Western nations express some degree of tolerance for homosexuality, compared to just 10 percent of those surveyed in Islamic societies. Similarly, Western publics are much more likely to support gender equality, divorce, and abortion, than are Islamic publics. Inglehart and Norris (2003) find that Finland, Sweden, West Germany, Canada, and Norway are at the top of the international gender equality scale, while Morocco, Egypt, Bangladesh and Jordan rank at the bottom, concluding that "An Islamic religious heritage is one of the most powerful barriers to the rising tide of gender equality."

As we have seen (see table 2.2), support for gender equality and tolerance of homosexuality are key indicators of the survival/self-expression values dimension—and a society's position on this dimension is strongly correlated with its level of democracy, as indicated by its scores on the Freedom House ratings of political rights and civil liberties. This relationship is remarkably powerful (r = .83) and it is clearly not a methodological artifact or an intracranial correlation, since the two variables are measured at different levels and come from different sources (Inglehart 2003). Virtually all of the societies that rank high on survival/self-expression values are stable democracies. Virtually all of the societies that rank low on this dimension have authoritarian governments. The correlation between survival/self-expression values and democracy is significant at a very high level, and probably reflects a causal linkage. But what causes what?

One interpretation would be that democratic institutions give rise to the self-expression values that are so closely linked with them. In other words, democracy makes people healthy, happy, nonsexist, tolerant and trusting, and instills postmaterialist values. This interpretation is appealing and if it were true, it would provide a powerful argument for democracy, implying that we have a quick fix for most of the problems in the world: adopt democratic institutions and live happily ever after.

Unfortunately, the experience of the Soviet Union's successor states does not support this interpretation. Since their dramatic move toward democracy in 1991, they have not become healthier, happier, more trusting, more tolerant, or more postmaterialist: most of them have moved in exactly the opposite direction. The fact that their people are living in economic and physical insecurity seems to have more impact than the fact that their leaders are chosen by free elections.

Democratic institutions do not automatically produce a culture that emphasizes self-expression values. Instead, it seems that economic development gradually leads to social and cultural changes that make democratic institutions more likely to survive and flourish. That would help explain why mass democracy did not emerge until a relatively recent point in history, and why, even now, it is most likely to be found in economically more developed countries—in particular, those that emphasize self-expression values over survival values.

This is cause for concern, but not a reason for resignation. During the past few decades, most industrialized societies have moved toward increasing emphasis on self-expression values, in an intergenerational cultural shift linked with economic development. And despite the relative weakness of democratic institutions in Islamic societies, there is evidence that the publics of these societies see democracy as a highly desirable goal.

Do Islamic Publics Reject Democracy?

According to the latest Freedom House rankings, almost two-thirds of the 192 countries around the world are now electoral democracies. But among the 47 countries with an Islamic majority, only one-fourth are electoral democracies—and none of the core Arabic-speaking societies falls into this category. Why has not democracy taken hold in these countries?

One response has been that the Islamic world lacks the core political values that gave birth to representative democracy in Western civilization. But those who have advanced this claim have presented little or no empirical evidence about whether Western and Muslim societies exhibit deeply divergent values. Indeed, very little empirical evidence has been

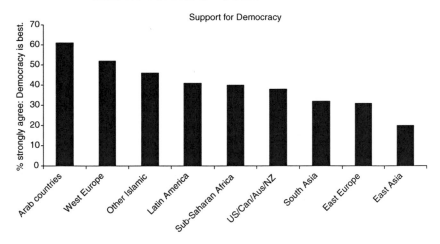

Figure 2.4   Support for democracy in nine cultural zones

Regional groupings. **Arab countries**: Algeria, Egypt, Jordan, Saudi Arabia, Morocco; **Other Islamic**: Albania, Azerbaijan, Bangladesh, Bosnia, Indonesia, Iran, Kyrgyzstan, Pakistan, Turkey; **Sub-Saharan Africa**: Nigeria, South Africa, Tanzania, Uganda, Zimbabwe; **Western Europe**: Austria, Belgium, Denmark, Finland, Germany, Greece, Iceland, Ireland, Italy, Luxembourg, Netherlands, Norway, Spain, Sweden, Switzerland, United Kingdom; **Eastern Europe**: Armenia, Belarus, Bulgaria, Croatia, Czech Republic, Estonia, Georgia, Hungary, Latvia, Lithuania, Macedonia, Moldova, Poland, Romania, Russia, Slovakia, Slovenia, Ukraine, Yugoslavia; **English-speaking**: Australia, Canada, New Zealand, United States; **Latin America**: Argentina, Brazil, Chile, Colombia, Dominican Republic, El Salvador, Mexico, Peru, Uruguay, Venezuela; **East Asia**: China, Japan, Republic of Korea, Taiwan; **South Asia**: India, Philippines, Singapore, Vietnam.

available about the beliefs of Islamic publics—until now. The two most recent waves of the WVS, conducted in 1995–96 and 2000–02, provide an extensive body of relevant evidence. These surveys included five Arab countries (Algeria, Egypt, Jordan, Saudi Arabia, and Morocco) plus nine other predominantly Islamic countries (Albania, Azerbaijan, Bangladesh, Bosnia, Indonesia, Iran, Kyrgyzstan, Pakistan, and Turkey). Because of the severe democratic deficit in Arab societies, these countries are analyzed separately from the other Islamic societies in the remainder of this chapter.

Despite claims of a clash of civilizations between the West and the rest, the evidence from the WVS reveals that at this point in history, democracy has an overwhelmingly positive image throughout the world. And the publics of Arab countries are particularly likely to endorse democracy, as figure 2.4 demonstrates. In response to the item "Democracy may have

Table 2.5 Support for democracy (Percent agreeing that "Democracy may have problems but it is better than any other form of government")

Denmark	99	Spain	92	Zimbabwe	87
Bangladesh	98	Japan	92	New Zealand	87
Egypt	98	India	92	S Africa	86
W Germany	97	Montenegro	92	Georgia	86
Iceland	97	Bosnia	92	Bulgaria	84
Austria	97	Argentina	91	Taiwan	84
Greece	97	Finland	91	Slovakia	84
Netherlands	96	S Korea	91	Hungary	83
Uruguay	96	Switzerland	91	Brazil	83
Azerbaijan	96	Puerto Rico	91	Ukraine	83
Croatia	96	Lithuania	91	Chile	82
Morocco	96	Slovenia	90	Pakistan	82
Norway	95	China	90	Macedonia	81
Albania	95	Estonia	90	Mexico	80
Luxemburg	95	Jordan	90	Philippines	79
Italy	94	Poland	89	Kyrgyzstan	78
N Ireland	94	Latvia	89	Britain	78
Sweden	94	Peru	89	Romania	78
Malta	94	Serbia	89	Moldova	78
France	93	Turkey	88	Saudi Arabia	74
Ireland	93	Tanzania	88	Armenia	73
Czech Rep	93	Algeria	88	Vietnam	72
E Germany	93	United States	87	Indonesia	71
Venezuela	93	Canada	87	Iran	69
Dominican Rep	93	Australia	87	Russia	62
Uganda	93	Belarus	87	Nigeria	45
Belgium	92	El Salvador	87		

Source: Data from most recent WVS (the 1999–2002 wave for most countries, from the 1995–96 wave for Uruguay, Azerbaijan, Norway, Dominican Rep.,Switzerland, Australia, Georgia, Taiwan, Brazil, and Armenia).

many problems but it is better than any other form of government," 61 percent of the publics of the five Arab countries agreed strongly—a figure higher than the 52 percent registered in 16 West European countries or the 38 percent strong agreement in the United States, Canada, Australia, and New Zealand. If we combine the percentage that "agrees" with those who "agree strongly," overwhelming majorities consider democracy the best form of government in all nine regions and in virtually every society. Table 2.5 shows the percentage that view democracy as the best form of government, in every country for which data are available. The figures range from a low of 69 percent in Iran, to highs of 98 percent in both Bangladesh and Egypt. Clearly, the publics of Arab countries (and

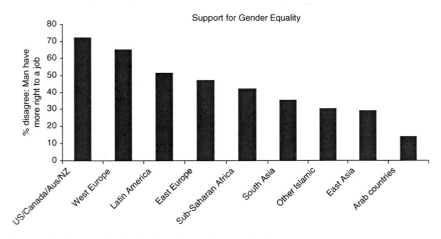

Figure 2.5   Support for Gender Equality in nine cultural zones

Regional groupings. **Arab countries**: Algeria, Egypt, Jordan, Saudi Arabia, Morocco; **Other Islamic**: Albania, Azerbaijan, Bangladesh, Bosnia, Indonesia, Iran, Kyrgyzstan, Pakistan, Turkey; **Sub-Saharan Africa**: Nigeria, South Africa, Tanzania, Uganda, Zimbabwe; **Western Europe**: Austria, Belgium, Denmark, Finland, Germany, Greece, Iceland, Ireland, Italy, Luxembourg, Netherlands, Norway, Spain, Sweden, Switzerland, United Kingdom; **Eastern Europe**: Armenia, Belarus, Bulgaria, Croatia, Czech Republic, Estonia, Georgia, Hungary, Latvia, Lithuania, Macedonia, Moldova, Poland, Romania, Russia, Slovakia, Slovenia, Ukraine, Yugoslavia; **English-speaking**: Australia, Canada, New Zealand, United States; **Latin America**: Argentina, Brazil, Chile, Colombia, Dominican Republic, El Salvador, Mexico, Peru, Uruguay, Venezuela; **East Asia**: China, Japan, Republic of Korea, Taiwan; **South Asia**: India, Philippines, Singapore, Vietnam.

Islamic societies in general) do not reject democracy: overwhelming majorities want it.

This does not mean that it will come automatically. As younger generations in the West have gradually become more supportive of gender equality, Islamic nations have remained the most traditional societies in the world. Commenting on the disenfranchisement of women throughout the Middle East, the United Nations Development Report observed in 2002 that "no society can achieve the desired state of well-being and human development, or compete in a globalizing world, if half its people remain marginalized and disempowered." The fact that gender equality tends to go hand in hand with democratization makes it disturbing that support for gender equality in Arab countries is lower than in any other region of the world. As figure 2.5 demonstrates, in the United States, Canada, Australia, and New Zealand, 72 percent of the public disagrees with the statement that "When jobs are scarce, men should have more right to a job than women." At the other end of the scale, only 14 percent of the publics of the Arab countries disagrees with this statement. Table 2.6 shows the levels of support for gender equality

44

Table 2.6 Support for gender equality % disagreeing that "When jobs are scarce, men have more right to a job than women"

Iceland	94	W Germany	53
Sweden	93	S Africa	53
Denmark	89	Austria	53
Netherlands	83	Russia	53
United States	82	Venezuela	53
Norway	80	Chile	51
Canada	77	Bulgaria	48
Ireland	76	Uganda	48
Estonia	75	Bosnia	48
N Ireland	74	Romania	47
Puerto Rico	73	Singapore	46
Greece	73	Poland	45
Croatia	73	Vietnam	45
Finland	73	China	43
Belgium	70	Malta	43
Latvia	69	Moldova	40
Colombia	69	Indonesia	40
France	68	Kyrgyzstan	39
Spain	68	Macedonia	35
Hungary	68	Albania	32
Slovenia	68	India	31
Britain	67	Turkey	31
Australia	67	Armenia	31
Peru	67	Nigeria	30
Dominican Rep	67	Azerbaijan	28
Luxemburg	66	S Korea	27
Czech Rep	65	Georgia	26
Lithuania	65	Iran	23
Belarus	64	Japan	21
New Zealand	64	Algeria	20
Argentina	61	Ghana	19
Portugal	61	Pakistan	18
Ukraine	61	Bangladesh	17
Mexico	59	Philippines	16
E Germany	59	Morocco	12
Italy	57	Jordan	12
Serbia	57	Egypt	10
Montenegro	57	Saudi Arabia	9
Tanzania	56	Taiwan	7
Switzerland	55	El Salvador	6
Zimbabwe	54	Brazil	2
Slovakia	54	Uruguay	2

Source: WVS (latest available survey for given country).

in jobs, within each society. Islamic publics, including the Arab publics, overwhelmingly view democracy as the best form of government. This is an important and encouraging finding. But they still lag on some of the important underlying attitudes of tolerance and equality that seem to help sustain democracy.

Conclusion

Islamic societies have relatively similar basic values in comparison with societies with other cultural traditions—but it is important to distinguish between mainstream Islamic societies and those that have experienced communist rule. The mainstream Islamic group forms a compact cluster on the global cultural map despite having a wide geographical dispersion, from Morocco to Indonesia. The ex-communist Islamic societies have much more secular-rational values than the mainstream Islamic societies, which emphasize traditional religious values strongly.

Strong majorities of the publics of all 14 Islamic societies view democracy as the best form of government but they rank relatively low on self-expression values, which are strongly linked with stable democracy. But they are not unique in this respect: societies with an Orthodox tradition, and the Soviet successor societies, rank even lower than the Islamic societies on this dimension. Although there is some tendency for Islamic societies to be characterized by low levels of tolerance and support for gender equality, even controlling for per capita GNP, these characteristics can largely be attributed to their relatively low levels of economic development. The Islamic societies, which are more prosperous than others, rank as high on self-expression values as do many of the new democracies in East Asia and Eastern Europe. There is no reason to doubt whether the Islamic publics' aspirations for democracy can be realized in the future, particularly if they attain reasonable levels of economic security.

Notes

1. Direct correspondence to Ronald Inglehart, Institute for Social Research, University of Michigan Ann Arbor, Michigan, 48106–1248; e-mail: RFI@umich.edu.
2. The WVS and European Values Surveys (EVS) have been carried out in more than 80 societies, with successive waves conducted in 1981–82, 1990–91, 1995–97 and 1999–2001; a fifth wave will be carried out in 2005–06. For detailed information about these surveys, see the WVS web sites at http://www.worldvaluessurvey.org (September 20, 2006), and the EVS web site http://www.europeanvalues.nl/index2.htm (September 20, 2006).
3. For details of these analyses at both the individual level and the national level, see Inglehart and Baker 2000.

References

Fish, M. Steven. 2002. "Islam and Authoritarianism." *World Politics* 55(1): 4–37.

Huntington, Samuel P. 1996. *The Clash of Civilizations and the Remaking of World Order*. New York: Simon and Schuster.

Inglehart, Ronald. 2003. "How Solid Is Mass Support for Democracy—and How Can We Measure It?" *PS: Political Science and Politics* 36(1): 51–57.

Inglehart, Ronald and Wayne Baker. 2000. "Modernization, Cultural Change and the Persistence of Traditional Values." *American Sociological Review* 65(1): 19–51.

Inglehart, Ronald and Pippa Norris. 2003. *Rising Tide: Gender Equality and Cultural Change Around the World*. Cambridge: Cambridge University Press.

Inglehart, Ronald and Christian Welzel. 2005. *Modernization, Cultural Change and Democracy: The Human Development Sequence*. New York: Cambridge University Press.

CHAPTER 3

Value Systems of Elites and Publics in the Mediterranean: Convergence or Divergence

JUAN DÍEZ-NICOLÁS

Elites and Publics

The study of elites and publics has always received great attention in the social sciences, since the early times (Lasswell 1936; Mannheim 1935; Mosca 1939/1896; Ortega y Gasset 1929; Pareto 1902–03). In general, the concept of elites has referred to social minorities and ruling minorities, mainly in the fields of politics, the military, the economy, business, and culture. In earlier times scholars did not differentiate so much among different types of elites, and referred to them as minorities in power, simply because there was a great overlap among the elites in different fields. The tendency to refer to elites as a compound mixture of minorities in different sectors of society persisted however for a long time, and were generally referred to as the "ruling class," "the power elite" (Mills 1956) or the like (Bottomore 1964; Lasswell 1952), though other authors preferred to discriminate among different types of elites, for example, "strategic elites" (Keller 1963), to designate minorities who had authority or power in different sectors of society (politics, religion, business, fashion, etc.). More recently there has been a proliferation of country studies of elites (some examples are Collier 1999; Eldersveld 1995; Lerner et al. 2004; Perthes 2004; Verba et al. 1987; Werbner 2004; Yoder 1999), whose findings are more difficult to generalize, as well as other more general works (Carlton 1996; Etzioni-Halevy 1997; Marger 1981;

Walden 2000). Most studies of elites, including those cited, refer to elites as very small social minorities who occupy power positions either in society at large or within some part of it. But, generally, there is little comparison with publics or masses, which usually appear in the background as a necessary complement to elites, since there would be no minorities without majorities. An important exception would be Kornhauser's fourfold classification of societies on the basis of accessibility of elites and availability of nonelites (Kornhauser 1959).

The approach that has been adopted in this research shares with most of the works in this area the assumption that elites influence publics though some recent research findings establish limitations of that influence (Druckman and Nelson 2003; Paul and Brown 2001), but does differ from them in several respects. First, the concept of elites is defined in a less rigid and more flexible manner to avoid the rigid elites-publics dichotomy and, instead, treat these two concepts as the poles of a continuum. In this respect, the analysis follows a similar but revised methodology that Galtung established four decades ago to construct a "social position" index as a tool to test his "center-periphery" theory (Galtung 1964, 1976). Second, rather than focusing on the values of elites, the values of elites and publics are always compared within and between societies (developed versus less developed, Mediterranean-European versus Mediterranean-Islamic).

Galtung's main assumption was that some social positions receive more rewards (economic, prestige, power) than others. He then selected eight sociodemographic characteristics that are rewarded differently by societies to construct the social position index, which produced a scale of nine categories.[1] Lower ratings received the name of "social periphery," while higher ratings on the scale received the name of "social center," and the extremes of the scale received the names of "extreme periphery" and "decision-making nucleus" respectively. As may be noticed, the conceptualization of "elites" and "publics" based on the social position index allows for greater flexibility, since each researcher may define elites-publics (center-periphery) differently (defining one or more positions in the scale as center or periphery), in order to meet specific research requirements. Social center (as the sum of the more socially rewarded positions) and social periphery (as the sum of the less socially rewarded positions) differ from each other in many respects. Individuals belong to the social center or the social periphery not because of their personal traits, but because of the different status they hold, which corresponds to social roles they perform in society.

According to Galtung's center-periphery theory, the center has more knowledge, particularly about policies, while the periphery shows little knowledge, particularly in regard to policies. As a consequence, the center has more opinions, while the periphery has fewer or no opinions. Therefore, as the center has more knowledge and opinions and has more access to mass media, communication flows generally from the center to the periphery (among other things because the center has more things to communicate). It also follows that the center will demand and show more social participation, especially through secondary (associations) and tertiary channels (mass media), while the periphery will demand and exhibit less social participation, manifested through primary channels (interpersonal communication). Therefore, new ideas and social values originate mainly in the center and from it they are disseminated to the periphery (and even if new values or ideas originate in the periphery, they will have to be adopted by some group in the center if they are to be disseminated to the rest of society). At this point it may be necessary to clarify that the center is by definition ideologically heterogeneous (no ideological characteristics are used to define center or periphery), so that new ideas in the periphery may always find some group in the center willing to accept them and disseminate them. Center and periphery differ in many other respects, but especially on their orientation to social change: the center will favor gradual change, reforms, while the periphery will be more absolutist, in favor of changing everything (radical or revolutionary change) or of no change at all (defense of the status quo). Most of the hypotheses of this theory have been verified repeatedly (Díez-Nicolás 1966, 1968, 1996; Halle 1966; van der Veer 1976), and they have also contributed to specify some of the main hypotheses of Inglehart's theory of cultural change (Díez-Nicolás 1999, 2000, 2004a), especially with respect to the emergence of the new values in favor of protecting the environment.

The main hypothesis that is tested here is another example of how Galtung's theory of the emergence and diffusion of new values can complement Inglehart's theory of cultural change. Thus, according to Inglehart's well-known hypotheses, postmaterialist, or self-expression values are more frequently found, at the macro level, in more developed societies, and at the micro level, in the upper strata of each society. Consequently, elites (the social center) in developed and less developed societies should be expected to share more similar values amongst themselves than with their respective publics (the social periphery), so that it should be possible to observe a convergence of values between elites at the same time that a divergence of values occurs between elites and their respective publics. The convergence of values between elites would be a consequence of their greater access to communication facilities (telephone, internet, travelling, interpersonal communication through professional meetings) and, as a result, to the greater possibilities of interaction between them. A second hypothesis that will be tested is that publics in developed and less developed societies should show the largest divergence in values, due to infrequent interaction between them.

Does Globalization Lead to Convergence?

Globalization is not a new process. It has been at work since the beginning of history, as human societies have grown from the early self-sufficient and independent communities to ever expanding and interdependent human communities in terms of population, elaborate technology, complex social organization, and with access to an expanding environment due to technological developments in the means of communication and transportations (Díez-Nicolás 1999; Duncan 1964; Hawley 1986). Fukuyama has observed that, after the fall of the Berlin Wall in 1989, there seems to be only one model of economic organization, the free market economy, and one model of political organization, the parliamentary democracy (Fukuyama 1991), and that all societies claim to have achieved or to be in the process of achieving both. The explicit assumption of this argument is that there is a universal convergence toward these two organizational systems, and that their universal acceptance will be more or less permanent (an assumption that leads to his conclusion about the end of history).[2] There is, however, an implicit assumption in Fukuyama: that if there is a more or less universal convergence toward the same models of economic and political organization, there should also be a similar process of convergence in values and beliefs systems. This assumption is tenable, because increasing economic interdependence worldwide (and consequently increasing interaction worldwide) leads to isomorphism of organizational arrangements (as it is observed regarding political and economic institutions as well as other institutional arrangements). And due to developments in the means of communication and transportation (satellites, internet, and movies), one should expect cultural convergence and isomorphism.

The explicit assumption about the institutional convergence in the economic and political realms seems to be supported by facts, and the implicit assumption regarding a certain convergence in values and beliefs systems has been supported by the results of extensive analysis of values surveys that were carried out by Inglehart and others. Just as societies still differ in the degree to which they have achieved a free market economy and parliamentary democracy, societies still differ, probably even more, in the degree to which they have achieved a certain cultural model characterized by a new value system. Inglehart has shown how most societies seem to be changing from survival values to self-expression values, from traditional values to rational-secular values, and how the values systems that accompanied the process of change from traditional to industrial society are again changing in the transition from industrial to postindustrial society (Inglehart et al. 2004). Welzel has also explained how these two processes are linked to produce a more encompassing process of human development characterized by a continuous drive toward values of emancipation that constitute the basis of democratic systems (Welzel 2003; Welzel et al. 2003). According to this theory, the new values are more widespread among the more developed societies, and within each society, among people with the higher socioeconomic status.

The methodological strategy of this chapter is twofold. First, comparisons at the macro level (using countries as units of analysis) must be made with great care. This is because survey data are not in some cases representative of the total population, but frequently neglect or underrepresent the lower strata (the social periphery). Second, comparisons at the micro level will likely show that there are different rhythms of change for different groups within each society. They also should show that the different rhythms of change cause some unexpected (and maybe undesired) consequences, the most important of them being that elites in less developed countries are approaching the value systems of elites in the more developed societies, while detaching themselves at the same time from the values of their respective social peripheries. This hypothesis would not contradict the previous hypothesis that the higher social strata acquire the new values earlier than the lower strata, just as more developed countries acquire them earlier than less developed countries, but it specifies that the different rhythms of change produce a convergence of elites in very different societies on a shared system of values, but at the same time a growing divergence between elites and publics in each society. It seems relevant to test this hypothesis on the basis of a massive amount of data that are provided by the EVS and the WVS.

Before analyzing these hypotheses about the Mediterranean region, it was thought relevant to test these hypotheses at a more general level by comparing countries with different degrees of development in the world as a whole. Assuming that findings should be similar at the world and the Mediterranean levels, the value of the findings would be enhanced. In fact, the comparison between developed European-Christian societies and less-developed Islamic societies in the Mediterranean can be considered a special case of the more general comparison between developed and less developed countries.

Measuring the Concepts of Elites and Development

To measure development, countries have been grouped according to cultural areas that are somewhat similar to Huntington's (Huntington 1996) classification of civilizations.[3] For each country four measures of development were obtained: economic, political, social, and cultural. GNP per capita is used to measure economic development. Political development is measured by Freedom House ratings of democracy (FHR). Social development is measured by the Human Development index (HDI). To measure cultural development, the two dimensions developed by Inglehart (1990, 1997), the survival-self expression dimension—equivalent to the former materialist-postmaterialist dimension (POSTMAT) in previous publications (Díez-Nicolás 2000; Inglehart 1977)—and the traditional-secular/rational dimension (TRADRAT) were used.

Taking countries as the units of analysis, the correlation coefficients among the five measures for 81 countries were all above .45 and statistically significant at the .01 level, with the only exception of the relationship between the two cultural values dimensions, as expected, since they are intended to measure two distinctive and independent dimensions of values.[4]

Furthermore, countries were grouped into the 13 world regions mentioned above, and averages in the same 5 variables have been calculated for each region, with a similar rank-order in each dimension. It may be noted that four regions (Anglo-Saxon, West European Catholic, West European Protestant, and Japan) rank higher than the rest in all five dimensions of development, with the only exception of the traditional-rational/secular dimension, in which Israel, East European Christian, and European Orthodox countries show greater secularization than Anglo-Saxon and West European Catholic countries. This finding has been confirmed in all waves of the values studies, and they suggest that traditional values based on religion have continued to play a more important role in some Western countries than they have played in countries that were under communist rule. One should underline the difference in the trajectory of development between the Anglo-Saxon and West European Protestant countries, probably due to the different paths taken by the Reformation in different parts of Europe. Thus, while

Lutherans (who subordinated religion to political power) remained in most of Central and Northern Europe, Calvinists (who subordinated political power to religion) became a minority established mainly in the Netherlands and Switzerland, which, after being prosecuted, escaped mainly to Great Britain (and from there to the New World as Pilgrims) and to South Africa. It should also be noted that Israel is a kind of frontier between the four more developed world regions and the less developed regions (figure 3.1).

In any case, the traditional-secular/rational dimension seems to be the only one that is less related to the other dimensions of development. The correlation coefficients among the five indicators of development are significant at the .01 level, except for the relationship between the two values dimensions. These significant correlation coefficients show that development in one dimension is associated with development in other dimensions, confirming that the different dimensions are all manifestations of the nonmaterial culture and, as such, instrumental social responses that human populations develop when interacting with their environment (Díez-Nicolás 2003). The strong relationships between the five dimensions facilitates classifying world regions as developed or less developed, precisely because it makes it unnecessary to specify what kind of development is being measured.

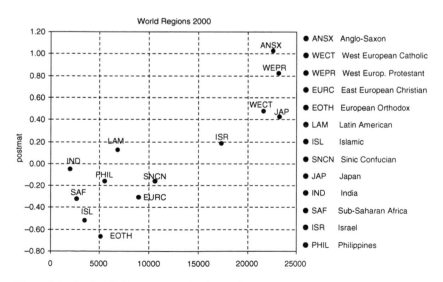

Figure 3.1 Survival/Self-expression values by GNP per capita

If the world regions are plotted on any two dimensions, they show a regular pattern of greater development (economic, political, social, or cultural) in the same areas, as well as a great gap between the more developed and the less developed. The Anglo-Saxon countries, the West European (Catholic and Protestant) countries, and Japan are classified as developed areas. The countries included in the other regions have been divided into two groups: (1) the East European Christian (EEC) and the European Orthodox (EO) countries, and (2) the remaining countries, considering the latter as less developed in general (i.e., taking all five dimensions into account). The EEC and EO countries, which include most of the former communist countries, are very low on the postmaterialist dimension, mainly due to their experience as economies based on state-socialism, though they rate very high on the traditional–secular/rational dimension (Inglehart 1990, 1997).

To measure elites, a revised version of the social position index developed by Galtung (Díez-Nicolás 1999, 2004a; Galtung 1964, 1976) has been constructed for this analysis. Thus, instead of dichotomizing the eight variables that Galtung used to construct the social position index, an effort has been made to measure them through several categories. In fact, only sex and age have been dichotomized, while four other indicators of social position have been measured on three-point scales (education, employment status, income, and size of habitat), and occupational prestige has been measured on a four-point scale. This modified version of the social position index varies between 0 and 13, and includes seven variables, while Galtung's index varied between 0 and 8, and included eight variables. The main difference between the two indices, apart from the number of categories in the scale, is that the variables are not given the same weight. Sex and age are given less weight, while occupation is given more weight, on the assumption that occupation is the main source of all kind of social rewards in present societies, not just economic rewards.[5] This explains why the social position index is more strongly correlated with employment status (r = .70) and profession (r = .68), and less strongly related (but still significantly) with sex, age, and size of place of residence (r > .30).

The fact that many countries lacked information on one or more of the variables used to construct the social position index caused the loss of a few thousand respondents (17 percent of the original 118,520 respondents), as well as the loss of ten countries.[6] The analysis was then based on the information for 71 countries, with a total N of 98,702 individuals. The distribution of these individuals is very close to a normal distribution, though a little skewed toward the lower end of the scale. For the purpose of this analysis, the world regions are divided into three categories, as explained, and the operationalization of the concept of elites is based on the distribution by social position, assuming that individuals closer to point 13 on the scale (high social position) are probably members of the elite in their society (defining elites in a very broad manner), while individuals closer to point 0 in the scale are most likely to be publics (nonelites) in their societies.

As table 3.1 illustrates, there seems to be no significant difference on the shape of the distribution on the social position index among the three groups of countries.[7] While it would seem normal that population distribution by sex and age, and even by size of habitat, might not be very different among countries, it is more difficult to accept that developed and less developed countries may have similar distributions of their adult populations with respect to education, income, employment, and occupation. This finding seems to indicate that the samples are not always representative of each country's population. A more detailed examination of the data shows that among the less developed countries one finds samples that are not proportionally representative of their populations; on the contrary, they seem to overrepresent some social sectors (the more educated, the higher incomes, the urban populations).

Table 3.1 Distribution of respondents by social position and degree of development, by world regions

Social position	More developed (AS+WEC+WEP)		Developing (EEC+EO)		Less developed (LA+SC+Ind+SSA+Ph)	
	N=	%	N=	%	N=	%
Low	71	.3	65	.3	241	.6
1	545	2.1	614	2.9	1.510	3.7
2	1,599	6.1	1,474	6.6	2,677	6.7
3	2,614	10.1	2,311	10.0	3,834	9.5
4	3,067	11.6	2,702	11.5	4,767	11.6
5	3,245	12.0	2,851	12.2	5,256	12.8
6	3,443	12.7	2,863	12.2	5,158	12.5
7	3,458	12.7	2,859	12.1	4,792	11.5
8	2,990	10.9	2,627	11.2	3,863	9.3
9	2,404	8.8	2,138	9.0	3,215	7.8
10	1,779	6.6	1,459	6.2	2,419	6.0
11	1,100	4.0	888	3.7	1,643	4.3
12	480	1.8	402	1.7	841	2.4
High	134	.5	82	.4	191	.6
Total	26,929	100.2	23,335	100.0	40,407	99.3

Source: Elaboration of data from WVSEVS_sb_v4.SAV, in Inglehart et al. 2004.

Thus, about 40 percent of respondents, both in more developed and less developed countries, have a low education, and about 20 percent in each group of countries have a high education, a finding that is a bit surprising. Similarly, 28 percent and 25 percent of respondents in less developed and more developed countries are on the upper layer of income in their countries, and about 10 percent in each group has high prestige occupations. Certainly this does not completely preclude a comparative analysis of countries, but it does impose very severe limitations on the comparison of country averages, or, for this purpose, of world regions' averages, because it is quite evident that in the case of developed countries samples seem to be proportionally representative of their populations, while samples in less developed countries seem to represent not their total populations, but their middle and upper socioeconomic strata.[8] It seems legitimate, however, to compare similar social position groups in more and less developed countries, even when their proportional representation does not correspond to their real weight in their country, though the underrepresentation of the lower social strata of less developed societies may introduce important distortions on the results.

Is There a Convergence of Values between Elites in Countries with Different Degrees of Development?

To test the main hypothesis of this research, the average measure of postmaterialist values based on Inglehart's four items scale[9] has been calculated for elites and nonelites in developed and less developed world regions (table 3.2).

Postmaterialist values vary directly with social position. The average index of postmaterialist values varies positively with social position, and the relationship holds in all three groups of countries. This finding mostly confirms the main hypothesis established by Inglehart in his early writings on cultural change, that is, that postmaterialist values are first adopted by the most developed societies and, within each society, by those in higher socioeconomic strata. However, though postmaterialist values are higher in developed countries, there is no significant difference when developing and less developed countries are compared. The data also confirms Galtung's theory that new values are adopted earlier and in greater proportion by the "social center" than by the "social periphery," both at the country and the individual levels.

According to the main hypothesis established for this research, developments in communication and transportation that go along with

Table 3.2   Distribution of respondents by social position and postmaterialism, by world regions

Social position	More developed		Developing		Less developed	
	$N =$	Postmaterialism	$N =$	Postmaterialism	$N =$	Postmaterialism
Low	71	1.73	65	1.48	241	1.55
1	545	1.77	614	1.47	1,510	1.55
2	1,599	1.80	1,474	1.53	2,677	1.60
3	2,614	1.87	2,311	1.56	3,834	1.68
4	3,067	1.94	2,702	1.60	4,767	1.71
5	3,245	1.98	2,851	1.64	5,256	1.71
6	3,443	2.03	2,863	1.67	5,158	1.72
7	3,458	2.05	2,859	1.70	4,792	1.74
8	2,990	2.08	2,627	1.73	3,863	1.76
9	2,404	2.13	2,138	1.73	3,215	1.81
10	1,779	2.19	1,459	1.81	2,419	1.82
11	1,100	2.24	888	1.84	1,643	1.87
12	480	2.29	402	1.89	841	1.86
High	134	2.42	82	1.95	191	1.95

Source: Elaboration of data from WVSEVS_sb_v4.SAV, in Inglehart et al. 2004.

globalization facilitate elites in less developed countries to acquire the values and lifestyles of elites in developed countries. But, in contrast with this process of convergence among elites, one finds a growing divergence of values between elites and their respective nonelites or publics. Data seems to confirm these two contrasting processes. Thus, if elites and nonelites are strictly defined as positions 13 and 0 in the social position index, the ratio of postmaterialism of elites in developed countries to elites in less developed countries is smaller (1.24) than the ratios between elites and publics in developed countries (1.40) and between elites and publics in less developed countries (1.26), though larger than the ratio between publics in developed and less developed countries (1.12). The hypothesis that elites' values in more and less developed countries, as measured by the postmaterialist index, are more similar to each other than to their respective publics is supported by the data, though the hypothesis that the greatest difference would be found between publics in more and less developed countries is not supported by the data. This finding is probably due to the fact that samples in less developed countries have underrepresented their lower social position strata (table 3.3).

Similar results are found if social position is grouped into four groups: 0–3 (social periphery), 4–6, 7–9, and 10–13 (social center), and countries are grouped into three categories according to their degree of development. Again, it appears that postmaterialism is greater among the elites and smaller among the publics in the three groups of countries. Elites in

58 Juan Díez-Nicolás

Table 3.3 Postmaterialism by social position, by world regions

Social position	More developed	Developing	Less developed
Elites (9–13)	2.23	1.83	1.85
2 (7–9)	2.08	1.72	1.77
1 (4–6)	1.99	1.64	1.71
Publics (0–3)	1.83	1.54	1.63

Source: Elaboration of data from WVSEVS_sb_v4.SAV, in Inglehart et al. 2004.

developed countries are the most oriented toward postmaterialism, while publics in less developed countries are the least postmaterialist, as expected. And when ratios are calculated, the ratio between the postmaterialist indexes of elites in developed and in less developed countries is slightly lower than the ratio between elites and publics in developed countries, but higher than the same ratio in less developed countries. This finding would seem to indicate that convergence between elites and publics in less developed countries is higher than between elites and publics in developed countries, a result that can legitimately be questioned when taking into account the more than likely assumption that the real lower social strata in less developed countries have been not only underestimated but probably neglected altogether. Consequently, the smallest ratio is found when comparing publics in developed and in less developed countries, something that very likely results from the fact that the lower strata of less developed countries have not been included in the samples of many less developed countries, and that what appears to be lower social positions are in fact middle social positions.

Elites and Publics in the Mediterranean

Comparing values of elites and publics in developed and less developed regions may hide very important internal differences. Most of the literature analyzing values has focused on comparing "the West" with Islam, since religion, and especially Muslim religion seems to make a significant difference on values, especially values related to gender inequality and the role of women in society, as well as on the influence of religion on politics (Inglehart 2003a, 2003b; Norris and Inglehart 2004). But, apart from the fact that neither Islam nor "the West" is a homogeneous category, the lack of homogeneity is especially acute regarding the role of religion and traditional social values in general (Díez-Nicolás 2003). In fact, while differences between Catholic and Protestant European countries seem to have decreased greatly over the past century, differences between these two groups of countries and Anglo-Saxon countries continue to exist regarding religious values, and some analysts would even argue that they have increased in recent decades (though with the exception of the United Kingdom, which in this respect is more similar to continental Europe than to other Anglo-Saxon countries).

The Mediterranean basin, on the other hand, offers the possibility to compare a relatively large number of developed countries that also seem to be relatively homogeneous in their cultural values (especially regarding religion) with a large number of less developed countries that share the common characteristic of being also relatively homogeneous in their Islamic beliefs (table 3.4).

Thus, eight European countries and eight Islamic countries that are either Mediterranean or close to the Mediterranean have been selected for this analysis.[10] Though Germany, Austria, and Switzerland cannot be considered Mediterranean from a geographical point of view, they have been selected because they are culturally closer to that region than would other Northern or Eastern European countries, with a mixture of Protestant and Catholic majorities and a high degree of economic development and democratic political stability. They also provide a balance to the number of countries on the Islamic side of the comparison.

Table 3.4   Distribution of Mediterranean European or Islamic respondents by social position

Social Position	European-Christians		Islamic	
	N =	%	N =	%
Low	54	.4	71	.5
1	365	2.9	537	3.9
2	909	7.1	1,131	8.3
3	1,426	11.1	1,511	11.0
4	1,660	13.0	1,583	11.6
5	1,628	12.7	1,730	12.6
6	1,684	13.2	1,768	13.0
7	1,661	13.0	1,607	11.7
8	1,343	10.5	1,326	9.7
9	944	7.4	1,006	7.3
10	653	5.1	722	5.3
11	294	2.3	437	3.2
12	139	1.1	218	1.6
High	31	.2	45	.3
Total	12,791	100.0	13,692	100.0

Source: Elaboration of data from WVSEVS_sb_v4.SAV, in Inglehart et al. 2004.

The subsample drawn from the previous larger sample of 71 countries and 98,702 individuals has been reduced to 16 countries and 26,501 individuals. Like in the larger sample, a surprising finding is that the distributions by social position in the eight European-Christian-developed countries and the eight Islamic-less developed countries do not differ significantly.[11] Thus, the social periphery (social position 0–3) represents 22 percent and 24 percent in European-Christian and in Islamic countries respectively, while the social center (social position 9–13) represents 16 percent and 18 percent respectively, suggesting that the lower social strata in Islamic countries are very underrepresented, while the higher social strata are overrepresented in their samples. This is an important problem for description and for using countries as units of analysis, but not for causal-explanatory analysis and for comparing segments of societies in European-Christian and in Islamic countries, though it may affect comparativeness by ignoring the very low strata in society, if they are not only underrepresented but not represented at all. As a matter of fact, the inclusion of the true lower socioeconomic strata in Islamic countries would increase the weight of the social periphery in absolute and relative terms, and consequently their values would gain greater weight when considering the average measures for each group (table 3.5).

As expected, postmaterialism is positively related to social position in both groups of Mediterranean countries (it is higher when the social

Table 3.5 Postmaterialism of Mediterranean European-Christian or Islamic respondents, by social position

Social Position	European-Christians		Islamic	
	N =	Postmaterialism	N =	Postmaterialism
Low	54	1.70	71	1.61
1	365	1.72	537	1.57
2	909	1.72	1,131	1.60
3	1,426	1.81	1,511	1.68
4	1,660	1.90	1,583	1.68
5	1,628	1.94	1,730	1.69
6	1,684	2.01	1,768	1.69
7	1,661	2.01	1,607	1.73
8	1,343	2.07	1,326	1.72
9	944	2.14	1,006	1.79
10	653	2.15	722	1.82
11	294	2.20	437	1.89
12	139	2.27	218	1.89
High	31	2.30	45	1.89

Source: Elaboration of data from WVSEVS_sb_v4.SAV, in Inglehart et al. 2004.

position is higher, with only minor exceptions in Islamic countries), and European-Christians of any social position are more postmaterialist than their Islamic counterparts. If one compares the values of postmaterialism indices among the four more extreme positions (0 and 13 in European-Christian and Islamic societies), they are, as expected, highest among the central nucleus of European-Christian societies and lowest in the extreme periphery of Islamic societies, with central nucleus of Islamic societies showing more postmaterialist attitudes than the extreme periphery of European-Christian societies. Differences in postmaterialist attitudes of the European-Christian central nucleus and its Islamic counterpart (as measured by the ratio between the two indexes) are smaller than between those of the central nucleus and the extreme periphery in European-Christian countries. But, once more, the other two differences are not the ones that would be expected, most likely because the social periphery in Islamic countries is underestimated or even not measured, so that postmaterialism is overestimated. A comparison of elites and publics in the two groups of countries, using different groupings of elites and publics, also confirms that the difference between European-Christian and Islamic elites is smaller than the difference between each elite and its corresponding public (though, again, the exception is the Islamic social periphery, probably due to the fact that the real social periphery in these countries was not represented in their samples).

It is a common finding that changes in different types of values follow different rhythms of change, especially when comparing political and religious values (Norris and Inglehart 2004). Therefore, the same comparative analysis shown has been replicated for more specific values: political values, moral-ethical values, attitudes toward migrants, religious values, and social exclusion values. Elites have been defined as social positions 9–13, publics as social positions 0–3, and social positions 4–8 have been excluded to make the contrasting differences more evident (table 3.6).

Convergence in political values between elites in Mediterranean European and Islamic countries is even more marked than when developed and less developed countries are compared because there is more internal homogeneity within these two groups of countries. Islamic elites give more importance to politics than European elites (probably because the latter have had democratic institutions for a long time now, while in Islamic countries there is a shorter, if at all, democratic tradition), and they are equally supporters of having a democratic political system. The finding that political democratic values are not incompatible with Islamic culture is not a novelty (Moaddel 2002; Tessler 2002).

Table 3.6 Indicators of political values of elites and publics in European-Christian and Islamic Mediterranean countries

	Importance of politics[a]	Having a Democratic political system[b]	Political action[c]	Discuss politics[d]	Interested in politics[e]
Elites-European/Christian	2.41	3.60	9.34	2.09	2.68
Elites-Islamic	2.53	3.60	7.33	1.92	2.46
Publics-European/Christian	2.00	3.43	7.31	1.61	1.99
Publics-Islamic	2.10	3.47	6.51	1.59	1.99

Notes:
[a] Importance of politics in R's life. Scale 1 (not at all important)–4 (very important).
[b] It is good or bad having a democratic system. Scale 1 (it is very bad)–4 (it is very good).
[c] Index of political action, based on answers to five indicators (signing a petition, joining in boycotts, attending lawful demonstrations, joining unofficial strikes, occupying buildings or factories) on a 3 point scale (have done, might do, would never do), so that the scale runs from 0 (would never do any of the five actions) to 15 (have done all five actions).
[d] When you get together with your friends, would you say you discuss political matters frequently, occasionally, or never? Scale 1 (never)–3 (frequently).
[e] How interested would you say you are in politics? Scale 1 (not at all)–4 (very interested).

Source: Elaboration of data from WVSEVS_sb_v4.SAV, in Inglehart et al. 2004.

It must also be pointed out that Islamic publics seem to be more supporters of democracy and give more importance to politics than European publics, something that may be a result of the already mentioned underrepresentation of lower strata in Islamic samples, or of some disengagement from politics on the part of European publics. There are fewer differences between European and Islamic elites with respect to the five indicators of political values than between each elite and its corresponding public. The same is also true with respect to attitudes toward immigration policy. European and Islamic elites are more favourable (2.69 and 2.59 in a scale of 1–4) toward immigrant workers than their respective publics (2.51 and 2.46) (table 3.7).

European-Christian and Islamic societies differ greatly, even more than developed and less developed world regions, with respect to moral and religious values. No convergence in these values between European-Christian and Islamic elites seems to exist, at least at present. Islamic elites seem to be slightly less religious than their publics (though they go to the mosque more frequently than their publics), but they are much more religious than European-Christian elites and also more religious than European-Christian publics. Islamic elites also tend to justify certain behaviors related to new morals or ethics less than European-Christian elites

Table 3.7 Indicators of moral and religious values for elites and publics in European and Islamic Mediterranean countries

	Moral justification[a]	Social exclusion[b]	Importance of religion[c]	Church attendance[d]	Importance of God[e]
Elites-European/Christian	22.95	1.94	2.30	3.65	5.64
Elites-Islamic	10.66	3.25	3.62	5.03	9.05
Publics-European/Christian	16.81	2.60	2.83	4.76	6.97
Publics-Islamic	9.11	3.65	3.79	4.46	9.54

Notes:

[a] Justification of homosexuality, abortion, divorce, and euthanasia. Scale from 1 (never) to 10 (always). The index varies between 4 (all are never justifiable) and 40 (all are always justifiable).

[b] Would not like to have as neighbors any of eight social groups (people with a criminal record, people of a different race, heavy drinkers, emotionally unstable people, immigrants/foreign workers, people who have AIDS, drug addicts, and homosexuals. Scale varies from 0 (no group is rejected) to 8 (all groups are not liked as neighbors).

[c] Importance of religion in R's life. Scale 1 (not at all important)–4 (very important).

[d] Apart from weddings, funerals, and christenings, about how often do you attend religious services these days? Scale of seven points: never or practically never, less often than once a year, once a year, only on special holidays, once a month, once a week, more than once a week.

[e] How important is God in your life? Scale varies from 1 = not at all, to 10 = very.

Source: Elaboration of data from WVSEVS_sb_v4.SAV, in Inglehart et al. 2004.

and publics. Islamic elites and publics also show more exclusionist attitudes toward certain social groups than European-Christian elites and publics, as expected, since social exclusion is higher in less developed countries than in more developed ones, especially with regard to immigrant workers (Díez-Nicolás 2004b).

High importance of work has been considered characteristic of industrializing societies, while leisure seems to be more important in postindustrial societies. Therefore, one should expect elites in European-Christian societies to attach greater importance to leisure, while elites in Islamic societies should be expected to give more importance to work. Data confirms that Islamic elites attach the greatest importance to work, a finding that implies that Islamic countries have embarked on their process of industrialization, though their publics seem not to follow them very closely (3.87 and 3.53 in a scale of 1–4). But European-Christian elites also give more importance to work than their publics (3.59 and 3.38, respectively). These findings, which are very similar to those found when comparing developed and less developed countries, show than even in developed societies work continues to be very important (more than politics and religion, as the data has shown), something that should not be a surprise since one's work or occupation continues to be the main source of income, and income is necessary to achieve and maintain the lifestyles and standard of living to which people aspire in present-day consumption societies. The importance of leisure, though greater in European-Christian elites and publics (3.29 and 3.06) than in Islamic elites and publics (2.96 and 2.84), is in all cases still lower than the importance of work.

Inasmuch as family values are usually closely related to moral and religious values, one would expect that differences between elites and publics in European-Christian and Islamic societies would follow a similar pattern to moral and religious values. To this effect an index of traditional family values has been constructed on the basis of answers to eight different questions.[12] There is no convergence between European and Islamic elites with respect to traditional family values and gender values, since they are closer to their respective publics than to each other. As expected, Islamic elites and publics are much more traditionally oriented toward family values (7.29 and 7.47 on a scale of 1–8) than their European-Christian counterparts (4.76 and 5.90 respectively). And values about gender equality leave no doubt that they constitute at present the greatest difference between European-Christian and Islamic societies (even in this case, where seven out of eight countries have a Catholic majority). While only 14 percent of European-Christian elites and 35 percent of European-Christian publics agree that when jobs are scarce men should have more right to a job than women, the proportions who agree with that statement in Islamic societies is 67 percent among the elites and 72 percent among the publics.

Discussion of Results

Results have verified the validity and reliability of the instrument designed to measure elites and publics on the basis of a modified version of Galtung's social position index. At the same time, data have strongly supported the hypothesis that there is a high and positive correlation between social position and postmaterialism. In three different groups of countries defined on the degree of development, as well as when comparing European-Christian and Islamic societies around the Mediterranean, it has been shown that the index of postmaterialism is higher among those who occupy higher social positions, and vice versa.

The central argument in this research has been that there is a convergence of values between elites in more developed and in less developed world regions, as well as between those in European-Christian and Islamic societies, which seems to be supported by the data. Thus, elites in European-Christian and Islamic societies seem to exhibit more similarities in their postmaterialist orientation with one another than they do with their respective publics. They also share greater similarities in terms of the five political indicators as well as in terms of their attitudes toward immigrant workers with one another than they do when compared with their respective publics.

However, this is not true with respect to moral and religious values, regarding social exclusion, or traditional and family values. When these values are considered, elites and publics of European-Christian societies manifest themselves as more tolerant and less religious, less exclusionist, and less traditionally oriented toward the family than elites and publics in Islamic societies. These differences are even greater than when comparing more developed and less developed countries.

The first modification of the main hypothesis stated, therefore, is that convergence of values among elites of European-Christian (more developed countries) and Islamic (less developed societies) is not the same regarding all kind of values. On the contrary, results seem to suggest that convergence is more evident with respect to political values and policy issues, but not with respect to moral, religious, family, and gender values. This finding is consistent with a similar result found when comparing values of immigrants to Spain with those of Spaniards and with those of their populations of origin. Immigrants showed values somewhat halfway between their populations of origin and the receiving Spanish population (Díez-Nicolás 2004b), but the data demonstrated that they were closer to Spaniards with respect to political and policy values than with respect to religious and family values. Apparently religious, moral, and family values are more difficult to change.

The second important modification is that some of the expected differences do not appear, or they do not appear with the expected intensity, because of the quality of the samples in less developed countries in general and in Islamic countries in particular, which are not really representative of their population. In these samples, the lower and more numerous socioeconomic strata are clearly underrepresented. Because of this underrepresentation, and given that postmaterialism seems to be much lower in the lower social positions, it seems plausible to think that Islamic and less developed countries would have significantly much lower scores on the postmaterialist scale, had those neglected lower social strata been included in the sample. This would have resulted in increasing the ratio of Islamic and less developed elites to their corresponding publics and the ratio of European-Christian (developed) to Islamic (less developed) publics. As a result, the second hypothesis concerning the divergence between elites and publics in less developed countries (or between European-Christian and Islamic societies) and the even greater divergence between developed (European-Christian) and less developed (Islamic) publics would have been supported.

The third important finding is that all results derived from the comparison of more developed and less developed societies have been replicated, even more clearly, when comparing the more internally homogeneous European-Christian societies and Islamic societies. But it has been repeatedly found that the real gap between the two value systems refers to religious and gender role values more than to other kinds of values, including particularly political and democratic values. And the divergence between European-Christian and Islamic publics are smaller than expected, probably due to the fact that social peripheries in Islamic countries are also underrepresented, as manifested by the similar distributions in social position in European and Islamic societies.

The final test of the hypothesis has been carried out by reducing even more the societies that have been compared. More specifically, elites have been defined as the "decision-making nucleus" (social positions 12 and 13), and publics have been defined as the "extreme social periphery" (social position 0 and 1). When comparing these very restricted concepts of elites and publics, it was found that the postmaterialist index followed even more perfectly the expected pattern. That is, European-Christian elites show a postmaterialism index of 2.17, followed by the Islamic elites (1.89), the European-Christian publics (1.72), and the Islamic publics (1.57). All other results are not only maintained, but reinforced.

The underrepresentation of the lower socioeconomic strata in less developed and Islamic societies is likely hiding part of the divergence of values between elites and publics in those societies, as well as between European-Christian (developed) and Islamic (less developed) publics. But there seems to be no reasonable doubt about the convergence of political and policy values between elites, though great differences persist with respect to religious and moral values. One follow-up research question would be to explore the consequences of greater convergence between elites in developed and less developed societies and growing divergence between elites and publics within each society, especially when these processes are examined in the context of growing social and economic inequalities both among countries and within countries.

Notes

1. The eight characteristics used by Galtung were: sex, age, education, income, occupation, sector of economic activity, habitat of residence, and centrality. These characteristics were dichotomized, and it was considered that men, adults (neither the young nor the elderly), the more educated, those with higher incomes, those that had nonmanual occupations, working in the second or third sectors of the economy, and those living in urban or metropolitan areas and in places that were more dynamic (i.e., that had net positive immigration or some other sign of economic dynamism) were more rewarded than individuals who did not meet each of those criteria. The social position index was the result of getting one point for each of the characteristics mentioned that was met, and therefore could theoretically vary from 0 to 8.
2. The discussion of Fukuyama's arguments has been presented elsewhere (Díez-Nicolás 2003) and therefore will not be repeated here.
3. Countries (81) included in each world area: *Anglo Saxon* (Australia, Canada, Great Britain, New Zealand, and USA). *West European Catholic* (Austria, Belgium, France, Ireland, Italy, Luxembourg, Malta, Netherlands, Portugal, Spain, and Switzerland). *West European Protestant* (Denmark, Finland, Germany, Iceland, Northern Ireland, Norway, and Sweden). *East European-Christian* (Croatia, Czech Republic, Estonia, Hungary, Latvia, Lithuania, Poland, Slovakia, and Slovenia). *European Orthodox* (Armenia, Bulgaria, Belarus, Georgia, Greece, Moldova, Romania, Russia, Ukraine, Macedonia, Serbia, and Montenegro). *Latin American* (Argentina, Brazil, Chile, Colombia, Dominican Republic, El Salvador, Mexico, Peru, Puerto Rico, Uruguay, and Venezuela). *Islamic* (Albania, Algeria, Azerbaijan, Bangladesh, Bosnia and Herzegovina, Indonesia, Iran, Jordan, Morocco, Pakistan, Turkey, and Egypt). *Sinic-Confucian* (China, Korea, Singapore, Taiwan, and Viet Nam). *Japan* (Japan). *India* (India). *Sub-Saharan Africa* (Nigeria, South Africa, Zimbabwe, Uganda, Tanzania). *Israel* (Israel). *Philippines* (Philippines).
4. Correlation coefficients: HDI-TRADRAT (.51), GNP-TRADRAT(.45), FHR-TRADRAT (.43), POSTMAT-TRADRAT (nonsignificant), HDI-POSTMAT (.60), GNP-POSTMAT (.80), FHR-POSTMAT (.57), HDI-GNP (.82), FHR-GNP (.68), HDI-FHR (.69).
5. Following Galtung's criteria regarding social rewards for different social positions, one point has been given to men and to respondents between 25 and 64 years of age (on the assumption that other characteristics being equal, men are socially more rewarded than women, and individuals 25–64 more rewarded than young individuals under 25 or those over 64 years). Education has been rated as 0 (incomplete secondary education or less), 1 (complete secondary education, including preparatory for university), and 2 (some university without degree or more). Employment status has been rated as follows: 0 (not employed), 1 (part-time employment), 2 (full-time and self-employed). Income has been rated country by country depending on their income distribution, aiming at three similar categories: 0 (low), 1 (medium), and 2 (high). Similarly, size of place of residence has been coded country by country to fit three categories: 0 (small), 1 (medium), and 2 (large). And occupation has also been coded country by country into four categories: 0 (never had an occupation), 1 (has or had a lower prestige occupation), 2 (medium prestige occupation), and 3 (high prestige occupation).
6. The countries that could not be included due to lack of information on some variable are: Georgia, New Zealand, Norway, China, El Salvador, Israel, Japan, Korea, Singapore, and Tanzania. Besides, one of the two data files for Colombia (1997) had to be excluded, as well as one of the two data files from Turkey (the WVS data file), because of the lack of information on some of the variables used to construct the social position index.
7. Indexes of dissimilarity are ± 1.9% between the percent distributions of more developed and developing countries, ± 4.0% between developing and less developed countries, and ± 4.4% between more developed and less developed countries.

8. The use of countries or any other territorial units, like regions, as units of analysis always presents some important problems, even when samples are totally proportional and representative, and especially when average measures are calculated, due to the potential differences in internal variation on the variables under scrutiny within the different units, manifested on the well-known "ecological fallacy" (Robinson 1950). But these problems are absolutely unsolvable when the samples are not proportionally representative and they are used for description. These problems are nevertheless less important when analysis is not descriptive but causal or explanatory.

9. Two of the four items measure materialism: maintain order in the nation and fight rising prices, and two other items measure postmaterialism: give people more say in important political decisions and protect freedom of speech. Since respondents were asked to mention which of these goals was the most important goal for their country, and which one was the second-most important, the scale had a theoretical range from 1 (no postmaterialist item was mentioned either as first or second choice) to 3 (the two postmaterialist items were chosen as first and second choices), with an intermediate category (2) for those who chose one materialist and one postmaterialist item.

10. The eight European countries are all Catholic except Germany: Austria, France, Germany, Italy, Malta, Portugal, Spain, and Switzerland, with a total of 12,794 individuals. The eight Islamic countries are: Albania, Algeria, Bosnia and Herzegovina, Iran, Jordan, Morocco, Turkey, and Egypt, with a total of 13,707 individuals.

11. The index of dissimilarity between the two percent distributions is ± 4,0%, that is, similar to the one found between the more developed and the less developed countries in table 3.1.

12. One point was given for agreement with the following statements: regardless of what the qualities and faults of one's parents are, one must always love and respect them; parents' duty is to do their best for their children even at the expense of their own well-being; a child needs a home with both a father and a mother to grow up happily; a woman has to have children in order to be fulfilled; marriage is not an outdated institution; a woman should not bring up a child as a single parent; a working mother cannot establish just as warm and secure a relationship with her children as a mother who does not work; both the husband and wife should contribute to household income. The scale runs from 0 (not traditional at all) to 8 (very traditional).

References

Bottomore, Tom 1964. *Elites and Society*. London: Watts.

Carlton, Eric. 1996. *The Few and the Many: A Typology of Elites*. Brookfield, Vermont: Ashgate Publishing Company.

Collier, Ruth B. 1999. *Paths towards Democracy: The Working Class and Elites in Western Europe and South America*. New York: Cambridge University Press.

Díez-Nicolás, Juan. 1966. "Posición Social y Opinión Pública." *Anales de Sociología* 2: 63–75.

———. 1968. "Social Position and Attitudes towards Domestic Issues in Spain." *Polls* 3(2): 1–15.

———. 1996. "Social Position, Information and Postmaterialism." *REIS* English edition, 153–65, Rumagraf, Madrid. Previously published in 1992 as "Posición Social, Información y Postmaterialismo." *Revista Española de Investigaciones Sociológicas* 57: 21–36.

———. 1999. "Industrialization and Concern for the Environment." In *Modern Society and Values*, edited by N. Tos, P.Ph. Moler and B. Malnar, pp. 331–60. Ljubljana, FSS and Mannhemim: ZUMA.

———. 2000. "La Escala de Postmaterialismo como Medida del Cambio de Valores en las Sociedades Contemporáneas." In *España 2000, entre el Localismo y la Globalidad. La Encuesta Europea de Valores en su Tercera Aplicación, 1981–1999*, edited by F. Andrés Orizo and J. Elzo, pp. 285–310. Madrid: Editorial Santa María

————. 2003. "Two Contradictory Hypotheses on Globalization: Social Convergence or Civilization Differentiation and Clash." In *Human Values and Social Change*, edited by R. Inglehart, pp. 235–63. Leiden-Boston: Brill.

————. 2004a. *El Dilema de la Supervivencia*. Madrid. Obra Social Cajamadrid.

————. 2004b. *Las Dos Caras de la Inmigración*. Madrid: IMSERSO.

Druckman, James N. and Kjersten R. Nelson. 2003. "Framing and Deliberation: How Citizens' Conversations Limit Elite Influence." *American Journal of Political Science* 47(4): 729–45.

Duncan, Otis D. 1964. "Social Organization and the Ecosystem." In *Handbook of Modern Sociology*, edited by Robert E. L. Faris, pp. 37–82. Chicago: Rand Mc Nally and Co. Eldersveld, Samuel J., Lars Stromberg, and Wim Derksen. 1995. *Local Elites in Western Democracies: A Comparative Analysis of Urban Political Leaders in the U.S., Sweden and the Netherlands*. Boulder: Westview Press.

Etzioni-Halevy, Eva. (ed.). 1997. *Classes and Elites in Democracy and Democratization: A Collection of Readings*. New York: Garland Pub.

Fukuyama, Francis. 1991. *The End of History and Last Man*. New York: The Free Press.

Galtung, Johan. 1964. "Foreign Policy Opinion as a Function of Social Position." *Journal of Peace Research* 1(3–4): 206–31.

————. 1976. "Social Position and the Image of the Future." In *Images of the World in the Year 2000*, edited by H. Ornauer, H. Wiberg, A. Sicinki, and J. Galtung, pp. 381–400. Paris: Mouton.

Halle, Nils H. 1966. "Social Position and Foreign Policy Attitudes: A Comparative Study of France, Norway and Poland." *Journal of Peace Research* 3(1): 46–74.

Hawley, Amos H. 1986. *Human Ecology. A Theoretical Essay*. Chicago: The University of Chicago Press.

Huntington, Samuel P. 1996. *The Clash of Civilizations and the Remaking of the World Order*. New York: Simon and Schuster.

Inglehart, Ronald. 1997. *Modernization and Postmodernization*. Princeton: Princeton University Press.

————. 1977. *The Silent Revolution*. Princeton: Princeton University Press.

Inglehart, Ronald. 1990. *Culture Shift in Advanced Industrial Society*. Princeton: Princeton University Press.

————. (ed.). 2003a. *Human Values and Social Change*. Leiden-Boston: Brill.

————. (ed.). 2003b. *Islam, Gender, Culture and Democracy*. Willowdale, ON: Sitter Publications.

Ingelhart, Ronald, Miguel Basáñez, Jaime Díez-Medrano, Loek Halman, and Ruud Luijkx (eds.). 2004. *Human Beliefs and Values*. Mexico: Siglo XXI Editores.

Keller, Suzanne. 1963. *Beyond the Ruling Class: Strategic Elites in Modern Society*. New York: Random House.

Kornhauser, William. 1959. *The Politics of Mass Society*. Glencoe, IL: The Free Press.

Lasswell, Harold. 1936. *Politics: Who Gets What, When, How?* New York: McGraw Hill.

————. (ed.). 1952. *The Comparative Study of Elites*. Stanford: Stanford University Press.

Lerner, Robert, Althea K. Nagai, and Stanley Rothman. 2004. *American Elites*. New Haven, CN: Yale University Press.

Mannheim, Karl. 1935. *Man and Society in an Age of Reconstruction: Studies in Modern Social Structure*. New York: Harcourt.

Marger, Martin. 1981. *Elites and Masses: An Introduction to Political Sociology*. New York: D. van Nostrand Co.

Mills, C. Wright. 1956. *The Power Elite*. New York: Oxford University Press.

Moaddel, Mansoor. 2002. "The Study of Islamic Culture and Politics: An Overview and Assessment." *Annual Review of Sociology* 28: 359–86.

Mosca, Gaetano. 1939/1896. *The Ruling Class.* New York: McGraw Hill.

Norris, Pippa and Ronald Inglehart. 2004. *Sacred and Secular: Religion and Politics Worldwide.* Cambridge, UK: Cambridge University Press.

Ortega y Gasset, José. 1929. *La Rebelión de las Masas.* Madrid: Revista de Occidente.

Pareto, Vilfredo. 1902–1903. *Les Systèmes Socialistes.* Paris: Giard.

Paul, David M. and Clyde Brown. 2001. "Testing the Limits of Elite Influence on Public Opinion. An Examination of Sports Facility Referendums." *Political Research Quarterly* 54 (4): 871–88.

Perthes, Volker. (ed.). 2004. *Arab Elites: Negotiating the Politics of Change.* Boulder: Lynne Riennner Publishers.

Tessler, Mark. 2002. "Do Islamic Orientations Influence Attitudes toward Democracy in the Arab World? Evidence from Egypt, Jordan, Morocco and Algeria." *International Journal of Comparative Sociology* 43(3–5): 229–49.

van der Veer, Kees. 1976. "Social Position, Dogmatism and Social Participation as Independent Variables." In *Images of the World in the Year 2000,* edited by H. Ornauer, H. Wiberg, A. Sicinki, and J. Galtung, pp. 621–36. Paris: Mouton.

Verba, Sidney, Steven Kelman, Gary Orren, Ichiro Miyake, Joji Watanuki, Ikuo Kabashima, and G. Donald Ferree. 1987. *Elites and the Idea of Equality: A Comparison of Japan, Sweden and the United States.* Cambridge, MA: Harvard University Press.

Walden, George. 2000. *The New Elites: Making a Career in the Masses.* London: Allen Lane.

Welzel, Christian. 2002. "Effective Democracy, Mass Culture and the Quality of Elites." *International Journal of Comparative Sociology* 43(3–5): 317–35.

Welzel, Christian, Ronald Inglehart, and H.D. Klingemann. 2003. "The Theory of Human Development: A Cross-Cultural Analysis." *European Journal of Political Research* 42(2): 341–80.

Werbner, Richard P. 2004. *Reasonable Radicals and Citizenship in Botswana: The Public Anthropology of Kalanga Elites.* Bloomington: Indiana University Press.

Yoder, Jennifer A. 1999. *From East Germans to German? The New Postcommunist Elites.* Durham, NC: Duke University Press.

CHAPTER 4

Muslim Immigrants in Western Europe: Persisting Value Differences or Value Adaptation?

THORLEIF PETTERSSON

Introduction

By the end of World War II, less than one million Muslims were living in Western Europe. Half a century later, the number had risen to some 15 millions, and Islam has become Europe's second largest religion (Hunter and Serfaty 2002; Lubeck 2002; Tibi 2002). Today, Muslims are a highly visible constituency in most European countries. The growing Islamic presence may exert a profound influence on both Islamic and Western cultures and identities. In comparison with other major religious traditions, Islam appears to exert a pervasive role in contemporary politics (for a review, see Moaddel 2002). An important issue therefore concerns whether this pattern will be retained in the European context, where religion and politics are mostly differentiated (Halman and Pettersson 2003; Pettersson 2003a). An equally interesting question asks whether traditional Islamic patterns for family life and gender roles will persist in the European setting, where traditional male-dominated family institutions and patriarchal structures are increasingly challenged by demands for gender equality, one-parent households, and various cohabitation arrangements (see Gelissen 2003). Value change among Muslim immigrants may also contribute to changing ethnic relations within Europe. Such value change may also have an impact on the relationships between different generations of immigrants. Finally, value change among the Muslim immigrants might also affect the relations between their countries of origin and their new home countries.Immigrants who cherish democratic values may contribute to the rise of democratic movements in their former home countries, and radical Islamists resorting to more extreme forms of political behavior might hamper the relations between their new home countries and their countries of origin. All these factors demonstrate why comparative analyses of the value systems among Muslim immigrants in Western Europe are of great interest. Research on religion and migration has become an increasingly important topic (Ebaugh 2003).

Islamic presence in Western Europe is certainly not new. During the eighth century, the Arabs conquered parts of South-Western Europe, and Islamic culture exerted a profound influence there until the fifteenth century. Between the fifteenth and the seventeenth century, the Turks came from southeast, and their cultural impact is still noticeable is this part of Europe. If these historical Islamic influxes into Europe were due to expanding Muslim empires, the contemporary Muslim presence in Europe is primarily the result of immigration. A first immigration wave came about as a heritage of European colonization of Islamic regions, for instance by France in Northern Africa, by Great Britain in India, and by the Netherlands in Indonesia. A second wave was due to Muslim labor migration, starting in the early postwar era. A third wave of Muslim immigration was due to family reunions, asylum seeking and illegal underground entries (Lubeck 2002). Due to low birth rates and ageing populations in many Western European countries, as well as political instability, more or less authoritarian rule, limited economic growth, and high unemployment rates in some of the Islamic countries, the contemporary Muslim immigration into Europe is likely to continue (Lubeck 2002). The increasingly visible Muslim presence has become a salient political issue in several Western European countries. As a consequence, stricter immigration policies have been introduced in order to reduce immigration rates.

Due to a variety of historical, economic, political, and cultural factors, the Muslims living in Western Europe can be divided into four groups (Lubeck 2002). The first group of *Europeanized Muslims* consists of those became (i.e., naturalized) citizens and their offspring. The latter tend to make a distinct Muslim generation, often perceiving itself as a kind of "Euro-version" of their parents. The second group, the *Muslim ethnic enclave* consists of immigrants with residence rights, but lacking citizen rights. Holders of work permits, contract workers, spouses, second-generation young Muslims, and students belong to this category. Since the average length of immigrant residenceship is about 15 years, and naturalization rates are low, this category is large. The third group could be called *illegal and underground Muslims* and consists of illegitimate immigrants, often living and working in the agricultural and/or informal sector. Finally, a fourth and lesser category comprises cosmopolitan *Muslim professionals and intellectuals*. This category also includes some European converts to Islam.

There are substantial differences among the European countries with regard to their immigration policies. This has also affected the development of different immigrant communities with different value orientations. Broadly speaking, European immigration policies differ along two dimensions. One concerns state policies in relation to the promotion or nonpromotion of ethnic minority cultures, while the other relates to the understanding of citizenship as either ethnic or civic. The combination of these four options tend to result in different mixes of immigrant assimilation and integration, for instance into ethnic communities, ethnic exclusions, assimilated civic communities, and multiculturalist societies, respectively (Borevi 2002; Hammar 1985). In the Netherlands, Muslim identities have become more or less institutionalized by the so-called pillarization policies,[1] and Dutch citizenship is comparatively easy to obtain for Muslim immigrants. In Germany, citizenship is defined by family descent, and naturalization rates are consequently very low. In addition, there are also differences in immigration policies between the various federal states in the German Federal Republic.

The long and diverse history of Muslim immigration into Western Europe and the different immigration policies in many Western European countries have made the Muslim immigrants a rather heterogeneous social, ethnic, religious, and cultural minority. It might therefore appear too simplistic to investigate them as one homogenous category. Yet, this chapter attempts to report on European Muslim immigrants in general. Nevertheless, due to a fairly innovative analytical design, the findings may still deserve attention.

The Structural, Cultural, and Identity

Incorporation of Muslim Immigrants

In migration research, the relations between the receiving majority society and the incoming immigrant minorities are often investigated with regard to three different dimensions. These are the structural incorporation, the cultural incorporation, and the identity incorporation of the immigrants (see Isajiw 1999). *Structural incorporation* relates to the physical and geographical boundaries that are applied to the immigrants, the socioeconomic strata that are open to them and the networks and informal relationships that are formed between them and the native citizens of the host society. *Cultural incorporation* refers to how the immigrants learn, accept, and ultimately internalize the dominant cultural patterns in the immigration society. This may include as different features as taking on common patterns of behaviors, ways of dressing, food habits, and eating traditions. Cultural incorporation can also include the acquisition of the language of the immigration country, and ultimately the adoption of the key attitudes and values of the host society. *Identity incorporation* refers to the development of new identities among the immigrants. For instance, they can start to see themselves as fully belonging to the new immigrant society. Their new personal identities can also cover several other dimensions, for instance in relation to their subjectively experienced ethnic and religious belongings. This kind of personal identity is often the result of primary socialization experiences during childhood and early adolescence, and it concerns the more or less immutable core of personality, showing up irrespective of the many different social roles one has to enact (Hammond 1992). But personal identity can also be thought of as including the more transient and changeable images of oneself as one moves from one social context to another (ibid). This type of identity, often achieved through secondary socialization processes can be more easily put "on and off."

Since the identity components that are acquired by primary socialization tend to be more resistant to change, and religious commitment is usually due to primary socialization during childhood, religious values and beliefs would—ceteris paribus—be less prone to change as a consequence of immigration. In contrast, work values and political values are generally acquired by secondary socialization during adult life (Pettersson 1988, 2003b). These values would therefore be more easily affected by migration. In other words, this issue comes to the fore when the so-called formative period for different kinds of values occurs in people's life. The formative period, for example, work values and political values, tends to occur during early adulthood, while for values related to family and religion, the formative period is more likely to occur during childhood.

Thus, one may assume international migration to have a larger impact on the values that are acquired by secondary socialization during late adolescence and adulthood as compared to the values that are acquired by primary socialization during childhood. As a consequence, at least first generation immigrants would be more likely to change their work values and political values than their religious values and family values. However, in this regard, one should also note that immigration into a new social context may, for example, provide women with new opportunities for power and leadership, including those in religious matters (Haddad and Lumis 1987; Miller et al. 2001). Further, the religious communities of the immigrants may take on organizational forms that were not established in the countries from which the Muslims emigrated. These new forms may in turn affect the religious values and beliefs of the immigrants, both among men and women (Furseth and Repstad 2003). Thus, when it comes to religious change among the immigrants, different factors may produce different outcomes, also with regard to the values that were internalized during primary socialization.

There are also other factors that may influence these outcomes. One has to do with whether the migration was individual or collective. Another concerns whether the immigrants' settlement took place in a community of like-minded immigrants or in areas that were dominated by members of the receiving majority society. This is to say that the degree of structural incorporation may influence the degree of cultural—or vice versa. A theoretical foundation for this assumption can be found in the importance that the sociology of knowledge attaches to the so-called plausibility structures. Thus, social relations to like-minded people are assumed to constitute the basic legitimation for peoples' worldviews and value structures (see Berger and Luckmann 1967).

In this chapter, yet another dimension of the international migration process deserves attention. Obviously, the effects of migration are likely to depend on the cultural distances between the countries of emigration and immigration, respectively. It is one thing to migrate from a country with a Christian tradition to another country belonging to the same tradition, but a completely different thing to migrate from a predominantly Islamic country to one predominantly Christian. The religious community in many Muslim emigration countries may at least partially correspond to what Troeltsch called a "church," something that one is born into and not something that one has voluntarily joined. In these societies, religious belonging is mostly collective-expressive in contrast to the "individual-expressive" form prevailing in most of the Western immigration countries (Hammond 1992). In the Islamic countries from which the Muslims have emigrated, religious belonging might have been more or less mandatory and taken for granted, while in their new home countries, religious identity is often seen as voluntary and a matter of personal choice. Not the least in these regards, immigration into Western Europe brings the Muslim way of life into fundamentally different cultural and religious setups.

One should not, however, easily assume the Muslim immigrants to come from one single homogenous culture. Rather, the Muslim world is almost as heterogeneous as that of the Western Christian. There are differences between the two major divisions in Islam: Sunni and Shi 'i. There are also differences between the historical core Islamic Arab countries, and the Islamic countries in South East Asia or sub-Saharan Africa. There are also the differences between Islam in a secular state like Turkey and Islam in a theocracy like Iran. And finally there are also differences between less developed Islamic countries like Pakistan, medium developed countries like Libya, and highly developed countries like Kuwait. One should not assume such different countries to form one homogenous and monolithic Islamic culture.

For instance, with regard to the political cultures of the predominantly Islamic countries, a recent investigation failed to distinguish a presumed homogeneous Islamic culture from the Protestant, Catholic, Orthodox, or Hindu worlds. The levels of political tolerance, the support for freedom, the political participation, and the search for alternatives to the democratic system were not fundamentally different in the Islamic countries (Esmer 2003). Another analysis concluded that there is little evidence that Islam and democracy are incompatible (Tessler 2003). And yet another comparative analysis has argued that Islam is not the cause of the lack of democracy in predominantly Muslim countries (Price 1999). However, should there be one major difference between Islamic and Western cultures, this difference has to do with "Eros far more than Demos" (Norris and Inglehart 2003).[2] Thus, where civic attitudes are concerned, the differences between the Islamic world and the West are often minor. On the other hand, religious authorities are found to be stronger in Islamic societies, although this is not exclusive for these countries. And finally, with regard to views on gender equality and sexual liberalization, a substantial cultural gap is often found between Islam and the West. This gap is said to have widened in recent years (Norris and Inglehart 2003).

But even if there are obvious differences in religious values between Islam and the West, it should also be noted that the Islamic societies are not homogeneous in this regard either. For instance, a recent comparative analysis of grassroot religious involvement in Egypt, Jordan, and Iran documented noticeable differences between these three countries.

The Iranians placed less emphasis on religion than the Egyptians and the Jordanians. This was explained by the fact that in Iran, a theocracy dominates the sociopolitical order, and that opposition groups often are formulated in reaction toward this regime. Therefore, the Iranians' withdrawal from religious involvement can be understood as a token of political opposition (Moaddel and Azadarmaki 2003). Among the three countries compared, Iran also showed the lowest percentage claiming cultural invasion from the West to be a serious problem.

However, even if Islamic communities, both within and outside Islamic countries, do not form a homogeneous culture, there is still one cultural divide that separates Western and Islamic cultures. This divide refers to family values, gender roles, sexual mores, and also partly to religious commitments. In these domains, Muslims tend to adhere to more traditional and less secularized views. These views are often internalized by primary socialization during childhood and early adolescence. As a consequence, these views would be more resistant to change than those that are internalized during the later phases of life and are related to, for example, work and politics.

Based on these theoretical propositions, this chapter investigates whether the Muslim immigrants into Western Europe differ in their value orientations from the European public. A series of comparisons are performed in order to answer a set of key research questions: What are the value differences between the Muslim immigrants and their new countrymen, and what are the value similarities? How are these differences and similarities affected by the Muslim migration into a new cultural and religious context? Do the value changes in relation to international migration differ for different kinds of value orientations, for instance, between those that are acquired by primary socialization processes during childhood and those that are acquired by secondary socialization experiences during the later parts of life? Has the Muslim immigration into Western Europe created new value differences that did not exist prior to the immigration, or has the migration processes dissolved those differences that existed before the migration started? What do these patterns of value change imply for the long-term cultural divide between Muslim immigrants and non-Muslim Europeans?

In order to answer these research questions, an appropriate analytical strategy must first be developed. This is done in the following section. In two subsequent sections, the data and the results are presented. In the concluding section, the findings are summarized and the investigation is critically assessed.

Analytical Strategy

In this chapter, a two-tiered comparative analytical strategy has been developed. A first set of comparisons contrasts the value profiles of the populations at large in two groups of countries. The first group consists of the Islamic countries from where the Muslim immigrants into Western Europe emigrated and the second group of the Western European countries to which they immigrated. In other words, these comparisons will investigate the value differences between the countries from which the Muslim immigrants originate and the countries to which they come. A second set of comparisons investigates value differences between a group of Muslim immigrants and a group of their new Western-European neighbors, matched to be as close as possible to the immigrants with regard to age, gender, family relations, the number of children, education, work status, income, and place of residence. The selected members of this latter group are also of a Christian denomination. To refer to the introductory theoretical discussion, the comparison between the immigrants and their new neighbors will at least partially control for the possible effects of the differential structural incorporation of the Muslim immigrants.

The logic of this comparative analytical strategy are outlined in figure 4.1. For a given value orientation such as religious values or work values, the two comparisons can in principle result in four different outcomes, which lead to four different conclusions. This can be described as follows: (1) In the case where there is a value difference between the countries of origin and the receiving immigration countries, and the same difference is also found between the Muslim immigrants and their socioeconomic "twins," the conclusion would be that the immigration has not caused any value change among the immigrants. Rather, the original value difference has remained after the immigration; (2) Where, however, there is a value difference between the countries of origin and the receiving countries, and this difference is *not* found between the Muslim immigrants and their new neighbors, the conclusion would be that the immigration has had an impact. The original value difference has dissolved, and the immigrants do not differ anymore from their new countrymen; (3) In the case where there is *no* value difference between the countries of origin and the receiving immigration countries, but where such a difference can be found between the immigrants and their new neighbors, the conclusion would be that the immigration has created a new value difference that did not exist prior to the immigration; (4) Where, however, no difference has been found between the

Is there a difference on a given value dimension between the muslim immigrants and their matched christian neigbors?	Is there a difference on a given value dimension between the countries from which the muslim immigrants originate and the european countries to which they have emigrated?	
	Yes	No
Yes	A previous value difference has remained: No impact of immigration	A new value difference has been created: Impact of immigration
No	A previous value difference has been dissolved: Impact of immigration	A previous value similarity has remained: No impact of immigration

Figure 4.1 Analytical scheme for the analysis of value change among Muslim immigrants into Western Europe

countries of origin and the receiving immigration countries, and where the immigrants and their new neighbors also appear to be similar, the conclusion would be that the immigration has not caused any value changes. In this case, the original value similarity has not been altered by the immigration.

For the sake of simplicity, the description of the analytical strategy did not mention that more moderate and gradual value changes can also occur. For instance, a given value difference between the countries of emigration and the countries of immigration cannot only remain or dissolve in toto with regard to the immigrants and their new neighbors. Rather, when these two groups are compared, the magnitude of this difference may have increased. It can also have decreased, although it remains statistically significant. Thus, the issue is not only whether a given difference has remained or been dissolved, but also a question of whether the size of this difference had changed or not (Hamberg 2000). Another possibility that is not dealt with in this paper is that members of the receiving local communities may also change their values as a result of the increased Muslim presence there.

In short, then, and temporarily disregarding the relative size of these value changes, Muslim immigrants into Western Europe can be differently affected by their migration into a new cultural, economical, and political context. In relation to their new neighbors, new value differences can be created and original value differences can dissolve. But original value differences can also persist, and previous value similarities can remain. Obviously, to investigate the conditions that may cause such multifaceted outcomes, a sensitive and differentiated analytical strategy is needed.

Data for the Analysis of Value Change among

Muslim Immigrants in Western Europe

In order to investigate the value differences between the Muslim immigrants in Western Europe and their native born new compatriots, data from the most recent wave of the EVS/WVS are used. In the following section, these data are presented.

The EVS/WVS Data Sets

The EVS/WVS project was launched at the end of the 1970s, and aimed at investigating fundamental value orientations in Western Europe. A large scale survey was conducted in more than 20 European countries. A second wave of surveys was fielded in 1990. This time, some 45 countries participated. At this time, many countries outside Europe joined the project. In 1995/1996, a third wave was conducted in about 55 countries around the world. In 1999–2000, the most recent wave was fielded in about 65 countries. This wave included for the first time a set of Islamic societies as Albania, Algeria, Egypt, Iran, Jordan, Morocco, Pakistan, and Indonesia. All in all, the EVS/WVS project covers about 80 percent of the world population, and about 75 different countries have participated in at least one of the four waves (for information on the EVS/WVS projects and issues such as sampling, questionnaires, response rates, etc., see e.g., Inglehart et al. 2004). In comparison with similar comparative projects like the European Social Survey (ESS), the International Social Survey Programme (ISSP), or the International Social Justice Project (ISJP), the EVS/WVS project is characterized by the simultaneous coverage of a great number of different value domains, the longitudinal design, and the global approach.

Self-Declared Muslims in

the EVS/WVS Data

In the 1999 EVS data set, as few as 109 self-declared Muslims were found among the respondents from the Western European countries. It must be strongly emphasized that this number is not reflecting the actual distribution of Muslim immigrants among these countries. That so comparatively few Muslim respondents are included is primarily related to sampling and language problems. The Muslim immigrants are often not included in the sampling frames that are used in the value studies. Should they be included, linguistic problems often prevent that they are interviewed. To relate to the introductory discussion, it seems reasonable to assume that the Muslims that are included in the EVS data set are primarily representative for the Europeanized Muslims and those who belong to the so called "Muslim ethnic enclave."

A Sample of Respondents Socioeconomically

Equal to the Muslim Immigrants

As already mentioned, for each of the Muslim immigrants in the EVS/WVS data, one socioeconomic "twin" from the same host country has been randomly selected. This native born respondent should be as close as possible to the immigrant with regard to gender, age, family status, employment, income, education, and place of residence. The respondent should also be member of the dominant Christian denomination in the country.

A Sample of Respondents from

Countries of Immigration

In order to compare the value systems of the countries of origin for the Muslim immigrants and the receiving immigration countries, respectively, two other subsets of the EVS/WVS data are used. The sample size for each of these subsets was arbitrarily set to 2,000.

To get a representative sample of native Europeans from the Western European immigration countries, the percentages for the national belongings of the sample of Muslim immigrants was used as a baseline. For instance, the German Muslims made 21.1 percent of the sample of Muslim immigrants, while the British Muslims made up 8.3 percent (see table 4.1). Therefore, the sample for the Western European countries to which the Muslim immigrants have immigrated should contain 21.1 percent German respondents, 8.3 percent British respondents, and so on. Accordingly, 420 respondents (21 percent * 2,000) should be randomly selected from the German EVS data file, while 166 respondents (8.3 percent * 2,000) should be randomly selected from the British file. The number of respondents for the remaining Western European countries was then determined by the same principles.

Table 4.1 Socioeconomic background data for a set of Western European Muslims and their matched Christian counterparts, respectively, from 8 West-European countries results from the 1999 EVS data

	Sample of Muslim immigrants (N = 109)	Sample of socio economically matched neighbors (N = 109)
Mean age	33.0	33.1
Men	55.0%	55.0%
Married	65.1%	66.1%
With children	57.5%	52.3%
Completed education at age	18.6	20.2
Employed	43.1%	51.4%
Mean household income	4.5	5.1
Population size of place of living	6.3	5.9

Notes:
a. Household income: Mean score on a 10 point scale
b. Population size: Mean score on a 8 point scale

A Sample of Muslim Respondents from

Islamic Countries of Origin

The EVS data set does unfortunately not contain any information on from which countries the Muslim immigrants have emigrated. Therefore, the countries of origin for these respondents must be estimated from other sources (AlSayyad and Castells 2002; Hunter 2002; Westerlund and Svanberg 1999). The following example demonstrates how these estimates have been calculated. As already mentioned, the German Muslims account for 21 percent of the entire sample of Muslim immigrants (se table 4.1 below). Therefore, 21 percent of the sample for the countries of origin should correspond to the German case. Since it is known that 67.9 percent of the German Muslims comes from Turkey, 21 percent * 67.9 percent * 2,000 = 136 randomly selected respondents in the Turkish WVS data set should be included in the sample for the countries of origin. The corresponding numbers of respondents from each of the possible countries of origin have then been calculated by the same principles.

Following these calculations, the sample from the countries of origin came to include randomly Muslim respondents from Morocco, Algeria, Egypt, Jordan, Turkey, Iran, Bangladesh, Pakistan, and Indonesia. These countries are the main countries of origin for the Muslim immigrants into Western Europe. It should be noted that the construction of this sample is based on the assumption that the Muslim immigrants who are identified in the EVS data file for the Western European countries have a similar national origin as the entire Muslim population in these countries. Although this assumption seems reasonable, it can also be questioned. However, given the available data, this assumption has been necessary in order to build the data file for the Islamic countries of origin.

Results

Socioeconomic Status and National
Belonging among the Four Samples

Table 4.1 summarizes some of the characteristics of the Muslim immigrants and the matched set of their new neighbors. Quite as expected from the sampling procedures, the immigrants are rather similar to their randomly selected socioeconomic and Christian "twins." However, it should be noted that a somewhat higher percentage of the immigrants have children (57.5 percent versus 52.3 percent and that a somewhat lower proportion of them are employed (43.1 percent vs. 51.4 percent). They also report somewhat lower household incomes. These differences indicate that it has been difficult to find a perfect match on all socioeconomic criteria between the Muslim immigrants and their native Christian neighbors. This reflects that the Muslim immigrants generally belong to the lower socioeconomic strata of the immigration countries.

Unfortunately, the EVS data on the Muslim immigrants do not clarify whether they are first, second, or third generation immigrants or for the years they have lived in Western Europe. The effects of these key dimensions of international migration can therefore not be assessed (cf. below on the findings on this from the European Social Survey data). Of the Muslim immigrants, about half the number appears to be naturalized. This estimate is indirectly made from their responses to a question on national pride. This question should only be asked to those who had received citizenship in the country where they lived. It cannot be decided whether some of these respondents are Muslim converts. However, it is rather unlikely that many of them should be so (cf. the above discussion on the different categories of Muslims living in Western Europe). The Muslims holding citizenship were equally distributed among all the immigration countries.

Table 4.2 National belonging among four samples of Muslims and Christians EVS/WVS data from the 1999/2000 waves

	Muslim immigrants (N = 109)	European socioecon. twins (N = 109)	Western immigration countries (N = 1938)	Countries of emigration for Muslim immigrants (N = 2007)	
France	1.0%	1.0%	0.2%	Muslim India	2.1%
UK	8.3%	8.3%	7.2%	Pakistan	2.2%
Germany	21.1%	21.1%	20.2%	Bangladesh	2.3%
Spain	2.8%	2.8%	4.1%	Turkey	40.2%
Netherlands	9.2%	9.2%	9.0%	Indonesia	2.9%
Belgium	53.2%	53.2%	55.4%	Morocco	18.9%
Denmark	4.6%	4.6%	4.1%	Iran	3.9%
				Bosnia	2.7%
				Algeria	24.7%
Sum	100.0%	100.0%	100.0%		100.0%

Table 4.2 reports the national belongings for the four samples. Quite as expected, the Muslim immigrants and their matched socioeconomic twins are identically distributed over the seven immigration countries. Also as expected, the sample for the receiving immigration countries shows a rather similar distribution of national belonging. In the sample for the Muslim emigration countries, the largest portions come from Turkey, Algeria, and Morocco, while lesser shares come from Iran, Indonesia, and Bosnia. This is quite in line with what is known about the national origins of the Muslims now living in Western Europe.

Results for the Analytical Strategy

As already mentioned, the comparisons between the four samples cover several of the value dimensions that have been investigated in previous studies of the EVS/WVS data. However, since the measurement techniques for these dimensions have not been thoroughly tested on data from the Islamic societies, I also investigate whether these measurements work equally well when applied in a Muslim context. To this end, a set of confirmatory factor analyses, based on structural equation modeling, has been applied (see Billiet 2003; Byrne 2001; De Vijver and Leung 1997).

All in all, five value dimensions are analyzed in this investigation. These are chosen to represent differences between the different kinds of socialization processes that were discussed in the theoretical introduction. The five value dimensions cover religious values, family values, moral values, work values, and values related to democracy and the civic society. The indicators that are used to tap these value dimensions are described in the Appendix.

Religious Values

With regard to religious values, two dimensions are investigated. These concern the level of religious involvement and the relationship between religion and politics. The level of religious involvement is measured by three items: How important God is in one's life, how important religion is in one's life, and one's views of church adequacy (how adequate one finds the teachings of one's religion to be in relation to family problems, moral problems, social problems, and spiritual problems). Views on the relationship between religion and politics are measured by two items: If one thinks that irreligious people are fit for public office or not and whether it would be better if more people with religious beliefs held public office. Previous studies have shown that these two items can be used to measure people's preferences for a differentiation between religion and politics (Halman and Pettersson 2003).

These two religious dimensions are related to secularization theory (Pettersson 2003a): The level of religious involvement is often used as an indicator of religious decline, while people's views on the relationship between religion and politics have been used as an indicator of the preferred differentiation between religion and secular society. The latter aspect is sometimes referred to as "secularization-in-mind" and the "compartmentalization" between religion and the secular. Compartmentalization can be thought of as the psychological parallel to macro-level differentiation between religion and the secular (Dobbelaere 2002). The results for the religious indicators are given in table 4.3.

The results show that for both Muslims and Christians, the factor structure is the same for the two sets of indicators. This demonstrates that the responses from the Muslim and Christian respondents can be meaningfully compared. The Islamic emigration countries score higher on each of the items for the two dimensions of religious values than the receiving immigration countries. When the Muslim immigrants are compared to their new countrymen, these differences remain. Thus, with regard to religious values, immigration to the more secularized Western European countries does not appear to have had any significant impact on the Muslim' religious values. The original differences with regard to religion seem to remain after immigration.

Table 4.3   Results from a set of factor analyses for five indicators of religious orientations together with the means for these indicators among four different samples of Muslims and Christians. Results from the 1999−2002 EVS/WVS data

| | Varimax rotated factor analyses:[a] | | | |
| | Muslim respondents | | Christian respondents | |
	Factor 1	Factor 2	Factor 1	Factor 2
Indicators:				
Importance of God	.66	.08	.86	.17
Importance of religion	.75	.19	.87	.03
Church adequacy	.71	.01	.57	.26
Politicians should be religious	.10	.82	.06	.87
Religious believers in publ. office	.11	.81	.25	.77
Explained variance	36.8%	21.2%	45.5%	21.0%

| *Comparisons of means:* | | | | |
| | A: Immigrants -Residents | | B: Groups of countries | |
	Immigrants to West Europe (n≈100)	Socioecon. immigr twins (n≈100)	Emigration countries (n≈1800)	Immigration countries (n≈1900)
Indicators:				
Importance of God	9.0	7.3***	9.7	7.2***
Importance of religion	3.7	2.9***	3.9	2.9***
Church adequacy	3.0	2.3*	3.1	2.2***
Religious politicians	2.9	2.2**	3.1	2.1***
Believers hold publ. office	3.4	2.7**	3.1	2.8***

Note: [a]Test of the same factor structure among two 50% samples of both Muslims and Christians, respectively: Chi-square: 15.5, 8 df, p = .05 AGFI = .98, RMSEA = .03, p = .94.
*** p < .001,**p < .01,* p < .05.

However, it should also be noted that for each of the five indicators, the Muslim immigrants demonstrate somewhat lower scores than their former countrymen, but higher scores than their new neighbors. This pattern might indicate that Muslim immigration to Western Europe is associated with some decreases in the immigrants' religious involvement, although not to the extent that they have adopted the lower levels that dominate among their new countrymen (cf. the above discussion on the relative sizes of these differences).

Family Values

The respondents' views on family values have been measured by five indicators. These measure two dimensions of family values. The first covers

Table 4.4 Results from a set of factor analyses for five indicators of family values together with the means for these indicators among four different samples of Muslims and Christians. Results from the 1999−2002 EVS/WVS data

| | Varimax rotated factor analyses:[a] | | | |
| | Muslim respondents | | Christian respondents | |
	Factor 1:	Factor 2:	Factor 1:	Factor 2:
Indicators:				
Child needs both parents	.63	.05	.62	.21
Dislike single mothers	.65	.13	.65	.16
Marriage not outdated	.67	.01	.68	−.15
Strict parent obligations	.08	.77	.14	.73
Strict child obligations	.06	.80	.01	.79
Explained variance	30.0%	20.6%	30.1%	20.7%

Comparisons of means:

| | A: Immigrants-Residents | | B: Groups of countries | |
	Immigrants to West Europe (n≈100)	Socioecon. immigr twins (n≈100)	Emigration countries (n≈1800)	Immigration countries (n≈1900)
Indicators:				
Child needs both parents	89.9%	77.1%*	95.3%	83.2%***
Dislike single mothers	69.7%	31.2%***	87.3%	36.0%***
Marriage not outdated	87.2%	73.4%*	85.8%	76.7%***
Strict parent obligations	85.3%	65.1%***	79.8%	71.9%***
Strict child obligations	84.4%	63.3%***	89.7%	62.3%***

Note: [a]Test of the same factor structure among two samples of both Muslims and Christians, respectively: Chi-square: 10.2, 8 df, p = .25, AGFI = .99, RMSEA = .02, p = .99.
*** p < .001,**p < .01,* p < .05.

preferences for a traditional family structure (marriage is not outdated but continues to be a viable option, dislike of single parents, a child needs both parents to grow up in a pleasant environment), while the second taps preferences for a strict family structure (parents are obliged to sacrifice for their children, children are obliged to honor and respect their parents). Table 4.4 shows the results for these five indicators.

The results demonstrate that the factor structure for the five indicators is the same for both Muslims and Christians. The responses to this set of indicators can therefore be meaningfully compared across the four samples. The Muslim emigrant countries are more in favor of both a traditional family structure and more strict family relations than the Western European countries. These differences remain when the Muslim immigrants are compared to their native countrymen. Thus, after immigration to Western Europe with its more liberal family values, the Muslim immigrants have kept their distinct views. However, it can also be noted that the Muslim immigrants demonstrate somewhat more liberal family values than their former countrymen. This suggests a minor liberalizing effect of the immigration processes. A similar pattern was found for the religious values.

Moral Values

The moral values among the four samples have been measured by five indicators. These relate to two dimensions. One concerns socioeconomic moral values. Three indicators measure these values (strict views on cheating on taxes, claiming social benefits that one is not entitled to, and

Table 4.5 Results from a set of factor analyses of five indicators for moral values together with the means for these indicators among four different samples of Muslims and Christians. Results from the 1999–2002 EVS/WVS data

| | Varimax rotated factor analyses:[a] | | | |
| | Muslim respondents | | Christian respondents | |
	Factor 1:	Factor 2:	Factor 1:	Factor 2:
Indicators: Strict views on				
Cheat on social benefits	.72	−.10	.80	−.04
Taking bribes	.75	.12	.63	.10
Cheat on taxes	.86	.13	.73	.16
Abortion	.04	.83	.06	.85
Euthanasia	.05	.83	.11	.83
Explained variance	37.0%	26.6%	36.3%	24.2%

Comparisons of means:

| | A: Immigrants-Residents | | B: Groups of countries | |
	Immigrants to West. Europe ($n \approx 100$)	Socioecon. immigr twins ($n \approx 100$)	Emigration countries ($n \approx 1800$)	Immigration countries ($n \approx 1900$)
Cheat on social benefits	7.8	8.2[n.s.]	9.1	8.9[**]
Taking bribes	8.7	8.9[n.s.]	9.8	9.2[***]
Cheat on taxes	7.4	7.7[n.s.]	9.5	8.1[***]
Abortion	8.7	6.1[***]	8.9	6.9[***]
Euthanasia	7.9	6.0[***]	8.9	5.8[***]

Note: [a]Test of the same factor structure among two samples of both Muslims and Christians, respectively: Chi-square: 15.0, 6 df, p = .02, AGFI = .98, RMSEA = .03, p = .98.[***] p < .001,[**]p < .01,[n.s.]No significance.

taking bribes). The second moral dimension concerns bioethical morality. This is measured by two items. These concern strict views on abortion and euthanasia, respectively. The results for the five moral indicators are reported in table 4.5.

The results from the factor analyses demonstrate that the factor structure for the five indicators is the same for the Muslim and the Christian respondents. Their responses can therefore be compared. The Muslim emigrant countries appear to have stricter views on each of the two moral dimensions than the Western immigrant countries. In contrast, the Muslim immigrants appear to be slightly more *permissive* on socioeconomic morality than their new neighbors. Even if there are no statistically significant differences for each of the single indicators, the combined mean score for the three indicators of socioeconomic morality suggests that the Muslim immigrants have become somewhat more permissive than their new countrymen. Thus, immigration into the more lenient Western European immigration countries seem to have brought about a more permissive economic morality among the Muslim immigrants, even to the extent that they may have become more permissive than their native countrymen.

However, when it comes to the bioethical issues, the Muslim immigrants have retained their stricter morality. In this case, immigration does not seem to have caused any moral changes. However, a weak and statistically uncertain tendency toward slightly more permissive views among the Muslim immigrants can be tentatively assumed from the comparison with their former countrymen.

Work Values

The respondents' work values have been measured by two dimensions. The first concerns work ethos. This dimension is measured by three indicators (one needs a job to develop one's talents, a job prevents laziness, work should always come before leisure). The second dimension concerns what kind of job one prefers. This dimension is tapped by two indicators (whether one prefers a job that gives opportunity for initiative and responsibility, respectively). The results for these five indicators are given in table 4.6.

The results show that the factor structure for the five indicators is the same for both Muslim and Christian respondents. The Muslim emigration countries show a significantly stronger work ethos than the immigration countries. The emigration countries also show stronger preferences for

Table 4.6 Results from a set of factor analyses of five indicators of work-related values together with the means for these indicators among four different samples of Muslims and Christians Results from the 1999−2002 EVS/WVS data

	Varrimax rotated factor analyses:[a]			
	Muslim respondents		Christian respondents	
	Factor 1	Factor 2	Factor 1	Factor 2
Indicators:				
Job develops talents	.76	−.02	.76	−.01
Job prevents laziness	.67	.26	.67	.09
Work comes first	.73	.02	.75	−.04
Initiative in job important	.07	.86	−.01	.82
Responsible job important	.08	.87	.04	.82
Explained variance	37.3%	25.4%	31.8%	26.7%

Comparisons of means:

	A: Immigrants-Residents		B: Groups of countries	
	Immigrants to West Europe (n ≈ 100)	Socioecon. immigr twins (n ≈ 100)	Emigration countries (n ≈ 1800)	Immigration countries (n ≈ 1900)
Indicators:				
Job develops talents	3.9	3.8[n.s]	4.0	3.7***
Job prevents laziness	3.4	3.4[n.s.]	3.9	3.3***
Work come first	3.1	3.0[n.s.]	3.9	3.0***
Intiative in job important	26.6%	55.1%***	66.5%	51.0%***
Responsible job important	42.2%	44.0%[n.s]	66.4%	48.4%***

Note: [a]Test of the same factor structure among two samples of both Muslims and Christians, respectively: : Chi-square: 17.0, 8 df, p = .03, AGFI = .98, RMSEA = .03, p = .98.
*** p < .001 [n.s.]No significance.

jobs that give opportunities to take initiatives and to show responsibility. However, these differences have dissolved when one compares the Muslim immigrants with their new neighbors. The immigrants show the same level of work ethos, and they appear to be less in favor of jobs where one can show initiative. For this indicator, an original difference in one direction has changed into a new difference in the opposite direction. However, the over-all impression of the results for the work values is that the original differences between the Islamic and the European countries have developed into a new similarity between the Muslim immigrants and their native countrymen. When the Muslim immigrants find themselves on the West European labor market, they seem to have adopted the same kind of work values as their new countrymen.

Democratic and Civic Values

In order to measure civic orientations, six indicators have been used. These cover three different dimensions. The first concerns attitudes toward democracy and is measured by responses to two statements (It is good to have a democratic system, and even if democracy may have its faults, democracy is still the best system). The second dimension concerns confidence in two of the main social institutions (the police and the civil service, respectively), while the third covers two key components of social capital (horizontal social trust and the importance of showing others respect as well as active involvement in both formal and informal social networks, respectively). The results for these six indicators are found in table 4.7.

Table 4.7 Results from a set of factor analyses of six indicators for democratic culture together with the means for these indicators among four samples of Muslims and Christians. Results from the 1999–2002 EVS/WVS data

	Varimax rotated factor analyses:[a]					
	Muslim respondents			*Christian respondents*		
	Fac 1	*Fac 2*	*Fac 3*	*Fac1*	*Fac 2*	*Fac 3*
Indicators:						
Good to have democracy	.84	−.01	.01	.86	.01	.03
Democracy best system	.85	.02	−.01	.84	.05	.01
Confidence in the police	−.06	.84	−.06	−.06	.82	.01
Confidence in the civil service	.08	.83	.10	.11	.81	.04
Social trust	−.05	.02	.72	.12	−.03	.75
Social networks	.05	.02	.75	−.08	.08	.76
Explained variance	31.7%	2.4%	16.7%	37.5%	18.3%	16.3%

Comparisons of means:

	A: Immigrants-Residents		*B: Groups of countries*	
	Immigrants to West. Europe (n≈100)	*Socioecon. immigr twins (n≈100)*	*Emigration countries (n≈1800)*	*Immigration countries (n≈1900)*
Good to have democracy	3.4	3.6[n.s.]	3.5	3.5[n.s.]
Democracy best system	3.4	3.5[n.s.]	3.4	3.5 ★★★
Confidence in the police	2.5	2.7[n.s.]	2.7	2.7[n.s.]
Confidence in civil service	2.3	2.4[n.s.]	2.5	2.4 ★★
Horizontal social trust	1.1	1.1[n.s.]	0.7	1.1 ★★★
Participat. social networks	1.7	1.8[n.s.]	1.5	1.5[n.s.]

Note: [a]Test of the same factor structure among two samples of both Muslims and Christians, respectively: Chi-square: 21.6, 14 df, p = .09, AGFI = .99, RMSEA = .02, p = .99. ★★★ p < .001, ★★ p < .01,[n.s.] No significance.

The results demonstrate that the factor structure for the six indicators for civic orientations is the same for both Muslims and Christians. Their responses can therefore be meaningfully compared. In several instances, the Muslim emigration countries and the Western European countries show similar orientations, while the few original differences that are found between these two groups of countries have disappeared when one compares the Muslim immigrants to their new neighbors. In short, the results demonstrate rather similar orientations toward civic society and democracy among Westerners and Muslims. These similarities do not appear to have been affected by the Muslim settlement in the Western European countries with their different political systems. Rather, the previous similarities seem to have remained.

Some Additional Findings from the

European Social Survey

Since the EVS/WVS data contains only a limited number of Muslim immigrants and contains no information on whether the respondents are first or second generation Muslim immigrants, it is of considerable interest to look for other data that may compensate for these shortcomings. The data from the 2002 wave of the European Social Survey (ESS) can serve to this end. For details on this survey, the reader is referred to the ESS webpage http://www.europeansocialsurvey.org/. Here it is sufficient to note that the ESS is conducted on fairly large samples, representative of the populations in some 25 European countries. The ESS questionnaire contains questions on some of the value orientations that have been analyzed in the analyses of the EVS/WVS data. The ESS data also allows comparisons between the first and second generation of Muslim immigrants in Western Europe.

The 2002 ESS data from Belgium, Denmark, England, France, the Netherlands, Luxembourg, Norway, Germany, Spain, and Sweden includes 276 self-declared Muslims. The majority of these (216 respondents) are first generation immigrants, born in an Islamic country. A minority of about 60 Muslim respondents is born in some of the Western European countries, but at the same time have at least one parent who is of foreign origin. These respondents constitute a selection of second generation Muslim immigrants in Western Europe. A recent analysis of these two generations of Muslim immigrants has demonstrated results that seem to parallel the findings from the EVS/WVS data (Pettersson and Esmer, 2005). A comparison of the levels of self-reported religiosity (how religious one is, how important religion is in one's life) among the two generations of Muslim immigrants showed that each of them scored higher than their new countrymen and also that the second generation demonstrated the same level as the first generation. However, when the two generations were compared with regard to overt religious behavior (prayer, attendance at religious services), the second generation scored lower than the first, but still higher than their new countrymen. This may indicate that the second generation has slowly begun to adopt the lower level of religious activity that dominates in the country where they now live. The slightly lower level of religious activity among the second generation may also be explained by fewer opportunities for religious participation, for instance because of migration to other places of living than where their parents live. Thus, with regard to religiosity, the ESS data indicate that the Muslim immigrants continue to demonstrate higher levels, but also that there might be a certain "leveling out" of the differences to their new countrymen, especially in the case of overt religious behavior among the second generation. As already demonstrated, the EVS/WVS data suggested a similar pattern.

The ESS data also allows an analysis of the civic orientations among the Muslim immigrants. The measure for this includes internal political efficacy, participation in political debates, protest behavior, and horizontal social trust. To a certain degree, this measure resembles the measures of civic orientations that were used in the analysis of the EVS/WVS data. The ESS measure for the civic orientation demonstrated that each of the two generations of Muslim immigrants scored lower than their new countrymen, but also that the second generations scored significantly higher than the first generation. In other words, it appears that the second generation has begun to approach the civic orientations of their new countrymen. The EVS/WVS data suggested a similar tendency.

Conclusion

This analysis of value change among Muslim immigrants in Western Europe started from the notion that the immigrants are of different historical, national, and ethnic backgrounds and also that they are met with different immigration policies with different aims. Accordingly, one should not treat them as one homogenous category. The analysis also started from the assumption that different kinds of value change may occur among the immigrants. Original value differences between Muslims and Western Christians may both persist and dissolve and old similarities may both remain and turn into new differences. It was furthermore noted that a number of different factors could affect these different outcomes. However, it was also argued that the value dimensions that are internalized by primary socialization during childhood and early adolescence would be least likely to change as a result of immigration into Western Europe. From this point of view, religious values and family values were assumed to be more resistant to value change among the Muslim immigrants than their work values and civic orientations.

This investigation has built on an analytical strategy that included two kinds of simultaneous comparisons. One set of comparisons investigated value differences between a group of Muslim immigrants and another group of their native Christian socioeconomic equals. These comparisons were said to control for the differential structural incorporation of the immigrants in their new home countries. In order to set the findings from these comparisons into perspective and to allow more detailed conclusions on the impact of immigration, they were compared to the findings from a second set of comparisons. These searched for differences between the value systems that prevailed in the immigrants' countries of origin and the countries into which they have immigrated. The two sets of comparisons were performed on the data from the most recent EVS/WVS wave, and they covered five value dimensions. These were religious values, family values, moral values, work values, and civic orientations.

The results showed that the factor structure for the indicators for these five value dimensions were similar for the Christian and Muslim respondents. In a general sense, this demonstrates that the value orientations of Muslims and Christians from Western Europe are equally structured. Besides the theoretical interest of this finding, the similar factor structure is also a necessary requirement for the comparison of value profiles among Muslims and Christians.

Even if the results for the measures of religion suggested that especially the second generation of Muslim immigrants had begun to slowly adapt to the lower levels of religious behavior among their new countrymen, the main result from the empirical analyses suggested that neither the religious values nor the family values among the Muslim immigrants were substantially affected by the immigration processes. Since these values tend to be internalized by primary socialization processes, this result is in line with the theoretical premises of this investigation. Although not obviously related to primary socialization processes, the Muslim immigrants also appeared to retain the stricter Muslim views on bioethical issues such as abortion and euthanasia. However, in value domains that tend to be acquired during secondary socialization, the Muslim immigrants appeared to have adapted to the cultural patterns that dominate in their new Western European environments. This finding is also expected from the theoretical premises. In socioeconomic moral matters, the immigrants seemed to have abandoned the stricter views that are found in their former Muslim home countries, even to the extent that they had almost become more permissive than their new countrymen. Likewise, they had also adapted to the weaker work ethos of their new compatriots, and their originally stronger emphasis on opportunities for initiative and responsibility in work life had become weaker. Finally, with regard to their prodemocratic and civic orientations, the few differences that were found between the immigrants' countries of origin and their new immigration societies seemed to have dissolved after immigration—especially the finding that the Muslim immigrants showed the same levels of social capital as their new neighbors deserves attention. This suggests that the Muslim immigrants have started to accumulate an important cultural resource for a good life.

The differentiated pattern of value change among the Muslim immigrants suggests that the issue is not whether the Muslim-Christian (or the Muslim-Western) value differences persist or dissolve among Muslim immigrants in Western-Europe. Rather, the results suggest that some of their original values tend to remain while others are likely to change. Those values that are acquired by primary socialization are likely to persist, while those that are internalized by secondary socialization are more likely to change. In a very general sense, these findings are also in line with the results from previous research that have shown that the main fault line between Islam and the Western world is primarily related to religious and family values and not to the values that apply to the public sphere, democracy, and the civic society. However, in this regard another group of findings from this investigation is also relevant. These findings indicated that the Muslim immigrants had slowly begun to approach the religious values and family values of their new countrymen. This may indicate that in the long run, the religious values and family values may also change among the Muslim immigrants.

Several modes of this investigation must be critically discussed. The analytical two-tiered strategy appears to have some obvious advantages. For one thing, this strategy was able to clarify rather differentiated cultural effects of international migration. However, in the present application, there were also some obvious drawbacks associated with this strategy. One problem relates to the relatively small sample size of the Muslim immigrants in the EVS/WVS data set. Even if the impact of different kinds of structural incorporation among these immigrants is kept under control by this analytical strategy, the small sample size nevertheless makes it more difficult to uncover existing value differences between the immigrants and their new countrymen. However, since the results were in line with the differentiated theoretical expectations, the comparatively small number of Muslim immigrants need not be evaluated as a major methodological flaw. It should also be noted that the ESS data, which include a greater number of Muslim immigrants, by and large showed similar findings as the EVS/WVS data.

Another problem with the sample of Muslim immigrants is the lack of key data on their country of origin, the length of their stay in the host society, and whether they are immigrants of the first, second, or third generation. In principle, one can even imagine that at least some of those who have been analyzed as immigrants in reality are native born converts to Islam. Considering the socioeconomic status of the immigrants, it is however unlikely that this should be the case for more than a few of them. The results form the 2002 ESS data helped illuminate the differences between different generations of Muslim immigrants. As already mentioned, these data showed similar tendencies as the EVS/WVS data. This added to the validity of the EVS/WVS data for the kinds of analyses that are presented in this investigation.

Another critical issue of this investigation concerns how representative the Muslim immigrants are for the Muslims in general in their various home countries. Thus, due to different self-selection processes, the Muslims who choose to immigrate into Western Europe might not have been entirely representative of their fellow countrymen at the time of emigration. They might, for instance, have scored lower on religiosity, work ethos, and socioeconomic morality, and higher on social trust. Although the data does not allow checks on this option, it seems less likely considering their present levels of religious commitment and their distinct traditional family values. Moreover, it should also be noted that even if such self-selection processes have been at work for the Muslim immigrants, the results from the comparisons between the immigrants and their new European compatriots would still be valid as a description of the present situation. Furthermore, even if the Muslim immigrants were not representative for the culture of their former home countries, this culture is likely to have determined how the immigrants have reacted in their relations to their new countrymen in the new cultural setting. In this regard, it should however also be noted that the data files that have been analyzed in this investigation do not, in all likelihood, include the illegal immigrants working in the informal sectors of society. Therefore, it must be strongly underlined that the findings only concern those Muslim immigrants that have become sufficiently established in order to be included in an investigation like the European Values Study or the European Social Survey.

In this sense, several dimensions of this investigation should be critically assessed and the results must be interpreted with care. However, the formats of this investigation and the findings it has generated also seem to merit consideration. The analytical strategy has uncovered interesting cultural effects of international migration, and the results have corroborated some key assumptions in socialization research. The results have also cast further light on some of the basic characteristics of Islamic culture. In these regards, this investigation of value change, value adaptation, and value persistence among Muslim immigrants in Western Europe has contributed new insights.

Appendix

The items that are used to measure the different value orientations can be described as follows. It should be noted that in some instances, the direction of the response scales has been recoded in relation to the original questionnaires.

Religious values are measured by the following five items:

1) Importance of God is measured by one question that asks, "How important is God in your life?" The responses were given on a 10 point scale, ranging from "Not at all important" (1) to "Very important" (10).
2) The importance of religion is measured by one question that asks, "How important is religion in your life?" The responses were given on a four-point scale, ranging from "Not at all important" (1) to "Very important" (4).
3) Church adequacy is measured by a set of four questions that ask whether one thinks that one's church/religious tradition gives adequate answers to (a) the moral problems and needs of the individual, (b) the problems of family life, (c) people's spiritual needs, and (d) the social problems facing our society today. Those who said "yes" to all four items received a score of 4, while those who did not say "yes" to any of them received a score of 0.
4) Views on the relation between religion and politics are measured by two questions. The first asks the respondent to agree or disagree to the statement "Politicians who do not believe in God are unfit

for public office." The responses were given on a 5 point response
scale, ranging from "Agree strongly" (1) to "Disagree strongly" (5).

5) The second question on the relation between religion and politics
asks the respondent to agree or disagree to the statement "It would be
better for (this country) if more people with strong religious beliefs
held public office." The responses were given on a 5 point response
scale, ranging from "Disagree strongly" to "Agree strongly."

Family values are measured by the following five items:

1) "If a woman wants to have a child as single parent but does not
want to have stable relation to a man, do you approve or disapprove?" The responses were given on a 2 point scale, ranging from
"Disapprove" (0) to "Approve" (1).

2) "If someone says that a child needs a home with both a father and a
mother to grow up happily, would you tend to agree or disagree?"
The responses were given a 2 point scale, ranging from "Disagree"
(0) to "agree" (1).

3) "Do you agree or disagree with the statement 'Marriage is an outdated institution'?" The answers were given on a 2-point scale,
ranging from "Tend to disagree" (0) to "tend to agree" (1).

4) "Which of the following statements best describes your views
about parents' responsibilities toward their children?" Those who
selected the alternative "Parents' duty is to do their best for their
children even at the expense of their own well-being" received a
score of 1, while those who chose another alternative, saying that
parents should not be asked to sacrifice their own well-being for
the sake of their children, received a score of 0.

5) "Which of the following two statements do you tend to agree
with?" Those who selected the alternative "Regardless of the qualities and faults of one's parents, one must always love and respect
them" got a score of 1, while those who chose the alternative
"One does not have the duty to respect and love parents who have
not earned it by their behavior and attitudes" received a score of 0.

Moral values are measured by the following five items:

The five items were chosen from a battery that was introduced by the
following: "Please tell me for each of the following statements whether
you think that it can always be justified, never justified, or something in
between." The responses were given on a 10-point scale, ranging from
"Never" (1) to "Always" (10).

Socioeconomic morality is measured by the responses to:

1) Claiming state benefits that you are not entitled to;
2) Cheating on tax if you have the chance; and
3) Someone accepting a bribe in the course of their duties.

Bioethical morality is measured by the responses to:

4) Abortion;
5) Euthanasia.

Work values are measured by the following five items:

In the case of job motivation, the respondents were asked to disagree or agree to three items. The responses were given on a 5 point response scale, ranging from "Disagree strongly" (1) to "Agree strongly" (5). The three items were:

1) To fully develop your talents, you need to have a job;
2) People who do not work turn lazy;
3) Work should always come first, even if it means less spare time.

Two items for the measurement of preferences of different kinds of jobs asked whether the respondent favored jobs that allowed him/her the following two options. If these two options were chosen, a score of 1 was given for each. If not, a score of 0 was applied to each:

4) An opportunity to use initiative;
5) A responsible job.

Democratic values and civic orientations are measured by the following six indicators:

Democratic orientations are measured by disagreements-agreements to two statements. The responses were given on a 4-point response scale, ranging from "Very bad/disagree strongly" (1) to "Very good/Agree strongly" (4). The two statements were:

1) Having a democratic political system;
2) Democracy may have its problems but it is better than any other form of government.

Confidence in social institutions are measured by two questions with response alternatives ranging from "None at all" (1) to "A great deal of confidence" (4). The two items asked about confidence in:

1) The police;
2) The Civil service.

Involvement in the civic society is measured by two indicators. These concern:

1) Horizontal social trust. Those who say that one can trust other people rather than to be very careful in relating to them, and that it is important to show other people respect received a score of 2, while those who do not endorse any of these two options get a score of 0.
2) Social networks. This indicator is calculated as the sum of two subindices. One concerns whether one meets friends, work mates, fellow church members, and fellow organizational members informally every week. On this subindex, the scores range from 0 to 4. The other index measures in how many organizations and social movements one is an active member. On this index, the scores range between 0 and 13.

Notes

1. "Pillarization policies" refers to those policies that are related to the societies divided between different religious traditions (e.g., Netherlands), where the various social policies (health care, labor unions, care for the old, etc.) are divided into two different blocks, depending on their belief in their religious tradition.
2. This means that the value differences between Muslims and Christians are more related to gender roles and sexual mores than to sociopolitical orientations (e.g., views on democracy).

References

AlSayyad, Nezar and Manuel Castells. 2002. "Introduction: Islam and the Changing Identity of Europe." In *Muslim Europe or Euro-Islam*, edited by Nezar AlSayyad and Manuel Castell. New York: Lexington Books, pp. 1–6.
Berger, Peter and Thomas Luckmann. 1967. *The Social Construction of Reality*. Garden City, NY: Doubleday.
Billiet, Jaak. 2003. "Cross-Cultural Equivalence with Structural Equation Modeling." In *Cross-Cultural Survey Methods*, edited by Janet Harkness, Fons van de Vijver and Peter Ph. Mohler, pp. 247–63. Hoboken: John Wiley and Sons.

Borevi, Karin. 2002. *Välfärdsstaten I det mångkulturella samhället.* Uppsala: Acta Universitatis Upsaliensis. Skrifter utgivna av Statsvetenskapliga föreningen i Uppsala.

Byrne, Barbara. 2001. *Structural Equation Modeling with AMOS.* London: Ludwig Erlbaum Associates.

De Vijver, Fons and Kwok Leung. 1997. *Methods and Data Analysis for Cross-Cultural Research.* London: Sage Publications.

Dobbelaere, Karel. 2002. *Secularization: An Analysis at Three Levels.* Bern: Publishing Group Peter Lang.

Ebaugh, Helen. 2003. "Religion and the new immigrants." In *Handbook of the Sociology of Religion,* edited by Michele Dillon, pp. 225–39. Cambridge: Cambridge University Press.

Esmer, Yilmaz. 2003. "Is There an Islamic Civilization?" In *Human Values and Social Change: International Studies in Sociology and Social Anthropology,* edited by Ronald Inglehart, pp. 35–68. Leiden: Brill.

Furseth, Inger and Pal Repstad. 2003. *Innføring i Religionssociologi.* Oslo: Universitetsförlaget.

Gelissen, John. 2003. "Cross-National Differences in Public Consent to Divorce: Effects of Cultural, Structural and Compositional Factors." In *The Cultural Diversity of European Unity,* edited by Wilhelmus Arts, Jacques Hagenaars, and Loek Halman, pp. 339–70. Leiden: Brill.

Haddad, Yvonne and Adair Lumis. 1987. *Islamic Values in the United States: A Comparative Study.* New York: Oxford University Press.

Halman, Loek and Thorleif Pettersson. 2003. "Religion und Politik in zetgenössischen Gesellschaft: Differenzierung oder Entdifferenzierung?" In *Politik und Religion, Sonderheft 33/2002, Politische Vierteljahresschrif,* edited by Michael Minkenberg and Ulrich Willems, pp. 303–22. Wiesbaden: Westdeutscher Verlag.

Hamberg, Eva. 2000. *Livsåskådningar, Religion och Värderingar i en Invardrargrupp.* Stockholm: CEIFO, Stockholms Universitet.

Hammar, Tomas. (ed.). 1985. *European Immigration Policy: A Comparative Study.* Cambridge: Cambridge University Press.

Hammond, Phillip. 1992. *Religion and Personal Autonomy: The Third Disestablishment in America.* Columbia: University of South Carolina Press.

Hunter, Shireen. 2002. (ed.). *Islam, Europe's Second Religion: The New Social, Cultural and Political Landscape.* London: Praeger.

Hunter, Shireen and Simon Serfaty. 2002. "Introduction." In *Islam, Europe's Second Religion: The New Social, Cultural and Political Landscape,* edited by Shireen Hunter, pp. xiii–xvii. London: Praeger.

Inglehart, Ronald, Manuel Basáñez, Jaime Díex-Medrano, Loek Halman, and Ruud Luijkx. (eds.). 2004. *Human Values and Beliefs: A Crosscultural Sourcebook Based on the 1999–2002 Values Surveys.* Mexico City: Siglo Veintiuno Editors.

Isajiw, Wsevolod. 1999. *Understanding Diversity: Ethnicity and Race in the Canadian Context.* Toronto: Thompson Educational Publishing.

Lubeck, Paul. 2002. "The Challenge of Islamic Networks and Citizenship Claims: Europe's Painful Adjustment to Globalization." In *Muslim Europe or Euro-Islam,* edited by Nezar AlSayyad and Manuel Castell, pp. 69–90. New York: Lexington Books.

Miller, Donald, John Miller, and Grace Dyrness. 2001. *Immigrant Religion in the City of Angels.* Los Angeles: Center for Religion and Civic Culture, University of Southern California.

Moaddel, Mansoor. 2002, "The Study of Islamic Culture and Politics: An Overview and Assessment." *Annual Review of Sociology* 28: 359–86.

Moaddel, Mansoor and Taghi Azadarmaki. 2003. "The Worldviews of Islamic Publics: The Cases of Egypt, Iran, and Jordan." In *Human Values and Social Change: International Studies in Sociology and Social Anthropology,* edited by Ronald Inglehart, pp. 69–89. Leiden: Brill.

Norris, Pippa and Ronald Inglehart. 2003. "Islamic Culture and Democracy: Testing the 'Clash of Civilizations' Thesis." In *Human Values and Social change: International Studies in Sociology and Social Anthropology*, edited by Ronald Inglehart, pp. 5–33. Leiden: Brill.

Pettersson, Thorleif. 1988. *Bakom Dubbla lås. En Studie av små och Långsamma Värdeingsförändringar.* Stockholm: Allmänna Förlaget.

———. 2003a. "The Relations between Religion and Politics in the Contemporary Western World." www.worldvaluessurvey.org/ accessed September 21, 2006.

———. 2003b. "Basic Values and Civic Education. A Comparative Analysis of Adolescent Orientations towards Gender Equality and Good Citizenship." www.worldvaluessurvey.org/, accessed September 21, 2006.

Pettersson, Thorleif and Yilmaz Esmer. 2005. *Annorlunda Folk. Om Invadrares Möte med Svensk Kultur.* Norrköping: Migrationsverket.

Price, Daniel. 1999. *Islamic Political Culture, Democracy, and Human Rights.* London: Praeger.

Tessler, Mark. 2003. "Do Islamic Orientations Influence Attitudes toward Democracy in the Arab World?" *International Journal of Comparative Sociology* 43(3–5): 229–49.

Tibi, Bassam. 2002. "Muslim Migrants in Europe: Between Euro-Islam and Ghettoization." In *Muslim Europe or Euro-Islam*, edited by Nezar AlSayyad and Manel Castell, pp. 31–52. New York: Lexington Books.

Westerlund, David and Ingvar Svanberg (eds.). 1999. *Islam Outside the Arab World.* Richmond Srre: Curzon Press.

PART 2

Political and Economic Consequences of Islam versus Rentier Economy

CHAPTER 5

Do Islamic Orientations Influence Attitudes toward Democracy in the Arab World? Evidence from the World Values Survey in Egypt, Jordan, Morocco, and Algeria

MARK TESSLER

The Absence of Democracy in the Arab World

Over the course of the past two decades, democratic currents have swept across much of the developing and postcommunist world. Whereas democratic regimes were a minority just a few years ago, electoral democracy is the predominant form of government among today's nation-states and guides the lives of more than half of the world's population (Karatnycky 2000). The Arab world, however, has been largely unaffected by this political revolution, by what Huntington has called the "Third Wave" of democratization (Huntington 1991). According to Freedom House, not a single Arab country qualifies as an electoral democracy (Karatnycky 2000; also Sivan 2000).

The 1980s and early 1990s did witness halting moves toward democratization in some Arab countries. Confronted with popular anger fuelled by economic conditions, government mismanagement and corruption, and the violation of human rights, a number of Arab governments enacted programs of political liberalization. For the most part, however, these reforms were part of a containment strategy designed to increase regime legitimacy at a time when calls for political change were widespread. Accordingly, and not surprisingly given their strategic purpose, most of these democratic experiments were slowed or even abandoned during the 1990s. By the end of the decade, as Lisa Anderson wrote in 1999, the political landscape was littered with "the remnants of so many of the democratic experiments—from the spectacular crash and burn of Algeria's liberalization to Tunisia's more subtle but no less profound transformation into a police state, from Egypt's backsliding into electoral manipulation [and repression of Islamic movements] to the reluctance of Palestinian authorities to embrace human rights" (Anderson 1999: 6).

This situation is acknowledged and lamented by Arab intellectuals as well as Western scholars. A Lebanese political scientist writes, for example, that unchecked authoritarian rule is "paving the way to a deep crisis in the fabric of society" (Khashan 1998: 43–44). Similarly, according to a Jordanian journalist, "one of the leading sources of instability and political-economic distortion in the Arab world is the unchecked use of state power, combined with the state's whimsical ability to use the rule of law for its own political ends" (Khouri 2000). Against this background, intellectuals from thirteen Arab countries attending a December 1999 conference in Amman, Jordan, issued a final communiqué emphasizing the need for "greater political freedoms and intellectual pluralism" (Al-Farawati 1999). Their concern, in the assessment of still another Arab scholar, is that "Arab countries do not allow freedom of thought . . . Where necessary, their surveillance spares neither the telephone nor the mail, neither the fax nor the Internet" (Talbi 2000: 62).

There are some partial exceptions to this depressing characterization. In Jordan, Morocco, Lebanon, Kuwait, and Qatar, for example, some would argue that there is continuing albeit uneven progress and that it is possible to have a meaningful debate about whether the glass is half full or half empty. In the Palestinian Authority, too, there have been accomplishments as well as setbacks in the struggle for democratic governance. Nevertheless, taken as a whole, the Arab world clearly stands apart from other world regions with respect to the authoritarian character of its governments and the limited influence of institutions and individuals working for democracy. This point is emphasized by the recent Arab Human Development Report of the United Nation's Development Programme, published in 2002. The report observes that, as in the 1980s, political openings remain "heavily regulated and partial" and political systems "have not been opened up to all citizens." Thus, the report continues, "political participation is less advanced in the Arab world than in other developing regions" and, with understatement, "transfer of power through the ballot box is not a common phenomenon" (AHDR 2002, Chapter 7).

Support for Democracy and the Influence of Islam

There is disagreement about the reasons for the persistence of authoritarian rule in the Arab world, just as there is uncertainty about the prospects for Arab democratization in the years ahead. Research on democratic transitions and consolidation has emphasized the importance both of structural factors, such as institutional reform and economic development, and of political culture. Both have been discussed in relation to the Arab world. On the one hand, many scholars have emphasized the resistance of Arab leaders to power sharing and meaningful reform (Brumberg 1995; Korany 1994; Sivan 1997). A widespread popular perception in the region, according to the report of a Moroccan political scientist, is that the primary motivation of many Arab kings, sultans, and presidents "is to remain in power and protect their personal interests . . . [and as a result they often have] to defend themselves against their own people" (Bennani-Chraibi 1994: 243). In the succinct assessment of a senior American analyst, much of the explanation for the political situation in the Arab world "lies in the fact that many Middle Eastern states have no greater enemy than their own governments" (Cordesman 1999).

Students of democratization also stress the importance of citizen attitudes and values, which is the focus of the present inquiry. Relevant orientations include both generalized support for democratic political forms and the embrace of specific democratic values, such as respect for political competition and tolerance of diverse political ideas (Rose et al. 1998). Thus, as summarized by one prominent scholar, a democratic citizen is one who "believes in individual liberty and is politically tolerant, has a certain distrust of political authority but at the same time is trusting of fellow citizens, is obedient but nonetheless willing to assert rights against the state, and views the state as constrained by legality" (Gibson 1995: 55).

Some analysts suggest that these normative orientations may be a precondition for democratic transitions (Huntington 1993). Much more common is the view that democratic values need not precede, but can rather follow, elite-led transitions involving the reform of political institutions and procedures (Rose 1997; Schmitter and Karl 1993). Indeed, according to this argument, attitudes and values conducive to democracy tend to emerge among the citizens of countries experiencing successful democratic transitions. At the very least, however, the presence of appropriate attitudes and values would seem to be necessary for democratic consolidation. As expressed by Inglehart, "Democracy is not attained simply by making institutional changes through elite-level maneuvering. Its survival depends also on the values and beliefs of ordinary citizens" (2000: 96).

Evidence in support of this assessment comes from a number of empirical investigations. According to a recent study of Taiwan and Korea, for example, the consolidation of democracy requires that "all significant political actors, at both the elite and mass levels, believe that the democratic regime is the most right and appropriate for their society, better than any other realistic alternative they can imagine" (Chu et al. 2001: 123). A cross-national study in Latin America makes the same point: an important factor "that has contributed to the greater survivability of Latin American democracies revolves around changes in political attitudes, toward a greater valorization of democracy" (Mainwaring 1999: 45). Thus, as Harik has noted with respect to the Arab world, "a democratic government needs a democratic political culture, and vice versa" (Harik 1994: 56).

There are differing scholarly opinions about whether citizen orientations conducive to democracy can emerge and flourish in the Arab world. The influence of Islam is the focus of particular attention in this connection (Tessler 2002). This is due, in part, both to the nature of Islam and to the religion's political resurgence during the past three decades. Islamic law includes numerous codes governing societal relations and organization. It guides that which is societal as well as personal, corporate as well as individual (Esposito 1992). As Voll explains, Islam is a total way of life; it represents a worldview (Voll 1994). This is one of the reasons that popular support for Islamist movements and parties has grown significantly in recent years (Tessler 1997).

Amid these assumptions, there have long been debates about Islam's proper role in political affairs, including, more recently, its compatibility with conceptions of governance based on democracy, pluralism, and popular sovereignty. Some observers, particularly some Western observers, assert that democracy and Islam are not compatible. Whereas democracy requires openness, competition, pluralism, and tolerance of diversity, Islam, they argue, encourages intellectual conformity and an uncritical acceptance of authority. According to the late Elie Kedourie, for example, the principles, institutions, and values of democracy are "profoundly alien to the Muslim political tradition" (Kedourie 1994: 5–6; also

Huntington 1984). Equally important, Islam is said to be antidemocratic because it vests sovereignty in God, who is the sole source of political authority and from whose divine law must come all regulations governing the community of believers. Thus, in the view of some observers, Islam "has to be ultimately embodied in a totalitarian state" (Choueiri 1996: 21–22; also Lewis 1994). Comparable assertions are sometimes advanced in debates about "Asian values," in which it is asked whether Confucianism's emphasis on consensus, order, obedience, and hierarchy is compatible with such democratic values as individual freedom and identity, diversity, competition, and political accountability (Flanagan and Lee 2000; Wei-Ming 2000; Welsh 1996; Zakaria 1994).

But many knowledgeable analysts reject the suggestion that Islam is an enemy in the struggle to establish accountable government. They point out that Islam has many facets and tendencies, making unidimensional characterizations of the religion highly suspect (Halliday 1995; Esposito and Piscatori 1991). They also report that there is considerable variation in the interpretations of religious law advanced by Muslim scholars and theologians, and that among these are expressions of support for democracy, including some by leading Islamist theorists (Abed 1995). Finally, they insist that openness, tolerance, and progressive innovation are well-represented among traditions associated with the religion, and are thus entirely compatible with Islam (Hamdi 1996; Mernissi 1992).

As the foregoing suggests, one can find within Islamic doctrine and Muslim traditions both elements that are and elements that are not congenial to democracy; and this in turn means that the influence of the religion depends to a very considerable extent on how and by whom it is interpreted. There is no single or accepted interpretation on many issues, nor sometimes even a consensus on who speaks for Islam. As one study demonstrated with respect to Islamic strictures about family planning and contraception, different religious authorities give different advice about what is permissible in Islam (Bowen 1993). In addition, serious doubts have been expressed about the motivation of some religious authorities, particularly in connection with pronouncements pertaining to governance. As one Arab scholar asks, "Can democracy occur if the *ulama* or jurists have sole charge of legal interpretation? May not the *ulama*'s ability to declare laws compatible or incompatible with the teaching of the shari 'a lead to abuse? There are numerous examples of *ulama* manipulating Islamic teachings to the advantage of [undemocratic] political leaders" (Al-Suwaidi 1995; 87–88).

Debates about the compatibility of democracy and Islam have for the most part focused on issues of theology, doctrine, and historical precedent.

Less has been said about whether and how Islamic conceptions and attachments influence the political attitudes and values of ordinary citizens. Further, when implications about the political orientations of ordinary citizens *are* proposed, it is almost always on the basis on deductive reasoning and analogy. Despite a few recent studies, empirical evidence about whether and how Islam helps to shape the political views of Muslim Arab men and women is extremely rare. Indeed, empirical research on the political orientations of ordinary citizens in the Arab world is something that has generally been lacking (Anderson 1999; also Hudson 1995; Tessler 1999). The availability of WVS data, recently collected in four Arab states, offers an important opportunity to begin filling this gap. The analysis of these data will shed light both on the degree of popular support for democracy and on the validity of competing positions in ongoing debates about whether Islam fosters antidemocratic attitudes among ordinary men and women in the Arab world.

Data and Methods

Questions about the impact of Islamic attachments on the attitudes toward democracy held by ordinary Arab men and women can usefully be investigated with data from the WVS. The four Arab countries in which the WVS has thus far been conducted are Egypt, Morocco, Algeria, and Jordan. Surveys in each country were carried out during the fourth wave of the WVS, and the data were therefore collected between 2000 and 2002. As elsewhere, each WVS project was designed and carried out in close collaboration with scholars from the participating country. The present author helped to direct the WVS in Algeria.

While no subset of states is completely representative of the Arab world, these four countries provide a strong foundation for insights that may be generalizable to much of the region. Egypt, Algeria, and Morocco are the most populous Arab countries; Egypt and Algeria are republics while Jordan and Morocco are monarchies; two of the countries have a legacy of French colonialism whereas in the other two Britain was the dominant imperial power prior to independence; and, finally, two were in the socialist camp and had a socialist orientation during much of the cold war and two have always been allied politically and ideologically with the Western bloc. This subset of countries does not include any of the Gulf Arab states, countries with small populations and substantial wealth that to a considerable extent have a distinctive political and cultural orientation. Nevertheless, overall, Egypt, Algeria,

Morocco, and Jordan encompass between them the political, economic, and social environments in which the vast majority of the Arab world's citizens reside. Accordingly, if data from the four countries suggest similar conclusions, these are likely to shed light on the attitudes of Arab citizens elsewhere. Alternatively, should there be differences among the four cases, it will be possible to offer insights about the conditionalities associated with particular patterns and relationships.

Five items from the WVS interview schedule have been used to measure attitudes toward democracy. These items are:

I am going to describe various types of political systems and ask what you think about each as a way of governing this country. For each one, would you say it is a very good, fairly good, fairly bad, or very bad way of governing this country?

V167. Having a democratic political system

I am going to read off some things that people sometimes say about a democratic political system. Could you please tell me if you agree strongly, agree, disagree or disagree strongly, after I read each one of them?

V169. In democracy, the economic system runs badly
V170. Democracies are indecisive and have too much quibbling
V171. Democracies are not good at maintaining order
V172. Democracy may have problems but it is better than any other form of government

Factor analysis was used to select these items from a slightly larger battery of questions pertaining to democracy. Factor analysis identifies items that cluster together and hence measure the same underlying concept, thereby increasing confidence in reliability and validity (Marradi 1981). Confidence is further increased, as is cross-national conceptual equivalence, by the similar pattern of factor loadings observed in all four countries. Two distinct sets of attitudes toward democracy were identified by factor analysis. One, reflecting the strong intercorrelation of items V167 and V172, concerns the degree to which respondents have a favorable attitude toward democracy. The second, reflecting strong correlations among the other three items, concerns the degree to which respondents believe there are important problems associated with democracy, regardless of whether they believe these make an alternative political formulae more desirable.

The two sets of attitudes identified by factor analysis are the dependent variables in the analysis to follow. V167 and V172 have been combined to form an additive index measuring the first of these dimensions, support for democracy. V169, V170, and V171 have been combined to form an additive index measuring the second of these dimensions, significance of the perceived drawbacks associated with democracy. Table 5.1 shows the distribution of responses to each of the two indices and its constituent items for each of the four countries. The table shows, first, that in all four countries attitudes toward democracy are much more likely to be favorable than unfavorable. While the distributions are skewed in favor of democracy to a greater degree in Morocco and Egypt than in Jordan and Algeria, even in the latter two countries most citizens have a favorable, if not a very favorable, attitude toward democracy. Second, again in each case, there is considerable variation in views about whether there are important problems associated with democracy. On average, roughly one-third of the respondents agree or agree strongly that democracies are not good at managing the economy, maintaining order, and acting decisively. Other respondents disagree, or in many instances disagree strongly, that such problems are associated with democracy.

Factor analysis was also used to select items measuring attitudes and attachments pertaining to Islam and two distinct dimensions were again identified. One of these concerns personal piety and religious involvement and the other concerns the role in public affairs of religion and religious leaders. The measure of personal religiosity resulting from this analysis is an additive index composed of two items dealing with mosque attendance and participation in mosque activities. A question requesting a subjective assessment of personal religiosity and another asking about the importance of God had high loadings on the same factor. But while these loadings increase confidence in the reliability and validity of all items, the latter two were not included in the personal piety index because their response distributions were highly skewed and contained little variance. For example, on a 10-point scale ranging from not at all important to very important, the proportion of respondents selecting a 10, meaning extremely important, in response to a question about God was 81.6 percent in Egypt, 94.8 percent in Algeria, 98.5 percent in Jordan, and 99.2 percent in Morocco. In the Egyptian case, another 14 percent chose an 8 or 9. This means that only with respect to mosque attendance and participation in mosque activities is there variance whose impact on political attitudes may be explored. With respect to religious conviction and personal piety, at least as measured by the WVS, the virtual absence of variance obviates questions about explanatory power of these characteristics.

Two measures of attitudes toward the role of Islam in public affairs have been established on the basis of this analysis. One is an additive

Table 5.1 Attitudes toward Democracy in Egypt, Jordan, Morocco, and Algeria

	Egypt %	Jordan %	Morocco %	Algeria %
V167 Having a democratic government in this country is				
Very good	67.9	51.2	81.5	60.4
Fairly good	30.6	43.5	14.5	32.3
Fairly bad or bad	1.5	5.3	4.0	7.3
V172 Despite it problems, democracy is better than any other form of government				
Strongly agree	63.6	39.1	77.3	48.5
Agree	34.1	51.2	18.6	39.9
Disagree or strongly disagree	2.3	9.7	4.1	11.6
Attitude toward democracy index				
Very favorable	52.1	28.6	71.6	41.4
Favorable	45.7	61.0	24.0	47.3
Somewhat favorable	1.6	7.9	2.7	5.6
Not favorable	.6	2.5	1.7	5.7
V169 In democracy, the economic system runs badly				
Strongly agree	3.1	7.4	15.1	9.2
Agree	15.0	25.1	20.7	22.0
Disagree	56.8	39.3	42.4	54.9
Strongly disagree	25.1	28.2	21.8	14.1
V170 Democracies are indecisive				
Strongly agree	3.3	9.7	28.2	15.3
Agree	25.7	34.0	43.6	47.9
Disagree	53.4	35.4	20.5	29.7
Strongly disagree	17.6	20.8	7.7	7.1
V171 Democracies are not good at maintaining order				
Strongly agree	3.2	8.2	18.1	9.4
Agree	17.0	24.9	23.0	23.0
Disagree	55.6	37.3	40.1	51.8
Strongly disagree	24.3	29.6	18.8	15.8
Index of agreement that democracy brings problems				
Strongly agree	2.6	7.6	17.9	11.7
Agree	16.5	27.0	28.6	28.0
Disagree	51.6	38.1	41.3	46.2
Strongly disagree	29.2	27.3	12.2	14.1

index composed of two intercorrelated items, and the second is a separate item that factor analysis indicates should not be combined with the others. The first two items, which load strongly on the same factor, ask respondents to agree or disagree with the following statements: "Politicians who do not believe in God are unfit for public office" and "It would be better for [this country] if more people with strong religious beliefs held public office." The third item, which asks respondents to agree or disagree that "Religious leaders should not influence how people vote in elections" loads strongly on a separate factor. Also loading on the second factor is an item that asks whether religious leaders should influence government decisions. There is a great deal of missing data on the latter question, however, and thus, while its correlation with the other item asking about the political influence of religious leaders offers evidence of reliability and validity, it has not been used to construct an additive index in order to avoid excluding a large number of respondents from the analysis.

Table 5.2 presents the distribution of responses to the two sets of measures pertaining to Islam: personal religiosity, or mosque involvement, and also to both the two-item index and the remaining item pertaining to the role of Islam in public affairs for each of the four countries. For personal religiosity, the table shows a bimodal pattern of mosque attendance and involvement in all four countries. In each case, a significant proportion of men and women participate regularly and frequently and as many if not more participate rarely or "almost never." Responses are particularly polarized in Egypt and Jordan, but the pattern is similar in Morocco and Algeria as well. There is considerable, albeit less, variation in all four countries with respect to attitudes about the role of Islam in public affairs. The distribution in Egypt is skewed in the direction of giving a greater role to Islam, and to a lesser extent this is the case in Jordan and Morocco as well. The greatest diversity of opinion regarding the political role of Islam is found in Algeria, where, for example, only one-third of the respondents agree or agree strongly that it would be better for the country if people with strong religious beliefs held public office.

Attitudes and attachments relating to Islam are the primary nondependent variables in the present study, the goal being to determine whether and to what extent these orientations account for variance in the attitudes toward democracy held by ordinary citizens. In addition, however, a number of other nondependent variables are included in the analysis for purposes of statistical control. These are age, education, sex, income, and residence, the latter referring to the size of the town in which the respondent lives. These variables have been selected both because they constitute important demographic characteristics and because research in other world regions has found that they are sometimes related to attitudes toward democracy (Bratton and Mattes 2001; Duch 1995; Mattes and Thiel 1998; Mishler and Rose 1999; Ottemoeller 1998; Seligson and Booth 1993; Shin and Shyu 1997; Waldron-Moore 1999). Finally, a measure of regime evaluation has been developed for inclusion in the

Table 5.2 Religious orientations in Egypt, Jordan, Morocco, and Algeria

	Egypt %	Jordan %	Morocco %	Algeria %
V30 How often do you spend time with people at your mosque				
Weekly	37.9	39.1	23.5	29.3
Monthly	19.5	18.3	10.5	10.2
Less		29.2	9.3	14.4
None at all	42.6	38.3	56.7	46.1
V185 Apart from weddings, funerals and christenings, about how often do you attend religious services				
More than once a week	22.4	28.9	32.4	25.2
Weekly	19.8	15.2	11.8	18.6
Less	32.8	13.3	19.1	37.5
Never, practically never	25.1	42.6	36.7	17.7
Index of Mosque involvement				
Very high	24.9	41.4	29.8	33.8
High	17.4	2.3	5.0	6.4
Low	45.4	12.5	21.3	22.5
Very low	12.3	43.8	43.9	37.3
V200 Politicians who do not believe in God are unfit for publ. office				
Strongly agree	73.7	73.9	66.5	53.5
Agree	18.5	12.3	15.3	21.5
Neutral		4.2	8.1	7.8
Disagree	2.6	2.4	4.2	8.2
Strongly disagree	5.2	7.2	5.9	9.0
Religious leaders should not influence how people vote in elections				
Strongly agree	34.2	38.5	41.3	11.8
Agree	26.8	33.5	23.6	21.0
Neutral	2.9	7.2	22.2	20.5
Disagree	12.8	8.8	6.8	21.5
Strongly disagree	23.2	11.9	6.1	25.2
V201 It would be better for [this country] if more people with strong religious beliefs held public office				
Strongly agree	53.2	30.3	30.6	13.8
Agree	33.7	31.4	22.8	20.4
Neutral	.8	6.6	18.7	19.0
Disagree	8.6	14.0	17.0	26.2
Strongly disagree	3.8	17.7	10.9	20.6
Index of attitudes about whether persons holding public office should be religious				
Strongly agree	73.4	51.0	40.7	25.2
Agree	14.9	16.7	30.3	28.1
Neutral	8.7	21.8	17.4	26.1
Disagree	2.6	7.9	7.5	13.8
Strongly disagree	.5	2.6	4.0	6.8

analysis, again because several studies have found this to be a determinant of attitudes toward democracy (Chu et al. 2001; Rose et al. 1998). The measure is an additive index composed of two highly intercorrelated items. One asks respondents how much or how little confidence they have in their national government. The other asks respondents how satisfied they are with the way the people now in national office are handling the country's affairs.

Findings and Conclusions

Tables 5.3 through 5.6 present regression analyses for Egypt, Morocco, Algeria, and Jordan, respectively. In each case, both the index measuring the degree to which attitudes toward democracy are favorable or unfavorable and the index measuring the degree to which respondents believe there are important problems associated with democracy are treated as dependent variables. The three measures pertaining to Islam, the five demographic variables, and the measure of regime evaluation are the nondependent variables in these regressions.

Taken together, the findings presented in tables 5.3 through 5.6 suggest that Islamic orientations and attachments have at most a very limited impact on views about democracy. With respect to personal religiosity, at least as measured by involvement in religious activities, there is not a single instance when this variable is related to attitudes toward democracy to a statistically significant degree. Further, there is only one instance when this variable is related to views about whether there are problems associated with democracy. This is the case in Egypt, where individuals with higher levels of involvement in religious activities are more likely than others to agree that democracy has drawbacks. The relationship is significant at the .05 level.

As noted earlier, there is very little variance associated with personal piety, belief in God, and self-reported religiosity, and so these questions from the survey instrument have almost no explanatory power. All that can be said is that most people claim to be pious and most also have a favorable opinion of democracy, thus suggesting, in the aggregate, that there is no incompatibility between Islam and democracy. Support for democracy, in other words, is widespread in Arab societies where most citizens have strong Islamic attachments.

To the extent that the preceding statement shifts the level of analysis, it does not address the central question of the present analysis: do views about democracy vary among men and women in the Arab world as a

Table 5.3 Multiple regression showing the influence of Islamic orientations on attitudes toward democracy in Egypt

	Favorable attitudes toward democracy	Agreement that democracy brings problems
Independent variables		
Greater Mosque involvement	.036	.050
	(1.533)	(2.056)*
Persons holding public office	.069	−.026
should be religious	(3.184)***	(−1.141)
Religious leaders should not	.031	.041
influence how people vote	(1.447)	(1.865)
Control Variables		
Positive evaluation of	−.004	−.107
government leaders	(−.167)	(−4.768)***
Higher education	.107	.034
	(4.356)***	(1.365)
Older age	.041	−.065
	(1.776)	(−2.683)***
Male sex	.093	−.052
	(3.905)**	(−2.106)*
Higher income	.072	−.021
	(3.019)***	(−.870)
Resides in larger town	−.065	.107
	(−2.789)***	(4.441)***

Note: The table shows standardized coefficients (betas) and gives *t* statistics in parentheses.* p < .05, ** p < .02, ***p < .01.

Table 5.4 Multiple regression showing the influence of Islamic orientations on attitudes toward democracy in Jordan

	Favorable attitudes toward democracy	Agreement that democracy brings problems
Independent variables		
Greater Mosque involvement	.039	−.084
	(.692)	(−1.477)
Persons holding public office	.062	−.046
should be religious	(1.684)	(−1.265)
Religious leaders should not	.016	−.151
influence how people vote	(.440)	(−1.242)
Control Variables		
Positive evaluation of	.102	−.151
government leaders	(2.716)***	(−4.041)***
Higher education	.073	−.124
	(1.800)	(−3.091)***
Older age	−.009	−.007

Continued

118

Table 5.4 Continued

	Favorable attitudes toward democracy	Agreement that democracy brings problems
	(−.227)	(−.172)
Male sex	.108	−.092
	(1.923)	(−1.635)
Higher income	.057	.085
	(1.510)	(2.244)*
Resides in larger town	−.078	.042
	(−2.106)*	(1.157)

Note: The table shows standardized coefficients (betas) and gives *t* statistics in parentheses. * p < .05, **p < .02, ***p < .01.

Table 5.5 Multiple regression showing the influence of Islamic orientations on attitudes toward democracy in Morocco

	Favorable attitudes toward democracy	Agreement that democracy brings problems
Independent variables		
Greater Mosque involvement	.008	.018
	(.182)	(.340)
Persons holding public office should be religious	−.042	.081
	(−1.017)	(1.641)
Religious leaders should not influence how people vote	.081	.129
	(2.040)*	(2.811)***
Control variables		
Positive evaluation of government leaders	.022	−.047
	(.541)	(−1.006)
Higher education	.102	−.119
	(2.374)**	(−2.398)**
Older age	.069	−.009
	(1.672)	(−.187)
Male sex	.051	−.145
	(1.164)	(−2.838)
Higher income	.027	−.150
	(.685)	(−3.249)
Resides in larger town	.016	.080
	(.395)	(1.711)

Note: The table shows standardized coefficients (betas) and gives *t* statistics in parentheses. * p < .05, **p < .02, ***p < .01.

Table 5.6 Multiple regression showing the Influence of Islamic orientations on attitudes toward democracy in Algeria

	Favorable attitudes toward democracy	Agreement that democracy brings problems
Independent variables		
Greater Mosque involvement	−.058	.084
	(−1.158)	(1.647)
Persons holding public office should be religious	.063	.049
	(1.551)	(1.182)
Religious leaders should not influence how people vote	.070	.190
	(1.794)	(4.657)★★★
Control Variables		
Positive evaluation of government leaders	.137	.037
	(3.500)★★★	(.900)
Higher education	.018	.055
	(.385)	(1.112)
Older age	.039	−.114
	(.817)	(−2.280)★
Male sex	−.003	−.034
	(−.062)	(−.712)
Higher income	−.058	−.004
	(−1.455)	(−.106)
Resides in larger town	.161	−.093
	(4.085)★★★	(−2.242)★

Note: The table shows standardized coefficients (betas) and gives t statistics in parentheses. ★ $p < .05$, ★★$p < .02$, ★★★$p < .01$.

function of the strength of their Islamic attachments. By contrast, the regressions presented in tables 5.3 through 5.6 bear directly on this question. Further, again, they suggest that personal religiosity has little influence of attitudes toward democracy. There is substantial variation with respect to mosque attendance and participation in religious activities in all four countries, and it is notable that those with higher levels of mosque involvement and those with lower levels have similar, and to a substantial extent favorable, views about democracy. Thus, in the ongoing debate about the compatibility of democracy and Islam, findings from the WVS suggest, so far as the individual level of analysis is concerned, that strong Islamic attachments do not discourage or otherwise influence support for democracy to any significant degree.

The pattern is only slightly different with respect to attitudes about political Islam. Since there are two measures of attitudes about the role of religious officials in public affairs and two indices measuring views about democracy, four relationships are observable in each of the four Arab countries for which WVS data are available. Of these 16 relationships, only 4 are statistically significant, one at the .05 level and three at the .01 level. One of these is in Egypt, none is in Jordan, two are in Morocco, and one is in Algeria. Thus, it is clear that in only a distinct minority of instances do attitudes about the political role of religion and religious leaders have an impact on attitudes toward democracy.

The conclusion that support for political Islam does not lead to unfavorable attitudes toward democracy among ordinary citizens becomes even more evident when the character of the statistically significant relationships is examined. First, only one of the four significant relationships, that in Egypt, involves views about whether persons holding public office should be religious. Moreover, the relationship involves judgments about democracy, not views about associated problems, and it is positive. In other words, those who deem it desirable that persons holding pubic office be religious have a *more* favorable attitude toward democracy than do others.

Second, although the remaining three significant relationships are in the opposite direction, they offer only limited support to those who would argue that Islam discourages prodemocracy attitudes and values. In these instances, those who disagree with the proposition that religious officials should not influence how people vote are less likely to have positive views about democracy. This pattern was observed in only three of the eight instances where relationships are reported, however, and in one of these the relationship is only significant at the .05 level. In addition, statistically significant relationships are found in only two of the four countries, Morocco and Algeria.

The nature of the dependent variables in these relationships is even more important. In two of the cases, the two that are significant at the .01 level, the dependent variable does not involve judgments about the desirability of democracy but rather about whether there are problems associated with democracy. Thus, these respondents do not necessarily have an unfavorable view of democracy or consider other forms of governance to be preferable. They are simply more likely than others to believe that democracy, whether or not desirable or preferable to alternatives, has certain potential drawbacks. In only one instance, then, that of the weak but nonetheless statistically significant relationship observed in Morocco, are persons *more* favorably disposed toward the influence of religion in political affairs *less* favorably disposed toward democratic governance.

Since these findings are much more similar than different across the four countries, it is worth recalling how much of the Arab world's diversity is encompassed by Egypt, Jordan, Morocco, and Algeria. The combined population of these countries is roughly 140 million, perhaps two-thirds of the population of all Arab states. Equally important, as noted earlier, the four countries for which data are available differ with respect to present-day political systems and, in addition, both pre- and postindependence political and ideological trajectories. Accordingly, cross-country comparisons approximate a "most different system" research design, which in turn increases confidence in generalizability when similar findings are observed. So far as the influence of religious orientations on attitudes toward democracy is concerned, this means that the very limited impact of Islamic attachments is a conclusion that in all probability applies to much of the Arab world.

Relationships involving the six control variables are not central to the present study, which is primarily concerned with assessing the degree to which religious orientations influence attitudes toward democracy. Nevertheless, given that research on the initiation, maintenance, and consolidation of democratic transitions seeks to identify the broader array of factors that either promote or hinder the emergence of democratic attitudes and values, some brief observations about the explanatory power of these nondependent variables may be of interest.

Findings from empirical research in other world areas are somewhat mixed regarding the relationship between demographic characteristics and attitudes toward democracy. On balance, however, there is at least some evidence that support for democracy is positively related to levels of education and socioeconomic status and to male gender. Findings from the present study are for the most part similar. For example, education is positively and significantly related to a more favorable judgment of democracy in at least one instance in three of the Arab countries for which data are available, Algeria being the only exception. Similarly, both male gender and income are positively and significantly related to such attitudes in Egypt and Morocco, although income is inversely related to one of the dependent variables in Jordan and these variables otherwise do not have explanatory power in either Jordan or Algeria.

Findings about residence are interesting in that the direction of the relationship is different in the two countries where this variable has the greatest influence. Residence is related to both dependent variables to a statistically significant degree in Egypt and Algeria, but in the former country prodemocracy attitudes are associated with residence in *smaller* towns and in the latter country they are associated with residence in *larger* towns and cities. Residence in smaller towns is also positively related to prodemocracy attitudes in Jordan. Finally, the influence of evaluations of the government and its leaders should be noted.

Statistically significant relationships involving the evaluation of political leaders are found in at least one instance in every country except Morocco, and in each case a favorable assessment of government leaders is positively correlated with a positive judgment about democracy.

It is beyond the scope of the present inquiry to speculate about the causes and consequences of these cross-national differences. Suffice it to say that the explanatory power of the factors here treated as control variables is not the same in Egypt, Jordan, Morocco, and Algeria, which suggests that future research should strive to shed light on the nature and determinants of cross-national variation in the process by which attitudes relating to democracy and governance are shaped in Arab and other Muslim-majority countries. Such research will be enriched to the extent that additional independent variables are incorporated into the analysis, and perhaps if additional dimensions of the dependent variable are considered as well. The purpose of the present study is more limited, however. It is to assess the role of religious orientations in shaping attitudes toward democracy, and the findings in this connection are clear and straightforward. Islamic attachments at most have only a very limited influence on attitudes toward democracy.

While these findings about Islamic attachments do not shed much light on how attitudes *are* formed, they address and offer important conclusions about an issue that is the focus of considerable debate among students of Arab and Muslim societies: do the religious orientations of ordinary citizens retard the emergence of a political culture supportive of democracy and thus help to explain the persistent authoritarianism of the countries in which these men and women live. The answer provided by WVS data, which is consistent with findings based on several less comprehensive data sets (Tessler 2002), is that Islam is not incompatible with democracy and does not discourage the emergence of attitudes favorable to democracy.

In conclusion, there is little evidence, at least at the individual level of analysis, to support the claims of those who assert that Islam and democracy are incompatible. The reasons that democracy has not taken root in the Arab world must therefore lie elsewhere, perhaps in domestic economic structures, perhaps in relations with the international political and economic order, or perhaps in the determination of those in power to resist political change by whatever means are required. But while these and other possible explanations can be debated, what should be clear is that cultural explanations alleging that Islam discourages or even prevents the emergence of support for democracy are misguided, indeed misleading, and thus of little use in efforts to understand the factors shaping attitudes toward democracy in the Arab world.

Note

This chapter originally appeared as a journal article: "Do Islamic Orientations Influence Attitudes Toward Democracy in the Arab World: Evidence from Egypt, Jordon, Morocco, and Algeria." *International Journal of Comparative Sociology* 2 (Spring 2003): 229–49, and is reprinted here with permission from Sage Press.

References

Abed, Shukri. 1995. "Islam and Democracy." In *Democracy, War, and Peace in the Middle East*, edited by David Garnham and Mark Tessler, pp. 116–32. Bloomington: Indiana University Press.

Al-Farawati, Oula. 1999. "Arab Intellectuals Review Challenges of Globalization." *Jordan Times* December 9–10.

Al-Suwaidi, Jamal. 1995. "Arab and Western Conceptions of Democracy." In *Democracy, War, and Peace in the Middle East*, edited by David Garnham and Mark Tessler, pp. 82–115. Bloomington: Indiana University Press.

Anderson, Lisa. 1999. "Politics in the Middle East: Opportunities and Limits in the Quest for Theory." In *Area Studies and Social Science: Strategies for Understanding Middle East Politics*, edited by Mark Tessler, Jodi Nachtwey, and Anne Banda, pp. 1–10. Bloomington: Indiana University Press.

Arab Human Development Report. 2002. New York: United Nations Development Programme; http://cfapp2.undp.org/rbas/ahdr2.cfm?menu=10, accessed September 21, 2006.

Bennani-Chraibi, Mounia. 1994. *Soumis et Rebelles: Les Jeunes au Maroc*. Paris: CNRS Editions.

Bowen, Donna Lee. 1993. "Pragmatic Morality, Islam, and Family Planning in Morocco." In *Everyday Life in the Muslim Middle East*, edited by Donna Lee Bowen and Evelyn Early, pp. 91–101. Bloomington: Indiana University Press.

Bratton, Michael and Robert Mattes. 2001. "Africans' Surprising Universalism." *Journal of Democracy* 12(1): 107–21.

Brumberg, Daniel. 1995. "Authoritarian Legacies and Reform Strategies in the Arab World." In *Political Liberalization and Democratization in the Arab World: Theoretical Perspectives*, edited by Rex Brynen, Bahgat Korany, and Paul Noble, pp. 229–59. Boulder: Lunne Rienner Publishers.

Choueiri, Youssef. 1996. "The Political Discourse of Contemporary Islamist Movements." In *Islamic Fundamentalism*, edited by Abdel Salem Sidahmed and Anoushiravam Ehteshami, pp. 19–33. Boulder: Westview Press.

Chu, Yun-han, Larry Diamond and Doh Chull Shin. 2001. "Halting Progress in Korea and Taiwan." *Journal of Democracy* 12(1): 122–36.

Cordesman, Anthony. 1999. "Transitions in the Middle East." Address to the eighth annual United States Middle East Policymakers conference. Washington, DC.

Duch, Raymond. 1995. "Economic Chaos and the Fragility of Democratic Transition in Former Communist Regimes." *Journal of Politics* 57(1): 121–58.

Esposito, John L. 1992. *Islam: The Straight Path*. New York: Oxford University Press.

Esposito, John L. and James P. Piscatori. 1991. "Democratization and Islam." *Middle East Journal* 45(3): 427–40.

Flanagan, Scott C. and Aie-Rie Lee. 2000. "Value Change and Democratic Reform in Japan and Korea." *Comparative Political Studies* 33(5): 626–59.

Gibson, James L. 1995. "The Resilience of Mass Support for Democratic Institutions and Processes in the Nascent Russian and Ukrainian Democracies." In *Political Culture and Civil Society in Russia and the New States of Eurasia*, edited by Vladimir Tismaneanu, pp. 53–111. New York: M. E. Sharpe.

Halliday, Fred. 1995. Islam and the Myth of Confrontation: Religion and Politics in the Middle East. London: I. B. Tauris.

Hamdi, Mohamed Elhachmi. 1996. "Islam and Democracy: The Limits of the Western Model." *Journal of Democracy* 7(2): 81–85.

Harik, Iliya. 1994. "Pluralism in the Arab World." *Journal of Democracy* 5(3): 43–56.

Hudson, Michael. 1995. "The Political Culture Approach to Arab Democratization: The Case for Bringing It Back in, Carefully." In *Political Liberalization and Democratization in the Arab World*, edited by Rex Brynen, Bahgat Korany, and Paul Noble, pp. 61–76. Boulder: Lynn Reinner Publishers.

Huntington, Samuel. 1984. "Will More Countries Become Democratic?" *Political Science Quarterly* 99(2): 193–218.

———. 1991. *The Third Wave*. Norman: University of Oklahoma Press.

———. 1993. "Democracy's Third Wave." In *The Global Resurgence of Democracy*, edited by Larry Diamond and Marc Plattner, pp. 3–25. Baltimore: Johns Hopkins University Press.

Inglehart, Ronald. 2000. "Culture and Democracy." In *Culture Matters: How Values Shape Human Progress*, edited by Lawrence E. Harrison and Samuel Huntinngton, pp. 80–96. New York: Basic Books.

Karatnycky, Adrian. 2000. "A Century of Progress." *The Journal of Democracy* 11(1): 187–200.

Kedourie, Elie. 1994. *Democracy and Arab Political Culture*. London: Frank Cass Publishers.

Khashan, Hilal. 1998. "History's Burden." *Middle East Quarterly* 5(1): 41–48.

Khouri, Rami G. 2000. "A View from the Arab World." *Jordan Times* July 5.

Korany, Bahgat. 1994. "Arab Democratization: A Poor Cousin." *PS: Political Science and Politics* 27(3): 511–13.

Lewis, Bernard. 1994. *The Shaping of the Modern Middle East*. New York: Oxford.

Mainwaring, Scott. 1999. "Democratic Survivability in Latin America." In *Democracy and Its Limits: Lessons from Asia, Latin America and the Middle East*, edited by Howard Handelman and Mark Tessler, pp. 11–68. Notre Dame: University of Notre Dame Press.

Marradi, Alberto. 1981. "Factor Analysis as an Aid in the Formulation and Refinement of Empirically Useful Concepts." In *Factor Analysis and Measurement in Sociological Research*, edited by Edgar F. Borgatta and David J. Jackson, pp. 11–49. London: Sage.

Mattes, Robert, and Hermann Thiel. 1998. "Consolidation and Public Opinion in South Africa." *Journal of Democracy* 9(1): 95–110.

Mernissi, Fatima. 1992. *Islam and Democracy: Fear of the Modern World*. Reading, Massachusetts: Addison-Wesley.

Mishler, William and Richard Rose. 1999. "Five Years after the Fall: Trajectories of Support for Democracy in Post-Communist Europe." In *Critical Citizens: Global Support for Democratic Government*, edited by Pippa Norris, pp. 78–99. Oxford: Oxford University Press.

Ottemoeller, Dan. 1998. "Popular Perceptions of Democracy: Elections and Attitudes in Uganda." *Comparative Political Studies* 31(1): 98–124.

Rose, Richard. 1997. "Where Are Postcommunist Countries Going?" *Journal of Democracy* 8(3): 92–108.

Rose, Richard, William Mishler, and Christian Haerpfer. 1998. *Democracy and Its Alternatives: Understanding Post-communist Societies*. Cambridge: Polity Press.

Schmitter, Philippe and Terry Lynn Karl. 1993. "What Democracy Is . . . and Is Not." In *The Global Resurgence of Democracy*, edited by Larry Diamond and Marc Plattner, pp. 39–52. Baltimore: Johns Hopkins University Press.

Seligson, Mitchell and John Booth. 1993. "Political Culture and Regime Type: Evidence from Nigaragua and Costa Rica." *Journal of Politics* 55(3): 777–92.

Shin, Doh Chull and Huoyan Shyu. 1997. "Political Ambivalence in South Korea and Taiwan." *Journal of Democracy* 8(3): 109–24.

Sivan, Emmanuel. 1997. "Constraints and Opportunities in the Arab World." *Journal of Democracy* 8(2): 103–13.

———. 2000. "Illusions of Change." *Journal of Democracy* 11(3): 69–83.

Talbi, Mohamed. 2000. "A Record of Failure." *Journal of Democracy* 11(3): 58–68.

Tessler, Mark. 1997. "The Origins of Popular Support for Islamist Movements: A Political Economy Analysis." In *Islam, Democracy, and the State in North Africa*, edited by John Entelis, pp. 93–126. Bloomington: Indiana University Press.

———. 1999. "Arab Politics and Public Opinion." Paper presented at U.S. Government interagency conference on "Next Generation Politics in the Muslim World." Washington, DC.

———. 2002. "Islam and Democracy in the Middle East: The Impact of Religious Orientations on Attitudes toward Democracy in Four Arab Countries." *Comparative Politics* 34(3): 337–54.

Voll, John. 1994. *Islam, Continuity, and Change in the Modern World.* Syracuse: Syracuse University Press.

Waldron-Moore, Pamela. 1999. "Eastern Europe at the Crossroads of Democratic Transition." *Comparative Political Studies* 32(1): 32 62.

Wei-Ming, Tu. 2000. "Multiple Modernities: A Preliminary Inquiry into the Implications of East Asian Modernity." In *Culture Matters: How Values Shape Human Progress*, edited by Lawrence E. Harrison and Samuel Huntington, pp. 256–66. New York: Basic Books.

Welsh, Bridget. 1996. "Attitudes Toward Democracy in Malaysia." *Asian Survey* 36: 882–903.

Zakaria, Fareed. 1994. "Culture Is Destiny: A Conversation with Lee Kuan Yew." *Foreign Affairs* 73(2): 109–26.

CHAPTER 6

The Egalitarian Face of Islamic Orthodoxy: Support for Islamic Law and Economic Justice in Seven Muslim-Majority Nations

NANCY J. DAVIS[1] AND
ROBERT V. ROBINSON

Introduction

The role that Islam plays in the economic circumstances and development of Muslim nations has been the subject of intense debate among Muslims and non-Muslims alike. Western critics of Islam or "Islamic civilization," such as Bernard Lewis (1990) and Samuel Huntington (1993), have decried its economic irrationality, incompatibility with democracy, and failure to separate religion and state, while scholars, such as Edward Said (2001: 11), have denounced such thinking as Orientalist essentialism that ignores "the internal dynamics and plurality" of Muslim nations. The debate is not just academic. Today, there are over 1.3 billion Muslims in the world and more than 50 predominantly Muslim nations. Some of the governments of these nations are meeting their citizens' economic needs, while many others are unable or unwilling to address these needs.

What to do about the depressed economic circumstances in which many Muslims live is the subject of much private concern, public discussion, and movement activism throughout the Muslim world. From the mid-nineteenth century on, the debate and mobilization on economic issues often centered on whether socialism or nationalism was the solution. Islamist (or Islamic fundamentalist) movements seeking the implementation of Islamic law (the shari 'a) in an Islamic state as the solution to economic problems began to form in the late 1920s, but public interest in such movements did not take off until most secular, putatively socialist and/or nationalist regimes failed to solve these problems during the 1960s, 1970s, and 1980s. Today, Islamists vie with Islamic modernists (or reformists), who see the best hope for economic progress in keeping Islam out of legal codes and maintaining strict separation of mosque and state (Kepel 1994: 13–23).

In this chapter, we move away from the public discourse and skir-mishes of movement leaders, academics, and media pundits to explore how moral cosmology—Islamic orthodoxy versus modernism—affects the economic beliefs of ordinary Muslims. Most scholarly accounts of religion and politics in predominantly Muslim countries have been his-torical or observational, relying on careful analyses of the speeches and writings of leaders of Islamist and modernist movements, of archival materials on the formation, political activities, and platforms of movement organizations, and, in many cases, on the author's direct experience with the Muslim world. While much has been learned from this work, because it is often not based on analyses of interviews with representative samples of Muslims, we know relatively little about how ordinary Muslim citizens make linkages between their religion and economic preferences (but see, e.g., Hassan 2002, Inglehart and Norris 2003, Moaddel 2004, 2006).

Throughout the world, religious traditionalists are commonly charac-terized as being to the political right of modernists. Yet, despite the con-ventional wisdom, our research in the United States, 21 European countries, and Israel has uncovered a surprising relationship: in many countries where Catholicism, Eastern Orthodoxy, Judaism, or Protestantism predominate, the religiously orthodox are to the right of modernists on cultural issues of abortion, sexuality, family, and gender, but to the left of modernists on issues of economic justice (Davis and Robinson 1996a, 1997, 1999a, 1999b, 2001). In this chapter, we exam-ine whether the less recognized element of this pattern—the tendency for the religiously orthodox to be more economically left than mod-ernists—holds in countries where Islam, another Abrahamic faith tradi-tion, predominates.

We analyze newly available national surveys of seven Muslim-majority nations (Algeria, Bangladesh, Egypt, Indonesia, Jordan, Pakistan, and

Saudi Arabia) to test two alternate arguments to explain how orthodoxy versus modernism affects attitudes toward economic justice among Muslims. Our own Moral Cosmology theory (Davis and Robinson 1999b, 2001, 2005), which we argue applies to all of the Abrahamic faith traditions, regardless of their specific theological tenets, posits that because the religiously orthodox are theologically communitarian in seeing individuals as subsumed by a larger community of believers and as subject to the timeless laws and greater plan of God, they are disposed toward economic communitarianism, whereby it is the society's responsibility to provide for those in need, reduce inequality, and intervene in the economy to meet community needs. Modernists, because they are theologically individualistic in seeing individuals themselves as responsible for their destinies and as having to make moral decisions in the context of the times, are inclined toward laissez-faire economic individualism, which sees the poor as responsible for their fates, supports wider income differences to promote individual initiative, and wants government to keep out of the economy. We test this theory, which does not depend on the specific content of faith traditions, against a logical counterthesis, based on what Islamic scripture says about economic matters, that limits the effect of Islamic orthodoxy versus modernism only to government responsibility for the needy. We find that Islamic orthodoxy—measured as the desire to establish Islamic law—is associated in these countries with the broad economic communitarianism expected by Moral Cosmology theory.

Theoretical Background

Moral Cosmology Theory

In *The Protestant Ethic and the Spirit of Capitalism* and his other works on religion, Weber was primarily concerned with differences *between* faith traditions (e.g, Catholicism, Protestantism, ancient Judaism) and their effects on economic beliefs and practices. Our Moral Cosmology theory, with its emphasis on differences *within* faith traditions among individuals holding different moral cosmologies, complements Weber's. Our argument is that cosmological differences between the religiously orthodox and modernists that had only just begun to appear when Weber wrote *The Protestant Ethic* (1904–05) exist today within all of the Abrahamic traditions and have similar effects, regardless of the specific tenets of these traditions, on economic and cultural beliefs. Because differentiation between the orthodox and modernist cosmologies is required for these cosmologies to affect political beliefs, our argument should hold only since modernist and orthodox theological strands became separate within each of the religions of the Book—for example, the development of Reform Judaism, which grew out of Enlightenment ideas and was formalized in documents like the Pittsburgh Platform of 1885; the rise of Islamic "modernism" in the late-nineteenth century; the appearance at the turn of the twentieth century of the "modernist" movement in Catholicism that nearly caused a schism in the Church; and the development of the split between mainline and fundamentalist churches in the United States and British Protestantism in the early twentieth century.

In discussing the effect of moral cosmology on cultural and economic attitudes, we begin with Hunter's (1991: 49) distinction between two "fundamentally different conceptions of moral authority." The *religiously orthodox* vision views God as the ultimate judge of good and evil, regards sacred texts as divinely revealed and hence inerrant and timeless, and sees the deity as playing an active role in people's everyday lives. In contrast, the *modernist*[2] vision views individuals as having to make moral decisions in the context of their times, sees religious texts and teachings as human creations that should be considered in cultural context along with other moral precepts, and regards individuals as largely determining their own fates.

Drawing out the theological and political orientations of these ideal-typical visions of moral authority—or what we prefer to call moral cosmologies, we argue that the religiously orthodox cosmology is theologically communitarian in that it regards individuals as subsumed by a larger community of like-minded believers who are all subject to the laws and greater plan of God (Davis and Robinson 1999b, 2001). In the orthodox cosmology, timeless religious truths, standards, and laws are seen as having been laid down once and for all by God—laws that the community must uphold and that everyone is obliged to obey. The theological communitarianism of the orthodox, we argue, inclines them to an authoritarian strand of cultural communitarianism, in which the community must enforce divinely mandated moral standards on abortion, sexuality, family, and gender. But theological communitarianism also inclines the orthodox to economic communitarianism or egalitarianism, whereby it is the state's responsibility to provide for those in need, reduce the gap between the rich and the poor, and intervene in the economy so that community needs are met. The communitarianism of orthodoxy entails watching over community members, giving it both a strict side and a caring one, and inclining its adherents toward cultural authoritarianism and economic egalitarianism.[3]

Orthodoxy, as we conceive it, does not refer to "doctrinal" orthodoxy or belief in the specific tenets of a faith tradition (e.g., the existence of heaven and hell, the divinity of Jesus), but to a broad theological orientation toward the locus of moral authority with which the orthodox of all of the Abrahamic faith traditions would agree. In other words, orthodox Catholics, Jews (with a small "o" to distinguish their cosmology from formal membership in the Orthodox branch of Judaism), Muslims and Protestants adhere to different religious tenets, but share the broad world view that the locus of moral authority is God, and that legal codes should reflect absolute and timeless divine law.

We argue that modernists, in contrast to the orthodox, are theologically individualistic in that they see individuals, and not a deity, as largely responsible for their own moral decisions and fates (Davis and Robinson 1999b, 2001). The modernist cosmology combines support for individual choice and freedom with an expectation of individual responsibility,[4] inclining its adherents to cultural individualism or libertarianism, whereby the resolution of pregnancy is seen as a woman's private decision, individual freedom in sexual expression is allowed, and husbands and wives should decide for themselves how to divide their labor or structure their partnership. The theological individualism of modernists also inclines them to laissez-faire economic individualism or inegalitarianism, whereby individuals are held responsible for their economic fortunes—good or bad—and the solution to poverty and inequality is greater effort and initiative by the poor themselves rather than government efforts to improve their lot, equalize incomes, or redistribute economic resources by nationalizing businesses. Our argument is, of course, probabilistic, not deterministic, and some modernists hold communitarian economic beliefs, such as socialism or communism. We argue and show that the individualism that characterizes both the modernist moral cosmology and laissez-faire economics inclines modernists toward such economic individualism more than toward economic communitarianism (see also Jelen 1990; Regnerus et al. 1998; Tamney et al. 1989).

While orthodoxy and modernism are ideal types, representing polar extremes, our Moral Cosmology theory treats cosmology as a matter of degree, with people's cultural and economic attitudes tending to reflect where they are on the continuum of orthodoxy/modernism (Davis and Robinson 1996a, 1996b, 1996c, 1997, 1999a, 1999b, 2001). In this chapter, we focus on the economic consequences of the continuum of moral cosmology for Muslims—the tendency for the Islamic orthodox to be more economically egalitarian than Islamic modernists.

Applying Moral Cosmology Theory to Islam

Islam, a religion of the Book along with Judaism and Christianity, has a sacred text that is taken by Muslims as divine revelation. The vast majority of Muslims—some scholars would say all—regard the Quran as divinely revealed, inerrant, and to be taken literally (Marty and Appleby 1992: 138). In this sense, (nearly) all Muslims are "orthodox," and a question about the literal truth of the Quran, such as the one we used (Davis and Robinson 1996a, 1996b, 1997, 1999b, 2001) to help distinguish the orthodox from modernists among Catholics, Jews, and Protestants based on their beliefs about the Bible, probably would not distinguish among Muslims. Yet one dimension of orthodoxy/modernism that does differentiate among Muslims is the extent to which they believe that the Quran and other sacred texts of Islam should be the sole basis of the legal system and the state. The establishment of Islamic law, which is based on sacred Islamic texts, is the fulfillment of the orthodox belief that it is the responsibility of the community to uphold timeless divine law. Orthodox Muslims differ from modernist Muslims in wanting Islamic law to constitute the sole legal foundation of the state, and it is this distinction and its consequences for economic attitudes that is our focus here.

The distinction between Muslims who would apply Islamic law in all realms of life and those who would not is central both to divisions within Muslim publics at large and to the agendas of many of the major political and intellectual movements of Muslims of the past century and a half. Since the Egyptian Hasan al-Banna founded the Society of Muslim Brothers in 1928, the goal of *Islamists* has been the implementation of the shari 'a in all realms of life as the sine qua non of an Islamic state (Ghadbian 2000: 78, Husain 2003: 13). The primacy of this goal reflects the fact that religion and state were once one in the first Islamic state of the seventh century, where Prophet Muhammad was both the religious and political leader. While orthodox Muslims are not monolithic in their interpretation of the shari 'a (Murphy 2003: 51), they share the desire to implement Islamic law as the sole legal foundation, rather than allow legal codes to emerge through pluralistic political negotiation and compromise between competing interests, including secular ones.

The economic communitarianism that Moral Cosmology theory expects among the orthodox of all of the Abrahamic faith traditions manifested itself historically and still today in many Muslim countries in practices of patrimonialism, whereby the clan or tribal leaders were/are responsible for the well-being of the community's needy. It can also be seen in "Islamic economics," which was developed in late-colonial India of the 1940s by Sayyid Abul A'la Mawdudi (1903–79), the Islamist founder of *Jamaat-i-Islami* (Party of Islam; Esposito 2003: 142). Apart from prohibiting *riba* (excessive interest) and collecting and distributing *zakat* (an obligatory charitable contribution to the poor) the details of Islamic economics are vague, although it appears that this would not involve as extensive control of the economy by the state as in socialist command economies, but would require a greater commitment—much of it voluntary on the part of believers—to looking out for the poor and to maintaining more equitable economic dealings than is true in laissez-faire capitalism (Fuller 2003: 26; Ibrahim 1982: 122–23).

Islamic "modernism," as the movement came to be called, emerged during the late-nineteenth century, especially in India and Egypt (Moaddel and Talattof 2000: 1). The theological individualism that Moral Cosmology theory assumes of modernists in all Abrahamic traditions can be seen in an important theological distinction made by early Islamic modernists. Moulavi Cherágh Ali (1844–95), a noted Indian modernist, distinguished between the *revealed* law of the Quran, which is immutable and timeless, and the *common* law, which is the product of Muslim history and reflects the circumstances of each age. He argued that since Islamic law was, in part, a product of the times, it could not constitute a timeless moral code for Muslims, thus necessitating a new legal frame in accord with the standards of modernity (Moaddel and Talattof 2000: 8–9; Ahmad 1967: 54–58). A distinction with similar implications was made by the Egyptian modernist, Muhammad Abduh (1849–1905), between *ibadat* (acts of worship) and *mu-amalat* (commercial or civil acts related to the affairs of the world). According to Abduh, while Islamic texts mandated specific rules regarding the worship of Allah, they included only broad principles on how humans should relate to each other, thus leaving it up to humans to apply these in specific circumstances. This not only allowed but required the application of *ijtihad* (independent reasoning) in the development of legal codes (Hourani 1983: 148; Moaddel 2005: 90).

The distinction of Cherágh Ali and Abduh allows humans much discretion in organizing their affairs, including their economic structures and individual economic behavior. An essay by an anonymous Indian modernist, originally published in 1877–80 and included in Moaddel and Talattof's (2000: 123–35) anthology, argued that Islamic laws prohibiting the taking of interest and limiting individual discretion in passing on estates were breeding "listlessness and inactivity" among Muslims in India, throwing many into poverty. The solution was not for government to provide free education, which only "lower[s] our character by rendering weaker the motives for the exercise of our energies and by diminishing our prudence or responsibility to ourselves," but to understand that "there is no connection whatsoever, either necessary or even contingent, between Religion in its pure sense and civil and juridical laws" (Anonymous 2000/1877–80: 124 and 132) Only the separation of mosque and state would result in "wider diffusion of habits of energy and patience, self-exertion and self-dependence." The essay concludes with an homage to the Indian modernist leader, Sir Sayyid Ahmad Khan (1817–98), who sought to reconcile Enlightenment values and natural law with Islamic belief through the application of *ijtihad* to sacred texts, and who was a strong advocate of laissez-faire capitalism and a limited role of government (Malik 1980).[5]

Muslim modernists today seek a strict separation of mosque and state and resist the implementation of Islamic law. Kurzman (1998: 19; 1999) notes that such Muslims object to the implementation of the shari 'a on several grounds, including that "divine revelation has left the form of government for human construction," that political power would corrupt religious rulers, and that the "Qur'an refers to the shari 'a as a path, not as a ready-made system of law, waiting to be put in practice."

While the writings of orthodox and modernist thinkers and the political positions of the movements they inspired seem to be in accord with Moral Cosmology theory, whether these movements represent the sentiments of ordinary Muslims is an empirical question that can be resolved only with data for individuals. We have found, for example, that in the United States, where the most visible movements and leaders appearing to represent the religiously orthodox have a conservative, laissez-faire economic agenda, the orthodox are to the left of modernists on economic issues in a national survey of Americans (Davis and Robinson 1996a, 1996b, 1997). Thus, in accord with Moral Cosmology theory, which expects similar effects of orthodoxy/modernism on economic attitudes in all of the Abrahamic faith traditions, we test the following hypothesis on nationally representative samples of Muslims:

H_1: Religiously orthodox Muslims, as indicated by their desire to implement Islamic law as the sole law of the land in their country, will be more economically communitarian or egalitarian than their modernist counterparts in supporting (1) government efforts to improve the lot of the poor and needy, (2) greater equality of incomes, and (3) government nationalization of private business and industry.

An Alternative Hypothesis: Islamic Scriptural
Directives on Economic Matters

Moral Cosmology theory is not denomination-specific in that it does not depend on the specific content of religious texts. It assumes that the orthodox of all of the Abrahamic faith traditions differ from modernists in their economic orientations, regardless of the specific doctrinal positions on economic matters in their religious texts. In our earlier analyses of Judeo-Christian traditions, we argued that the Torah and the Bible are ambiguous regarding economic matters (Davis and Robinson 1996a, 1999b). Yet are there clear economic messages in Islam that might impel those who seek to build a state around it to endorse communitarian economic relations? We test Moral Cosmology theory against the logical counterthesis that the tenets of Islam on economic matters can explain any tendency for the more text-bound Islamic orthodox to be more communitarian than Islamic modernists.

In contrast to the sacred texts of Judaism and Christianity, the Quran is very specific about the obligation of every Muslim to give to the poor, orphaned, and widowed, "In order that [wealth] may not (merely) make a circuit between the wealthy" (Quran 59: 7, Abdullah Yusuf Ali translation). The third of five pillars of the faith, *zakat* (purification), requires Muslims with the financial means to give at least 2.5 percent of their net assets (not just their income) annually to the needy (Husain 2003: 10, Kuran 2004: 19). The institution of *zakat* changed during Muhammad's lifetime from voluntary private charity in Mecca, where he and his followers were in a minority and powerless, to a compulsory obligation of the faith, with specific rates, collected and distributed by state-run institutions, once Muhammad and his followers migrated to Medina in 622 and established the first Islamic state (al-Shiekh 1995: 366–37). The *Hadith* (2: 24: 537), the sacred text that records the sayings of the Prophet, reports Muhammad as saying, "Allah has made it *obligatory* for them to pay *zakat* from their property; it is to be *taken* from the wealthy among them and given to the poor" (emphasis added). Among the countries considered here, *zakat* is collected and distributed by the state in Pakistan and Saudi Arabia; in the other countries, because they are largely secular states, it is left to individuals to make contributions directly to the needy or to organizations serving them (al-Shiekh 1995: 366–67).

While the Quran is clear in requiring those with financial means to give to the poor and in providing mechanisms whereby the state will look out for the needy, it neither enjoins economic equality nor questions the right of individuals to hold private property (Kamali 2002: 136–38). State ownership of property is not directly addressed; contemporary proponents and opponents of government ownership alike cite scripture to support their stances, suggesting that Islam takes no clear position on this (Kuran 2004: 33, 111). In the Quran (20: 131), differences in wealth and property are viewed as a test by Allah of the charitableness of the wealthy but as unimportant after death. While there is a spiritual equality of believers before Allah, there is no assumption that such equality does or should hold in human societies (Kamali 2002; Marlow 1997). A well-known proverb attributed to the Prophet states that "Men are equals like the teeth of a comb; one has precedence over another only in well-being" (quoted in Marlow 1997: 18).

We conclude that while Islamic texts mandate efforts to provide for those in need, they do not enjoin equality of income or wealth, nor sanction violation of the private property, nor take a clear position on government ownership of industry as a means of meeting community needs. Thus, we test Moral Cosmology theory (H_1), which posits broad egalitarian/communitarian effects of orthodoxy in all religions of the Book, against a hypothesis based strictly on the economic directives of Islamic texts, which limits the effect of orthodoxy versus modernism to the clear economic directive of Islam that it is the state's responsibility to care for the needy:

H_2: Religiously orthodox Muslims, as indicated by their desire to implement Islamic law as the sole law of the land in their country, will be more supportive than their modernist counterparts of government efforts to care for the needy, but will not differ from modernists in their desire for more equal incomes or their willingness to nationalize private property or businesses.

Standard of Living and Economic Beliefs

Governments of Muslim-majority nations differ in their ability or willingness to meet the economic needs of their citizens. We expect that failure to meet material, educational, and health needs will increase popular demand for economic reform, while maintenance of a high standard of living will reduce the desire for such reform. Hashmi (2004), for example, has shown that the failure of Bangladesh's socialist-secular-Bengali-nationalist government during the 1970s to bring about the promised socialist utopia increased the popularity of Islamist groups calling for social justice and economic reform. Thus we hypothesize:

H₃: The lower a country's standard of living (life expectancy, literacy, school enrollments, and per capita GDP), the greater will be support for government efforts to improve the lot of the poor and needy, reduce inequality of incomes, and nationalize private business and industry.

How strong an effect that support for implementation of Islamic law has on the desire for egalitarian economic reforms should depend on the country's standard of living. In countries where people's basic needs are not being met by the state, the desire to implement the shari 'a will be more strongly associated with egalitarian positions than in countries where these needs are being met; the general condition of the population in the former countries more seriously fails to meet communitarian economic norms. Thus we hypothesize:

H₄: In countries with low standards of living (life expectancy, literacy, school enrollments, and per capita GDP), support for implementing Islamic law will be more strongly associated with support for government efforts to improve the lot of the poor and needy, reduce inequality of incomes, and nationalize private business and industry than in countries with higher standards of living.

Rationalism and Islamic Economics

Contrasting the economic rationality or self-interest assumed by free market economists with the voluntary communitarians on the part of Muslims of all classes assumed by Islamic economics, Kuran (2004: 42) describes the task of Islamic economics as "to transform selfish and acquisitive *Homo economicus* into a paragon of virtue, *Homo Islamicus*." Kuran's argument is that Islamic economics, not Islamic theology, assumes this communitarianism; a classic study of the terms used in the Quran argued that Islamic theology is couched in the language of commerce, trade, and economic rationalism: "The mutual relations between God and man are of a strictly commercial nature. Allah is the ideal merchant . . . Life is a business, for gain or loss. He who does a good or an evil work ['earns' good or evil], receives his pay for it, even in his life" (Torrey 1892: 48).

We contrast the assumption of voluntary communtarianism in Islamic economics with a rational choice, "underdog principle" that posits that the advantaged will be less economically communitarian than the disadvantaged, each group reflecting its economic self-interest (Robinson and Bell 1978):

> H_5: Muslims with more education, higher income, or who are in the middle or upper class will be less supportive of government efforts to care for the needy, of efforts to equalize incomes, and of government nationalization of businesses and industry than those who are less educated, poorly paid, and in the working class or unemployed.

If, however, there are no socioeconomic differences in Muslims' economic attitudes and if these attitudes are communitarian, this would support the assumption of Islamic economics that the advantaged can be counted upon in the establishment of a more just Islamic state.

Data and Methods

Data

The data with which we test our hypotheses are from the fourth wave of the WVS, conducted from 1999 to 2003, which surveyed 81 societies. Our sample consists of Muslims living in seven Muslim-majority countries: Algeria (surveyed by Mark Tessler and Ronald Inglehart), Bangladesh (surveyed by Q. K. Ahmad and Nilufar Banu) Egypt (surveyed by Mansoor Moaddel), Indonesia (surveyed by Nadra Muhamad Hosen), Jordan (surveyed by Mansoor Moaddel and Mustafa Hamarneh), Pakistan (surveyed by Farooq Tanwir), and Saudi Arabia (surveyed by Mansoor Moaddel). The years and sample sizes of the surveys are in the Appendix Table. The surveys of six other Muslim-majority nations in the WVS (Albania, Azerbaijan, Bosnia–Herzegovina, Iran, Morocco, and Turkey) did not include our key independent variable— support for Islamic law. Analyses are limited to respondents aged 18 years and older who self-identify as Muslim. In Algeria, which is 99 percent Muslim, the religion of the respondents was not asked; thus we include every respondent. In some of our analyses, we pool the samples for all seven countries into a single sample, weighting each sample proportional to the size of the country's Muslim population.

The seven countries examined here are among the most populous and influential Muslim nations in the world. They include Indonesia, with the world's largest Muslim population, Pakistan with the second largest, and Bangladesh, Egypt, and Algeria, with the fourth, fifth, and ninth largest Muslim populations. Adding Jordan and Saudi Arabia, just under half of the

138   Nancy J. Davis and Robert V. Robinson

world's 1.3 billion Muslims lives in these countries. Standards of living in these countries range from low to moderate. The United Nations' (2001) HDI, an index of standard of living based on life expectancy, literacy, school enrollment rates, and per capita GDP, ranges from .47 in Bangladesh (the same as Haiti, the poorest country in the Western Hemisphere) to .75 in Saudi Arabia (the same as Brazil; see Appendix Table). Four of these countries—Algeria, Egypt, Indonesia, and Saudi Arabia—are what Mahdavi (1970) calls "rentier states," whose government and economy depend on substantial rents from oil and hydrocarbon sales (Saudi Arabia and Algeria), transit charges (Egypt, from the Suez Canal), or revenue from tourism (Bali in Indonesia, and to a lesser extent Egypt). In rentier states, only a small proportion of the population is involved in the enterprises creating most of the nation's wealth, making most people's income less dependent on their own efforts and skills than on who they know (personal relationships and crony capitalism), their ethnicity, or their citizenship (Moaddel 2002: 376–78). Political democracies do not exist or are highly compromised in these countries. Freedom House (2001, table 6.1), which rates the political climate of countries,[6] reports that in 2000–01 denial of political freedoms and civil liberties varied from moderate in countries like Bangladesh and Indonesia (3.5 on a 1–7 scale, where 7 represents few political rights and freedoms) to extremely high (7.0) in Saudi Arabia (see Appendix Table).

Measures

Independent Variables

Support for implementing the shari 'a. To measure the orthodoxy/modernism continuum among Muslims we use a question on support for establishing Islamic law as the sole basis of jurisprudence: I would like to know your views about a good government. Which of these traits is (1) very important, (2) important, (3) somewhat important, (4) least important, or (5) not important for a good government to have? It should implement only the laws of the shari 'a. We recode responses so that high values indicate support for implementing the shari 'a while low values indicate opposition to this (1 = 5, 2 = 4, 4 = 2, 5 = 1). Using the degree of support for implementing the shari 'a to measure Islamic orthodoxy/modernism is consistent with the orthodox desire to establish and uphold what they see as divinely ordained eternal laws that apply to all members of the community, and with the contrary modernist belief that legal codes should reflect the times and draw upon multiple sources, including secular ones. In our research on Judeo-Christian nations, we used agreement with the statement "Right and wrong should be based on God's laws," among other items, to distinguish the orthodox from modernists (Davis and Robinson 1996a, 1996b, 1997, 1999a, 1999b, 2001).

While implementation of the shari 'a has both religious and political implications, this is not surprising in the case of Islam since Muhammad unified religion and the state in the first Islamic state of the seventh century. Nonetheless, under the possibility that the most politicized Muslims might be both more supportive of establishing Islamic law solely for political motives (Woltering 2002: 1134) and more favorable toward economically progressive policies, we control for *Discusses Politics*, based on the question: "When you get together with your friends, would you say you discuss political matters (3) frequently, (2) occasionally, or (1) never?" We use this to indicate the most rudimentary level of politicization—debating political issues with others—in the absence of measures of higher levels of political involvement. If support for implementing the shari 'a is merely capturing politicization, then inclusion of this variable should reduce its effects on economic attitudes.

It could also be argued that any effect of support for implementing the shari 'a on economic attitudes may be due to an underlying nationalism or rejection of the West (including Western jurisprudence, foreign economic domination, debt dependency on the West, neoliberal economic restructuring required by the IMF or World Bank, and globalization) that could produce egalitarian economic stances. Thus, we control for *National Pride*, the best indicator of nationalistic values in the WVS, and strongly linked, in a recent survey of nationalism in Iraq, to oppositional attitudes toward foreign occupation (Moaddel et al. 2005). Respondents were asked: "How proud are you to be [NATIONALITY]," and responses are coded (1) not at all proud, (2) not very proud, (3) quite proud, or (4) very proud.

Socioeconomic variables. In our models, *Education* is in nine ordered categories ranging from (1) no formal education to (9) university-level education, with degree. *Household Income* before taxes, counting all wages, salaries, pensions, and other income, is coded in deciles by the local investigators in each country (with 1 as the lowest decile and 10 as the highest). Occupation/employment status is a dummy variable series identifying *Owner/Manager, Professional, White Collar, Blue Collar, Army, Student, Housewife/Retired,* and unemployed (reference category).

Control variables. Mosque Attendance is how often, apart from weddings and funerals, the respondent attends religious services, and ranges from (1) never or practically never to (7) more than once a week. We also control for *Age*, coded in years; gender, coded as (1) *Male* and (0) female; marital status, measured as (1) *Single* and (0) married, widowed, or divorced; and *Urban*, measured as size of town in eight categories from (1) under 2,000 to (8) 500,000 or more.

In analyses of the pooled sample of seven countries, we test for the additive effect of standard of living (under H_3) and the interactive effect of this with support for Islamic law (under H_4). The United Nation's (2001) HDI is used as a measure of standard of living. The Gini coefficient, a measure of economic inequality, is unavailable for Saudi Arabia and has far less effect on economic attitudes than HDI in the remaining countries. We also control for *Repression*, or the country's 2000–01 rating by Freedom House.

Dependent Variables: Economic Attitudes

We analyze the effect of moral cosmology and socioeconomic characteristics on three economic attitudes that contrast communitarian/egalitarian economic policies with individualistic policies. *Everyone Provided For* is the respondent's self-placement on a 1–10 scale, where "1" indicates complete agreement that "people should take more responsibility to provide for themselves" and "10" complete agreement that "the government should take more responsibility to ensure that everyone is provided for." *More Equal Incomes* is the respondent's placement on a 1–10 scale, where "1" is complete agreement that "we need larger income differences as incentives for individual effort" and "10" that "incomes should be made more equal." *More Government Ownership* is the respondent's placement on a 1–10 scale, where "1" indicates complete agreement that "private ownership of business and industry should be increased" and "10" that "government ownership of business and industry should be increased."

Results

Support for Implementing the shari 'a and Economic Attitudes

Table 6.1 shows the distribution by country of support for implementing Islamic law. We order the countries from low to high on the HDI

Table 6.1   Attitudes toward implementation of the shari 'a among Muslims in seven Muslim-majority countries, WVS, 2000–03

Country (HDI)	A good government "should implement only the laws of the shari 'a."					Total
	Very important	Important	Somewhat important	Least important	Not important	
Bangladesh (.47)	21.7	23.6	23.8	21.8	9.2	100.1% 1120
Pakistan (.49)	36.4	25.1	30.9	6.3	1.2	99.9% 1949
Egypt (.64)	48.0	34.0	9.4	7.8	0.9	100.1% 2800
Indonesia (.68)	15.0	37.6	25.8	12.3	9.3	100.0% 875
Algeria (.69)	36.7	34.9	15.5	7.3	5.5	99.9% 1177
Jordan (.71)	53.7	26.2	13.2	3.3	3.6	100.0% 1121
Saudi Arabia (.75)	73.8	14.7	7.3	2.6	1.7	100.0% 880
Pooled Sample	29.1	30.5	23.5	11.2	5.6	99.9% 9847

since we expect this to be the key country-level variable affecting support for egalitarian economic policies (H₃) and how this support relates to support for Islamic law (H₄).

The desire to implement Islamic law is widely held among Muslims in the seven Muslim-majority nations considered here.[7] There is, however, considerable variation across countries, with Saudi Arabians showing the strongest support and Indonesians the least. Popular support for implementing Islamic law in all realms of life is loosely connected to which domains the shari 'a currently covers in each country. In Saudi Arabia, where the shari 'a is the sole basis of the legal code, nearly three-fourths of the population (73.8 percent) regards implementation of this as "very important" to good government. In countries where Islamic law applies only to family matters, lower levels of support are found for instituting the shari 'a as a total system of law (53.7 percent in Jordan, 48.0 percent in Egypt, 36.7 percent in Algeria, 36.4 percent in Pakistan, and 15.0 percent in Indonesia). In Bangladesh, where Islamic law has no role in the legal system, 21.7 percent regard establishing the shari 'a in all realms of life as "very important." The strong popular support in Saudi Arabia, Jordan, and Egypt for implementing the shari 'a suggests that were these countries to become less repressive, the democracies established might not resemble what Western promoters of democracy in the Muslim world would envision. (Davis and Robinson forthcoming) While very few respondents say that implementation of the shari 'a is "not important," disinterest in this is highest in Bangladesh and Indonesia (9.2 and 9.3 percent, respectively), perhaps due to the presence and influence of Hindus in the former and of Christians, Hindus, and Buddhists in the latter, and the resulting syncretic nature of Islam in these countries (Nash 1991: 715; SBS World Guide 2003: 64, 347).

The distinction among Muslims in these nations is not between equal-sized groups of the religiously orthodox and modernists. As we found in our analyses of predominantly Christian and Jewish nations, populations rarely fall into polarized camps along cosmological lines. Instead, there is a continuum of belief, and in some countries the distribution is skewed toward the orthodox pole, in others it is approximately normal, while in still others it is skewed toward the modernist pole (Davis and Robinson 1996a, 1996b, 1996c, 1997, 1999a, 1999b, 2001). Moral cosmology is a matter of degree, and we show below that the strongest advocates of the shari 'a are more egalitarian in their economic positions than those who are less enthusiastic, or not at all, about implementing this.

In table 6.2, we show the means by country on the three economic attitudes considered here. Recall that responses range from 1 (economically individualistic) to 10 (economically communitarian), making the midpoint 5.5. Among Muslims in these countries, popular support is greatest for government taking more responsibility to ensure that everyone is provided for, as opposed to individuals taking more responsibility for themselves (6.06 in the pooled sample). Preferences between making incomes more equal and increasing income differences as an incentive to individual effort lean toward the latter (4.24 in the pooled sample). The relative disinterest in equalizing incomes may be because the Quran does not enjoin economic equality but does mandate *zakat* to care for those in need. Yet more surprisingly, since the Quran also appears to hold private property as inviolable and takes no clear position on nationalization of businesses, Muslims support increasing government ownership of economic resources (5.64) almost as much as they support increasing government efforts to care for the needy.

To put the economic stances of Muslims in a global context, Norris and Inglehart (2004: 171, table 7.4) report that residents of predominantly Muslim nations surveyed in the WVS are more likely than residents of predominantly Catholic, Eastern Orthodox, or Eastern (Asian) nations, but not Protestant nations, to favor increased government

Table 6.2 Means and standard deviations of economic attitudes among Muslims in seven Muslim-majority countries, WVS, 2000–03

Country (HDI)	Everyone provided for			More equal incomes			More government ownership		
	Mean	SD	N	Mean	SD	N	Mean	SD	N
Bangladesh (.47)	5.55	3.45	1294	3.40	2.82	1293	5.28	3.38	1291
Pakistan (.49)	7.13	1.92	1647	7.17	2.15	1461	5.11	1.65	1259
Egypt (.64)	6.61	2.76	2830	2.77	2.06	2830	6.70	2.86	2830
Indonesia (.68)	5.97	3.13	895	3.84	2.34	883	5.86	2.66	885
Algeria (.69)	6.11	3.01	1252	2.91	2.57	1261	5.06	3.19	1192
Jordan (.71)	6.96	2.87	1099	3.56	2.72	1107	5.83	2.98	1040
Saudi Arabia (.75)	5.19	2.58	999	4.19	2.37	999	5.58	2.48	983
Pooled Sample	6.06	2.98	9854	4.24	2.83	9566	5.64	2.79	9268

responsibility for everyone, more likely to support greater government ownership than the residents of all except Eastern Orthodox and Eastern nations, but less likely to favor equalizing incomes than residents of all except Eastern Orthodox nations.

Explaining Economic Attitudes

We begin our analyses of the determinants of economic attitudes by showing the zero-order associations between support for implementing Islamic law and economic egalitarianism in table 6.3, Model 1. From our Moral Cosmology theory (H_1), we expect support for implementing the shari 'a, as an indicator of religious orthodoxy among Muslims, to be associated with communitarian economic attitudes, including support for the government taking more responsibility to provide for everyone, a more equal income distribution, and greater government ownership of businesses and industries. The alternate hypothesis (H_2), based on the specific economic tenets of Islam, posits a narrower effect of orthodoxy, only on support for increased government responsibility for everyone. We find strong confirmation in the bivariate associations for the broad effects expected under Moral Cosmology theory. The desire to implement Islamic law as the sole legal foundation of the state is positively and significantly associated with support for greater government effort to provide for everyone in six of the seven countries (the exception being Saudi Arabia), with wanting to equalize incomes in three countries (Pakistan, Indonesia, and Algeria), and with support for increased government ownership in six countries (the exception being Indonesia). The effects of orthodoxy on support for greater government effort to care for the needy could be explained by both hypotheses, but the totality of effects, including those on support for equalizing incomes and greater government ownership of businesses, can be explained only by Moral Cosmology theory.

The effects of support for Islamic law on economic attitudes are remarkably robust as successive sets of controls are added in Models 2 through 4. In Model 2, we add controls for gender, age, marital status, urban residence, and mosque attendance; only 3 of the 15 effects of support for Islamic law become nonsignificant. Adding further controls for education, income, and occupation in Model 2 reduces none of the effects of support for Islamic law to nonsignificance, indicating that little of the economic communitarianism of supporters of the shari 'a is due to a tendency for them to be less economically advantaged. The addition of politicization and national pride in

Table 6.3 OLS regression coefficient of support for implementing the shari 'a in models explaining economic attitudes among Muslims in seven Muslim-majority countries, WVS, 2000–03

Country and Model (HDI)	Everyone provided for	More equal incomes	More government ownership
Bangladesh (.47)			
(1) No controls	0.648★	−0.012	0.512★
(2)+Male, age, single, urban, Mosque attendance	0.683★	0.059	0.591★
(3)+Education, income, occupation	0.641★	0.006	0.574★
(4)+Discusses politics, national pride	0.635★	0.029	0.628★
R²	0.150	0.128	0.125
N	1040	1047	1042
Pakistan (.49)			
(1)No controls	0.302★	0.230★	0.082★
(2)+Male, age, single, urban, Mosque attendance	0.182★	0.067	0.038
(3)+Education, income, occupation	0.180★	0.065	0.039
(4)+Discusses Politics, National Pride	0.193★	0.075	0.047
R²	0.216	0.205	0.096
N	1610	1425	1229
Egypt (.64)			
(1)No controls	0.249★	−0.013	0.155★
(2)+Male, age, single, urban, Mosque attendance	0.235★	−0.016	0.141★
(3)+Education, income, occupation	0.188★	−0.023	0.098★
(4)+Discusses politics, national pride	0.206★	−0.029	0.103★
R²	0.072	0.018	0.054
N	2678	2678	2678
Indonesia (.68)			
(1)No controls	0.549★	0.146★	0.048
(2)+Male, age, single, urban, Mosque attendance	0.536★	0.211★	0.037
(3)+Education, income, occupation	0.524★	0.198★	0.016
(4)+Discusses politics, national pride	0.453★	0.192★	0.010
R²	0.086	0.085	0.031
N	834	826	823
Algeria (.69)			
(1)No controls	0.238★	0.176★	0.228★
(2)+Male, age, single, urban, Mosque attendance	0.262★	0.190★	0.221★
(3)+Education, income, occupation	0.224★	0.152★	0.226★
(4)+Discusses politics, national pride	0.222★	0.152★	0.221★
R²	0.062	0.071	0.040
N	1098	1105	1056

Continued

Table 6.3   Continued

Country and Model (HDI)	Everyone Provided For	More Equal Incomes	More Government Ownership
Jordan (.71)			
(1)No controls	0.161★	0.104	0.277★
J(2)+Male, age, single, urban, Mosque attendance	0.138	0.121	0.313★
(3)+Education, income, occupation	0.116	0.072	0.278★
(4)+Discusses politics, national pride	0.113	0.074	0.281★
R^2	0.026	0.050	0.051
N	1072	1072	1020
Saudi Arabia (.75)			
(1)No controls	0.134	−0.005	0.271★
(2)+Male, age, single, urban, Mosque attendance	0.139	−0.001	0.281★
(3)+Education, income, occupation	0.152	−0.003	0.299★
(4)+Discusses politics, national pride	0.164	−0.007	0.278★
R^2	0.015	0.021	0.089
N	868	866	853

★$p<.05$.

Model 4 also has no effect on the significance of support for Islamic law, suggesting that any tendency for such supporters to be more politicized or nationalistic is not responsible for their communitarian stances on economic justice. Note that effects of support for Islamic law on the desire for increased government responsibility for all and nationalization of businesses are stronger in countries with low standards of living (especially Bangladesh) than in those with higher living standards (Saudi Arabia and Jordan). We explore these relationships further in analyses of the pooled sample shortly.

The proportions of variance explained (R^2s) in the three economic attitudes by the independent variables in Model 4 are modest, as earlier analyses of similar economic beliefs in the United States, Europe, and Israel have found (e.g., Davis and Robinson 1996a, 1997, 1999b, 2001; Form and Hanson 1985; Knoke et al. 1987). Nonetheless, the overall F-tests for Model 4 are significant in every case except for *Everyone Provided For* in Saudi Arabia and *More Government Ownership* in Indonesia, and the pattern of positive effects of religious orthodoxy on communitarian economic attitudes is clear. With all controls, 12 out of the 21 possible associations of support for Islamic law as the sole legal basis of the state with egalitarian economic attitudes are significant. We estimate the probability of obtaining this many significant coefficients by chance very conservatively at .0000176.[8] Had we posited an opposite effect of orthodoxy among Muslims, we would have found no support for this in any of the seven nations. We conclude from these analyses of each country that there is strong support for the broad effects of religious orthodoxy on egalitarian economic beliefs that our Moral Cosmology theory posits.

To further examine the economic effects of support for Islamic law and how these vary depending on country-level factors (e.g., standard of living, political repression), we conduct Ordinary Least Squares (OLS)analyses on the pooled sample for the seven countries. These analyses are shown in table 6.4.

Support for establishing the shari 'a is positively associated in the pooled sample with wanting greater government responsibility for everyone, more equal incomes, and increased government ownership of businesses and industries. The effects of support for Islamic law on greater government responsibility and greater government ownership are robust when successive sets of controls are added in Models 2 through 5. While the effect of support for the shari 'a on equalizing incomes disappears when controls for HDI, repression, and interactions with support for the shari 'a are added in Model 5, the interaction of support for Islamic law with mosque attendance is significant. Thus, supporters of Islamic law who go to the mosque frequently are especially likely to favor equalizing incomes, perhaps because they are receiving reinforcement for their communitarian beliefs from like-minded clergy and fellow worshipers (see Brooks 2002; Starks and Robinson 2005). With all controls added (Model 5), the standardized coefficients (not shown) indicate that support for establishing Islamic law is the single-most important factor in support for greater government responsibility to care for everyone and the third-most important factor (after education and HDI) in support for increased government ownership of businesses.

We made no prediction as to the effect of mosque attendance on economic communtarianism. The inconsistent effects of mosque attendance—positive on equalizing incomes but negative on greater government ownership (Model 5)—may arise for a number of reasons. Mosques differ in type from government-controlled to independent, in theological orientation, in whether a political message is delivered, and in the content of that message. Attendance may occur for nonreligious reasons (e.g, out of a desire to appear faithful or socially acceptable to others, to make business or political contacts, or for purely social reasons). Nonattendance need not indicate a lack of religious commitment; it can arise from distrust of the religious leadership, for example, because this is appointed by, accommodates to, or colludes with a largely secular and/or corrupt regime. Most important, while the communitarianism of

Table 6.4 OLS regression models explaining economic attitudes, pooled sample of Muslims in seven Muslim-majority countries, WVS, 2000–03

Variables & Models	Models				
	1	2	3	4	5
Everyone Provided For					
Model 1					
shari 'a	0.558★	0.548★	0.486★	0.489★	0.421★
Model 2					
Mosque attendance		0.021★	0.032★	0.030	−0.003
Model 3					
Education			−0.156★	−0.172★	−0.121★
Household income			−0.112★	−0.113★	−0.083★
Owner/Manager			0.532	0.519	0.455
Professional			0.208	0.219	0.164
White Collar			0.536	0.524	0.552
Blue Collar			0.448	0.467	0.457
Army			0.884	0.894	0.740
Student			0.129	0.122	0.084
Housewife/Retired			0.534	0.562	0.458
Model 4					
Discusses Politics				−0.191★	−0.230★
National Pride				−0.252★	−0.367★
Model 5					
HDI					−1.971★
Repression					0.325★
shari 'a x attendance					0.017
shari 'a x HDI					−1.380★
shari 'a x repression					−0.210★
Constant	4.021	3.987	4.732	6.119	6.534
R²	0.050	0.051	0.082	0.086	0.106
N	9006	9006	9006	9006	9006
More Equal Incomes					
Model 1					
shari 'a	0.166★	0.146★	0.064★	0.065★	0.029
Model 2					
Mosque attendance		0.193★	0.213★	0.216★	0.148★
Model 3					
Education			−0.194★	−0.186★	−0.052★
Household income			−0.190★	−0.188★	−0.126★
Owner/Manager			0.561	0.552	0.555
Professional			0.290	0.272	0.339
White Collar			0.805	0.799	1.068
Blue Collar			0.453	0.429	0.663
Army			1.456	1.447	1.441
Student			0.670	0.659	0.696
Housewife/retired			0.966	0.946	0.759

Continued

Table 6.4   Continued

Variables & Models	Models				
	1	*2*	*3*	*4*	*5*
More Equal Incomes (Continued)					
Model 4					
Discusses politics				0.212★	0.171★
National pride				0.021	−0.283★
Model 5					
HDI					−7.994★
Repression					0.568★
shari 'a x attendance					0.055★
shari 'a x HDI					−1.505★
shari 'a x repression					−0.065★
Constant	3.705	2.923	3.813	3.232	5.848
R^2	0.005	0.021	0.089	0.091	0.181
N	8746	8746	8746	8746	8746
More Government Ownership					
Model 1					
shari 'a	0.201★	0.230★	0.216★	0.217★	0.204★
Model 2					
Mosque attendance		−0.125★	−0.121★	−0.124★	−0.108★
Model 3					
Education			−0.105★	−0.116★	−0.163★
Household Income			0.073	0.072	0.060
Owner/Manager			−0.045	−0.051	−0.126
Professional			0.274	0.284	0.119
White Collar			0.640	0.634	0.417
Blue Collar			0.214	0.229	0.013
Army			0.285	0.292	0.114
Student			0.451	0.445	0.374
Housewife/Retired			0.215	0.232	0.256
Model 4					
Discusses politics				−0.163★	−0.181★
National pride				−0.155★	−0.078
Model 5					
HDI					4.006★
Repression					−0.006
shari 'a x attendance					0.000
shari 'a x HDI					−1.332★
shari 'a x repression					−0.022
Constant	4.971	6.049	5.933	6.896	5.247
R^2	0.008	0.024	0.035	0.037	0.056
N	8442	8442	8442	8442	8442

Note: Model 2 also includes age, gender, marital status, and urban residence.

★p<.05, one-tailed test (two-tailed for mosque attendance, repression, and shari 'a x repression).

orthodoxy is a broad worldview that is not limited in its implications to the narrow community of fellow worshipers, the sense of community created through mosque attendance may be limited to the specific congregation. In a U.S. study, Ryle and Robinson (2006) found that the orthodox cosmology was the strongest predictor of a sense of community with neighbors, friends, fellow congregants, coworkers/fellow students, and ethnic group members, while frequent attendance at religious services had no effect in promoting such feelings beyond attachment to fellow congregants.

The Islamist economic program of "Islamic economics" assumes that advantaged Muslims will voluntarily opt for more egalitarian economic relations (Kuran 1997, 2004). From the underdog principle (Robinson and Bell 1978), we hypothesized (H₅) to the contrary, that class matters; advantaged Muslims will be less supportive of government efforts to care for the needy, equalize incomes, and nationalize businesses. The economic self-interest expected by the underdog principle is evident in these models, with highly educated people and those with high household incomes being less supportive of communitarian economic reforms, with one exception that we discuss later. Contrary to this principle, unemployed people are less supportive of increasing government responsibility for everyone and equalizing incomes than almost any other occupational category, although otherwise there is no systematic effect of class/occupation (e.g., between owners/managers and blue collar workers) on economic attitudes. Overall, there is more support for the rational choice, underdog principle than for the voluntary communitarianism assumed by Islamic economics.

Discussing politics frequently or having a strong sense of national pride, when added in Model 4, do not diminish the effects of support for Islamic law on economic attitudes. Muslims who discuss politics frequently are less likely to want greater government responsibility for the needy and greater government ownership but more likely to want incomes to be equalized. An interaction term, testing the possibility that supporters of Islamic law who are politicized are exceptionally egalitarian, is not significant for any of the economic attitudes (details available on request). Nor are the effects of orthodoxy due to any tendency for nationalistic Muslims to be both more supportive of Islamic law out of an anti-West sentiment, and more egalitarian or anticapitalist in their economic views. Muslims with strong pride in their country are actually less favorable toward increasing government responsibility for everyone and equalizing incomes.

As we hypothesized under H₃, high standards of living (HDI) are negatively related to support for government taking more responsibility for everyone and for equalizing incomes, apparently reflecting the feeling that when the country as a whole is doing reasonably well economically, there are fewer needy to take care of (or that they are less deserving of help) and less necessity for government to support the poor or equalize incomes. Interestingly, with a two-tailed test, HDI is *positively* related to support for increased government ownership of businesses, suggesting that Muslims in high-HDI countries may feel that state ownership ensures prosperity. High income and white collar occupation are also positively associated with support for government ownership (had we used two-tailed tests). This may indicate support among high status groups for the crony capitalism and family patronage systems that characterize the rentier economies of some of the nations (Algeria, Egypt, Indonesia, and Saudi Arabia) in our study. Those who are better off in such states are likely to benefit directly from state control of productive resources through their association with government elites (Fandy 1999: 34–36; Moaddel 2002: 77).

To test whether support for Islamic law has a stronger effect on economic egalitarianism in countries with lower standards of living, as we hypothesized under H₄, we include interactions of support for the shari 'a with HDI in Model 5. The significant negative effects of these interactions indicate that, as expected, the lower the country's standard of living, the greater the effect that support for Islamic law has on all three economic attitudes. Failing to meet the needs of the citizenry strengthens effects of Islamic orthodoxy on the desire for egalitarian economic reform.

Political repression, which is only modestly correlated with HDI (–.079), is associated with a desire for greater government responsibility for everyone and more equal incomes, possibly because repressive governments are less likely to look out for those in need. Interestingly, the more repressive the government, the less effect that support for the shari 'a has on wanting greater government responsibility for everyone and more equal incomes. In politically repressive regimes, orthodox Muslims, who are the objects of government repression in some of these countries, may prefer that Islamic nongovernmental organizations (NGOs), rather than the state, provide for the poor and needy. As we discuss in a short while, this is the strategy that most Islamist movements have adopted when faced with government repression and corruption (Carapico 2000).

Discussion and Conclusions

Through analyses of seven Muslim-majority nations, we tested two alternate hypotheses linking orthodoxy versus modernism in Islam with economic attitudes. Our Moral Cosmology theory assumes similar effects of moral cosmology on economic (and cultural) attitudes within all of the Abrahamic faith traditions. Specifically, we argue that the theological communitarianism of the religiously orthodox inclines them to favor communitarian/egalitarian economic arrangements (and communitarian/authoritarian cultural policies that seek to impose what they see as divinely ordained standards on abortion, sexuality, family, and gender). In contrast, the theological individualism of modernists disposes them toward individualistic, laissez-faire economic arrangements (and individualistic/ libertarian cultural policies). While Moral Cosmology theory does not depend on the specific content of Islam, the alternate hypothesis, based on specific tenets of Islam with regard to economic matters, limits the effect of orthodoxy only to government aid to the needy, which is supported by the Islamic pillar of *zakat*, and posits no effects on equalizing incomes or government ownership of businesses.

We found that in all seven societies, orthodoxy—measured as support for the implementation of Islamic law (the shari 'a) as the sole legal foundation of the state—is associated with support for one or more of the following economic reforms: greater government responsibility to provide for everyone, equalization of incomes, or increased government ownership of business. That orthodoxy is linked in these countries, not only with support for government provision for those in need, but with support for other communitarian economic policies that are not enjoined by Islamic texts, supports our Moral Cosmology theory linking orthodoxy to communitarian economic policies in all of the Abrahamic traditions. In additional analyses not reported in this chapter but available on request, we tested the argument of Moral Cosmology theory that orthodoxy is associated with cultural communitarianism or authoritarianism, and found that support for the implementation of Islamic law is significantly related in each of the seven countries to two or more of the following: (1) agreement that "when jobs are scarce, men should have more right to a job than women," (2) agreement that abortion is never justifiable, (3) agreement that homosexuality is never justifiable, and (4) agreement that divorce is never justifiable.

Thus, the link between religious orthodoxy and economic communitarianism that we found earlier in societies that are predominantly Protestant (Norway, United States), mixed Protestant and Catholic

(West Germany), Catholic (Austria, Ireland, Italy, Poland, Portugal), Eastern Orthodox (Bulgaria, Romania), and Jewish (Israel; Davis and Robinson 1996a, 1997, 1999a, 1999b, 2001) holds in seven predominantly Muslim societies as well—18 societies in all. We caution, however, that without survey data or in-depth interviews of ordinary people for earlier periods, it is impossible to know whether the general tendency for the religiously orthodox to be to the left of modernists on economic issues holds throughout the period since the decades around the turn of the past century when the orthodox and modernist cosmologies became separate in the Abrahamic faith traditions or is a more contemporary pattern.

While we found evidence of economic communitarianism among ordinary orthodox Muslims, is there also evidence of this in Islamist movements in Muslim-majority nations? We noted that in politically repressive societies, support for Islamic law is less strongly related to a desire for greater government responsibility for everyone and equalizing incomes, and we suggested that orthodox Muslims may, in such states, prefer that economic needs of the citizenry be addressed by Islamic NGOs (Carapico 2000). In highly repressive Egypt of the 1930s, the Muslim Brotherhood began to establish a broad network of welfare agencies, clinics and hospitals, factories that offer better wages and benefits than state-run companies, day care centers, youth clubs, unemployment agencies, and so on. After the 1992 Cairo earthquake, it was the Brotherhood, not the government, that stepped in to provide medical assistance, shelter, food, and clothing for the victims (Walsh 2003: 34). This "state within a state" (Esposito 2003: 71), while not the first choice of Islamists seeking to establish an Islamic state, became a model for "re-Islamization from below" (Kepel 1994: 33) that has been widely adopted throughout the Muslim world. Eschewing government funds and drawing on *zakat* contributions (as would an Islamic state), these welfare networks demonstrate that Islamist organizations can outperform secular governments in providing social services to citizens (Fuller 2003: 27; Ghadbian 2000: 80; Marty and Appleby 1992: 150; Woltering 2002: 1134).[9]

The cosmological and class differences that we found among Muslims in support for communitarian economic measures suggest that an Islamist call for communitarian economic change would draw support from orthodox Muslims and from those at the bottom of educational and income hierarchies. One of the attractions of Islamist movements arguably is their emphasis on economic reform (Husain 2003: 42) and their efforts to address, with varying degrees of success,[10] human needs that established governments have been unwilling or unable to meet (Fuller 2003: 27).

The landslide victory in the 2005 Iranian presidential election of Islamist Mahmoud Ahmadinejad over Akbar Hasmeni Rafsanjani, a reformist/modernist, shocked Western observers, who had assumed that cultural liberties initiated by outgoing reformist president, Muhammad Khatami, would continue. In a country where the official jobless rate was 11 percent and inflation 14 percent, Ahmadinejad promised to put the poor at the top of his agenda, pledged to renationalize the oil industry and redistribute its wealth, and condemned the reformists' reintroduction of private banks and privatization of state-own industries for increasing the gap between the rich and the poor (*Business Week* 11/7/2005, *The Economist* 27/7/05). *The New York Times* reported that, "while [Ahmadinejad] often invoked God and his faith, he has usually done so in the context of populist proposals to lower prices, raise salaries and create jobs" (Slackman 2005: 1) Ahmadinejad's critique of corruption and cronyism in Iran's rentier economy and his social conservatism contrasted sharply with Rafsanjani's neoliberalism (ending subsidies for bread, gas, and utilities; accelerating privatization; and encouraging foreign investment) and cultural progressivism (*Business Week* 28/6/05). While some might view Ahmadinejad's populism as strictly instrumental, he garnered 62 percent of the vote, drawing especially on the orthodox Muslim poor and unemployed (*The Economist* 27/7/05). Yet encouraging as Ahmadinejad's victory have been for Islamists throughout the Muslim world, the weaker commitment to economic communitarianism that we found among well educated and highly paid Muslims suggests a problem for proponents of "Islamic economics," who assume that an Islamic state could rely on advantaged classes to willingly build an economically just society.

We conclude that while *zakat*, the pillar of Islam requiring Muslims to provide for those in need, may reinforce the tendency for Muslims who support implementation of the shari 'a in all realms of life to be more economically egalitarian, the tendency for such Muslims to go beyond the tenets of their faith in supporting equalization of incomes or nationalization of businesses and industries cannot be attributed to Islam per se, but rather to the economic communitarianism that we have argued characterizes the orthodox of all of the Abrahamic faith traditions. The culturally authoritarian impulse of orthodox Islam regarding the position of women, abortion, sexuality, and family has been well documented by other scholars (e.g., Hassan 2002; Inglehart and Norris 2003; Moaddel 1998), but as we have shown, among Muslims who want religion to be at the core of the state, there is an economically egalitarian face as well.

Appendix Table

Characteristics of the surveys and populations of seven Muslim-majority nations

Country	Survey Characteristics		Population Characteristics		
	Year	*N*	*Percent Muslim*	*Human Development Index (HDI)*	*Political Repression*
Bangladesh	2000	1499	88	.47	3.5
Pakistan	2002	2000	97	.49	5.5
Egypt	2001	3000	94	.64	5.5
Indonesia	2001	1004	92	.68	3.5
Algeria	2002	1282	99	.69	5.5
Jordan	2001	1233	96	.71	4.0
Saudi Arabia	2003	1014*	99	.75	7.0

Note: Percent Muslim is from CIA World Factbook, https://www.cia.gov/cia/publications/factbook/index.html, September 28, 2006. HDI is from United Nations (2001) http://hdr.undp.org/statistics/, 28 September 2006. Political repression, which ranges from 1(low) to 7 (high), is from Freedom House http://www.freedomhouse.org/, September 28, 2006.

*For Saudi citizens only.

Notes

1. The authors are listed alphabetically. This chapter originally appeared as an extended journal article: "The Egalitarian Face of Islamic Orthodoxy: Support for Islamic Law and Economic Justice in Seven Muslim-Majority Nations." *American Sociological Review* 71(2): 167–90, and is reprinted here in shortened form with permission from the American Sociological Association. We wish to thank our respective universities for financial support during our 2003–04 sabbatical in Paris and Sydney, as well as our colleagues in the Department of Sociology and Social Policy at the University of Sydney and the School of Sociology and Anthropology at the University of New South Wales. We especially thank Mansoor Moaddel, Michael Humprey, Jeff Kenney, Brian Powell, Brian Starks, Robert Van Krieken, and Melissa Wilde for their helpful comments. Address correspondence to: Robert V. Robinson, Department of Sociology, Indiana University, Ballantine Hall 744, 1020 East Kirkwood Avenue, Bloomington, IN 47405; e-mail: robinsor@indiana.edu.
2. We use "modernist" for this ideal type because it avoids the political connotation attached to Hunter's "progressive," a connotation that we have shown to be incorrect for economic issues.
3. The communitarianism of the orthodox is corroborated by Ryle and Robinson's (2006) finding for Americans that orthodoxy is the single-most important factor promoting feelings of community across a wide range of sources of community (their neighbors, friends, fellow congregants, coworkers or fellow students, and ethnic group members).
4. The individualism of modernists is corroborated by Starks and Robinson's (forthcoming) finding that modernists in the United States are more likely than the orthodox to prefer that children "think for themselves" over "obey."
5. Consistent with our expectation that modernism is also associated with cultural individualism or freedom of expression, the modernist/reformist activism of Islamic feminists in the Muslim world often involves application of *ijtihad* to sacred texts in order to challenge patriarchal interpretations offered by orthodox Muslims (Moghadam 2002: 1144).
6. The index combines scores on 10 political rights and 15 civil liberties. (www. freedomhouse.org) September 22, 2006.
7. Hassan (2002) found high levels of agreement with the statement "Muslim society must be based on the Qur'an and *shari 'a* law" in his surveys of Pakistan, Egypt, and Indonesia (93% in each), and little agreement with the statement that "It is not practical or realistic to base a complex modern society on the *shari 'a* law" (17%, 10%, and 21%, respectively). A survey by the Pew Research Center for the People and the Press (2003) found that when asked "How much of a role do you think Islam should play in the political life of our country," 73% of Jordanians, 74% of Bangladeshis, 82% of Indonesians and 86% of Pakistanis answered "very large" or "fairly large" as opposed to "fairly small" or "very small."
8. We assume that the three dependent variables (economic attitudes) are perfectly correlated, and estimate the probability of obtaining 12 of 21 (or 4 of 7 since the three items are assumed to be perfectly correlated) outcomes with .05 probability as $7!/(4! \ 3!) \times (.05)^4(.95)^3 = .0000176$. However, the highest correlation among any two of the economic attitudes is only .123; if we instead assume that these are independent (i.e., their correlation is zero), the probability is $21!/(12! \ 9!) \times (.05)^{12}(.95)^9 = .0000000000452$.
9. Not all "welfare Islam" has been initiated by orthodox movements. The *Muhammadiyah* movement in Indonesia, while it scrupulously avoids politics, is modernist in its opposition to the implementation of the shari 'a, but has established a welfare network and school system that serves needs unmet by the state (Fuad 2002; Nash 1991).
10. An ethnography of Islamic NGOs in Egypt, Jordan, and Yemen found them to be more effective in providing employment for the many unemployed and underemployed professionals (doctors, nurses, social workers) and in building ties among middle-class service providers and clients than in addressing the needs of the poor (Clark 2004).

References

Ahmad, Aziz. 1967. *Islamic Modernism in India and Pakistan: 1857–1964.* London: Oxford University Press.

al-Shiekh, Abdallah. 1995. "Zakat." In *The Oxford Encyclopedia of the Modern Islamic World*, edited by John L. Esposito, pp. 366–70. Oxford: Oxford University Press.

Anonymous. 2000/1877–80. "Social Liberalism and Laissez-Faire Capitalism." In *Contemporary Debates in Islam*, edited by Mansoor Moaddel and Kamran Talattof, pp. 123–34. New York: St. Martin's Press.

Brooks, Clem. 2002. "Religious Influence and the Politics of Family Decline Concern: Trends, Sources, and U.S. Political Behavior." *American Sociological Review* 67(2):191–211.

Carapico, Sheila. 2000. "NGOs, INGOs, GO-NGOs and DO-NGOs: Making Sense of Non-Governmental Organizations." *Middle East Report* 214: 12–15.

Cherágh Ali, Moulavi. 1883. *The Proposed Political, Legal, and Social Reforms in the Ottoman Empire and the Other Mohammadan States.* Bombay: Education Society Press.

Clark, Janine. 2004. *Islam, Charity, and Activism: Middle Class Networks and Social Welfare in Egypt, Jordan and Yemen.* Bloomington, IN: Indiana University Press.

Davis, Nancy J. and Robert V. Robinson. 1996a. "Are the Rumors of War Exaggerated? Religious Orthodoxy and Moral Progressivism in the United States." *American Journal of Sociology* 102(3): 756–87.

———. 1996b. "Religious Orthodoxy in American society: The Myth of a Monolithic Camp." *Journal for the Scientific Study of Religion* 35(3): 229–45.

———. 1996c. "Rejoinder to Hunter: Religious Orthodoxy—An Army without Foot Soldiers?" *Journal for the Scientific Study of Religion* 35(3): 249–51.

———. 1997. "A War for America's Soul? The American Religious Landscape." In *Cultural Wars in American Politics: Critical Reviews of a Popular Myth*, edited by Rhys H. Williams, pp. 39–61. New York: Aldine de Gruyter.

———. 1999a. "Religious Cosmologies, Individualism, and Politics in Italy." *Journal for the Scientific Study of Religion* 38(3): 339–53.

———. 1999b. "Their Brothers' Keepers? Orthodox Religionists, Modernists and Economic Justice in Europe." *American Journal of Sociology* 104: 1631–65.

———. 2001. "Theological Modernism, Cultural Libertarianism and Laissez-Faire Economics in Contemporary European Societies." *Sociology of Religion* 62(1): 23–50.

———. 2005. "Sacralizing the Public Sphere in Egypt, Israel, Italy and the United States: The Muslim Brotherhood, *Shas, Comunione e Liberazione*, and the Salvation Army." Paper presented at the annual meetings of the Pacific Sociological Association, Portland, Oregon.

———. Forthcoming. "Freedom on the March? Bush's Democracy Doctrine for the Muslim World. *Contexts.*

Esposito, John L. 2003. "Islam and Civil Society." In *Modernizing Islam: Religion in the Public Sphere in the Middle East and Europe*, edited by John L. Esposito and Francois Burgat, pp. 69–98. New Brunswick, NJ: Rutgers University Press.

Fandy, Mamoun. 1999. *Saudi Arabia and the Politics of Dissent.* New York: Palgrave.

Form, William and Claudine Hanson. 1985. "The Consistency of Stratal Ideologies of Economic Justice." In *Research in Social Stratification and Mobility*, vol. 4, edited by Robert V. Robinson, pp. 239–69. Greenwich, CT: JAI Press.

Freedom House. Freedom in the World, 2000–2001. 2001. New York: Freedom House.

Fuad, Muhammad. 2002. "Civil Society in Indonesia: The Potential and Limits of Muhammadiyah." *Sojourn* 17(2):133–63.

Fuller, Graham. 2003. *The Future of Political Islam.* London: Palgrave MacMillan.

Ghadbian, Najib. 2000. "Political Islam and Violence." *New Political Science* 22(1): 77–88.

Halliday, Fred. 2003. *Islam and the Myth of Confrontation: Religion and Politics in the Middle East.* London: I.B. Tauris.

Hashmi, Taj I. 2004. "Islamic Resurgence in Bangladesh: Genesis, Dynamics and Implications." In *Religious Radicalism and Security in South Asia,* edited by Satu P. Limaye, Mohan Malik, and Robert G. Wirsing, pp. 35–72. Honolulu: Asia-Pacific Center for Security Studies.

Hassan, Riaz. 2002. *Faithlines: Muslim Conceptions of Islam and Society.* Oxford: Oxford University Press.

Hourani, Albert. 1983. *Arabic Thought in the Liberal Age: 1798–1939.* Cambridge: Cambridge University Press.

Hunter, James Davison. 1991. *Culture Wars: The Struggle to Define America.* New York: Basic Books.

Huntington, Samuel P. 1993. "The Clash of Civilizations?" *Foreign Affairs* 72(3): 22–49.

Husain, Mir Zohair. 2003. *Global Islamic Politics. Second Edition.* New York: Longman.

Ibrahim, Saad Eddin. 1982. "Islamic Militancy as a Social Movement: The Case of Two Groups in Egypt." In *Islamic Resurgence in the Arab World,* edited by Ali E. Hillal Dessouki, pp. 117–37. New York: Praeger.

Inglehart, Ronald and Pippa Norris. 2003. "The True Clash of Civilizations." *Foreign Policy*135: 6270.

Jelen, Ted. 1990. "Religious Belief and Attitude Constraint." *Journal for the Scientific Study of Religion* 29(1): 118–25.

Kamali, Mohammad Hashim. 2002. *Freedom, Equality and Justice in Islam.* Cambridge: Islamic Texts Society.

Kepel, Giles. 1994. *The Revenge of God: The Resurgence of Islam, Christianity, and Judaism in the Modern World.* University Park, PA: Pennsylvania State University Press.

Knoke, David, Lawrence E. Raffalovich, and William Erskine. 1987. "Class, Status, and Economic Policy Preferences." In *Research in Social Stratification and Mobility,* vol. 6, edited by Robert V. Robinson, pp. 141–58. Greenwich, CT: JAI Press.

Kuran, Timur. 1997. "The Genesis of Islamic Economics: A Chapter in the Politics of Muslim Identity." *Social Research* 64(2): 301–39.

———. 2004. *Islam and Mammon: The Economic Predicaments of Islamism.* Princeton: Princeton University Press.

Kurzman, Charles. (ed.). 1998. *Liberal Islam: A Sourcebook.* New York: Oxford University Press.

———. 1999. "Liberal Islam: Prospects and Challenges." *Middle Eastern Review of International Affairs* 3(3): 11–19.

Lewis, Bernard. 1990. "The Roots of Muslim Rage." *Atlantic Monthly* 266(3): 47–60.

Mahdavi, Hussein. 1970. "Patterns and Problems of Economic Development in Rentier States: the Case of Iran." In *Studies in the Economic History of the Middle East,* edited by M. A. Cook, pp. 428–67. Oxford: Oxford University Press.

Malik, Hafeez. 1980. *Sir Sayyid Ahmad Khan and Muslim Modernization in India and Pakistan.* New York: Columbia University Press.

Marlow, Louise. 1997. *Hierarchy and Egalitarianism in Islamic Thought.* Cambridge: Cambridge University Press.

Marty, Martin E. and R. Scott Appleby. 1992. *The Glory and the Power: The Fundamentalist Challenge to the Modern World.* Boston: Beacon Press.

Moaddel, Mansoor. 1998. "Religion and Women: Islamic Modernism versus Fundamentalism." *Journal for the Scientific Study of Religion* 37(1): 108–30.

———. 2002. "The Study of Islamic Culture and Politics: An Overview and Assessment." *Annual Review of Sociology* 28: 359–86.

———. 2004. "Prospects for Change in Saudi Arabia." *Footnotes* 32(8): 1, 8–9.

———. 2005. *Islamic Modernism, Nationalism, and Fundamentalism: Episode and Discourse.* Chicago: University of Chicago Press.

———. 2006. "The Saudi Public Speaks: Religion, Gender, and Politics." *International Journal of Middle East Studies* 38(1): 79–108.

Moaddel, Mansoor, Ronald Inglehart, and Mark Tessler. 2005. "Foreign Occupation and National Pride: The Case of Iraq." Unpublished manuscript, University of Michigan.

Moaddel, Mansoor and Kamran Talattof. (eds.). 2000. *Contemporary Debates in Islam: An Anthology of Modernist and Fundamentalist Thought*. New York: St. Martin's Press.

Moghadam, Valentine M. 2002. "Islamic Feminism and Its Discontents: Toward a Resolution of the Debate." *Signs: Journal of Women in Culture and Society* 27(4): 1135–71.

Murphy, Caryle. 2003. "In the Throes of a Quiet Revolution." In *The Muslim World*, edited by Geoffrey Orens, pp. 49–52. New York: H.W. Wilson Company.

Nash, Manning. 1991. "Islamic Resurgence in Malaysia and Indonesia." In *Fundamentalisms Observed*, edited by Martin E. Marty and Scott Appleby, pp. 691–739. Chicago: University of Chicago Press.

Norris, Pippa and Ronald Inglehart. 2004. *Sacred and Secular: Religion and Politics Worldwide*. Cambridge, England: Cambridge University Press.

Pew Research Center for the People and the Press. 2003. *Views of a Changing World*. Available at www.people-press.org (accessed 8/1/05).

Regnerus, Mark D., Christian Smith, and David Sikkink. 1998. "Who Gives to the Poor? The Influence of Religious Tradition and Political Location on the Personal Generosity of Americans Toward the Poor." *Journal for the Scientific Study of Religion* 37(3): 481–93.

Robinson, Robert V. and Wendell Bell. 1978. "Equality, Success and Social Justice in England and the United States." *American Sociological Review* 43(2): 125–43.

Ryle, Robyn R. and Robert V. Robinson. 2006. "Ideology, Moral Cosmology and Community in the United States." *City and Community* 5(1): 53–70.

Said, Edward. 2001. "A Clash of Ignorance." *The Nation* 273(12): 11–13.

SBS World Guide. 2003. *SBS World Guide: The Complete Fact File on Every Country, 11th Edition*. South Yarra, Australia: Hardie Grant Books.

Slackman, Michael. 2005. "Victory Is Seen for Hard-Liner in Iranian Vote." *New York Times* 25 June, 2005, Section A, p. 1, column 5.

Starks, Brian and Robert V. Robinson. Forthcoming. "Moral Cosmology, Religion and Adult Values for Children." *Journal for the Scientific Study of Religion*.

———. 2005. "Who Values the Obedient Child Now? The Religious Factor in Adult Values for Children, 1986–2002." *Social Forces* 84(1): 343–59.

Tamney, Joseph B., Ronald Burton, and Stephen D. Johnson. 1989. "Fundamentalism and Economic Restructuring." In *Religion and Political Behavior in the United States*, edited by Ted G. Jelen, pp. 67–82. New York: Praeger.

Torrey, Charles C. 1892. *The Commercial-Theological Terms in the Koran*. Leyden, Netherlands: E.J. Brill.

United Nations. 2001. *Human Development Indicators: 2001 Report* (online at http://hdr.undp.org/reports/global/2001/en/pdf/back.pdf September 22, 2006.

Walsh, John. 2003. "Egypt's Muslim Brotherhood: Understanding Centrist Islam." *Harvard International Review* 24(4): 32–36.

Woltering, Robert A.F.L. 2002. "The Roots of Islamic Popularity." *Third World Quarterly* 23(6): 1133–43.

CHAPTER 7

The Rentier State: Does Rentierism Hinder Democracy?

The Rentier Mentality Hypothesis Tested in Seven Middle Eastern Countries

BI PURANEN[1] AND OLOF WIDENFALK

Introduction

The Concept of the Rentier State

Given the persistence of authoritarianism in almost all Islamic countries in the modern period, there has been a strong tendency to establish a causal connection between Islam and authoritarianism. An alternative explanation derived from the rentier-state model may render this connection spurious, as it advances a compelling explanation of authoritarianism. Far from being an outcome of Islamic culture or the legacy of historical Islam, this model focuses on the effect of the availability of enormous petrodollars on the structure and functions of the state in Islamic countries. The concept of the rentier state, or the rentier economy, applies to a country that relies on substantial external rent in the form of the sale of oil, transit charges (Suez Canal), or tourism. Rentier economy has far-reaching political, social, and cultural consequences. First, only a small fraction of the population is directly involved in the creation of wealth. As a result, modern social organizations associated with productive activities have been developed only to a limited extent. Second, the work-reward nexus is no longer the central feature of economic transaction, where wealth is the end result of the individual's involvement in a long, risky, and organized production process. Wealth is rather accidental, a windfall gain, or situational, where citizenship becomes a source of economic benefit. To acquire wealth requires different types of subjective orientation, which researchers called "rentier mentality" and "rentier ethics." Noneconomic criteria, such as proximity to the ruling elite and citizenship, become the key determinants of income. Rentierism thus reinforces the state's tribal origins, as it regenerates the tribal hierarchy consisting of varying layers of beneficiaries with the ruling elite on top, in an effective position of buying loyalty through their redistributive power. As the state is not dependent on taxation, there is far less demand for political participation—no taxation, no representation (Beblawi and Luciani 1987; Mahdavy 1970; Moaddel 2002).

In recent years, the hypothesis has been tested more broadly both geographically and as an explanatory variable in studies of democracy. Most of rentier-state analyses have been case descriptions, like Mahdavy's (1970) that tested the rentier model in the case of Iran. However, there are insufficient empirical cross-national analyses of the rentier model.

Rentier, Repression, and Modernization Effects

Ross (2002) is among the most recent scholars who attempted to test the rentier hypothesis, using empirical data. Instead of asking Londregan and Poole's (1996) question—"Does high income promote democracy?"—Ross asks an alternative question: "Does oil hinder democracy?" Using pooled time-series cross-national data from 113 states between 1971 and 1997, he showed that oil exports are strongly associated with authoritarian rule. Ross tests three casual mechanisms of which the rentier effect is one, with the other two being the "repression effect" and the "modernization effect." He uses three different components to test and validate a possible rentier effect. These are (1) the "taxation effect" (low taxes—low demand on accountability), (2) the "spending effect" (patronage), and (3) the "group formation" effect (blocking the formation of independent social groups).[2]

The second causal mechanism tested was the "repression effect." Resource wealth allows their governments to spend more on internal security, thus blocking democratic aspirations.[3] The rentier and repression effects works through the state, and the indicators used are mainly official statistics tapping governmental incomes and expenditures.

The third main effect of "modernization" is a mechanism supposed to tap social life and values. When Ross' analysis leaves indicators tapping governmental use of fiscal and military expenditures to continue the analysis within the field of modernization, the analysis gets problematic. Using eleven indicators from official statistics, Ross tries to test the modernization theory as it is interpreted by Inglehart. Inglehart argues that two types of social changes have a direct impact on the likelihood that a state will become democratic:

1. Rising educational level
2. Rising occupational specialization

It was proposed that low levels of occupational specialization, education, health services, media participation, and urbanization will help explain the problem of developing democracy within resource-rich states.[4] Regression analysis, however, provides weak support for this proposition. Ross thus concludes that the tests may collectively provide a quantitative support for both the rentier effects and the repression effects, but that the modernization thesis needs to be modified or revised.

With the exception of Ross' study, most quantitative studies of democracy overlook the significance of oil as an explanatory variable. The problem, however, is that there are difficulties with cross-national comparisons since there are hardly any democracies in the region—whether oil-based economies or not. This has led to speculations whether it is culture rather than oil or religion that could explain the slow process of democratization. Furthermore, there are very few studies on the views of the citizens of the region, and most analyses are based on aggregated official statistics. The very few extrant qualitative studies have been country-level case studies with little possibility for generalization about the impact of oil on democracy.

Is There a Rentier Mentality?

In this chapter the focus is on citizen attitudes and values. Is there such a thing as a "rentier mentality" or a "rentier mood"? We use the empirical findings from the WVS 1981–2002, using both individual and national level data to test the rentier concept. The idea is that it is the mentality and the basic values among the people not the oil or the rentier state structure per see that decides the future of democracy and welfare. We hypothesize that people in rentier states have a high degree of self-expression but keep rather traditional values. Further more, if oil impedes democracy, countries lacking oil would be more developed when it comes to attitudes toward democracy. We also hypothesize that people in nonoil states place more emphasis on work than do people in rentier states.

The analysis is completed in four steps:

- Initially, we characterize rentier states using the two dimensions, traditional/secular rational and survival/self-expression, developed by Inglehart. We compare rentier states with other kinds of societies in the world; we focus the rest of the study on seven countries in the Middle East region,[5] where the WVS has been conducted[6]: Jordan, Morocco, and Turkey without oil, and Algeria, Saudi Arabia, Iran, and Egypt with oil.
- We then test the rentier state concept by analyzing citizen attitudes toward democracy in the seven countries.
- Moreover we will test the rentier mentality hypothesis by a battery of questions measuring attitudes to work and leisure.
- Finally, we examine the attitudes among citizens at the aggregated country level to see how political and sociological structures in the seven Middle East countries affect the expression of a rentier mentality, and do a more detailed analysis on Saudi Arabia.

Research design

A country is defined as a rentier state if the following criteria are fulfilled:

- At least 70 percent of the value of exports divided by GDP should come from either oil, natural gas, or minerals (table 7.1).
- The net energy import is negative (table 7.2).
- Oil/natural gas should be discovered no later than the 1960s (table 7.3).
- The structure of the economy should be low on industry and services as fractions of GDP (table 7.1).

The following countries within the WVS fulfill the criteria to qualify as the rentier states: Saudi Arabia, Venezuela, Algeria, Egypt, Iran, and Nigeria. Indonesia and Mexico could be defined as semirentier states where oil is vital but not totally dominant. Further Norway, Kazakhstan, and Azerbaijan are too young as oil producing nations to be included.

Table 7.1   Fuel exports as % of Merchandise exports 1999

Saudi Arabia	89
Nigeria	99
Iran	98
Algeria	96
Venezuela	81
Azerbaijan	69
Egypt	37★ (1980:64%)
Indonesia	23 (1980:72%)
Mexico	7★★ (1980:67%, 1990:38%)
Norway	50
Morocco	2
Jordan	0
Turkey	1

Source: World Bank 2000.

Table 7.2   Classification of Economies[a]

		Industry/labor force %[b]	Industry/GDP %[c]	Net energy import[d]
Algeria	middle-income/loIr	31	44	−273
Iran	middle-income/loIr	23	37	−127
Venezuela	middle-income/loIr	27	42	−245
Mexico	middle-income/loIr	24	28	−55
Indonesia	middle-income/loIr	14	41	−101
Egypt	low income	21	21	−67
Nigeria	low income	7	32	−484
Azerbaijan	low income		47	
Saudi Arabia	middle income/upper	20	50	−435

Notes: [a]World development Report 1996, table 1.
[b]World Development Report, Industry, percentage of Labor force, 1990, table 4, 1996.
[c]World Development Report Industry percentage of GDP, 1994, table 12, 1996.
[d]Net energy import as a percentage of energy consumption, World Development Report, table 8, 1996.

Analysis and Results

We start our analysis by locating the rentier states among other types of societies, on the two dimensions, traditional/secular rational and survival/self-expression, developed by Ronald Inglehart. These dimensions are based on factor analysis of ten items, five in each dimension (see Inglehart and Baker 2000 for details) at the aggregated country level.[7]

Table 7.3   Worldwide oil production since 1940 for selected countries[a]

1940	1950	1960	1970	1980	1990	2000
		Algeria				
		Nigeria				
Iran						
Egypt						
Indonesia						
Argentina						
Colombia						
Venezuela						
Peru						
Mexico						
US						
Saudi Arabia						
		China				
		Brazil				
			Chile			
					Norway	
						Kazakhstan
						Azerbaijan
						Russia

Note: [a]Smaller quantities are not included.
Source: International Petroleum Atlas, 2002.

The survival/self-expression dimension taps values of subjective well-being and self-expression that emerges in postindustrial societies with high levels of security. The traditional/secular rational dimension taps values such as tolerance for abortion and homosexuality, male dominance in economic and political life, and respect for authorities. The two dimensions for the different societies, expressed as intergenerational change, show that the rentier states have high self-expression values—actually, higher than any other type of society except industrial democracies (figure 7.1). On the traditional/secular rational dimension, however, the rentier states are among the most traditional (figure 7.2).

In order to do a more focused test of the rentier effect while trying to exclude cultural or geographical side effects, we have selected seven countries in the Middle East region: Saudi Arabia, Egypt, Algeria, and Iran (countries with oil), and Morocco, Jordan, and Turkey (countries without oil), for a further analysis. Figure 7.3 shows the location of the seven countries with respect to the two Inglehart dimensions. As expected, rentier states are rather high on the survival/self-expression axis. Saudi Arabia is highest in self-expression values, and also an extreme

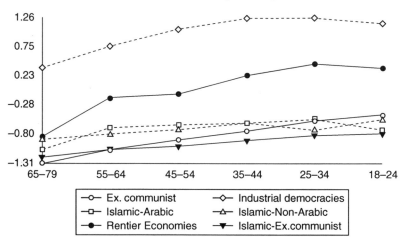

Figure 7.1 Intergenerational changes in Survival/Self-expression values in different types of societies

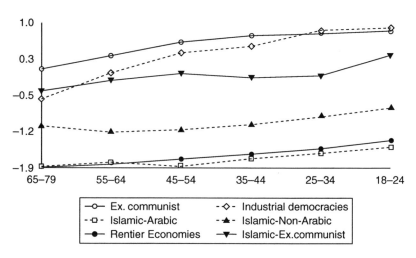

Figure 7.2 Intergenerational changes in traditional/secular rational values in different types of societies

outlier on the traditional/secular rational axis. Nonoil countries are located on the survival end of the survival/self-expression axis. On the traditional/ rational secular axis, two of the nonoil societies are located among the rentier states; Turkey, however, is more secular than any other country.

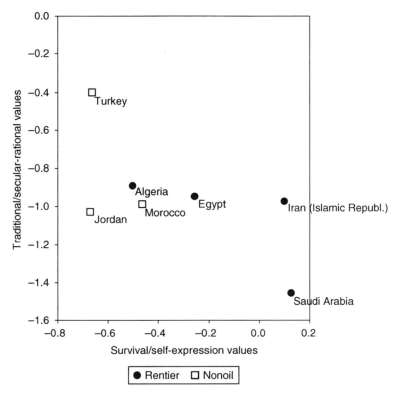

Figure 7.3 The seven Middle East countries in the study on Inglehart's cross-cultural map

To evaluate the effect of oil-economy on attitudes toward democracy and work ethics in the seven countries we used 13 items from the WVS interview schedule. These questions were selected from a larger set of questions by factor analysis. Furthermore, items with a great deal of missing data, such as a large proportion of nonrespondents within a country, were excluded from the analysis. In the first set of seven questions related to the state and government, three distinct factors were extracted in a principal component factor analysis (table 7.4). The *first* relates to democratic performance, and reflects the intercorrelation between three items concerning the degree to which respondents think that there are problems associated with democracy. The *second* reflects the intercorrelation between two items concerning confidence in civil services and major companies, and the *third* relates to a general attitude toward democracy and government (democratic ideals) and reflects the

Table 7.4   Factor analysis on the seven items concerning democratic values. The components explain 63% of the variance

	Democratic performance	Confidence in civil services and major companies	Democratic ideals
Government more responsibility			.829
Confidence: The civil services		.824	
Confidence: Major companies		.822	
In democracy, the economic system runs badly	.774		
Democracies are indecisive	.807		
Democracies are not good at maintaining order	.815		
Democracies are better than any other			.582

Extraction Method: Principal Component Analysis. Rotation Method: Varimax with Kaiser Normalization.

intercorrelation between two items. Several investigators have argued for a similar distinction between the ideals of democracy and the evaluation of its actual performance (Norris 1999; Norris and Inglehart 2003). In previous studies democratic ideals have included an item concerning the approval of a democratic political system. However, this item is missing for Saudi Arabia and replaced by another intercorrelated item asking the respondent if the government should take more responsibility or if people should take more responsibility to provide for themselves. Most people, 89 percent in all seven countries, agree or agree strongly that democracy is better than any other form of political system. When evaluating how democracies work in practice, it is found that the answers are more evenly distributed, and between 50 percent and 75 percent of respondents in each country is positive in judgments. Positive responses in all the dimensions represent higher approval for democratic values and higher confidence in companies and civil services.

In a second set of six items, which tap values of work-ethics and social life, three distinct factors were identified by principal component factor analysis (table 7.5). The *first* one is constructed from two items that concern the degree to which the respondent wants to spend more time with

Table 7.5 Factor analysis on the five items concerning work ethics and social life. The components explain 61% of the variance

	Friends and leisure time	Technology and family life	Money and work
Friends important	.778		
Leisure time	.785		
Less emphasis on money			.788
Less importance placed on work			.745
More emphasis on technology		.761	
More emphasis on family life		.781	

Extraction Method: Principal Component Analysis. Rotation Method: Varimax with Kaiser Normalization.

friends and leisure. The *second* one reflects two items concerning the degree to which the respondent wants to place more emphasis on technology and family life, and the *third* from two items that concern the degree to which the respondent wants to place more emphasis on work and money. For these items, it is important to note that, in general, most people (87 percent) think that friends are important or very important, while the figure for leisure time is somewhat lower (69 percent). Most people (91 percent) think that work is important and 60 percent thinks it is good to place more emphasis on money. About 87 percent emphasize on technology while 96 percent emphasizes on family life.

We used the factor scores as dependent variables in multiple linear regressions to test the effect of rentier state on the dimensions identified. The type of state (rentier/nonoil) was entered as a dummy variable with nonoil states being zero, hence the model analysis: the effect of living in rentier states compared to living in nonoil states. In the analysis we also entered five variables for the purpose of statistical control: gender, age, education, income, and social class. These variables have been selected both because they constitute important demographic and social characteristics and because research has found that they are sometimes related to attitudes toward work. The data was entered in two blocks, the first block including only control variables, and the second block also including the type of state in order to compare the effect of the full model with the model including only control variables.

For the democratic values we find a slight agreement with the rentier hypothesis. The approval of democratic ideals is significantly higher in nonoil countries after controlling for the background variables in the regression model (table 7.6). However, the approval of democratic

Table 7.6   Results from a GLM on democratic issues

Source	Approval of democratic performance			Confidence in major companies & Civil services			Approval of democratic ideals		
	B	Beta	Sig.	B	Beta	Sig.	B	Beta	Sig.
Constant	−.532		★★★	−.386		★★★	−.149		★
Sex	−.096	−.050	★★★	−.141	−.071	★★★	.049	.025	★
Age	.027	.039	★★★	−.011	−.015		−.001	−.002	
Education	.012	.031	★	.029	.072	★★★	−.038	−.095	★★★
Income	.045	.104	★★★	.020	.044	★★★	.020	.046	★★★
Social class	.044	.045	★★★	.086	.085	★★★	.093	.092	★★★
Rentier states	.313	.163	★★★	.112	.057	★★★	−.092	−.047	★★★
R² Block 1 (Control variables only)	.032		★★★	.020		★★★	.020		★★★
R² Block 2 (Controls + type of state, oil/ non-oil)	.055		★★★	.023		★★★	.022		★★★
N	7039			7039			7039		

Note: ★ p< 0.05, ★★ p< 0.01, ★★★ p< 0.001.

performance and confidence in civil services and big companies is higher in rentier than in nonoil states (table 7.5). Hence, people in nonoil states have a high approval for democratic ideals, but they are more negative than people in rentier states in their judgment of how the democratic system performs. It should be stressed, however, that only a small fraction of the variance (2–6 percent) is explained by the models and that the high level of significance is largely the result of the large number of cases in the study.

The relationships between the two dimensions on democratic values, at the aggregated country level, are depicted in figure 7.4. This figure shows that Egypt is a positive outlier both in terms of democratic ideals and performance. If Egypt is removed, all nonoil countries have higher approval for democratic ideals compared to the rentier states. As expected from the regression analysis, nonoil states are somewhat more negative in terms of approval of democratic performance.

In terms of work ethics and social life, we do not see patterns that agree with the rentier hypothesis. Contrary to what is predicted by this hypothesis, people in rentier states want to place significantly less emphasis on friends and leisure, less emphasis on technology and family

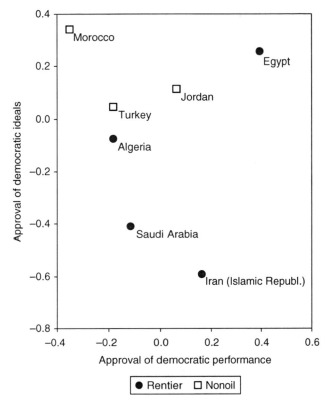

Figure 7.4 Two dimensions of democratic values for the seven countries (mean scores) in the study

life, and more emphasis on work and money than do people in nonoil countries (table 7.7). The same caution that was called upon regarding the statistics in the earlier paragraph should also be applied in these analyses. However, the constancy among the three models indicates that there is no support for a rentier effect in terms of work ethics and social life at the individual level.

If we look at the two dimensions, (1) emphasis on friends and leisure and (2) emphasis on work and money, at the country level, we see a substantial variation between countries (figure 7.5). Interestingly, Saudi Arabia, maybe the most pronounced oil-state in the study, is located in the lower left of the figure—that is, less emphasis on work and money and more emphasis on friends and leisure—that agrees with our predictions of a rentier mentality. On the other hand, in the upper right corner

Table 7.7   Results from a GLM on work ethics and social life

Source	Less emphasis on friends and leisure			Less emphasis on family and technology			More emphasis on money and work		
	B	Beta	Sig.	B	Beta	Sig.	B	Beta	Sig.
Constant	−.341		***	−.146		*	−.220		***
Sex	.003	.002		.021	.011		−.001	−.001	
Age	.036	.052	***	−.009	−.014		.015	.021	*
Education	−.060	−.150	***	−.002	−.006		−.001	−.002	
Income	.012	.026	*	−.002	−.004		−.003	−.007	
Social class	.063	.063	***	.024	.025		−.014	−.014	
Rentier states	.496	.251	***	.122	.065	*	.589	.297	***
R^2 Block 1 (Control variables only)	.035		***	.001			.008		***
R^2 Block 2 (Controls + type of state, oil/ nonoil)	.092		***	.004		***	.088		***
N	10192			10192			10192		

Note: * $p < 0.05$, ** $p < 0.01$, *** $p < 0.001$.

another rentier state, Egypt, stands out. Thus, even though we cannot see a rentier effect at the individual level there is a variation explicable between rentier states. In Saudi Arabia at least there may be a rentier mentality in terms of work ethics and social life. It is worth noting, however, that two nonoil countries, Morocco and Turkey, are also found in the lower right of the figure.

To further investigate this idea we conducted a more detailed analysis of Saudi Arabia. In a subset of the above dimensions, we studied the differences among ethnic groups within the country, namely people with Saudi Arabian citizenship (Saudis), people from other Arabic countries (Arabs) and non-Arabs who are basically in the country to work.[8] The rentier effect predicts that the Saudis, who presumably get a larger share of the oil wealth, will show more of a rentier mentality than will Arabic and other guest workers who have to work harder for their earnings. Figure 7.6 shows that this is, at least to some extent, confirmed when comparing the Saudis and other Arabs. Arabs have a higher approval for democratic ideals and performance and want to place somewhat less emphasis on friends and leisure and more emphasis on work and money (figure 7.7). However, Arabs are slightly more traditional than Saudis (figure 7.8). Somewhat

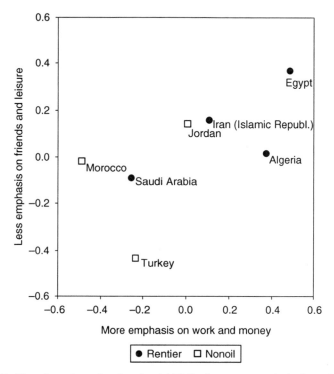

Figure 7.5 Two dimensions of work and social life for the seven countries in the study

surprising, non-Arabs (most of which presumably are guest workers from South East Asia) show less approval of democratic values, place less emphasis on work and money and are more traditional than any of the other two groups (figures 7.6–7.8). This is, however, a small group.

Discussion

During the past decades several investigators have proposed rentierism as an explanation for the hindered development toward democracy in the Middle East region. The underlying mechanisms may be both structural (i.e., oil incomes could be used by authoritarian leaders to strengthen control and security) and individual (i.e., people develop a rentier mentality). Rentier mentality could be characterized as low sense of coherence in the understanding of the linkage between productivity and economic status. Work inplace is not required in order to get a decent standard of living—the public good is produced in any case. Economic

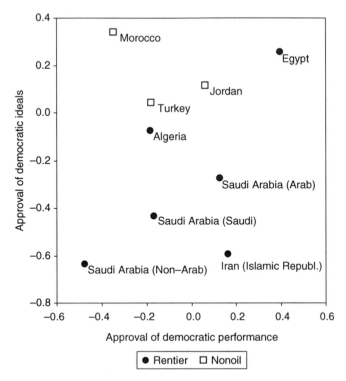

Figure 7.6 Two dimensions of democratic values for the seven countries in the study with Saudi Arabia subdivided into the three ethnic groups in the country

goods are supposed to be produced somewhere else but are still used for consumption. Thus we are back to Lenin and his definition of a rentier state, but with the important difference that in Lenin's theories it was Western colonial societies taking the wealth and now it is the governments of the rentier states that enrich themselves. If a rentier mentality is present among people in oil-exporting states, we would expect them to prioritize leisure time before work. Furthermore, we would expect them to express less approval of a democratic system, since not only wealth but also security is provided for by a strong authoritarian leadership.

The results from this report, however, indicate a somewhat more complicated picture. First, rentier states are characterized by a high degree of self-expression and postmaterialist life styles, accompanied by traditional cultural values. Secondly, only with regard to approval of democratic ideals is there an agreement with the predicted expression of a rentier mentality. The approval of democratic performance and emphasis on

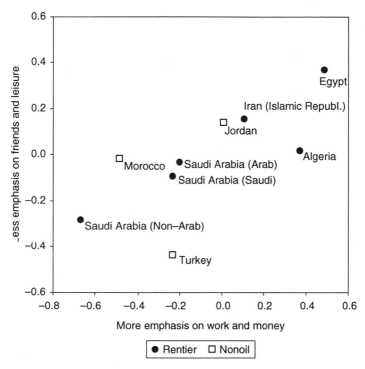

Figure 7.7 Two dimensions of work and social life for the seven countries in the study with Saudi Arabia subdivided into the three ethnic groups in the country

work and money is actually higher in rentier states than in nonoil countries. Thirdly, there are important differences between countries. Egypt shows higher approval for democracy and places less emphasis on friends and leisure and more emphasis on work and money than most Middle East countries in the study, whereas Saudi Arabia has lower approval for democracy and place less emphasis on work and more emphasis of friends and leisure than do people in most other rentier states in the study.

The lack of expression of a rentier mentality in rentier states may have several reasons. One may be a feeling of insecurity with low trust, high work ethics, importance of family, and low occupational differentiation, even if the state is defined as an autocracy dependent on oil exports. This may be the case, for example, in Egypt, that is still defined as a low income country and where incomes from oil export are relatively small (tables 7.1 and 7.2).

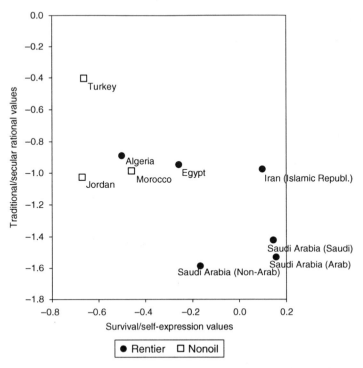

Figure 7.8   The seven countries in the study on Inglehart's cross-cultural map with Saudi Arabia subdivided into the three ethnic groups in the country

The political turbulence in the region may be another reason behind a feeling of insecurity and low trust. In Saudi Arabia, on the other hand, where oil incomes are high and not only people's wealth but also their security is provided for by a strong authoritarian leadership, we see more of a rentier mentality. The question is; will the majority of young unemployed men in countries like Saudi Arabia leave it that way? This study is based on data from 2001 and there are more recent indications of a change in attitudes both with regard to democracy and women's rights.

Another interesting issue is to what extent the high approval for democratic values found, not only in this study but also in several other studies, is "real" or to a large extent the result of "lip service." It is possible that democracy means a different thing to people in Middle East autocracies than it does to people in industrial democracies.

Some rentier states outside the Middle East region were left out in this study—for example, Nigeria and Venezuela and the semirentier states

Indonesia and Mexico. Preliminary analyses of these data indicate that there is a regional effect such that South American countries like Venezuela and Mexico share the same values, a rather low approval of democracy and low emphasis on work and leisure. Nigeria is similar while Indonesia on the other hand, with a rather high approval of democracy and a high emphasis on work.

The variation in democracy and work related values, among and within rentier states in this study, further stresses the importance of within state structures for the development of rentier mentalities. These structures involve, for example, ties of friendship, tribal affilations and proximity to the ruling elite (Moaddel 2002). Hence, it is important for future research on the rentier mentality concept to measure and include these types of parameters in the analyses.

Future research may also involve an extended application of the rentier concept. Is it, for example, possible to develop a rentier mentality without actually being a rentier state? If societies scoring high on self-expression, sustainability, and responsibility develop values while lacking linkage between democracy, productivity, economic status, and public good, can rentier mentalities develop in a production economy? Rentierism may serve as a raw model for attitudes toward democracy and work in a much larger context than just developing countries with large incomes from oil export.

Conclusion

Does rentierism hinder democracy? This study indicates that high incomes from oil export may affect people's demand for political partic-ipation, in terms of approval of democracy. The results are however far from unambiguous. In oil-exporting countries like Egypt, the approval of democracy is higher than in most nonoil countries. However, the example of Saudi Arabia suggests that with a combination of strong lead-ership, a high level of security, and networks for distribution of resource wealth, a more rentier oriented mentality may develop.

Notes

1. Correspondence to bi@bikupan.se.
2. To test the taxation effect Ross compares different types of taxes: personal and corporate taxes indicates democracy while taxes on trade, external grants, and right-of-way fees indicate author-itarian regimes. The spending effect is measured as government consumtion as a percentage of GDP by all levels of government and all types of spending (including wages). If the spending

effect is valid higher levels of spending should result in less democracy. The third variable measures the share of GDP accounted for by government activity—as government increase in size (relative to domestic economy) they are more likely to prevent the formation of civic institutions and social groups that are independent from the government. The regressions on taxes are highly significant and positive. The spending effect is also highly significant in the hypothesized direction. Finally, the group formation effect is also highly significant: the larger the government, the less movement toward democracy.

3. Ross measures the size of the military budget as a fraction of GDP and the size of the military personnel as a fraction of the labor force. Oil exports are positively and significantly correlated with military spending but mineral exports are negatively and significantly associated with military spending.

4. The indicators used are International Labor Force (ILO) statistics of men and women in industry, and services. Educational levels are measured through UNESCO statistics on the enrollment of men and women in secondary school and college. Physical health is measured by life expectancy at birth, media participation is measured through statistics collected by International Telecommunications Union on number of telephone mainlines and televisions. Finally urbanization is measured by UN statistics on part of states' population living in urban areas. The results from the regressions are somewhat Irak, the variables measuring education, life expectancy, urbanization, and televisions per capita are not significant; however the variables measuring occupational specialization are highly significant.

5. We use the World Bank's defintion of "Middle East" that includes North Africa: Algeria, Bahrain, Egypt, Iran, Iraq, Israel, Jordan, Kuwait, Lebanon, Libya, Malta, Morocco, Oman, Qatar, Saudi Arabia, Syria, Tunisia, United Arab Emirates, and Jemen. Of these countries the following are included in the WVS of 2002: Algeria, Egypt, Iran, Israel, Jordan, Malta, Morocco, and Saudi Arabia.

6. For the countries at the Arabic Peninsula we are lacking values surveys except for Saudi Arabia.

7. Values are taken from WVS Wave 4. Values for Saudi Arabia were kindly provided us by Professor Ronald Inglehart.

8. Number of people in the three ethnic groups in the WVS data set from Saudi Arabia: Saudis 1026, Arabs 353, and non-Arabs 123.

References

Beblawi, Hazem and Giacomo Luciani (eds.). 1987. *The Rentier State.* London, New York, Sydney: Croom Helm.

Inglehart, Ronald and Wayne E. Baker. 2000. "Modernization, Cultural Change, and the Persistence of Traditional Values." *American Sociological Review* 65(1): 19–51.

Londregan, John B. and Keith T. Poole. 1996. "Does High Income Promote Democracy?" *World Politics* 49(1): 1–30.

Mahdavy, Hussein. 1970. "Patterns and Problems of Economic Development in Rentier States: The Case of Iran." In *Studies in the Economic History of the Middle East*, edited by Michael A. Cook, pp. 428–67. Oxford: Oxford University Press.

Moaddel, Mansoor. 2002. "The study of Islamic Culture and Politics: An Overview and Assessment." *Annual Review of Sociology* 28: 359–86.

Norris, Pippa. (ed.). 1999. *Critical Citizens: Global Support for Democratic Governance.* Oxford: Oxford University Press.

Norris, Pippa and Ronald Inglehart. 2003. "Islamic Culture and Democracy: Testing the Clash of Civilization Thesis." In *Human Values and Social Change: Findings from the World Values Surveys*, edited by Ronald Inglehart, pp. 5–33. Leiden, Boston: Brill.

Ross, Michael L. 2002. "Does Oil Hinder Democracy?" *World Politics* 53(3): 325–61.

PART 3

Determinants of Self-Rated Health and Attitudes toward Religion, Gender and Democracy

CHAPTER 8

Social Structure versus Perception: A Cross-National Comparison of Self-Rated Health in Egypt, Iran, Jordan, and the United States

KRISTINE J. AJROUCH[1] AND
MANSOOR MOADDEL

Introduction

In the historical traditions of sociology one finds ample evidence that well-being relates to broader social processes. This association was proposed in Marx's theory of alienation, Durkheim's studies of suicide, and Weber's focus on life-chances as the key factor defining one's position in the social hierarchy. Over time, sociological inquiries increasingly attended to different aspects of well-being, with health constituting one branch of scholarship. In the classical tradition, however, determinants of health were constructed almost exclusively in terms of variations in such social structural arrangements as age, gender, race/ethnicity, and socioeconomic status. These factors are certainly important. People become ill, and their location in social stratification with regard to age, gender, race/ethnicity, and social class influences the nature of medical attention they receive. Furthermore, people of high socioeconomic status stand a better chance of remaining healthy because they may access higher quality housing, food, and material conditions that enhance life-circumstances. There are, however, considerable variations among individuals within each of these structural arrangements.

In recent years, social scientists have recognized the causal inadequacy of the association between these structural factors and health status. This is because the empirical relationships were either often weak or nonexistent or there were considerable in-group (e.g., class, age, gender) variations. As a result, empirical studies have departed from exclusively assessing the effects of social structural variables on well-being in favor of attending to such subjective factors as perceived control as a potential mediator between structural arrangements and health (Bisconti and Bergeman 1999; Bobak et al. 1998; Bosma et al. 1999; Lachman and Weaver 1998; Marmot 2003; Marmot et al. 1998;). This chapter builds on these new theoretical developments by assessing the effect of two additional variables—happiness and religiosity—on health. In this study, our objective is to formulate a model that considers the relative significance of structural, ritualistic, and perceptual variables in order to assess their significance in explaining cross-national variations in self-rated health. By considering these variables, we wish to contribute to a more general and abstract theoretical debate in sociology—social structure versus perception. While we do not attempt to take position against one perspective by exclusively leaning on the other, this chapter offers sufficient empirical evidence to reintroduce the perspective spearheaded by Charles Horton Cooley's famous dictum, "the imagination that we have of one another is the solid fact of society." Another contribution this chapter makes is its attempt to widen the empirical range of the sociological determinants of health by focusing on a selected number of Islamic countries—Egypt, Iran, and Jordan—compared to the United States. Most of the extant social-science research on predictors of health has thus far focused on industrialized countries of Europe and the United States. The Middle East represents an area of the world that receives little attention, yet is home to a growing number of the world populace and increasingly draws media attention due to political instabilities. What predicts health status in the Middle East? Do theoretical models developed in the U.S. and Europe societies apply to Islamic societies? What factors—structural or perceptual— have wider cross-national explanatory power?

Measuring Health: Self-Reports

In this study, respondents offer self-assessments of their health. Although there may be alternative measures of health based on one's medical records or assessment by a health care professional, the current measure is widely used in the literature and is demonstrated to have considerable predictive power. For example, empirical evidence demonstrates that self-definitions of health often link to various aspects of physical health including level of functional ability, morbidity, and mortality (Benyamini et al. 2000; Idler and Kasl 1995). Self-ratings of health also connect to the frequency with which individuals access the health care system, patterns of use, and overall health care costs (Bobak et al. 1998; Vingilis et al. 2002). However, little attention has been focused on its determinants, leading to growing concerns about what exactly drives such ratings (Spiers et al. 2003; Vingilis et al. 2002). As a case in point, Krause and Jay (1994) discovered from indepth interviews that specific referents used to evaluate one's health in a U.S. sample differed by age, education, and race. Also essential to consider is that self-rated health constitutes a measure gathered in various studies across nations, and so it stands that evaluation of one's health may differ depending on the national or cultural context (Janevic et al. 2000).

Theoretical Developments

Until recently, the social-scientific study of health was governed by models that emphasized such social structural factors as gender, class, and race. The concern with structural arrangements often attended directly to issues of inequality and social exclusion (Marmot 2003; Pearlin 1992). In the United States, for example, inequalities of gender, class, and race have been found to associate with health status and mortality. With regard to gender, chronic illness is more prevalent among women, but men die an average of seven years earlier than women (Barer 1994; Verbrugge 1985). Class is measured by various socioeconomic indicators including education, income, and occupational prestige (Liberatos et al. 1988). Low levels on each dimension are found to relate to poor health with those of lower socioeconomic position experiencing the onset of health problems earlier—that is, often in midlife—than do their higher positioned counterparts (House et al. 1994). Racial status influences health in that minorities, even those with high education and high income, tend to experience stress from exposure to racism and discrimination (Smith and Kington 1997).

Perceived Control

More recent developments, however, emphasize differences among individuals within groups (Marmot 2003). In other words, attention is increasingly focused on the processes that mediate the association between structural factors and health (Bisconti and Bergeman 1999). *Perceived control*, the meaning of which rests with the individual designating the level of control he or she commands, represents one subjective measure that researchers draw from in order to account for inequalities based on social position (Bisconti and Bergeman 1999; Bobak et al. 1998; Bosma et al. 1999; Lachman and Weaver 1998; Marmot et al.1998). Perhaps the most articulate argument put forth about the necessity of moving beyond absolute measures of inequality to better understand the link between structural arrangements and health may be found in Marmot (2003). Marmot acknowledges that inequality is associated with health status, but he argues for a refined theoretical model to include factors that indicate relative positions in the social hierarchy. For instance, while research has established the link between education and health (i.e., Ross and Wu 1995), this link is mediated through perceived control (Marmot 2003; Ross and Van Willigen 1997). That is, higher education enhances perception of control because it increases one's skill and confidence, hence ability to solve problems, leading to upward occupational mobility that in turn provides resources, status, and power. "Power, then, appears an important way that position in the social hierarchy is translated into greater risk of ill health" (Marmot 2003: S18). Additionally, a Netherlands cohort study demonstrated that those with lower education levels (only primary school) experience a higher risk of dying than those with a university or higher vocational education. However, those with low education levels but higher perceived control retained substantially lower mortality ratios. The authors conclude that the link between education and mortality is explained, at least partially, by perceived control (Bosma et al. 1999). This line of research enhances the explanatory power of the determinants of health by suggesting that while structural arrangements are undoubtedly important, the individuals' perception of their situation remains a critical factor.

This perception, however, may be influenced by one's position in the social hierarchy. In a representative sample of U.S. respondents, Ross and Mirowsky (2002) found that a gender gap exists in personal (perceived) control, but it is greater among older individuals, and over time women's sense of control declines more than it does among men. Furthermore, higher education is positively correlated with higher levels of perceived control, and economic hardship and heavy burdens of domestic work are associated with lower levels of perceived control (Ross and Mirowsky 2002). While age, gender, and education seem to differentially associate with perceived control and health status, income level and social class represent other critical variables conveying differential power levels that also link to health status (Marmot 2003).

Happiness and Health

The effect of perceived control in mediating the relationship between social structure and health is empirically established in various studies. However, the question of how higher control contributes to better health remains undertheorized. One way that control may enhance health would be through a reduction in the emotional stress and alienation that are generally believed to be associated with powerlessness. Another way is to argue that perceived control has the additional effect on individual well-being by promoting a positive state of mind— making him/her happier.

In a recent effort to develop valid health measures for the World Health Organization, happiness emerged as the most important component in describing quality of life (Skevington 1997). Moreover, good health is often considered a consequence of happiness (Rogers and Zaragoza-Lao 2003; Veenhoven 1988). The directionality of the association between happiness and health remains unclear, however. A main obstacle involves the question of causality, does good health lead to happiness, or is it the other way round where being happy produces good health? The issue of mind over matter, that is, perceptions possessing the power to determine objective states of being, receives anecdotal attention, but little empirical examination (Burch 2001). The study by Rogers and Zaragoza-Lao (2003) observed this relationship indirectly by examining whether communities that offer more "cultural" events in the way of museums, parks, and other recreational facilities may also lead to healthier children since other studies suggest that the existence of such resources leads to happier children. Rogers and Zaragoza-Lao conclude that children living in communities that offer such leisure pursuits are more likely to be healthier, and suggest, "communities that have made an investment in the happiness of children may be encouraged to find that this also may extend to children's health" (289). In this analysis we draw from the theoretical viewpoint which posits that perceptions of situations result in objective consequences that shape lived experience; in other words a situation defined as real is real in its consequences (Thomas and Thomas 1928).

Happiness has been linked to health, most recently by Stack and Eshleman (1998) who demonstrate a direct and strong association between these using data from 17 nations. Lacking, however, is an examination of happiness as a potential mediator between social stratification and health, or for that matter, a more detailed examination of how happiness may relate to other social psychological measures such as perceived control. The prevalence of happiness correlates with social factors such as age, gender, socioeconomic status, and sociopolitical factors (Gerdtham and Johannesson 2001; Inglehart and Klingemann 2000; Stack and Eshleman 1998). Previous studies drawing from the WVS suggest that women report higher levels of happiness than men in younger years, but during older years the relationship reverses so that it is men who report higher levels of happiness (Inglehart 2003). Additionally, Inglehart and Klingemann (2000) advance the idea that historical and cultural characteristics, including political and economic institutions, impinge on levels of happiness within nations.

In this study, we test the effect of structural variables and perceived control on happiness and its association with self-rated health.

Religiosity and Health

Social scientists have long emphasized the significance of religion in social processes. Besides Durkheim's pioneering work on religion and individual well-being, many social scientists have addressed the effects of performing religious rituals on broad social processes in transforming the obligatory and constraining into something desirable. "The irksomeness of moral constraint," said Turner (1967: 3), "is transformed into the 'love of virtue.' " Rituals are believed to transcend the limitations of social structure "and reconfigure it along communitarian lines" (Alexander 1991: 27). In recent decades, sociologists of religion have also tried to systematically assess the linkages between religiosity, on the one hand, and happiness and health on the other. For example, some studies have supported the relationship between religiosity and happiness (Francis and Stubbs 1987; Francis et al. 2000), while other studies indicated that the relationship varies according to the measure of happiness used and the samples studied (Robbins and Francis 1996). Lewis (2002) discovered that when happiness is operationalized in terms of the depression-happiness scale there is no association with either attitudinal or behavior measures of religiosity. Likewise, there exists considerable literature on the relationship between religiosity and health (Benson 1997; Carroll 1991; Levin 1996). However, while some studies connected religiosity to recovery from acute illness (Ai et al. 1998), one study indicates that strong religious beliefs may actually slow the process of recovery (King et al. 1999).

We include structural, ritualistic, and perceptual variables in order to arrive at a more complete explanation of social factors affecting health. These include such measures of social hierarchy as age, gender, education, income, and social class. We also include religiosity to assess the effect of ritual performance on health. The perceptual variables are intended to capture the social psychological processes and are indicated by measures of perceived control and happiness.

Model of the Study and Hypotheses

We propose to examine the pathways that influence health by introducing happiness as a mediator between the standard structural measures of social position and health as well as between perceived control and health. Based on previous findings, we first predict direct effects of structural arrangements on the perceptual variables and self-rated health across countries:

> H_1: younger age, being male, higher levels of education, social class, and income will be associated with higher ratings of perceived control, happiness, and self-rated health.

The second hypothesis involves an examination of the role of religiosity. Religiosity is thought to positively associate with perceived control, happiness, and self-rated health.

> H_2: religiosity will have a positive effect on self-rated health, perceived control, and happiness.

Perceived control will mediate the relationship between structural variables and health, and happiness will mediate the relationship between both the structural relationship and health and perceived control and health.

> H_3: perceived control will be positively associated with self-rated health, diminishing the observed associations that exist between the objective measures of interest and self-rated health.

> H_4: happiness will be positively associated with self-rated health, diminishing the observed associations that exist between objective measures of interest as well as between perceived control and self-rated health.

Egypt, Iran, Jordan, and the United States

The hypotheses mentioned are tested using comparable survey data collected in Egypt, Iran, Jordan, and the United States. Being considerably diverse in terms of the level of economic development, history, culture, and social and political institutions, these four countries provide a unique opportunity to test the degree to which the pattern of relationships among the specified variables hold cross-nationally.

The United States is among the world's most advanced industrial democracies. Individualism, freedom of choice, and hard work are highly valued. Combined with universally available education, these values represent the main channel for social mobility and status attainment, which are in turn believed to bring empowerment, happiness, and better quality of life. Egypt, Iran, and Jordan are developing societies, which, although all are predominantly Muslim, have followed diverse patterns of cultural and political developments. Egypt and Jordan are secular states, having a predominantly Sunni Muslim population. Iran, on the other hand, is predominantly Shi 'i and has a theocratic government. While freedom of choice and hard work are also valued in these societies, authoritarian political environments and a rentier economy are believed to contribute to the persistence of patrimonialism (Beblawi 1987; Brynen 1992; Luciani 1988). Furthermore, Jordan while having the most educated public among Arab countries tends to stress more on family and tribal affiliations, at the same time, its economy depends on remittance money sent back home by several hundred thousands of its expatriates working in Persian Gulf countries (Moaddel 2002a). Rapid population growth in Iran and Egypt over the past decades considerably constrained the state's ability to promote economic development and job creation. Both countries have a very young population, demanding jobs and better living conditions, cultural fulfillment, and political inclusion. On the societal level, while Iranians are dominated by a religious government, they are less religious and more nationalistic than either Jordanians or Egyptians. This difference is more pronounced among educated Iranians, as both the educated public and women appear to be at the forefront of the demand for reform. In Jordan and Egypt, educated individuals, while being considerably critical of their governments, are (in contrast to Iran) sympathetic to Islamic activism (Moaddel 2002a; Moaddel and Azadarmaki 2002). These variations may thus affect the way the social structural factors, ritual performances, and perception affect self-rated health. Critical questions include: What is the invariant aspect of this determination across all four countries? What aspects are country specific? To what degree are there divergences on the determinants of health between the United States, on the one hand, and these three Islamic countries, on the other?

Comparing structural arrangements as well as perceptions within each nation offers a unique opportunity to broaden scientific knowledge and refine theoretical models on the social determinants of health. Social scientists have documented in the Western world, as well as those previously communist countries, that sociodemographic factors are associated with health status, and often times "perceived control" serves as an intervening variable (Bobak et al. 1998, 2000; Lachman and Weaver 1998; Marmot et al. 1998). Some suggest that the political and economic organization of a country and its national character determine the prevalence and nature of psychosocial resources such as perceived control and happiness (Carlson 1998; Inglehart 2003; Stack and Eshleman 1998). Our analysis examines these associations in Islamic countries, and by comparison how they differ and/or are similar to the United States. On the whole, applying social science theory and method to Islamic countries provides an occasion to empirically document social life in an understudied part of the world, and ultimately suggest ways to enhance health status and overall quality of life.

Methodology and Measures

We conducted path analysis to estimate the causal connections among the observed variables. An identical model was tested for each country using AMOS (Arbuckle 1995). AMOS is a structural equation model program that allows for model specification through an intuitive path diagram to show hypothesized relationships among variables. The following fit indices were used: chi-square/df, and CFI. A good fit was indicated by a chi-square/df of less than 5, and CFI greater than .90. Initial AMOS analyses were performed with structural parameters free to vary. Using structural equation modeling, a model was drawn to test the associations between all variables hypothesized to influence self-rated health for each country. We set the significance level at .01. The final models presented were evaluated after eliminating nonsignificant paths.

Self-Rated Health

Respondents were asked for a global rating of their health, *self-rated health*, with the following question:

All in all, how would you describe your state of health these days? Would you say it is: (1) very good; (2) good; (3) fair; (4) poor.

Responses were recoded, and larger numbers indicated better health
(1 = 4, 2 = 3, 3 = 2, 4 = 1).

Structural Measures

The structural variable of *age* in this study was gathered by asking year of
birth; and *gender* is a dummy variable, where 0 = male and 1 = female.
We include education, income, and class as measures of respondents'
socioeconomic status. *Education* is a dummy variable, where 0 = vocational or less and 1 = high school degree or more. *Income* is a 10 point
scale where the respondent designates a monthly household income
category including all sources. While the lived experience in each country may differ, that is, the lowest income category may differ in dollar
amounts across countries, within each country respondents choose their
monthly household income from a 10 point scale, ensuring to some
extent similar groupings across countries. The same holds true for
education where the curriculum may differ depending on the national
context, but education levels completed are uniform in terms of vocational training versus university studies. We do not include occupation
in this study due to the difficulty of developing status codes for occupations that are equivalent across national contexts. Instead, we have included
the variable *social class*, where the respondent is asked to determine
whether they rank themselves as upper, upper middle, lower middle,
working, or lower class. Responses were recoded so that larger numbers
indicated higher class.

Ritual Performance

Religiosity comprises behavioral characteristics as opposed to attitudinal.
The respondent indicates the number of times she/he goes to places of
worship for prayer (excluding occasions such as funerals and weddings)
ranging from more than once a week (1) to never (7). Responses were
recoded, so that larger numbers indicated higher levels of religiosity
(1 = 7, 2 = 6, 3 = 5, 5 = 3, 6 = 2, 7 = 1).

Perceptual Measures

Perceived control and happiness are hypothesized to be the indirect
pathways through which the structural variables and self-rated health are
associated. In order to measure *happiness*, the respondent answered the

following question:

Taking all things together, would you say you are: (1) very happy; (2) quite happy; (3) not quite happy; (4) not at all happy.

Perceived control is indicated by asking respondents to rate the amount of control they perceive in their life on a 10-point scale from 1 (not at all) to 10 (a great deal) through the following question:

Some people feel they have completely free choice and control over their lives, while other people feel that what they do has no real effect on what happens to them. Please use the scale to indicate how much freedom of choice and control you feel you have over the way your life turns out.

While each of these subjective measures are single indicators, past research has demonstrated each to represent fairly reliable measures of the given social psychological construct (Angel and Gronfein 1988; Sastry and Ross 1998; Stack and Eshleman 1998).

Data

The data for this study were drawn from national values surveys carried out in Egypt, Iran, Jordan, and the United States during 2000–02. Although the surveys in Egypt, Iran, and Jordan contain questions specifically designed for Islamic countries, the surveys include identical questions that allow for cross-national comparison with the United States. The data are based on national representative samples of the adult population of each respective country. Samples drawn from Egypt ranged in age from 16 to 73, N = 3,000; from Iran the age range of the sample was 15 to 97, N = 2,532; in Jordan age ranged from 18 to 93, N = 1,223, and from the United States age ranged from 18 to 86, N = 1,200. The original version of the questionnaire was formatted in English, and translated into Persian and Arabic; the survey was then translated from Persian and Arabic back into English by translators who had not seen the original English version, and compared with the original survey item by item in order to ensure reliability.

Results

The descriptive statistics for each of the variables for all four nations are presented in table 8.1. Approximately half the number of the sample in

Table 8.1. Means and standard deviations of analytic variables by country

	Egypt (N=3000)		Iran (N=2532)		Jordan (N=1223)		U.S.A. (N=1200)	
	Mean	*SD*	*Mean*	*SD*	*Mean*	*SD*	*Mean*	*SD*
Age	38	(15)	34	(15)	36	(15)	42	(16)
Gender	0.49	(0.50)	0.46	(0.50)	0.51	(0.50)	0.50	(0.50)
Education	0.22	(0.42)	0.49	(0.50)	0.38	(49.00)	0.57	(0.49)
Social class	2.73	(1.02)	2.96	(1.02)	2.89	(0.93)	3.13	(0.93)
Income	6.04	(2.65)	5.03	(1.70)	3.57	(2.08)	5.60	(2.61)
Church attendance	4.29	(2.25)	4.61	(1.45)	3.88	(2.65)	4.55	(2.04)
Perceived control	7.1	(2.50)	6.62	(2.30)	7.26	(2.49)	7.98	(1.83)
Happiness	3.06	(0.57)	2.81	(0.88)	2.91	(0.65)	3.32	(0.61)
Self-rated health	2.79	(0.85)	2.99	(0.81)	3.06	(0.83)	3.23	(0.78)

each country was female. Also presented are the mean scores on perceived control, happiness, and self-rated health. Note that the respondents in the United States report highest ratings on each dimension, followed by Egypt, Jordan, and then Iran. While we do not test for statistical significance due to the limitations of combining data sets from different countries, results nevertheless offer some indication of how these variables are distributed within the populations of interest.

A model of determination is tested against the empirical data from the four countries under investigation. Findings indicate points of divergence and convergence in the determinants of health among these countries. Two interesting findings stand out. First, the countries diverge with respect to the effects of the structural and ritualistic variables on self-rated health. Second, these countries converge with respect to the links between the perceptual variables—perceived control and happiness—and health.

Country Specific Model of Determination

Since there are considerable variations in respect to the effects of structural and ritualistic variables on self-rated health, we first present the result for each country and then we discuss the pattern of relationships that is common to all these countries.

Model for Egypt

Figure 8.1 presents the significant paths (standardized coefficients) resulting from the AMOS analysis. The chi-square/df fit index = 1.47, and the CFI = 1.00. The first and second hypotheses, positing an association between age, gender, education, income, and social class, as well as religiosity, with perceived control, happiness, and self-rated health are partially supported. The resulting AMOS model presenting only those links that emerged as significant consists of the structural variables of age, gender, education, and social class. Income, nor religiosity is significantly related to perceived control, happiness, or self-rated health. Age has a significant effect on perceived control health so that older age is associated with more perceived control ($\beta = -12$). Older age is also associated with lower ratings of health ($\beta = -.31$), a pattern that emerges within all four nations. However, in Egypt gender and education also directly influence health so that being male ($\beta = -.13$) and higher levels of education ($\beta = .07$) are associated with higher ratings of health.

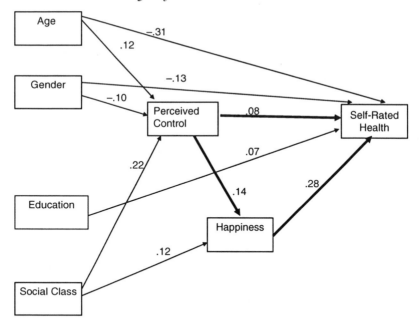

Figure 8.1 Path diagram and standardized structural coefficients for Egypt. Chi-square/df = 16.20/11, CFI = 1.00
Note: All structural coefficients shown are significant at or below *p* < .01.

Indirect influences constitute the remaining pathways between gender, class, and self-rated health. Specifically, gender and class influence self-rated health through perceived control. Sobel test indicates perceived control partially mediates the associations between both gender (x = −2.75, p < .01) and social class (x = 2.93, p < .01) with health (Sobel 1982). That is, gender and class are related to self-rated health because being male and higher social class rankings link to more perceived control, which in turn links to higher self-ratings of health.

Class is also positively associated with happiness. According to the Sobel test, happiness operates as a mediator with regard to social class (x = 6.23, p < .001). Results indicate that while higher social class is associated with higher self-ratings of health, this association is explained by happiness. In effect those of higher social class report higher health status because they report higher levels of happiness.

Model for Iran

In figure 8.2, the path analysis shows results for Iran. The chi-square/df fit index = 1.69, and the CFI = 1.00. The resulting model includes all

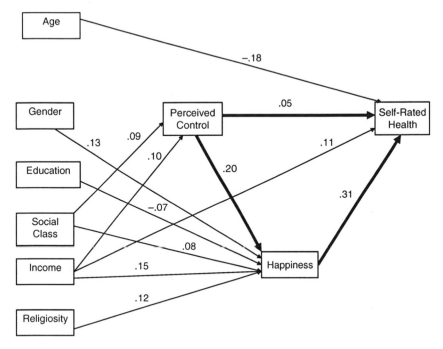

Figure 8.2 Path diagram and standardized structural coefficients for Iran. Chi-square/df = 15.19/9, CFI = 1.00
Note: All structural coefficients shown are significant at or below $p < .01$.

structural variables of age, gender, education, social class, income, and religiosity. Direct influences on self-rated health occurred with regard to age $(\beta = -.18)$, and income $(\beta = .11)$. While those with higher income levels also have higher levels of control, which in turn is associated with higher ratings of health, the indirect effect of income on health via perceived control is not significantly different from zero, and hence no mediation is detected. Social class does not directly influence self-rated health, but does so indirectly through both control and happiness. Those with higher social class are more likely to perceive more control and be happier. Tests for mediation reveal that perceived control does diminish the effect of social class on health status (x = 2.57, p < .01). Results demonstrate that those with higher social class have better health because they perceive more control in their lives.

Gender, education, social class, income, and religiosity each link to happiness levels. That is, being male, having vocational training or less, higher social class rankings, higher income, and more religiosity are related to higher levels of happiness. Happiness partially mediates the associations between income and self-rated health (x = 8.32, p < .001); those who report higher income have better health in part because they are happier.

Model for Jordan

Figure 8.3 presents the path analysis results from Jordan. The chi-square/df fit index = 2.93, and the CFI = .99. The resulting model includes the structural variables of age, gender, social class, and income. Direct influences on self-rated health occurred with regard to age (β = −.34), gender (β = −.14), and social class (β = .17); older age, being male, and higher social class all relate to higher ratings of health. However, in Jordan, indirect effects of age, gender, class, and income on health emerge as well, although the indirect effects are not significantly different from zero, that is, there are no mediation effects. Females who are happy are more likely to report higher self-ratings of health. However, being female is associated with lower levels of perceived control, and lower levels of perceived control are associated with poor

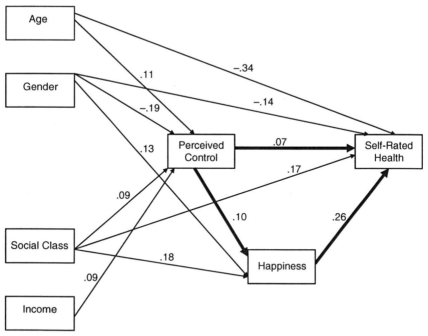

Figure 8.3 Path diagram and standardized structural coefficients for Jordan. Chi-square/df = 26.40/9, CFI = .99

Note: All structural coefficients shown are significant at or below *p* < .01.

health. Social class also links to health through happiness and perceived control. Those with higher social classes are happier and perceived more control over their lives, and higher level of happiness and perceived control link to better health.

Model for United States

Figure 8.4 presents the path analysis results from the United States. The chi-square/df fit index = 2.39, and the CFI = .99. The resulting model includes the structural variables of age, social class, and religiosity. Direct influences on self-rated health occurred with regard to all variables in the model: age ($\beta = -.10$), social class ($\beta = .16$) and religiosity ($\beta = .08$). However, in the United States, indirect effects of class and religiosity on health emerge as well, through happiness, where the indirect effects of

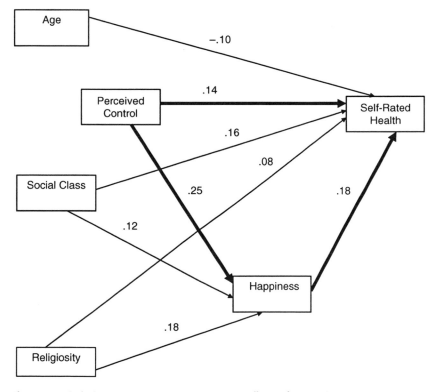

Figure 8.4 Path diagram and standardized structural coefficients for United States. Chi-square/df = 31.04/13, CFI = .99

Note: All structural coefficients shown are significant at or below *p* < .01.

class and religiosity on health via happiness are significantly different from zero. Specifically, higher class (x = 3.26, p < .01) and more religiosity (x = 3.97, p < .001) lead to higher levels of happiness, which then link to higher self-ratings of health. That is, the direct relationships between social class and self-rated health, as well as between religiosity and self-rated health diminishes slightly when happiness is added to the model. These results suggest that those who have higher social class and attend more religious services are healthier, in part, because they are happier. Of significant interest is that none of the structural variables (age, gender, education, social class, income, or religiosity) links to perceived control.

General Determinants of Health

Regarding the effects of structural variables, age consistently had a negative effect on health for all countries; older age is associated with lower self-rated health. Another consistent finding is that higher social class links to higher level of happiness. Additionally, a positive association emerges in Islamic countries between social class and perceived control; higher social class links with higher perceived control, an association not present in the United States.

The effects of gender are interesting by its absence in the case of the United States and presence in Islamic countries. Although there is no gender effect that is common among Islamic countries, where relationships do exist, the links often support the notion of gender hierarchy undermining women's health and perceived control. In Egypt and Jordan, being female is associated with lower self-rated health and perceived control. On the other hand, women are reported to be happier than men in Iran and Jordan.

While the pathways influencing self-rated health vary within each country, a common feature persistent and strong across nations encompasses significant paths between perceived control, happiness, and self-rated health, a well-being triangle that occurs through perceptual measures. In all four countries, perceived control directly links to self-rated health, but perceived control is also connected to self-ratings of health through happiness. That is, the association between perceived control and self-rated health is partially mediated by happiness (see bolded arrows drawn in figures 8.1 through 8.4). Analysis demonstrates that the indirect effect of perceived control on health through happiness is significantly different from zero: Egypt x = 13.67, p < .001; Iran x = 7.65, p < .001; Jordan x = 3.18, p < .01; USA x = 5.34, p < .001. Hence it appears that perceived control partially effects health through the presence of happiness levels, regardless of the country in which one resides.

Discussion

Drawing from the literature on the determinants of health status, this chapter examined the role of two perceptual variables: perceived control and happiness, as potential mediators between structural arrangements and health status in a cross-national context. It is unique in that it focuses on Islamic countries, and contrasts findings to a comparable sample of the U.S. public. Results uncover different associations within each country, but perhaps more striking are the similarities across nations.

We first address the commonalities that emerge from country to country, followed by a discussion of the effects on health within each country that seem to be a function of national specificity. Limitations are discussed, and then implications are presented.

Cross-National Commonalities

The Well-Being Triangle

The most notable results from this study involved the finding that perceptual factors are critical indicators of self-rated health in all four countries. Both perceived control and happiness link to self-rated health so that in Egypt, Iran, Jordan, and the United States higher levels of control and higher levels of happiness are associated with higher self-ratings of health. More specifically, however, within each country the association between perceived control and health diminishes when we introduce happiness into the model. Previous research assumes that perceiving one has control over one's life is always positive (Lachman and Weaver 1998; Ross and Mirowsky 2002). This study provided further support for this finding. Additionally, however, we hypothesized that perceiving control over one's life is also beneficial when it results in happiness. If one perceives control over his/her life and is not content, then perceived control is not necessarily beneficial to well-being. Hence, the association between perceived control and health status occurs through the presence of happiness. This raises the issue of reality defined by perception as opposed to objective criteria. As W.I. Thomas suggested almost 100 years ago, a situation defined as real is real in its consequences. Most of what matters in self-rated health is perception.

Health does not seem to be affected by objectively measured stratification indictors as much as on how well people define their state of mind. Perhaps when people do realize that their location in the social hierarchy has tremendous consequences for their health, it is then that they begin to express themselves politically. These findings point to the power of perceptions in defining reality.

Age

Our analyses demonstrated that on a cross-national level one significant, recurring association emerged between age and self-rated health. Older age is associated with lower ratings of health. This result puts forward the possibility that the aging process may produce similar concerns in Islamic countries as in the United States, and highlights the import of aging as a global issue. In other words, it is not only in the United States that aging implies increased health care concerns. Health status among the elderly is an issue in Islamic countries as well, and so as these nations encounter increasing aged populations, matters of health will be paramount.

Social Class in Islamic Countries

Of significant interest is the consistent statistically significant link between social class and perceived control in Islamic countries, an association that does not emerge in the United States. In fact perceived control mediates the association between social class and health in both Egypt and Iran. Results demonstrate that those with higher social class have better health because they perceive more control in their lives. The association between social class and perceived control may exist because class is more vertical in Islamic countries, where higher class infers more power. For instance, language connotes class differentials in Islamic countries because terminology exists to differentiate those with more status and simultaneously denotes power disparities. Language of familiarity juxtaposed to language of formality constitutes the mode by which communication upholds status differences and hence discrepancies in power (Khuri 1990). In the United States, however, while stratification based on class status remains a reality, it is outwardly minimized in that no specific formal expressions or interaction rituals exist to connote power differentials in everyday relations. It may also be that the "American Dream" or belief that all have the opportunity to move up in class contributes to the belief that class differences are less legitimate.

In other words, the ideal that no one person is better than another because of their class permeates the American value system, and hence produces a perception that power differentials are not shaped by class status.

Education

Of notable absence in these analyses is the lack of association between education and health in all of the countries with the exception of Egypt. Education is considered a reliable and valid measure of stratification, particularly as it relates to health (Liberatos et al. 1988; Ross and Wu 1995). While one may surmise that education does not capture the same processes of stratification in Islamic countries as it does in the West, the fact that education is absent from the model in the United States makes this notion irrelevant. It may be the way in which education was measured, that is respondents indicate the highest degree, as opposed to the number of years, does not capture the variation that exists within each country. Future studies should gather more detailed measures of education to gauge with more precision whether to determine this variable is important in Islamic countries.

Country Specific Pathways

Egypt

Most of what we know with regard to gender and well-being (including health) stems from research conducted in the United States. Gender differences in health generally demonstrates women rating their health poorer than do men (Bisconti and Bergeman 1999; Vingilis et al. 2002). Previous studies suggest that the difference in self reports are tied to social roles and illness behaviors; that is women are more likely to verbalize health problems even though men and women may have similar conditions (Verbrugge 1976, 1989). However, testing whether perceptions mediate the association between gender and health is not often examined. While some studies control for gender while testing whether perceiving control mediates the association between socioeconomic inequalities and health (Bobak et al. 1998, 2000), and others examine how gender relates to perceived control (Ross and Mirowsky 2002), we directly tested for any mediation effects to determine if the effect of gender on health exists because of different levels of control men and women perceive. Only in Egypt is the association between gender and health mediated by a psychosocial variable. While men rate their health higher than do women, this occurs in part because men perceive more control in their lives than do women.

Additionally happiness serves as a mediator between social class and health in Egypt. It is the only Islamic country that demonstrates this pattern, highlighting the divergent ways that people in Islamic countries experience stratification.

Iran

All structural variables of interest play some role in the model predicting self-rated health in Iran. In particular, the numerous associations between structural arrangements and happiness require some explanation. Being female, lower education, higher class, higher income, and more religiosity are all associated with higher levels of happiness in Iran.

Some research addresses gender and happiness cross-nationally, relaying that analyses of happiness rarely detect gender differences within nations (Inglehart 2003). Inglehart (2003) explains this pattern in terms of aspiration adjustments; that is most people adjust and adapt to the advantages or disadvantages incurred during their lifetime. Iran, however, has a recently active feminist movement. As a result, it may be that women's active participation in public life translates into detectable increases in happiness. Research has shown, at least in the United States, that when women participate in the public sphere they become more content (Coontz 1992).

A unique finding is that those with higher education levels tend to be less happy in Iran. One may surmise that this effect emerges from the fact that higher education leads to less satisfaction with the current political situation in Iran, and hence lower levels of happiness. That is, because others (see Inglehart and Klingemann 2000) demonstrate a link between governing structures and happiness levels within nations, the same processes may be at work in Iran. The positive effect of religiosity on happiness also makes sense in Iran, given the religious nature of the government. Those who participate in religious service tend to approve of the existing system than those who do not. As a result, life may be less stressful than for those who are less religious who are probably less supportive of the religious regime.

The positive effect of social class on perceived control and happiness in Iran may be due to the high correlation between income and social class. Naturally, when one's subjective class position is consistent (that is, highly correlated) with his/her income that person would feel less status inconsistency and objective reinforcement (income) of his/her subjective class assignment. The significant effects of income on control, happiness, and health may also be due to the relatively high correlation between income and class.

Jordan

In Jordan, there emerge no mediation effects of perceived control or happiness. However, the structural variables of gender, class, and income are significantly associated with perceived control. Being male, higher social class, and higher income link to higher levels of control. Also, being female and higher social class link to higher levels of happiness. These findings may reflect the recent economic changes in Jordan. Jordanian men now often find employment in Gulf countries (i.e., Oman, Kuwait, Saudi Arabia), sojourning and leaving women alone for long periods of time. Gender differences in happiness may reflect this pattern in that women enjoy temporary stretches of time without the responsibility of caring for their husbands. That is, we are able to detect different happiness levels between men and women within a country due to recent economic arrangements of Gulf employment. Furthermore, Jordan is the only nation in this study that experiences open trade with the United States. Increased money from employment in Gulf countries along with open trade relations with the United States. highlights the import of income. The influx of money from these arrangements may explain why income emerges as important in Jordan.

United States

The United States presents a distinct situation in that perceived control does not operate as a mediator between structural arrangements and health, but happiness does. The direct relationships between social class and self-rated health, as well as between religiosity and self-rated health diminish slightly when happiness is added to the model. Recent findings suggest that the association between structural arrangements and health status occurs through psychosocial factors such as perceived control, with the bulk of such findings coming out of Europe and the United States (Bisconti and Bergeman 1999; Bobak et al. 1998; Bosma et al. 1999; Lachman and Weaver 1998; Marmot et al. 1998). Notably, our findings do not demonstrate that perceived control functions as a mediator between structural variables and health status in the United States; indeed none of the structural variables analyzed in the U.S. sample links to perceived control. This finding invites a rethinking about perceived control, and how it relates to health status.

On the other hand, happiness partially mediates the association between social class and health. Higher social class is associated with more happiness, which then reduces the amount of explained variance class has on health. The link between class and happiness may again reflect the nature of the class structure in the United States, which deemphasizes power relations and instead emphasizes happiness in the sense of attaining the materialistic comforts of the American dream. In other words, higher social class signifies having "made it" or having acquired the status of the upper middle class that lacks any real power, but may be able to afford the home, car, and vacation opportunities to which they aspire.

Notably, only in the United States do we find a significant association between religiosity and self-rated health, which is partially mediated through happiness. This fact may point to the differences in the role and function of religion between the United States and Islamic countries. Based on these findings, one may suggest that in the United States, religion appears to be part of individual identity as a process, whereby individuals rationally assess, rethink, seek, and negotiate their relationships with diverse religious choices available to them. In the Islamic context, on the other hand, religion appears to be part of the structure (organized body of information) of individual identity. People follow religion because it is part of the structure of their society, without religion having the kind of utilitarian functions that might have motivated individuals in the United States to seek religious benefits (staying healthier and happier). This finding is note-worthy because while religion often shapes social structural positions and seems to underpin many social movements in the Islamic countries under study (Moaddel 2002a, 2002b), it does not emerge as key to well-being as indicated by self-ratings of health in Egypt, Iran, or Jordan. Conversely, religion is a private matter in the United States, absent from public encounters as the United States strives to maintain separation between church and state. It may be that because religion is officially absent from politics in the United States that it serves as a source of comfort and hence relates to happiness levels as well as to self-defined health status.

Implications

Theoretical developments suggest that factors influencing health, such as social position hierarchies, are mediated by perceived control. We pro-pose that while perceived control undoubtedly affects health, it does so through the presence of happiness. Perceiving control over one's life may produce both positive and negative results. For instance, if one perceives control over one's life, but then is unable to influence life-events in a desired manner, frustration and stress may arise. On the other hand, if life events operate in the desired manner when one perceives control over such happenings then we may suppose that the result is happiness, which then influences self-ratings of health. Of significance is the consistent finding between perceived control, happiness, and self-rated health. In all four models results demonstrate that perceived control exerts both a direct and indirect (through happiness) effect on health.

Applying social science theory and method to the countries of the Middle East offers many advantages—however, some limitations to this study and caveats to interpretation of results should be noted. The first is the cross-sectional nature of the data, which prohibits making causal inferences about the mutual effects of perceived control, happiness, and self-rated health. The second is the need to conduct more comparative studies, where Islamic societies are compared to non–Islamic societies. Follow-up studies should consider the rapidly changing norms in Middle Eastern societies, particularly with the globalization of economies, and its potential impact on stratification systems within each country.

While limitations are present in this study, it nevertheless provides critical empirical evidence on Islamic countries, and how they differ from and converge with their American counterpart. The inclusion of happiness as a principal variable in the search to uncover the role of psychosocial factors in health status furthermore enhances theoretical understandings of social processes and how structural positions impinge on well-being generally. In sum, results point to new areas of inquiry for further research and continued theoretical refinement of the psychosocial process by which well-being emerges.

Note

1. Direct correspondence to Kristine J. Ajrouch (KAjrouch@emich.edu) and Mansoor Moaddel (MMoaddel@emich.edu), Department of Sociology, Anthropology, and Criminology, Eastern Michigan University, Ypsilanti, MI 48197. This study has been supported by Grants from The National Science Foundation (SES-0097282) the Ford Foundation, and Bank of Sweden Tercentenary Foundation, and the National Institute of Aging (R03 AG19388-01).

References

Ai, Amy L., Ruth Dunkle, Christopher Peterson, and Steven Bolling. 1998. "The Role of Private Prayer in Psychological Recovery Among Midlife and Aged Patients Following Cardiac Surgery." *The Gerontologist* 38(5): 591–601.

Alexander, Bobby C. 1991. "Correcting Misinterpretations of Turner's Theory: An African-American Pentecostal Illustration." *Journal for the Scientific Study of Religion* 30(1): 26–44.

Angel, Ronald and William Gronfein. 1988. "The Use of Subjective Information in Statistical Models." *American Sociological Review* 53(3): 464–73.

Arbuckle, James L. 1995. *Amos for Windows. Analysis of moment structures (Version 3.5).* Chicago, IL: Small Waters.

Barer, Barbara M. 1994. "Men and Women Aging Differently." *International Journal of Aging and Human Development* 38(1): 29–40.

Beblawi, Hazem.1987. "The Rentier State in the Arab World." In *The Rentier State*, edited by Hazem Beblawi and Luciani Giacomo, pp. 49–62. London: Croom Helm.

Benson, Herbert. 1997. *Timeless Healing.* New York: Fireside.

Benyamini, Yael, Ellen. L Idler, Howard Leventhal, and Elaine A. Leventhal. 2000. "Positive Affect and Function as Influences on Self-Assessments of Health: Expanding our View beyond Illness and Disability." *Journals of Gerontology* 55B(2): 107–16.

Bisconti, Toni. L. and Cindy S Bergeman. 1999 "Perceived Control as a Mediator of the Relationships among Social Support, Psychological Well-Being and Perceived Health." *The Gerontologist* 39(1): 94–103.

Bobak, Martin, Hynek Pikhart, Clyde Hertzman, Richard Rose, and Michael M. Marmot. 1998. "Socioeconomic Factors, Perceived Control and Self-Reported Health in Russia: A Cross-Sectional Survey." *Social Science and Medicine* 47: 269–79.

Bobak, Martin, Hynek Pikhart, Richard Rose, Clyde Hertzman, and Michael M. Marmot 2000. "Socioeconomic Factors, Material Inequalities, and Perceived Control in Self-Rated Health: Cross-Sectional Data from Seven Post-Communist Countries." *Social Science and Medicine* 51(9): 1343–50.

Bosma, Hans, Carola Schrijvers, and Johan P. Mackenbach. 1999. "Socioeconomic Inequalities in Mortality and Importance of Perceived Control: Cohort Study." *British Medical Journal* 319(7223): 1469–70.

Brynen, Rex. 1992. "Economic Crisis and Post-Rentier Democratization in the Arab World: The Case of Jordan." *Canadian Journal of Political Science* 25(1): 69–97.

Burch, Druin. 2001. "Health Promotion." *The Lancet* 358(9285): 936.

Carlson, Per. 1998. "Self-Perceived Health in East and West Europe: Another European Health Divide." *Social Science and Medicine* 46(10): 1355–66.

Carroll, Stephanie. 1991. "Spirituality and Purpose in Life in Alcoholism Recovery." *Journal of Studies of Alcohol* 54(3): 297–301.

Coontz, Stephanie. 1992. *The Way We Never Were: American Families and the Nostalgia Trap.* New York: Basic Books.

Francis, Leslie J., Susan H. Jones, and Carolyn Wilcox. 2000. "Religion and Happiness: During Adolescence, Young Adulthood and Later Life." *Journal of Psychology and Christianity* 19(3): 245–57.

Francis, Leslie J. and Michael T. Stubbs. 1987. "Measuring Attitudes Towards Christianity: From Childhood to Adulthood." *Personality and Individual Differences* 8(5): 741–43.

Gerdtham, Ulf-G and Magnus Johannesson. 2001. "The Relationship between Happiness, Health, and Socio-Economic Factors: Results Based on Swedish Microdata." *The Journal of Socio-Economics* 30(6): 553–57.

House, James S., James M. Lepkowski, Ann M. Kinney, R. P. Mero, Ronald C. Kessler, and A. Regula Herzog. 1994. "The Social Stratification of Aging and Health." *Journal of Health and Social Behavior* 35(3): 213–34.

Idler, Ellen L. and Stanislav V. Kasl. 1995. "Self-Ratings of Health: Do They Also Predict Change in Functional Ability?" *Journals of Gerontology* 50B(6): S344–53.

Inglehart, Ronald F. 2003. "Gender, Aging and Well-being." In *Islam, Gender, Culture and Democracy: Findings from the Values Surveys*, edited by Ronald Inglehart, pp. 391–408. Willowdale, ON: De Sitter Publications. 2003.

Inglehart, Ronald F. and Hans-Dieter Klingemann. 2000. "Genes, Culture, Democracy, and Happiness." In *Subjective Well-Being across Cultures*, edited by Ed Deiner and Eunkook M. Suh, pp. 165–83. Cambridge, MA: MIT Press.

Janevic, Mary R., Kristine J. Ajrouch, Alicia Tarnowski, Hiroko Akiyama, and Toni C. Antonucci. 2000. "The Social Relations-Physical Health Connection: A Comparison of Elderly Samples from the United States and Japan." *The Journal of Health Psychology* 5(4): 413–29.

Khuri, Fouad I. 1990. *Tents and Pyramids*. London: Saqi Books.

King, Michael, Peter Speck, and Angela Thomas. 1999. "The Effect of Spiritual Beliefs on Outcome from Illness," *Social Science and Medicine* 48(9): 1291–99.

Krause, Neil M. and Gina M. Jay. 1994. "What Do Global Self-Rated Health Items Measure?" *Medical Care* 32(9): 930–42.

Lachman, Marjorie. E. and Suzanne L. Weaver. 1998. "The Sense of Control as a Moderator of Social Class Differences in Health and Well-Being." *Journal of Personal and Social Psychology* 74(3): 763–73.

Levin, Jeffrey. 1996. "How Religion Influences Morbidity and Health: Reflections on Natural History, Salutogenesis and Host Resistance." *Social Science and Medicine* 43(5): 849–64.

Lewis, Christopher A. 2002. "Church Attendance and Happiness Among Northern Irish Undergraduate Students: No Association." *Pastoral Psychology* 50(3): 191–95.

Liberatos, Peggy, Bruce G. Link, and Jennifer L. Kelsey. 1988. "The Measurement of Social Class in Epidemiology." *Epidemiological Reviews* 10(1): 87–121.

Luciani, Giacomo. 1988 "Economic Foundations of Democracy and Authoritarianism: The Arab World in Comparative Perspective." *Arab Studies Quarterly* 10(4): 457–75.

Marmot, Michael G. 2003. "Understanding Social Inequalities in Health." *Perspectives in Biology and Medicine* 46(3): S9–23.

Marmot, Michael G., Rebecca Fuhrer, Susan L. Ettner, Nadine F. Marks, Larry L. Bumpass, and Carol D. Ryff. 1998. "Contribution of Psychosocial Factors to Socioeconomic Differences in Health." *The Millbank Quarterly* 76(3): 403–48.

Moaddel, Mansoor. 2002a. *Jordanian Exceptionalism: An Analysis of State-Religion Relationship in Egypt, Iran, Jordan, and Syria*. New York: Palgrave.

———. 2002b. "The Study of Islamic Culture and Politics: An Overview and Assessment." *Annual Review of Sociology* 28: 359–86.

Moaddel, Mansoor and Taqhi Azadarmaki. 2002. "The World Views of Islamic Publics: The Cases of Egypt, Iran, and Jordan." *Comparative Sociology* 1(3–4): 299–319.

Pearlin, Leonard. 1992. "Structure and Meaning in Medical Sociology." *Journal of Health and Social Behavior* 33(1): 1–9.

Robbins, Mandy and Leslie J. Francis. 1996. Are Religious People Happier?: A Study among Undergraduates." In *Research in Religious Education*, edited by Leslie J. Francis, William K. Kay, and William S. Campbell, pp 207–17. Leominster: Gracewing.

Rogers, Mary A. M. and Emily Zaragoza-Lao. 2003. "Happiness and Children's Health: An Investigation of Art, Entertainment, and Recreation." *American Journal of Public Health* 93(2): 288–89.

Ross, Catherine E. and John Mirowsky. 2002. "Age and the Gender Gap in the Sense of Personal Control." *Social Psychology Quarterly* 65(2): 125–45.

Ross, Catherine E. and Marieke Van Willigen. 1997. "Education and the Subjective Quality of Life." *Journal of Health and Social Behavior* 38: 275–97.

Ross, Catherine E. and Chia-Ling Wu. 1995. "The Links between Education and Health." *American Sociological Review* 60: 719–45.

Sastry, Jaya and Catherine E. Ross. 1998. "Asian Ethnicity and Sense of Personal Control." *Social Psychological Quarterly* 61(2): 101–20.

Sobel, Michael E. 1982. "Asymptotic Intervals for Indirect Effects in Structural Equation Models." In *Sociological Methodology*, edited by Samuel Leinhart, pp. 290–312. San Francisco: Jossey-Bass.

Skevington, Suzanne M. 1997. "Developing Items for the WHOQOL: An Investigation of Contemporary Beliefs about Quality of Life Related to Health in Britain." *British Journal of Health Psychology* 2(1): 55–72.

Smith, James. P. and Raynard S. Kington. 1997. "Race, Socioeconomic Status, and Health in Late Life." In *Racial and Ethnic Differences in the Health of Older Americans*, edited by Linda G. Martin and Beth J. Soldo, pp. 106–61. Washington DC: National Academic Press.

Spiers, Nicola, Carol Jagger, Michael Clarke, and Antony Arthur. 2003. "Are Gender Differences in the Relationship between Self-Rated Health and Mortality Enduring? Results from Three Birth Cohorts in Melton Mowbray, United Kingdom." *Gerontologist* 43(3): 406–11.

Stack, Steven and J. Ross Eshleman. 1998. "Marital Status and Happiness: A 17 Nation Study." *Journal of Marriage and Family* 60(2): 527–36.

Thomas, William. I. and Dorothy S. Thomas. 1928. *The Child in America*. New York: Knopf.

Turner, Victor. 1967. *The Forest of Symbols: Aspects of Ndembu Ritual*. Ithaca, NY: Cornell University Press.

Veenhoven, Ruut. 1988. "The Utility of Happiness." *Social Indicators Research* 20(4): 333–54.

Verbrugge, Lois. 1976. "Sex Differentials in Morbidity and Mortality in the U.S." *Social Biology* 23(4): 275–96.

———. 1985. "Gender and Health: An Update on Hypotheses and Evidence." *Journal of Health and Social Behavior* 26(3): 156–82.

———. 1989. "The Twain Meet: Empirical Explanations of Sex Differences in Health and Mortality." *Journal of Health and Social Behavior* 30(3): 282–304.

Vingilis, Evelyn R., Terrance J. Wade, and Jane S. Seeley. 2002. "Predictors of Adolescent Self-Rated Health: Analysis of the National Population Health Survey." *Canadian Journal of Public Health* 93(3): 193–97.

CHAPTER 9

The Saudi Public Speaks: Religion, Gender, and Politics

MANSOOR MOADDEL[1]

Introduction

The fact that 15 of the 19 terrorists who attacked the World Trade Center and the Pentagon on September 11, 2001 were Saudi citizens inevitably raised serious questions about the social conditions that have produced such violent personalities capable of the mass taking of innocent lives and devastating an entire city, if not a nation. Answers were quick to come by, as the U.S. media pointed to the Saudi culture. Charges were made that the youth were brainwashed by the most extremist school in Islam, namely, Wahhabism. The Saudi educational institutions were also blamed for promoting anti-Semitism, anti-Western attitudes, and intolerance of other religions. Saudi society was also condemned for having a corrupt and backward political system. Naturally, in this land of intolerance and authoritarianism, resorting to violence by its inhabitants became a foregone conclusion (Baer 2003; Gold 2003; Schwartz 2002).

Recent scholarly studies have provided a more balanced picture of the cultural forces operating in the kingdom. However, there is little knowledge of how Saudis view the significant issues facing their society. We fill this void by analyzing the value orientations of Saudi citizens toward such key issues as the form of government, religion, religious tolerance,

gender relations, marriage, and Western culture, using the findings of
the values survey that was carried out in the kingdom in 2003. We also
use the results of similar values surveys in Egypt, Iran, Jordan, and the
United States to assess the similarities and differences in value orientations
between Saudi citizens and the public of these countries.

Furthermore, focusing on such key organizing principles of the kingdom as religion, gender, and politics, we try to explain religiosity and
attitudes toward women and democracy. What are the major factors that
affect the religiosity of the Saudi public? What is the connection
between religiosity and gender? To what extent does gender affect variations in daily prayer and mosque attendance? How does one explain
attitudes toward polygamy and the norm of wife obedience? Does education promote religiosity? Is there a connection between religiosity and
attitudes toward gender inequality? How are variations in attitudes
toward democracy related to variations in other attitudes and nonattitudinal characteristics of the respondents? Finally, are the extant sociological generalizations that are based on the experiences of the West
applicable to Saudi society?

In drawing from sociological models to explain the worldviews of
Saudis, we pay particular attention to Saudi Arabia's specific national and
historical context. We depart from the modernization perspective that
presumes societies as instances of a universal process of modernization,
secularization, and value generalization. We also abandon the postulate
that people's culture is shaped by the society's location in the hierarchically organized structure of the world capitalist system and the external
dictates of the world economy (although we concede that the rentier
economy to a degree has shaped the public's worldviews). Although we
use general variables to explain Saudis' value orientations, the linkages
among these variables are interpreted in terms of the country's specific
historical context in which these variables are embedded.

State Formation, Economic Development,

and Cultural Change

The incorporation of the disparate regions of the Hijaz, Asir, Hasa, and
Najd into the unified kingdom of Saudi Arabia in 1932 resulted in the
emergence of a new political community shaped by the military and religious alliance that in the span of thirty years (1902–32) brought Abd
al-Aziz ibn Abd al-Rahman al-Saudi, the founder of the kingdom, to
power. Key in the success of al-Saud was not only the effectiveness of the

ikhwan tribal warriors who supported him and a favorable international environment, but also his alliance with the Wahhabi movement whose *mutawwa'a* volunteers played a crucial role in legitimizing his rule, domesticating the population in the name of Islam and enforcing Saudi authority under the guise of a vigorous program to convert the people of Arabia to "true" Islam (al-Rasheed 2002; Okruhlik 2002). However, the necessity to establish order and finance state bureaucracy prompted Saudi rulers to engage in shifting coalitions with influential groups and social classes in different periods in the twentieth century.

In this process, the material foundations, institutional constructs, and ideational system of the autonomous nomadic tribes, the tribal armies, the guilds, and the smaller merchants who were instrumental in al Saud's success but later became antithetical to administrative centralization and the formation of national markets were destroyed. Instead, a business–government coalition between the Hijazi commercial elites and the Nejdi rulers was formed. The 1970s oil boom freed the government from the political constraints that naturally come with taxation and set the stage for another major shift in the state-society relations. The state's new spending, favoring the Nejdi commercial interests, precipitated the decline of the traditional merchant class. As a result, many old Hijazi merchant families disappeared into the ranks of retailers. The decline in the importance of the Jeddah Chamber of Commerce and the rise of the Riyadh chamber reflected the dissolution of the 1960s pact between the state and the traditional commercial elite. Each shift in state-class/group relations resulted in the narrowing of the social basis of the state (Chaudhry 1997).

Parallel with the changes in state–society relations were such structural changes as the state's bureaucratic expansion, occupational differentiation, sedentarization of tribes, urbanization, demographic growth, and impressive rates of economic development, which was made possible by the availability of vast petrodollars. The speed of change was particularly striking in the past decades of the twentieth century. The kingdom's population of 5 million in 1974 jumped to 12 million in 1992 (Krimly 1999), reaching an estimated 24 million in 2002, including 6 million foreigners (ICG 2004). A staggering part of this change is the high rate of urbanization; the urban population jumped from 16 percent of the total population in 1950 to 49 percent in 1970 and 80 percent in 1990. Riyadh underwent an even more spectacular growth. From a population of 88,000 in 1950, the city grew to 667,000 in 1974, reaching 3 million in 1997 (Krimly 1999) At the same time, the nomadic population dropped from being the majority earlier in the past century to between 5 percent and 25 percent of the population by 1993 (Champion 2003) The gross domestic product, also jumped from almost 23 million Saudi rials (SR) in 1970 to 547 million SR in 1997 (Krimly 1999). Driving the engine of the Saudi economy, the oil boom of the 1970s brought an unprecedented fortune to the kingdom (Champion 2003).

These structural changes coupled with the vulnerability of the single-commodity export economy to fluctuations in oil prices and demands in the world market,[2] the rising economic inequality,[3] and the monolithic religious discourse imposed on society by the official clerics set the stage for the rise of diverse political and cultural movements in the kingdom. Among them, two opposing groups came into the limelight, vying for the cultural control of the Saudi society. One group adhered to an Islamic awakening (al-Sahwa al-Islamiyya) and demanded the reorganization of the kingdom on the virtuous Islamic state that they believed had existed under the Prophet and the Rashidun caliphate. The other was the liberals and reformers, who called for a substantial restructuring of the country's social and political life, the establishment of a constitutional monarchy, elected institutions, separation of power, freedom of expression, egalitarian gender relations,[4] and recognition of the rights of the Shi 'i minority (Dekmejian 1994, 2003; Okruhlik 2002; al-Rasheed 1998).

The regime responded to these developments by first attempting to coach and coopt Islamic activists. Following the 1979 Mecca incident, where Muslim militants led by Juhaiman al-Utaibi forcibly took control of the sacred mosque (Okruhlik 2002), it allocated large sums of money to the religious institutions, increased mosque construction, reinforced the Islamic content of the schools' curricula, and further empowered the religious police. By 1986, more than 16,000 of the kingdom's 100,000 students were enrolled in Islamic studies, and by the early 1990s, one-quarter of all university students were studying in religious institutions (Okruhlik 2002; Prokop, 2003). One unintended result was the rise of a new generation of shaykhs and professors, who were sympathetic to al-Sahwa, incensed by the subservience of the official clerics, and denounced the state's failure to live up to Islamic values (ICG 2004). The regime also initiated some measures of reforms, which after 9/11 were somewhat expanded as a result of pressure from abroad. These included announcing the members of the Shura council in 1993; the expansion of its membership from 60 to 90 in 1997; the crown prince's decision to meet with reformers and to sponsor three rounds of national dialogue on religion, extremism and moderation, and women in 2003; and the Council of Ministers' issuance of a decree allowing women to obtain commercial licenses in their own names (Dekmejian 1998; Fandy 1999; ICG 2004; Layish 1987).

These events are indicative of the changes that were transpiring in the kingdom, but we know little about how Saudis view these changes. How religious are Saudis compared to the citizens of other Islamic countries? Is there considerable support for the conservative religious establishment? Are women more religious than men in the kingdom? In what terms, religious or nationalist, do Saudi citizens define their identity? What are the attitudes of Saudis toward religious authorities, gender relations, marriage, and democracy?

Values Surveys in Egypt, Iran, Jordan, and Saudi Arabia

Comprehensive values surveys of national representative samples of 3,000 Egyptian, 2,532 Iranian, 1,224 Jordanian, and 1,526 Saudi adults were carried out in 2001–03.[5] Except for some modifications and omissions of items due to the national context, an identical questionnaire was used for the four Islamic countries. The surveys in Egypt, Iran, and Jordan were completed in 2001 and in Saudi Arabia in 2003. All these surveys were based on face-to-face interviews. For illustration, we also present the findings of the values survey of a national representative sample of 1,200 American adults, which was carried out in the United States in 2000.[6]

The pan-Arab Research Center carried out the survey in Saudi Arabia using a multistage probability sampling procedure. The sample included 1,026 Saudi citizens and 500 foreign residents and equal number of men and women. The respondents were selected randomly from the northern, southern, central, eastern, and western regions, including Jeddah, Taif, Makkah, Riyadh, Qassim, Hail, Dammam/Khobar, Abha/Khamis, and al-Madinah. The households were the final sampling units, from which respondents were randomly selected. In terms of age, 29 percent were 15–24 years old, 29 percent were 25–34, 27 percent were 35–44, 11 percent were 45–54, and 4 percent were 55 or older. The majority of the respondents identified themselves as members of either the upper middle class (48 percent) or the lower middle class (34 percent); the rest identified themselves as upper class (10 percent) or working or lower class (8 percent). In terms of education, 80 percent of the respondents had less than a university education whereas 20 percent had a university education.

One of the objectives of these comparative values surveys was to understand the value orientations of the Islamic publics toward some of the same sociopolitical and cultural issues that were also points of contention and debate among Muslim intellectual leaders in the modern period. Included among these issues were (1) the role of religion in society; (2) the social status of women; (3) form of government; (4) national identity; and (5) the relationship with the outside world, most notably, the Western countries (Boullata 1990; Enayat 1982; Hourani 1983; Laroui 1976; Moaddel 2005; Sharabi 1970).

Religion and Religiosity

Religious beliefs are widespread among the respondents in all four countries. Among Saudis, 99 percent said that they were Muslim and 1 percent said they were Christian or Hindu. Among Egyptians, 94 percent said they were Muslim, and 6 percent said they were Christian. These figures for Jordan were 95 percent and 5 percent, and for Iran they were 97 percent and 1 percent, respectively. At least 94 percent of all respondents said that they believed in all of the following: God, life after death, the existence of the soul, heaven, and hell. Fully 90 percent of Saudi citizens said that religion was very important in their lives, as did 97 percent of Egyptians, 96 percent of Jordanians, and 79 percent of Iranians.

Although the Islamic publics are unanimous in terms of these basic religious beliefs, they display variations in terms of self-described religiosity, participation in religious services, attachment to religious or national identity, and attitudes toward religious authorities. On many of these measures, the Saudi public appears to be less religious than either Egyptians or Jordanians.

Self-Described Religiosity

According to table 9.1, a lower percentage of Saudis (62 percent) described themselves as religious than Iranians (82 percent), Jordanians (85 percent), Egyptians (98 percent), or even Americans (81 percent). There may be cross-national differences in the meaning of being religious. In the United States, in particular, there is a strong tradition of religious pluralism and the meaning of religiosity varies across diverse groups in the country. As a result, Americans may have a different conception of religiosity and lower emotional attachments to religious beliefs than the Islamic publics. The extent to which the yardstick of religiosity in the kingdom is different from that in the other Islamic countries is hard to tell. However, the magnitude of the difference in self-described religiosity between Saudis, on the one hand, and Iranians, Jordanians, and Egyptians, on the other hand, is significant and thus warrants a reexamination of the prevalent perception of Saudi Arabia as a very conservative and religious society.

Table 9.1 Religion and Religiosity: Self-described religiosity, religious authorities, mosque attendance, and identity

	Saudi Arabia			Iran			Jordan			Egypt			United States		
	Male	Female	Total	Male	Female	Total	Male	Female	Total	Male	Female	Total	Male	Female	Total
Independently of whether you go to religious services or not, would you say you are:															
A religious person	63%	62%	62%	83%	82%	82%	75%	94%	85%	98%	99%	99%	76%	86%	81%
Not a religious person	26%	31%	28%	4%	2%	3%	24%	5%	14%	2%	1%	1%	20%	11%	16%
A convinced atheist	0%	0%	0%	1%	1%	1%	0%	0%	0%	0%	0%	0%	2%	1%	1%
Participation in religious services: Apart from weddings, funerals, and baptisms, about how often do you attend religious services these days?															
More than once a week	17%	8%	13%	12%	11%	12%	56%	2%	28%	23%	22%	22%	13%	20%	16%
Once a week	25%	6%	15%	16%	13%	15%	24%	8%	16%	19%	20%	20%	24%	33%	29%
Less than once a week	58%	86%	72%	68%	72%	70%	20%	90%	56%	55%	55%	58%	63%	47%	55%
NA/ DK	0%	0%	0%	4%	4%	4%	0%	0%	0%	0%	0%	0%	0%	0%	0%
Religious authorities give adequate answers to social problems.															
Yes	67%	67%	67%	45%	49%	47%	53%	66%	60%	77%	82%	79%	40%	47%	43%
No	20%	21%	21%	33%	25%	29%	40%	26%	33%	20%	14%	17%	55%	48%	51%
NA/ DK	13%	11%	12%	22%	27%	24%	7%	8%	8%	3%	5%	4%	6%	6%	6%
Religious versus national identity															
Above all, I am a Muslim.	76%	73%	75%	58%	64%	61%	69%	75%	72%	78%	81%	79%	NA	NA	NA
Above all, I am a Saudi, Iranian, Jordanian, or Egyptian.	18%	16%	17%	37%	31%	34%	19%	11%	15%	10%	9%	10%	NA	NA	NA
Above all, I am an Arab.	7%	10%	9%	0%	0%	0%	10%	8%	9%	1%	1%	1%	NA	NA	NA
Above all, I am Palestinian.	0%	0%	0%	0%	0%	0%	3%	7%	5%	0%	0%	0%	NA	NA	NA
Other	0%	1%	0%	5%	5%	5%	0%	0%	0%	11%	9%	10%	NA	NA	NA
Above all, I am a Muslim.	76%	73%	75%	58%	64%	61%	69%	75%	72%	78%	81%	79%	NA	NA	NA
Total	517	509	1026	1361	1171	2532	594	630	1224	1540	1460	3000	600	600	1200

Note: All values are percentages; DK, don't know; NA, not available.

In terms of gender differences, if we consider 5 percent difference as significant, except in Jordan and the United States, men and women do not differ significantly in self-described religiosity. In Jordan, a much higher percentage of female respondents (94 percent) described themselves as religious than male respondents (75 percent). These figures for the United States were 86 percent and 76 percent, respectively.

Participation in Religious Services versus Daily Prayers

Mosque attendance in Saudi Arabia in comparison with other countries further reinforces the conclusion that Saudis are not necessarily more religious than the publics of other Islamic countries. Only 13 percent of Saudi citizens indicated that they attended mosques more than once a week. This figure was 12 percent for Iranians, 28 percent for Jordanians, and 22 percent for Egyptians. As table 9.1 shows, both Iranian and Saudi publics did not attend mosques as often as the citizens of the other two Islamic countries. Among Americans, 16 percent indicated that they attended church more than once per week.

There are gender differences in mosque attendance cross-nationally. In Saudi Arabia and Jordan, mosque attendance was significantly higher among men than among women. That is, 17 percent of men and 8 percent of women in Saudi Arabia and 56 percent of men and 2 percent of women in Jordan indicated that they attended mosques more than once a week. For Egypt and Iran, there was no significant gender difference; for the United States, once again, significantly more women (20 percent) than men (13 percent) attended church more than once a week.

Considering daily prayer, Saudis were more religious than Iranians. About 87 percent of the Saudi public indicated that they perform the five daily prayers, whereas this figure for Iranians dropped to 48 percent. This question was not included in the Egyptian and Jordanian surveys. If religiosity is measured in terms of daily prayer, women were more religious than men in Saudi Arabia, as 82 percent of men and 92 percent of women indicated that they prayed five times daily. For Iranians, these figures were 49 percent and 46 percent, respectively. Therefore, there is no significant gender difference among them (not shown in table 9.1).

Attitudes toward Religious Authorities

A large percentage of the Islamic publics affirmed that religious authorities adequately responded to people's spiritual needs, moral problems, family needs, and social problems. For example, in reference to social problems, religious authorities enjoyed the greatest support among Egyptians, as 79 percent indicated that these authorities respond adequately to social problems. This figure for the Saudi, Jordanian, Iranian, and American publics were 67 percent, 60 percent, 47 percent, and 43 percent, respectively. There was no significant gender difference in attitudes toward religious authorities in Saudi Arabia and Iran. However, there were such differences in Jordan (66 percent of women versus 53 percent of men), Egypt (82 percent of women versus 77 percent of men), and in the United States (47 percent of women versus 40 percent of men). Here again, 5 percent or more difference is considered significant.

Religious versus National Identity

Saudis consider religion as the most important element of their identity. In terms of adherence to territorial nationalism, however, they are more nationalist than Egyptians, as nationalist as Jordanians, and less nationalist than Iranians: 75 percent of Saudis defined themselves as Muslims above all; whereas 17 percent defined themselves as Saudis above all, compared with 61 percent and 34 percent for Iranians; 72 percent and 15 percent for Jordanians; and 79 percent and 10 percent for Egyptians, respectively. It is noteworthy that Arab identity among the three Arab countries is weak. Less than 9 percent of the Saudi and Jordanian publics defined themselves as Arabs above all, but this figure for Egyptians was only 1 percent. It thus appears that after religion, territorial nationalism is the distant second-most important component of identity for the publics of these countries.

There are some variations in identity among men and women. While more female than male respondents for Iran (64 percent versus 58 percent), Jordan (75 percent versus 69 percent), and Egypt (81 percent versus 78 percent) defined themselves as Muslims above all, in Saudi Arabia, it was just the opposite: more men than women (76 percent versus 73 percent) defined themselves as such. The gender difference for Egypt and Saudi Arabia, however, is not significant.

In self-described religiosity, mosque attendance, and to some extent identity, Saudis are less religious than Egyptians or Jordanians. They are more like Iranians than their Arab counterparts. This is astonishing given that the kingdom is officially a religious state, the Islamic way of life is rigorously enforced by the religious police, school curricula are heavily loaded with religious education, and Wahhabi thought has maintained a strong grip on religious institutions (Prokop 2003). This apparently inverse correlation between the religiosity of the state and the religiosity of the public may lend credence to a theory in the sociology religion that proposes that religious pluralism is the natural state of religion and when the state becomes involved in religious affairs and imposes a monolithic religious discourse on the public from above, the overall religiosity of the public declines (Bainbridge 1995; Finke and Stark 1988; Iannaccone 1991). It is thus little wonder that like Iranians, the religious nature of the state has made Saudi citizens less religious instead of making them more so. Egypt and Jordan, by contrast, are ruled by secular governments. Yet, their publics appear to be more religious than the Iranian or Saudi public.

Furthermore, considering gender differences in religiosity among the five countries, we can conclude that, among the U.S. public, women tend to be consistently more religious than men in terms of self-described religiosity, participation in religious services, and attitudes toward religious authorities. In contrast, among the four Islamic countries, gender differences do not follow a consistent pattern. Gender differences are both specific to the country and depend on the question asked. However, the notion that women are generally more religious than men, although perhaps true in the United States, is not supported by the findings from these four Islamic countries.

Attitudes toward Democracy

The survey questionnaire carried several items to measure the respondents' attitudes toward democracy. One of these items refers to democracy as an ideal system of government. Among the Saudi respondents, despite the rejection of democracy by both the Saudi rulers and clerics, a clear majority expressed favorable attitudes toward democracy, as 58 percent espoused the view that democracy is the best form of government, compared with 23 percent who disagreed. These figures were 42 percent and 19 percent for Iran; 75 percent and 9 percent for Jordan; 91 percent and 2 percent for Egypt; and 85 percent and 12 percent for the United States.

The findings also show that except for Egypt, Saudi Arabia, and the United States, there are significant gender differences in attitudes toward democracy among the Iranian (45 percent of men versus 38 percent of women) and Jordanian (80 percent of men versus 72 percent of women) publics. We may thus conclude that there is either no gender difference in attitudes toward democracy or a significantly higher number of men than women favor democracy (table 9.2).

A relatively large percentage of "don't knows" on the issue of democracy may be indicative of people's lack of knowledge about democracy and that opinions toward democracy may shift in one way or another, if or when

Table 9.2 Attitude toward democracy: Democracy may have problems, but it is the best form of government

	Saudi Arabia			Iran			Jordan			Egypt			United States		
	Male	Female	Total	Male	Female	Total	Male	Female	Total	Male	Female	Total	Male	Female	Total
Agree	60%	57%	58%	45%	38%	42%	80%	72%	75%	90%	91%	91%	85%	85%	85%
Disagree	22%	25%	23%	19%	18%	19%	7%	10%	9%	3%	2%	2%	13%	12%	12%
DK	18%	19%	18%	35%	45%	40%	13%	18%	16%	7%	7%	7%	3%	3%	3%
Total	517	509	1026	1361	1171	2532	594	630	1224	1540	1460	3000	600	600	1200

Note: All values are percentages; DK, don't know.

these people form opinions. It may also be the case that people were afraid to express their opinion. This is true in Saudi Arabia and Iran, where 18 percent of the respondents said they did not know and 40 percent refused to answer. Officially, the Jordanian and Egyptian governments adhere to democracy. The respondents in these two countries might have felt less intimidated than those in Saudi Arabia and Iran. When only those who expressed opinions on this issue are taken into account, an overwhelming majority of the respondents in all the countries are in favor of democracy: 71 percent of Saudis, 69 percent of Iranians, 89 percent of Jordanians, 99 percent of Egyptians, and 88 percent of Americans (figure 9.1).

Attitudes toward Women

On gender relations, our findings displayed a cultural gap between the U.S. and Islamic publics. The latter held biased attitudes toward women, whereas Americans had a predominantly egalitarian view of gender relations. Only 7 percent of Saudis disagreed with the statement, "When jobs are scarce, men should have more right to a job than women." This figure was 22 percent for Iranians, 12 percent for Jordanians, and almost 0 percent for Egyptians, but for Americans it was 81 percent. On political leadership, 23 percent of Saudis disagreed with the statements, "Men make better political leaders than women do." This figure was higher for Iranians (30 percent), and lower for Jordanians (13 percent) and Egyptians (15 percent). For Americans, in contrast, the figure was 73 percent. On university education, a smaller percentage of Saudis (38 percent) disagreed with the statement, "A university education is more important for a boy than for a girl," than Iranians (59 percent), Jordanians (61 percent), or Egyptians (69 percent). The figure for Americans, in contrast, was 91 percent (table 9.3).

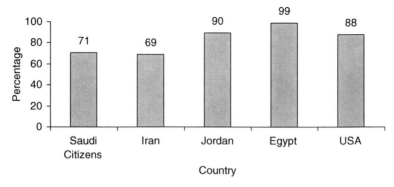

Figure 9.1   Democracy is the best form of government

Table 9.3 Attitudes toward women: Right to a job, leadership, education, polygamy, and obedience

	Saudi Arabia			Iran			Jordan			Egypt			United States		
	Male	Female	Total	Male	Female	Total	Male	Female	Total	Male	Female	Total	Male	Female	Total
When jobs are scarce, men should have more right to a job than women															
Agree	75%	61%	68%	76%	61%	69%	87%	74%	80%	93%	86%	90%	11%	9%	10%
Neither	18%	28%	23%	4%	5%	4%	7%	8%	7%	6%	14%	10%	10%	6%	8%
Disagree	6%	9%	7%	16%	28%	22%	6%	18%	12%	1%	0%	0%	79%	84%	81%
DK / NA	1%	1%	1%	4%	6%	5%	1%	0%	0%	0%	0%	0%	0%	1%	1%
Men make better political leaders than women do															
Agree	79%	65%	72%	67%	50%	59%	93%	79%	86%	90%	78%	84%	26%	18%	22%
Disagree	16%	30%	23%	25%	37%	30%	6%	19%	13%	10%	21%	15%	68%	78%	73%
DK / NA	4%	5%	4%	9%	13%	11%	1%	2%	2%	0%	1%	1%	6%	5%	5%
A university education is more important for a boy then for a girl															
Agree	68%	50%	59%	40%	31%	36%	50%	27%	38%	39%	22%	31%	7%	8%	7%
Disagree	29%	47%	38%	54%	64%	59%	49%	72%	61%	61%	77%	69%	90%	92%	91%
DK / NA	3%	3%	3%	6%	5%	5%	1%	0%	1%	0%	0%	0%	3%	1%	2%
It is acceptable for a man to have more than one wife															
Agree	58%	31%	45%	14%	8%	11%	30%	8%	19%	13%	7%	10%	NA	NA	NA
Neither	26%	26%	26%	16%	5%	11%	14%	6%	10%	12%	6%	9%	NA	NA	NA
Disagree	15%	41%	28%	68%	85%	76%	56%	86%	71%	74%	87%	80%	NA	NA	NA
DK / NA	2%	2%	2%	2%	2%	2%	0%	0%	0%	1%	0%	0%	NA	NA	NA
A wife must always obey her husband															
Agree	91%	72%	81%	61%	40%	52%	85%	63%	74%	82%	74%	78%	NA	NA	NA
Neither	8%	19%	13%	17%	19%	18%	5%	10%	7%	11%	14%	12%	NA	NA	NA
Disagree	1%	9%	5%	20%	39%	29%	10%	27%	19%	7%	12%	9%	NA	NA	NA
DK / NA	0%	0%	0%	1%	2%	1%	0%	1%	0%	0%	0%	0%	NA	NA	NA
Total	517	509	1026	1361	1171	2532	594	630	1224	1540	1460	3000	600	600	1200

Note: All values are percentages; DK, don't know; NA, not available.

On polygamy and obedience, the attitudes of the Saudi public were conservative and unfavorable to women. Only 28 percent of Saudis disagreed with polygamy in contrast with 80 percent of Egyptians, 71 percent of Jordanians, and 76 percent of Iranians. This does not mean that a majority of Saudis agreed with polygamy: 45 percent indicated that it was acceptable for a man to have more than one wife, while 26 percent neither agreed nor disagreed. These figures were 11 percent and 11 percent for Iran, 19 percent and 10 percent for Jordan, and 10 percent and 9 percent for Egypt. Likewise, on obedience, 81 percent of the Saudi respondents agreed that a wife must always obey her husband, compared with 52 percent of Iranians, 74 percent of Jordanians, and 78 percent of Egyptians. Only 5 percent of Saudi citizens disagreed with this statement, compared with 29 percent of Iranians, 19 percent of Jordanians, and 9 percent of Egyptians.

On all of the five gender-related questions, there were significant differences between the Islamic and the U.S. publics. There were also significant differences between men and women in all of the Islamic countries. Thus, the cultural fault line that separates the U.S. and Islamic publics may run through the cultural landscape of the four Islamic countries, as well.

We can conclude that (1) the cultural gap between the U.S. and Islamic publics is on issues related to gender equality and treatment of women, although all five countries have similar orientations in religiosity and attitudes toward democracy; (2) in the United States, women are more religious than men, but in Islamic countries this is not necessarily the case; (3) there are major differences between men and women on gender-related issues across all four Islamic countries; and (4) there is no majority support for polygamy, and Iranians, Jordanians, and Egyptians overwhelmingly reject the institution altogether.

Attitudes toward Women, Children, Work, and Marriage

In addition to religiosity, political attitudes, and attitudes toward women, conservatism can also be measured in terms of attitudes toward marriage and gender roles (table 9.4). A traditionalist perspective may consider that having children is a woman's primary source of fulfillment. If this is the case, then Saudi citizens are far less traditionalist than either Jordanians or Egyptians. Among Saudis, 33 percent did not consider it necessarily the case that a woman needs to have children in order to feel satisfied, compared with 47 percent of Iranians, 9 percent of Jordanians, 12 percent of Egyptians, and 81 percent of Americans. Likewise, in terms of attitudes toward marriage, a higher percentage of Saudis and Iranians were critical of the institution of marriage than the publics of

Table 9.4 Woman, work and children, and attitudes toward marriage

	Saudi Arabia			Iran			Jordan			Egypt			United States		
	Male	Female	Total	Male	Female	Total	Male	Female	Total	Male	Female	Total	Male	Female	Total
A woman has to have children in order to be fulfilled															
Needs children	61	65	63	44	46	45	90	89	89	88	88	88	16	12	14
Not necessary	34	33	33	46	47	47	8	10	9	11	12	11	78	84	81
DK	5	3	4	9	7	8	2	1	2	1	0	1	6	3	5
Marriage is an outdated institution															
Agree	18	13	15	17	18	17	12	12	12	4	4	4	12	9	10
Disagree	81	84	83	66	68	67	88	86	87	94	95	95	87	90	89
DK	2	3	2	17	14	16	1	2	1	2	1	1	2	1	1
What is the basis for marriage?															
Parental approval	42	58	50	42	39	41	NA	NA	NA	NA	NA	NA	NA	NA	NA
Love	56	40	48	48	50	49	NA	NA	NA	NA	NA	NA	NA	NA	NA
DK/NA	3	3	3	10	11	10	NA	NA	NA	NA	NA	NA	NA	NA	NA
A working mother can establish just as warm and secure a relationship with her children as a mother who does not work															
Agree	59	58	59	73	70	72	36	56	46	37	54	45	74	81	78
Disagree	36	35	35	18	25	21	61	42	52	62	45	54	25	17	21
DK	5	7	6	9	6	7	3	2	2	1	1	1	2	2	2

Note: All values are percentages; DK, don't know; NA, not available.

other countries, as 15 percent of Saudis and 17 percent of Iranians considered marriage an outdated institution, compared with 12 percent of Jordanians, 4 percent of Egyptians, and 10 percent of Americans. On these measures, there is no significant gender difference.

To be sure, for Americans the statement that marriage is an outdated institution probably implies a preference for cohabitation and raising children out of wedlock. For Saudis and Iranians, however, it probably means disapproval of the current practice of marriage. In Saudi Arabia, getting married, including the *mahr* (dowry paid by the groom to the bride) and festivities and the provision of the basic necessities to start and maintain a household, are quite expensive. In Friday sermons, preachers repeatedly discuss the extravagant cost involved in getting married. Charities are organized exclusively to help people who cannot afford marriage. And almost every bank in the kingdom provides loans for marriage. It is common to read in the newspapers that an increasing number of people are getting married late or are in no position to marry. To curb the growing cost of marriage, the government recently capped the upper limit of *mahr* to SR 30,000. The Saudis' critical attitude toward marriage may thus reflect their dismay at the prevalent situation rather than a negative attitude toward the institution per se.

On the question of the basis for marriage, parental approval, or love, the findings of the surveys indicate that Saudis are not as conservative as one might think. About 50 percent of Saudi citizens said that marriage should be based on parental consent, and 48 percent indicated that it should be based on love. For Iran, these figures were 41 percent and 49 percent, respectively. These findings are amazing, given that both countries are officially based on gender segregation and male domination. Particularly in Saudi Arabia, where there has been no state feminism from above and the mixing of the sexes is prohibited, the fact that almost 50 percent of the respondents prefer marriage to be based on love may be indicative of the existence of a fairly strong desire for social reforms among the public. How can people fall in love without meeting one another at some public place, interacting with one another for some time, and coming into some physical, emotional, and intellectual contact? Although it is not clear how Saudis would answer this question, we may speculate that those who pre-fer love to be the basis for marriage also prefer the modification or even elimination of the current institution of gender segregation. However, in Saudi Arabia, men were more supportive of love as the basis for marriage than women; in Iran, the difference was not significant.

There are also variations in attitudes toward traditional gender roles. An answer to the question of whether "a working mother can establish just as warm and secure a relationship with her children as a mother who does not work" may have different interpretations, depending on the social context. In the United States, where men and women have equal rights, working outside the home may be a matter of one's choice. In the Islamic Middle East, where women are often discouraged to participate in public activities, attitudes against women's work may well be indicative of conservatism. If this is true, then Saudi citizens appear to be less conservative than Egyptians or Jordanians but more conservative than Iranians: 59 percent of Saudis agreed that a working mother can establish as warm and secure a relationship with her children as a mother who does not work outside the home, compared with 78 percent of Americans, 72 percent of Iranians, 46 percent of Jordanians, and 45 percent of Egyptians. There was no significant gender difference for Saudis (59 percent of men versus 58 percent of women) and Iranians (73 percent of men versus 70 percent of women). There were significant gender differences among Jordanians (36 percent of men versus 56 percent of women), Egyptians (37 percent of men versus 54 percent of women), and Americans (74 percent of men versus 81 percent of women).

Determinants of Religiosity and Attitudes toward Women and Democracy

Religion, women, and democracy are among the most contested categories in the intellectual debates about the future of the kingdom. There are, however, variations among Saudis in religiosity and attitudes toward women and democracy. These variations may be a function of factors specific to each respondent, variations in socialization, alternative lifestyles and cultural outlooks, and the respondents' location in the social hierarchy. While it may not be possible to measure all of these factors in survey research, we focus on some of the key social attributes and beliefs of the respondents in order to explain these variations.

Determinants of Religiosity

Religiosity can be defined in varied ways, including the degree of one's adherence to religious beliefs, how such beliefs shape one's identity or affect daily activities, and the extent of participation in religious rituals, such as attending religious services at the mosques or performing daily prayers. Performance of rituals, however, may be a better indicator of religiosity than beliefs. Presuming that ritualistic practices presuppose beliefs but beliefs do not necessarily lead to such practices, we use two indicators of religious rituals as measures of religiosity: participation in mosque services (mosque attendance) and daily prayer:

- How often do you attend religious services, apart from funerals, in the mosque these days?
  1 = daily or more than once a week, 2 = once a week, 3 = once a month, 4 = only on special holy days, 5 = once a year, 6 = less often, 7 = practically never
- How many times do you pray daily?
  1 = 5 times, 2 = 4 times, , 4 = 2 times, 5 = 1 time, 6 = less often

The determinants of religiosity may include such factors as one's definition of self as religious (self-described religiosity), identification with religion (above all Muslim), age, education, gender, social class, income, and marital status. To explain the social determinants of religiosity, two statistical models are advanced. In the first model mosque attendance is the dependent variable and in the second model daily prayer.

Education, gender, marital status, identity, and self-described religiosity are measured as dummy variables (education: 0 = below university education, 1 = university education; gender: 0 = female, 1 = male; marital status: 0 = married, 1 = single, widowed, or separated;[7] identity: 0 = above all Muslim, 1 = above all Saudi or Arab; self-described religiosity: 0 = religious, 1 = not religious). Class is measured in terms of the respondents' self-assigned class membership (1 = upper class, 2 = upper middle class, 3 = lower middle class, 4 = working class, 5 = lower class), and income is based on a monthly household income divided into 15 categories, ranging from less than SR 2,000 (coded as 1) to more than SR 30,000 (coded as 15). Model I is:

Mosque attendance = prayer self-described religiosity + identity + class + income + education + gender + age + marital status

Model II is:

Prayer = self-described religiosity + identity + class + income + education + gender + age + marital status

The results of regression analysis are reported in table 9.5. In Model I, self-described religiosity, class, and age have positive effects, whereas income and female status have negative effects on mosque attendance. That is, describing themselves as religious people, members of the upper classes, lower income groups, men, and older people attend mosques more often than those who describe themselves as not religious people, members of the lower classes, higher income groups, women, and younger people. Given that Saudi society discourages the participation of women in public functions, it is natural that women attend religious services significantly less frequently than men. Daily prayer, however, is positively affected by self-described religiosity, Muslim identity, university education, and female status.

That university education has no significant effect on mosque attendance and a weak effect on daily prayer may modify the validity of the critics of the Saudi educational institutions as promoting conservatism, and at one remove extremism. Although our data cannot assess the quality and the orientation of the institutions of higher learning in the kingdom, and it may well be the case that they were organized to promote a conformist, or even intolerant, culture, they do not have the effect of making people more religious. In contrast, it can be stated that university education does not make Saudis less religious either.

Gender is the only nonattitudinal variable having strong effects on both prayer and mosque attendance. On mosque attendance, only income has a strong negative effect, while class and age have weak positive effects. On prayer, only education has a weak positive effect. Thus, if we define mosque attendance as the public side of religion and prayer as the private side, then there appears to be two different unrelated religious orders in

Table 9.5 Determinants of religiosity: Mosque attendance and Daily Prayer

Independent variables	Dependent variables	
	Mosque participation β	Prayer β
Daily prayer	−.020	
Describe self as a religious person	.185****	.265****
Muslim Identity	.051	.158****
Class	.082*	.010
Income	−.203****	−.014
University education	.020	.065*
Female	−.372****	.141****
Age	.079*	.022
Married	−.030	.022
Analysis of variance	$F_{9,805} = 23.826$****	$F_{8,806} = 15.026$****

Note: *p < .1, **p < .05, ***p < .01, ****p < .001 (two-tailed tests).

Saudi Arabia. On the public side, religion is the realm of men. On the private side, it is primarily the realm of women (Doumato 2000).

Determinants of Attitudes toward Women

People's value orientations toward gender relations cover a wide range of topics. Tables 9.3 and 9.4 present people's attitudes toward women and work outside the home, university education, political leadership, and the family. These orientations are interrelated. For example, where a woman has the opportunity to earn a university degree and obtain employment outside the home, she has more resources to change the nature of power relations in the family to her favor. She may question the norm of wife obedience and reject the institution of polygamy. Alternatively, a familial context that promotes egalitarianism may also encourage women to obtain a university education and seek employment outside the home.

Because the family is the immediate context of early gender socialization, explaining attitudes toward polygamy and wife obedience is important. This is so because such attitudes may give legitimacy to the practice of polygamy and the institution of male domination in the family. Understanding the social determinants of these attitudes provides insights into the social structure of Saudi society and the process of cultural change.

We propose that variations in these attitudes may be related to variations in the respondents' age, gender, education, class, income, marital status, and religiosity. We also propose a causal relationship between attitudes toward polygamy and attitudes toward wife obedience. Although there are degrees of reciprocal causations between these two variables, we propose that there is a higher likelihood that the belief in polygamy presupposes the belief in wife obedience than vice versa. This may be true because, among Saudi citizens, attitudes in favor of wife obedience were much more widespread than attitudes in favor of polygamy. According to table 9.3, 81 percent of Saudi citizens believe that a wife must always obey her husband whereas 45 percent agree with polygamy. Furthermore, considering the joint distribution of these two variables in table 9.6, the probability (prob.) that a randomly selected individual from the sample believes in wife obedience (obed.) given that that individual already believes in polygamy (polyg.) is .89:

prob. (obed. | polyg.) = prob. (obed. ∩ polyg.)/polyg. = 408/458 = 0.89).

Table 9.6 Joint Distribution of wife obedience and polygamy: A wife must always obey her husband

Polygamy	Agree	Neither	Disagree	Total
Agree	408	35	15	458
Neither	209	48	10	267
Disagree	203	53	27	283
Total	820	136	52	1,008

However, the probability that a person believes in polygamy given that that person believes in wife obedience is .50:

prob. (polyg.|obed.) = prob. (obed.∩polyg.)/obed. = 408/820 = 0.50).

The corollary of this argument also holds. That is, the probability that a person disagrees with wife obedience given that the person disagrees with polygamy is .095:

prob. (no obed.| no polyg.) = prob. (no obed.∩nopolyg.)/no. polyg. = 27/283 = 0.095).

In contrast, the probability that a person disagrees with polygamy given that that person disagrees with wife obedience is .52:

prob. (no polyg.| no obed.) = prob. (no obed.∩nopolyg.)/no. obed. = 27/52 = 0.52).

Based on these propositions, we test two statistical models. Model I is:

polygamy = obedience + mosque attendance + prayer + self-described religiosity + identity + education+income + class + gender + marital status + age

Model II is:

obedience = mosque participation + prayer + self-described religiosity + identity + education + income + class + gender + marital status + age

The regression results for both models are reported in table 9.7. In Model I, obedience, self-described religiosity, Muslim identity, university education, and gender have significant effects on attitudes toward

Table 9.7   Determinants of attitudes toward women: Polygamy and Obedience

Independent Variables	Dependent Variables	
	Polygamy β	Obedience β
Obedience	.139★★★★	
Mosque participation	.023	−.139★★★★
Daily prayer	−.032	−.023
Describe self as a religious person	.115★★★	.165★★★★
Muslim Identity	−.060★	−.014
Class	.038	.068★
Income	−.027	−.039
University education	−.057★	.029
Female	−.287★★★★	−.329★★★★
Age	−.024	−.016
Married	.032	.046
Analysis of variance	$F_{11,789} = 12.778$★★★★	$F_{10,802} = 11.022$★★★★

Note: ★p < .1, ★★p < .05, ★★★p < .01, ★★★★p < .001 (two-tailed tests).

polygamy. Obedience and self-described religiosity have positive effects on attitudes toward polygamy, while Muslim identity, university education, and gender have negative effects. Income, class, age, mosque attendance, and daily prayer have no significant effect on attitudes toward polygamy.

In Model II, self-described religiosity and class have positive effects on attitudes in favor of wife obedience, while mosque attendance and female gender have negative effects. Other factors like daily prayer, Muslim identity, income, university education, age, and marital status have no significant effect on attitudes toward wife obedience.

One of the most interesting findings of both models is that, except for self-described religiosity, other indicators of religiosity have no *positive* effect on the attitudes that promote gender hierarchy. Muslim identity has a negative effect on polygamy, while mosque attendance has a strong negative effect on wife obedience. These findings raise questions about the connection between the attitudes in favor of gender hierarchy and religiosity in the kingdom.

Determinants of Attitudes toward Democracy

The existence of considerable support for democracy among the Saudi public is enigmatic, given that the country's religious and political orders rest on views that are inimical to the formation of a democratic form of government. Furthermore, unlike other Middle Eastern countries, the kingdom has no prior historical experience of secularism and liberal nationalism. To explain how a large section of Saudi citizens arrived at democracy as an ideal form of government, we first try to identify and operationalize the variables that are proposed in the literature as causal factors shaping the individual's attitudes toward democracy. Using the least square regression techniques, we then test the significance of each of these variables in explaining the respondents' attitudes toward democracy as an ideal form of government.

Private ownership

Scholars have long debated the relations of the institutionalization of private property to the rise of democracy. The signing of the Magna Carta by King John of England in 1215, although an attempt by the nobility to control the king's power of taxation, is considered the beginning of political pluralism and democracy in that country. Over the years, this event is believed to have given rise to the intellectual and institutional foundation for the development of democracy and the rule of law. Other social scientists have further stressed the connection between capitalism and freedom (Friedman 2002). In contrast, another view has noted that this may not be necessarily so because the property owners have often collaborated with authoritarian rulers in suppressing popular democratic movements from below (Evans 1979; Hendersen 1977; O'Donnell 1978).

Although this chapter cannot settle this debate, we presume that the relationship between attitudes toward private property and democracy depends on the nature and the public standing of the property owning classes as well as the state's role in the economy. If the state heavily intervenes in the economy to serve the interests of the ruling elite and high-ranking bureaucrats, we may propose that the movement for democratic change is associated with the demand for privatization. Conversely, if the state is aligned with the property owning classes, the demand for democratic change may also be associated with critical attitudes toward these classes. As a result, the idea of privatization may have little appeal to the supporters of democracy.

We consider two factors in assessing the relationship between private property and democracy. One is attitudes toward private property in contradistinction to government ownership. The other refers to the effect of social class on democracy, which is discussed later. To examine the significance of attitudes toward private property in fostering attitudes toward democracy, two items in the survey questionnaire are selected for analysis. The first tabs the respondents' stand in favor of private ownership or government ownership:

How would you place your views on this scale?
1 = you agree completely that private ownership of business and industry should be increased
10 = your agree completely that government ownership should be increased
1 = private 2 3 4 5 6 7 8 9 10 = government

   Because democracy entails taming the state and given the Saudi state's extensive control of the economy, we propose that attitudes in favor of democracy are promoted by the desire to relax the state's control of business and industry and expand private ownership. That is, the more a person favors private ownership of business and industry, the more that person tends to agree with democracy as the best form of government. Second, to ensure that favorable attitudes toward private ownership are not confounded by poor state performance, the respondents' assessment of the public sector performance is included in the analysis. This variable may also independently shape the public's political views. Frederick Weil, for example, analyzed the effect of people's subjective assessment of the economy on political support and discovered that "performance positively affects political confidence but not support for democracy" (Weil 1989: 694). However, here, given the authoritarian nature of the state, people's negative opinion of the public sector may prompt them to express support for a democratic alternative.

   People have different views about the public sector in this country. Here is a scale for rating how well this sector is doing.
   1 = very bad
   10 = very good
   What point on this scale would you choose to describe how well the government is doing?
   1 = very bad 2 3 4 5 6 7 8 9 10 = very good

Tolerance

The development of democracy is linked to citizens' tolerance of alternative viewpoints. Tolerance is necessary for a stable and sustained functioning of political pluralism, where diverse viewpoints are publicly expressed and debated without the outbreak of serious destabilizing conflict. Citizens' intolerance, by contrast, is inimical to democracy because it constrains individual political liberty and promotes conformist culture. Tolerance of other groups promotes the democratic principle of majority rule and minority rights (Gibson 1992a). In Saudi Arabia also, tolerance of other religions and viewpoints is an integral part of the movement for democratic change. Some opinion writers have questioned elements of Wahhabi discourse, suggesting a link between certain attitudes promoted by the religious establishment and the rise of extremism (ICG 2004; Okruhlik 2002). Intolerance is also believed to have been promoted by school textbooks (Prokop 2003).

Tolerance is measured in such a variety of ways as one's attitudes toward Jews and members of other religious groups, communists, immigrants, and homosexuals with respect to whether members of these groups should be allowed to hold office, and as tolerance of least-liked groups for individual respondents (Gibson 1992b; Sullivan et. al. 1981). In the context of Saudi Arabia, some of these measures are irrelevant. For example, given that there are no Jews or communists in the country and that homosexuality may have a different meaning in the Saudi context than it does in Western societies,[8] these indicators may not be useful. There are, however, two other measures of tolerance that are consistent with these studies and at the same time relevant to Saudi cultural context. One is religious tolerance, measured by the respondents' willingness to accept the followers of other religions as neighbors, and the other is approval of divorce.

Religious tolerance is important because the religious institutions in the kingdom are monopolized by the Wahhabi school, whose founder did not even recognize Shi 'ism, one of the two main sects in Islam. The Shi 'is in Saudi Arabia are treated less favorably than they are in many other Persian Gulf states (al-Rasheed 1998; Doran 2004; Fuller 1999; Prokop 2003). Thus, a person expressing willingness to accept members of other religions as neighbors is a fairly valid measure of that person's universalism and liberation from the bounds of a conformist culture. Approval of divorce, in contrast, by itself is not indicative of a democratic mind.[9] In principle, approval or disapproval of divorce may have nothing to do with democracy. One may even argue that since divorce, like polygamy, has always been common in Saudi Arabia, approval of divorce may represent continuity, not a break with tradition. Nevertheless, given the growing gender awareness in the kingdom, where polygamy is considered the principal cause of divorce, approval of divorce may reflect individual willingness to break away from the

constraints of tradition and tolerate and accept change.[10] Both of
these indicators may reflect emerging attitudes in Saudi society.

Religious tolerance: Do you mind having people of other religion as
neighbors?
1 = Yes 2 = No
Approval of divorce: 1 = it is never justifiable 10 = it is always justifiable
1 = never justifiable 2 3 4 5 6 7 8 9 10 = always justifiable

Western Culture

To what extent are prodemocracy attitudes affected by the seriousness of
the Western cultural threats facing the nation in the public perception?
In what way does this perception shape their attitudes toward democracy? The past experience of liberal nationalism in Islamic countries
displayed an affinity between the support for democracy and favorable
attitudes toward the West. Muslim intellectual leaders in such diverse
countries as Algeria, Egypt, India, Iran, and Syria around the turn of
the twentieth century considered it appropriate to emulate the Western
model of democracy and constitutionalism. Nowadays, the West enjoys
little popularity in Islamic countries. Values surveys in Egypt, Iran, and
Jordan, however, indicated that critical attitudes toward the West are
inversely related to the ruling regime's orientation toward Western
countries. In Iran, where the state has an avowedly anti-Western orientation, the public appears to be much less concerned with Western cultural invasion than either the Egyptian or Jordanian public, where the
ruling regimes are American allies (Moaddel and Azadarmaki 2003). It
thus appears that Western popularity among the publics living under
unpopular authoritarian regimes in the Middle East is an inverse function of these regimes' degree of alliance with the West.

A similar logic might be applicable to Saudi Arabia. Given that the
kingdom does not recognize democracy, the supporters of democracy
are naturally in the opposition.[11] Given that the kingdom has been a
U.S. ally, the opposition tends to be critical of the West. We may thus
propose that the more the respondents are concerned with Western cultural invasion, the more they favor democracy. The pertinent question
that measures public perception of the importance of Western cultural
invasion is the following:

Every country faces a number of regional and international problems.
To what extent do you consider cultural invasion by the West to be

(1) very important (very serious), (2) important,(3) somewhat important, (4) least important, or (5) not an important problem?

Laws According to the People's
Wishes versus the shari 'a

How do attitudes toward making laws according to the people's wishes and attitudes toward the shari 'a relate to democracy? The moderniza- tion theory considers the separation of religion and the state not only an inevitable outcome of modernity, but also a precondition for the devel- opment of democratic rule making. Rooted in the Europe-centered rationalist school, to which belonged Thomas Hobbes, Voltaire, David Hume, James Mill, Jeremy Bentham, and J.S. Mill, among others, this theory is part of the notion of a universal history of social evolution in which religion was to wither away as society moved through the evolu- tionary process, fueled by progress in science and technology. This per- spective is further systemized in different manners in the works of Durkheim, Marx, Weber, and, later in the mid-twentieth century, Parsons. From this perspective it follows that the modern democratic individual prefers lawmaking based on the people's choices and the separation of religion and politics. The followers of the modernization theory in Islamic countries have argued that because the shari 'a laws are "discovered" or "recognized" by religious scholars and not enacted by the people's representatives, they are therefore inimical to democracy (Safran 1961).

In the 1970s, researchers began to question the modernization the- ory, arguing that it applies only to the experience of the West (Gillis 1970) and should not be generalized to other places (Hermassi 1976). Others, like Tilly (1973), argued that the theory is weak in explaining conflict and change even in Europe. Alternative explanations of cul- tural change in less developed countries are offered by the world sys- tem theory and the subaltern studies, proposing that the hierarchical structure of the world capitalist economy and the inequality in the distribution of power have undermined the autonomous development of culture in less developed countries. As a result, cultural change in these countries has occurred in a manner that ensured the continued hegemony of the core nations (Cooper 1994; Mallon 1994; Mitchell 1988; Prakash 1994). Further questioning the modernization theory, the historical experience of modern cultural change in many Islamic countries in the late nineteenth and early twentieth centuries has shown instances of compatibility between Islam and democracy, as an influential section of the ulama spearheaded the movement against monarchical absolutism and for constitutional change. For such diverse Islamic scholars as Egyptian Abduh, Syrian al-Kawakibi, and Iranian Na'ini, Islamic political theory was compatible with constitutionalism. For these leaders, however, rational laws must be shaped by Islam, not on the grounds that Islamic laws are immutable. On the contrary, for them Islam was capable of adapting to modern life, the hallmarks of a perfect Muslim community being law and reason. Abduh, in particular, argued that European laws and institutions cannot be successfully transplanted to Egypt. For him, Islam contained the universalistic creed that could transcend the cultural duality generated in his country as a result of modernization and thus form a moral basis of modern Egypt (Hairi 1977; Hourani 1983). However, there were also other Muslim theologians who believed Islam and democracy were incompatible.

We argue that the relationship between religion and democracy in the Islamic world is historically contingent, depending on the ulama's relationship with the ruling regime. When they were tied to an authoritarian regime, the democratic movement tended to display distinctly anticlerical and secularist attitudes, as was the case in late-nineteenth-century Iran and Turkey. The experience of the democratic movement in Saudi Arabia may parallel these cases, where the Muslim clerics are allied with the regime and oppose democracy. Thus, within the specific historical context of Saudi Arabia, where the conservative religious establishment purportedly defends the shari 'a and the status quo, we can propose (1) a negative relationship between attitudes toward the shari 'a and attitudes toward democracy; and (2) a positive relationship between attitudes toward laws according to the people's wishes and attitudes toward democracy.

Two questions measure the respondents' assessments of a good government—one that makes laws according to people's wishes or one that implements the shari 'a only.

Which of these traits is (1) very important, (2) important, (3) somewhat important, (4) least important, or (5) not important for a good government to have?

1. Make laws according to the people's wishes
2. Implement only the laws of the shari 'a

Religiosity

In the Saudi context, religiosity may indicate adherence to traditional values that are unfavorable to democracy. We use all four of the indicators of religiosity (mosque attendance, daily prayer, self-described religiosity, and Muslim identity) to assess their effects on attitudes toward democracy.

One may argue that mosque attendance subjects the individual to the conservative preaching of the clergy, reinforcing the belief in the supremacy of the religious laws over all other laws. Likewise, daily prayers would strengthen a person's attachment to religiously sanctioned values and norms. Finally, self-described religiosity and Muslim identity may be indicative of adherence to conservative religious values that are contrary to the alternative principle of organizing one's political community. All four of these measures, we thus propose, have negative effects on attitudes toward democracy.

Education

Modern education may promote favorable attitudes toward democracy insofar as it enhances people's awareness of the world's cultural diversity, the temporal nature of scientific discoveries, and the limits of the monolithic discourse promoted by religious institutions—all encouraging tolerance of alternative viewpoints and pluralism. Thus, the higher is one's education, the more favorable is one's attitude toward democracy.

Social Class

The effects of social class on democracy may vary according to social and historical context. Members of upper classes have easier access to education than lower classes. Through travel or involvement in modern activities, they are also exposed to cultural diversity and become familiar with democratic ideas. At the same time, wealthy individuals may benefit from the existing regime, and democracy may undermine their interests. This is especially true under the Saudi rentier economy, where ties to the ruling elites are keys to economic success.

The effects of class may also be a function of the way this variable is measured. In this study, we measure class in terms of the respondents' self-assigned class membership and monthly household income.

Age, Gender, and Marital Status

The variables of age, gender, and marital status are also included in the analysis in order to assess intergenerational, gender, and marriage effects on attitudes toward democracy.

Model

We use these variables to formulate a statistical model on democracy— attitudes toward Western culture, privatization, public sector performance, tolerance, laws according to the people's wishes, shari 'a, mosque attendance, daily prayer, self-described religiosity, Muslim identity, class, income, education, gender, marital status, and age.

Democracy = Western culturalinvasion + privatization + public sector performance + religious tolerance + approval of divorce + law according to people's wishes + shari 'a + mosque attendance + daily prayer + self-described religiosity + Muslim identity + class + in come + education + gender + marital status + age

Findings

Table 9.8 shows the results of the regression model. Except for self-described religiosity, education, age, and marital status, all other variables have significant effects on attitudes toward democracy.[12] An interesting finding is the positive effect of the perception of Western cultural invasion on attitudes toward democracy. That is, the more the respondents

Table 9.8 Determinants of attitudes toward democracy: Dependent variable: Democracy may have problems but it is the best for of government

Independent variables	β
Western cultural invasion	.168****
Privatization	.078**
Public-sector performance	−.073*
Religious tolerance	.080**
Divorce tolerance	.101***
Laws according to people's wishes	.099***
Laws of the shari 'a	−.105***
Mosque attendance	−.089**
Daily prayer	−.075*
Describe self as a religious person	−.008
Muslim identity	−.085**
Class	.174****
Income	−.144***
University education	.001
Female	−.095**
Age	.067
Married	−.044
Analysis of variance	$F_{17,595}, 5.627$

Note: *p < .1, **p < .05, ***p < .01, ****p < .001 (two-tailed tests).

consider Western cultural invasion to be a serious problem, the more they support democracy. This relationship is not only counterintuitive, for democracy is part of the Western tradition, but also contrary to the past experience of liberal nationalism in the Middle East, where liberal nationalists were also pro-Western. In the Saudi context, however, prodemocracy groups may be suspicious of the West partly because of its support of the unpopular authoritarian regime.

Attitudes toward privatization and public sector performance also have significant effects on attitudes toward democracy. People who favor the expansion of private ownership of business and industry in opposition to government ownership tend to favor democracy. Likewise, people who give a poor mark to public sector performance favor democracy. That is, the prodemocracy attitude is critical of the government not simply because it is authoritarian but also because of its poor performance. Both measures of tolerance (religious tolerance and tolerance of divorce) are also positively connected to attitudes in favor of democracy.

Support for making laws according to the people's wishes has a positive effect on attitudes toward democracy, while support for implementing the shari 'a has a negative effect. Except for self-described religiosity, all of the other three indicators of religiosity have negative effects on attitudes toward democracy. These findings are remarkable within the religious and political context of Saudi Arabia. Because four of the five religion-related variables (support for the shari 'a, mosque attendance, daily prayer, and Muslim identity) have negative effects on attitudes toward democracy, one may conclude that religion in the kingdom is a conservative and counterdemocratic force. The effects of class and monthly household income on attitudes toward democracy are contradictory. Whereas self-rated class membership has a positive effect on democracy—that is, the higher one's self-reported class background, the more favorable one's attitudes toward democracy—monthly household income has negative effects on democracy. That is, people with higher incomes tend to have less favorable attitudes toward democracy than people with lower incomes. The positive effect of class on democracy may be indicative of the emergence of a new (subjectively defined) influential class, whose members are dissatisfied with the government. This conclusion is reinforced considering that about 80 percent of the respondents from the upper classes agree that democracy is the best form of government, whereas this figure is about 71 percent for those who identify themselves as members of the middle class, 61 percent of the working class, and 40 percent for the lower class. The effect of income on attitudes toward democracy is negative. This may be a consequence of the Saudi rentier economy. According to the rentier economy model, a country's reliance on substantial external rent in the form of the sale of oil, transit charges (Suez Canal), tourism, or remittance funds (Jordan) has far-reaching political, social, and cultural outcomes. One such outcome is that the work-reward nexus is not the key feature of economic activities and accumulation of wealth, where wealth is the end result of the individual involvement in a long, risky, and organized production process. Wealth is rather accidental, a windfall gain, or situational, where citizenship becomes a source of economic benefit. To acquire wealth requires different types of subjective orientation, which Hazem Beblawi calls "rentier mentality" and "rentier ethics." Noneconomic criteria, such as ties to the ruling elite, are the key determinants of income. Rentierism thus reinforces the state's tribal origins, because it regenerates the tribal hierarchy consisting of varying layers of beneficiaries with the ruling elite on top, in an effective position of buying loyalty through their redistributive power. As the state is not dependent on taxation, there is far less demand for political participation (Beblawi and Luciani 1987). If this argument is correct and one's income is related to one's connection to the state, then people with higher incomes would prefer the existing arrangement over a democratic system.

Our findings also show that men are more supportive of democracy than women. Although women may benefit considerably from democratization of Saudi Arabia, the current gender difference may be indicative of either women having a relatively lower level of political awareness, being discouraged to participate in the public political debate as a result of the rigid system of gender segregation, or having little interest in a democracy that is dominated by men. With the increasing involvement of women in the public demand for democratic change, we may expect a change in this relationship. Finally, that university education has no significant effect on attitudes toward democracy can be interpreted differently. On the one hand, it is consistent with the view that the Saudi educational institutions have failed to promote democratic ideas because of their anti-Western biases, fear about dealing with non-Muslims, and lack of appreciation of the varieties of schools of thought in Islam (Doumato 2003). On the other hand, it means that these institutions, despite overtly trying to promote religious and political conservatism, have not been successful in producing conservative individuals. Thus, we may conclude that university education in Saudi Arabia neither promotes nor hinders political conservatism.

Conclusions

The foregoing analysis displays a picture of the worldview of the Saudi public that is different from the view of the society portrayed by the action of militant Islamic groups. Although by Western standards Saudi Arabia is a conservative society, compared with other Islamic countries like Egypt and Jordan, Saudis are not as conservative as one might expect. In fact, they are less religious than either Egyptians or Jordanians. In terms of their attitudes toward marriage, almost half of Saudis prefer love, rather than parental approval, as the basis for marriage. A larger percentage of Saudis than either Egyptians or Jordanians considers marriage to be an outdated institution. On such issues as those related to religiosity, marriage, women, and work and children, Saudis are closer to Iranians than to Egyptian or Jordanian Arabs. The similarities between Saudi and Iranian citizens in terms of religiosity and their differences from Egyptians or Jordanians may indicate the effect of the state's culture on people's attitudes. It appears that the religiosity of the Iranian and Saudi states have made the publics of these societies less religious instead of making them more so.

Mosque attendance and daily prayer have multiple determinations. However, except for the strong positive effects of self-described religiosity, these two variables are affected by different sets of factors. On mosque attendance, male gender has a strong positive effect and income a strong negative effect, while class and age have weak positive effects. On daily prayer, female gender and Muslim identity have strong positive effects, while education has a weak positive effect. Because male gender is the only nonattitudinal variable that has a strong positive effect on mosque attendance and female gender has a strong positive effect on daily prayer, and because mosque attendance is the public side of religious ritual and daily prayer is the private side, gender is the crucial line dividing the public from private spheres of religious activities in Saudi society. Likewise, nonattitudinal factors have no strong effect on attitudes toward polygamy and wife obedience: only university education has a weak negative effect on attitudes toward polygamy, class has a weak positive effect on wife obedience, and indicators of religion have inconsistent effects on these variables. Again, gender is the only nonattitudinal variable that strongly affects attitudes toward gender hierarchy.

Our findings on the determinants of attitudes toward democracy are consistent with the extant sociological generalizations. Insofar as these attitudes are connected positively to attitudes toward privatization, negatively to attitudes toward public sector performance, and positively to tolerance and attitudes toward making laws according to the people's wishes, our findings are consistent with some of the sociological generalizations that also relate the development of Western democracy to the rise of the free enterprise system, tolerance, and rational (secular) lawmaking. We may also interpret the inverse relationship between religious variables (attitudes toward the shari 'a, mosque attendance, daily prayer, and

Muslim identity) and democracy as qualified support for the secularization thesis on the conflict between religion and democracy.

These similarities, however, do not mean that Saudi Arabia represents an
instance of the democratic path that has already been traversed by the West.
Almost all of the sociological determinants of attitudes toward democracy
specified in this chapter make sense within the country's specific historical
context. That favorable attitudes toward democracy are connected to
favorable attitudes toward privatization is not because the rise of private property or privatization inherently generates democratic attitudes. It is because,
for the Saudi public, both the state (i.e., the realm of politics) and the lion's
share of the country's national economy are monopolized by the nonrespon-
sive and authoritarian ruling family. Naturally, we may expect that the desire for
privatization, which means dismantling the economic monopoly of the ruling
family, promotes attitudes toward democracy, which means limiting the political power of the ruling regime. Furthermore, since the state is authoritarian,
critical attitudes toward public sector performance may also dictate attitudes
in favor of democracy. If the state was based on a constitutional monarchy, in
which the members of the economically dominant classes had a monopoly
over the parliament, which was the case in Egypt in the 1930s and 1940s and
Syria in the late 1940s and 1950s, critical attitudes toward the state's economic
performance would go hand in hand with critical attitudes toward parliamentary politics, giving rise to various antidemocratic supranationalist
ideologies (Gershoni and Jankowski 1995; Khoury 1987).

Likewise, that attitudes toward democracy are inversely connected to
religiosity and to attitudes toward the shari 'a should not be interpreted
as religion is inherently undemocratic and therefore must decline for
democracy to rise. These linkages exist because of the state-cleric
alliance that has dominated the country. These clerics have displayed
considerable ruthlessness in suppressing dissent, repressing religious
minorities, and blocking any change in the culture that might undermine their institutional power. It is thus natural to expect favorable
attitudes toward democracy correlating inversely with attitudes toward
the shari 'a and religiosity. In fact, there are also historical precedents
showing the rise of liberal constitutional and anticlerical ideas in opposition to the state-religious alliances that were dominant in society.
The rise of anticlerical constitutionalism in late-nineteenth- and early-
twentieth-century Iran was in response to the monarch-ulama alliance,
and the rise of the liberal Arabist ideas in Syria around the same general
period was due to Sultan Abdülhamid's pan-Islamic despotism.[13]

Democratic movements in the Islamic Middle East in the first half of the
twentieth century had generally a pro-Western orientation. The Saudi

case appears to be departing from this historical pattern, as those who are concerned with Western cultural invasion also tend to be more in favor of democracy. This last finding can be explained in terms of Western support for the unpopular Saudi government. Furthermore, although the positive effects of class on democracy is consistent with historical experiences of liberal-nationalist movement in countries like Egypt and Syria, where merchants and landowners tended to favor parliamentary politics, the negative connection between income and attitudes toward democracy in Saudi Arabia may be due to the effect of the rentier economy because those in high income brackets may benefit from the policies of the rentier state and thus become less favorable to democratic change.

Although the actual development of favorable attitudes toward democracy and democratic movements are shaped by the specific national historical contexts within which they are embedded, there is one element that may universally give rise to democratic movement: the human desire and struggle for empowerment to control the socioeconomic and cultural environment. For the Saudi to become empowered, it seems, there must be more tolerance in their society, less involvement of the regime and the religious police in their lives, more laws according to their wishes, and less dictating from the West.

Notes

1. Professor of sociology at Eastern Michigan University, Ypsilanti, Mich. 48197, USA, and Research Affiliate at the Population Studies Center, Institute for Social Research, University of Michigan, Ann Arbor, Mich. 48108, USA; e-mail: mmoaddel@umich.edu. This study was supported by three grants from the NSF (SES-0242861, SES-0097282, SES-0139908), a grant from the Ford Foundation, and a grant from the Bank of Sweden Tercentenary Foundation. This chapter originally appeared in the *International Journal of Middle East Studies* 38(1): 79–108, and is reprinted here with permission from Cambridge University Press. Comments by Kristine Ajrouch, Alethea Helbig, Robert Robinson, and three anonymous reviewers for the *International Journal of Middle East Studies*, as well as the assistance of Mari Nukii are gratefully acknowledged.
2. For data on fluctuations in export earnings that contributed to a sharp increase or decrease in economic activities and GDP growth, see Champion 2003: 80, table 3.1.
3. The oil boom also increased income inequality, particularly in agriculture, where 82% of private land was held by 16.2% of the landowning population, making Saudi Arabia's one of the most inequitable land tenure systems in the world: see Chaudhry 1997: 156, 176.
4. Although they constitute 58% of the university graduates in Saudi Arabia, women make up only 5% of the labor force: see Cordesman 2003: 175–76.
5. The surveys were conducted under the supervision of Abdul-Hamid Abdul Latif, Ain Shams University, Cairo; Taghi Azadarmaki, University of Tehran; Mustafa Hamarneh and Fares al-Braizat, University of Jordan, Amman; and Tony Proudian, Pan Arab Research Center, Jeddah.
6. The principal investigators for the U.S. values survey, carried out in late 1999 and early 2000, were Ronald Inglehart and Virginia Hodgkinson. See also Inglehart et al. 2004.

7. In the sample, 564 (55%) were married, 29 (3%) were divorced, 10 (1%) were separated, 15 (1.5%) were widowed, and 408 (40%) were single.

8. There was little variation in the responses to the homosexuality question: 86% marked "1," and 6% marked "2" on a 10-point scale ("1" meaning "never justifiable," and "10" meaning always justifiable).

9. It has been argued that approval of divorce may lie at the core of value transition in the direction of modernity and political democracy: see Norris and Inglehart 2002: 18.

10. In addition to the data showing a negative correlation between approval of divorce and support for polygamy (r 5 [minus sign].1, p , .001), a study in Saudi Arabia concluded that the practice of polygamy is the principal cause of divorce in the kingdom: see BBC News, April 30, 2001, available at: http://news.bbc.co.uk/1/hi/world/middle_east/1304886.stmSeptember . 28, 06.

11. By pushing forward the idea of the formation of a constitutional monarchy as the only way for the kingdom to establish political stability and defeat extremism, some of the prodemocracy groups may portray themselves as the regime's stronger supporters. Nevertheless, there is no denying that the regime considers these groups a threat. For example, the group of reformers who were involved in preparing the petition calling for a constitutional monarchy were summoned to a stormy meeting with the interior minister, Prince Nayef, during which they were reprimanded and, in some cases, threatened with prison sentences. A few weeks later, Crown Prince Abdullah delivered a speech that mixed support for gradual change with a thinly veiled warning to more activist reformers. In March 2004, the regime went a step further, arresting a dozen proreform activists (ICG 2004: 18).

12. About 18% of the responses to the question of democracy were "don't know" and thus excluded from analysis. To assess whether this exclusion affected the validity of the findings, we created a weight variable as an inverse function of the predicted probability of the responses to the question of democracy. The predicted probability was obtained by creating a dummy variable: "don't knows" were coded as "0," and other responses were coded as "1." Then, using binary logistic regression technique, this dummy variable was regressed on all of the independent variables to assess whether the characteristics of the respondents affected the likelihood of responding. Each case was then automatically given a predicted value, and the weight variable was calculated as an inverse function of these predicted values. The results of the regression analysis using the weight variable were not significantly different from the results not using the weight variable. Therefore, "don't knows" did not significantly affect the findings.

13 . For an analysis of the Iranian Constitutional Revolution, see Afary 1996; Bayat 1991. For analyses of Arabism and Arab nationalism, see Antonius 1961; Dawisha 2003; Dawn 1973; Haim 1962; Khalidi et al. 1991; Khoury 1983; Tauber 1993; Zeine 1973.

References

Afary, Janet. 1996. *The Iranian Constitutional Revolution, 1906–1911.* New York: Columbia University Press.

al-Rasheed, Madawi. 1998. "The Shi'a of Saudi Arabia: A Minority in Search of Cultural Authenticity." *British Journal of Middle Eastern Studies* 25(1): 121–38.

———. 2002. *A History of Saudi Arabia.* Cambridge: Cambridge University Press.

Antonius, George. 1961. *The Arab Awakening: The Story of the Arab National Movement.* London: Hamish Hamilton.

Baer, Robert. 2003. *Sleeping with the Devil: How Washington Sold Our Soul for Saudi Crude.* New York: Crown Publishers.

Bainbridge, William Sim. 1995. "Social Influence and Religious Pluralism." *Advances in Group Processes* 12: 1–18.

Bayat, Mongol. 1991. *Iran's First Revolution: Shi 'ism and the Constitutional Revolution of 1905–1909*. Oxford: Oxford University Press.

Beblawi, Hazem and Giacomo Luciani. (ed.). 1987. *The Rentier State*. London: Croom Helm.

Boullata, Issa. 1990. *Trends and Issues in Contemporary Arab Thought*. Albany: State University of New York Press.

Champion, Daryl. 2003. *The Paradoxical Kingdom: Saudi Arabia and the Momentum of Reform*. New York: Columbia University Press.

Chaudhry, Kiren Aziz. 1997. *The Price of Wealth: Economies and Institutions in the Middle East*. Ithaca, NY: Cornell University Press.

Cooper, Frederick. 1994. "Conflict and Connection: Rethinking Colonial African History." *American Historical Review* 99(5): 1516–45.

Cordesman, Anthony H. 2003. *Saudi Arabia Enters the Twenty-First Century*. Westport, CO: Praeger.

Dawisha, Adeed. 2003. *Arab Nationalism in the Twentieth Century: From Triumph to Despair*. Princeton, NJ: Princeton University Press.

Dawn, Ernest C. 1973. *From Ottomanism to Arabism: Essay on the Origins of Arab Nationalism*. Chicago: University of Illinois Press.

Dekmejian, R. Hrair. 1994. "The Rise of Political Islamism in Saudi Arabia." *Middle East Journal* 48(4): 627–43.

———. 1998. "Saudi Arabia's Consultative Council." *Middle East Journal* 52(2): 204–18.

———. 2003. "The Liberal Impulse in Saudi Arabia." *Middle East Journal* 57(3): 400–13.

Doran, Michael Scott. 2004. "The Saudi Paradox." *Foreign Affairs* 83(1): 35–51. Doumato, Eleanor Abdella. 2000. *Getting God's Ear: Women, Islam and Healing in Saudi Arabia and Gulf*. New York: Columbia University Press.

———. 2003. "Manning the Barricades: Islam According to Saudi Arabia's School Texts." *Middle East Journal* 57(2): 230–47.

Enayat, Hamid. 1982. *Modern Islamic Political Thought*. London: Macmillan.

Evans, Peter. 1979. *Dependent Development: The Alliance of Multinational State and Local Capital in Brazil*. Princeton, NJ: Princeton University Press.

Fandy, Mamoun. 1999. "Cyber Resistance: Saudi Opposition between Globalization and Localization." *Comparative Studies of Society and History* 41(1): 140.

Finke, Roger. and Rodney Stark. 1988. "Religious Economies and Sacred Canopies." *American Sociological Review* 53: 41–49.

Friedman, Milton. 2002. *Capitalism and Freedom*. Chicago: University of Chicago Press.

Fuller, Graham E. 1999. *The Arab Shi'a: The Forgotten Muslims*. New York: St. Martin's Press.

Gershoni, Israel and James P. Jankowski. 1995. *Redefining the Egyptian Nation, 1930–1945*. Cambridge: Cambridge University Press.

Gibson, James L. 1992a. "The Political Consequences of Intolerance: Cultural Conformity and Political Freedom." *American Political Science Review* 86(2): 338–56.

———. 1992b. "Alternative Measures of Political Tolerance: Must Tolerance Be 'Least-Liked'?" *American Journal of Political Science* 36(2): 560–77.

Gillis, John R. 1970. "Political Decay and the European Revolutions, 1789–1848." *World Politics* 22(3): 344–70.

Gold, Dore. 2003. *Hatred's Kingdom: How Saudi Arabia Supports the New Global Terrorism*. Washington, DC: Regnery Publishers.

Haim, Sylvia G. 1962. (ed.). *Arab Nationalism: An Anthology*. Berkeley: University of California Press.

Hairi, Hadi. 1977. *Shi 'ism and Constitutionalism in Iran*. Leiden: E.J. Brill.

Hendersen, Barrie. 1977. "Chilean State after the Coup." *Socialist Register* 14: 121–42.

Hermassi, Elbaki. 1976. "Toward a Comparative Study of Revolutions." *Comparative Studies in Society and History* 18(2): 211–35.

Hourani, Albert. 1983. *Arabic Thought in the Liberal Age (1798–1939)*. Cambridge: Cambridge University Press.

Iannaccone, Laurence R. 1991. "The Consequences of Religious Market Structure: Adam Smith and the Economics of Religion." *Rationality Sociology* 3(2): 156–77.

Inglehart, Ronald, Miguel Basáñez, Jaime Díez-Medrano, Loek Halman, and Ruud Luijkx. (eds.). 2004. *Human Beliefs and Values: A Cross-Cultural Sourcebook Based on the 1999–2002 Values Surveys*. Mexico City: Siglo.

International Crisis Group (ICG). 2004. *Can Saudi Arabia Reform Itself?* ICG Middle East Report no. 28(10).

Khalidi, Rashid, Lisa Anderson, Muhammad Musli, and Reeva S. Simon. (eds.). 1991. *The Origins of Arab Nationalism*. New York: Columbia University Press.

Khoury, Philip S. 1983. *Urban Notables and Arab Nationalism: The Politics of Damascus 1860–1920*. Cambridge: Cambridge University Press.

———. 1987. *Syria and the French Mandate: The Politics of Arab Nationalism, 1920–1945*. Princeton, NJ: Princeton University Press.

Krimly, Rayed. 1999. "The Political Economy of Adjusted Priorities: Declining Oil Revenues and Saudi Fiscal Policies." *Middle East Journal* 53(2): 258.

Laroui, Abdallah. 1976. *The Crisis of Arab Intellectuals*. Los Angeles: University of California Press.

Layish, Aharon. 1987. "Saudi Arabian Legal Reform as a Mechanism to Moderate Wahhabi Doctrine." *Journal of the American Oriental Society* 107(2): 279–92.

Mallon, Florencia E. 1994. "The Promise and Dilemma of Subaltern Studies: Perspectives from Latin American History." *American Historical Review* 99(5): 1491–515. Mitchell, Timothy. 1988. *Colonising Egypt*. Cambridge: Cambridge University Press.

Moaddel, Mansoor. 2005. *Islamic Modernism, Nationalism, and Fundamentalism: Episode and Discourse*. Chicago: University of Chicago Press.

Moaddel, Mansoor and Taghi Azadarmaki. 2003. "The Worldviews of Islamic Publics: The Cases of Egypt, Iran, and Jordan." In *Human Values and Social Change: Findings from the Values Surveys*, edited by Ronald Inglehart, pp. 69–90. Leiden: E.J. Brill. Norris, Pippa and Ronald Inglehart. 2002. "Islamic Culture and Democracy: Testing the 'Clash of Civilizations' Thesis." In *Human Values and Social Change: Findings from the Values Surveys*, edited by Ronald Inglehart, pp. 5–33. Leiden: E.J. Brill.

O'Donnell, Guillermo. 1978. "Reflections on the Pattern of Change in the Bureaucratic-Authoritarian State." *Latin American Research Review* 13(1): 3–38.

Okruhlik, Gwenn. 2002. "Networks of Dissent: Islamism and Reform in Saudi Arabia." *Current History* 101(651): 22–28.

Prakash, Gyan. 1994. "Subaltern Studies as Postcolonial Criticism." *American Historical Review* 99: 1475–90.

Prokop, Michael. 2003. "Saudi Arabia: The Politics of Education." *International Affairs* 79(1): 77–89.

Safran, Nadav. 1961. *Egypt in Search of Political Community*. Cambridge, MA: Harvard University Press.

Schwartz, Stephen. 2002. *The Two Faces of Islam: The Houses of Sa'ud from Tradition to Terror*. New York: Doubleday Publishers.

Sharabi, Hisham. 1970. *Arab Intellectuals and the West*. Baltimore: Johns Hopkins University Press.

Sullivan, John L., George E. Marcus, Stanley Feldman, and James E. Piereson. 1981. "The Sources of Political Tolerance: A Multivariate Analysis." *American Political Science Review* 75(1): 92–106.

Tauber, Eliezer. 1993. *The Emergence of the Arab Movements*. London: Frank Cass.

Tilly, Charles. 1973. "Does Modernization Breed Revolution?" *Comparative Politics* 5(3): 425–27.

Weil, Frederick D. 1989. "The Sources and Structure of Legitimation in Western Democracies: A Consolidated Model Tested with Time-Series Data in Six Countries since World War II." *American Sociological Review* 54(5): 694.

Zeine, Zeine N. 1973. *The Emergence of Arab Nationalism*. Delmar, NY: Caravan Books.

PART 4

Events and Changes in Values and Perceptions

CHAPTER 10

Events and Value Change: The Impact of September 11, 2001 on the Worldviews of Egyptians and Moroccans

MANSOOR MOADDEL AND

ABDUL-HAMID ABDUL-LATIF

Introduction

The significance of an historical event depends on the meaning it carries for the social actors it potentially affects. That meaning is not haphazardly produced but rather structured by the nature of the political and cultural context in which social actors are embedded. That meaning determines whether and how individuals, and entire societies, reexamine their attitudes toward and beliefs about historically significant issues. We tested this proposition by examining how the attitudes of Egyptians and Moroccans were affected by the terrorist act perpetrated by al-Qaeda on 9/11, which was ostensibly carried out not only to avenge the presumed trauma Muslim nations have suffered because of the American-led "Jewish-Crusade" alliance, but also to rally the Islamic publics behind their banner for the construction of a virtuous Islamic order. Based on survey data, our findings indicate that these publics displayed more favorable attitudes toward democracy, gender equality, and secularism after 9/11 than they did before. Accordingly, the event influenced the attitudes of the Egyptian and Moroccan publics in ways contrary to those intended by the radical Islamists. Some effects were also moderated by the respondents' age, education, and gender. We discuss how these results contribute to the growing body of literature on the role of events in historical and social processes.

The 19 terrorists who were responsible for the horrific violence of September 11, 2001 on the U.S. soil were all from Arab countries. Fifteen hijackers were Saudis, and the remaining four were from Egypt, the United Arab Emirates, and Lebanon. In attacking the "far enemy," these Muslim terrorists were convinced that they would be handsomely rewarded in paradise (Schwartz 2002: 171). Their act was also part of a larger project to establish a universal virtuous Islamic order. Speaking with the authority of an Islamic theologian, as a revolutionary strategist, and as a calculating propagandist, the leadership of al-Qaeda warned and proclaimed that jihad was the only solution to the problem of Muslim decline and that "all other methods that tried to evade assuming the burdens of jihad" were futile as shown by the betrayal of the peaceful Algerian Islamic movement, and that "the Jewish-Crusade alliance, led by the United States, will not allow any Muslim force to reach power in any of the Islamic countries" (cited in Sageman 2004: 20, 23). Furthermore, its literature asserted that the violence carried out by a small, dedicated vanguard of Islamic *mujahedin* would receive the grateful acclamation of the Muslim nations, create a reserve of fighters, show the weakness of the enemy, publicize the issues, reject compliance and submission to decadent regimes, provide legitimacy to Muslim fighters, spread fear and terror within the ranks of local agents of the United States, and expose the "ugly" face of Americans as the U.S. forces retaliate against them—all effects presumed to win over the Muslim publics (Gunaratna 2002: 75; Sageman 2004: 22).

Less than a month after 9/11, al-Qaeda leader Osama Ben Laden issued a statement that sanctioned the violence against the United States. In doing so, he broadcasted his view of the trauma Muslims have endured in recent history, and thus eulogized the terrorists as "vanguards of Islam," naturally expecting other Muslims to follow suit:

> There is America, hit by God in one of its softest spots. Its greatest buildings were destroyed, thank God for that. There is America, full of fear from its north to its south, from its west to its east. Thank God for that.
>
> What America is tasting now is something insignificant compared to what we have tasted for scores of years. Our nation (the Islamic world) has been tasting this humiliation and this degradation for more than 80 years. Its sons are killed, its blood is shed, its sanctuaries are attacked, and no one hears and no one heeds.

When God blessed one of the groups of Islam, vanguards of Islam,
they destroyed America. I pray to God to elevate their status and bless
them (september11news.com/OsamaSpeeches.htm 11/9/2005: 2).[1]

That 9/11 had a dramatic impact on both the U.S. foreign policy and
the American public at large is hardly debatable, although only the
future can tell the full nature and extent of this impact. This event also
gained enormous publicity globally and the terrorists received universal
condemnation for their mass destruction of human lives and property.
However, it is not clear how much 9/11 and the al-Qaeda's representation of Muslim trauma affected the attitudes of the Islamic publics. In
what way did the event of 9/11 attain meaningfulness for these publics?
To what extent did the terrorists have "illocutionary success," to use
Alexander's (2004: 12) latest phrase, in shaping the mass public opinion
in Islamic countries? Were they able to win Muslims over to their
worldviews on gender, religion, and politics? Did the Islamic publics
become more supportive of the shari 'a? Is such a gruesome violence as
9/11 an effective means of causing attitudinal changes in the direction
expected by the perpetrators? We attempt to answer these questions for
two Muslim Arab countries—Egypt and Morocco—for which before
and after 9/11 values survey data are available.

By gaining insight into the dynamic of change in public opinion in these
two countries before and after 9/11, we also attempt to contribute to sociological knowledge about the relationship between events and attitude
change. We draw from two diverse traditions of comparative historical
sociology and public opinion research in order to more clearly theorize
about events and their effects on social processes. We propose that
incidents may not have automatic societal consequences. Rather, they
become eventful when and if they are inserted into the existing process of
cultural debates, framing contest, and political conflict.

Theoretical Development: Events and Change

Historical sociologists who expressed misgivings about the unilinear
evolutionary image of change projected by the universal history paradigm did so by pointing, among other things, to the outbreak of an
event not only as a historical marker that separates one era from another
but also as a key explanatory variable that contributes to rapid changes in
social relations, bringing into relief a new cultural pattern. Featured
prominently in their works were such notions as the revolutionary break

with the past as a precondition for the emergence of different forms of modern social organization (Moore 1966), the presence of historical conjuncture that makes the articulation of ideology and social structure possible (Wuthnow 1989), and the disruptive influence of changes in external conditions on the intellectual network that unleashes creativity (Collins 1998).

Sewell's (1996) work, however, is among the first to theorize about events, arguing that significant changes in social life are rarely continuous, incremental, or smooth in character. Rather, they come "clustered into relatively intense bursts" (843). Even when incremental changes are accumulated, they often result "in a building up of pressures and a dramatic crisis of existing practices rather than a gradual transition from one state of affairs to another" (843). For Sewell, the moments of accelerated changes "are initiated and carried forward by historical events" (ibid). Historical events are thus important to theorize about because "they reshape history, imparting an unforeseen direction to social development and altering the nature of the causal nexus in which social interactions take place" (ibid).

Sewell's analysis of the French Revolution has focused on the microsituational historical processes in the short period preceding the revolution that were punctuated and thrust forward by unfolding occurrences, involving simultaneously the actions (e.g., taking the Bastille), interpretations (e.g., popular violence as a legitimate popular revolution), signification (new meanings given to such terms as "revolution," "people," "liberty," and "despotism"), and articulation of action to conception of French men and women that in one week (July 12–17, 1789) produced and signified "the taking of the Bastille" (851), an historical event that became synonymous with the French Revolution. Although lacking the knowledge about how the French public thought and perceived the unfolding events, Sewell's description makes a convincing case for the relationship between events and the process of change in people's perceptions and values.

Events also form a key element in Moaddel's (2005, 2001) episodic-discourse model of ideological production. By partitioning history into distinct episodes, he argues, events introduce discontinuities into the process of cultural change. An episode is a bounded historical process that has a beginning and an end, displaying certain distinctiveness by virtue of its discontinuity from the preceding and following episodes. By causing ruptures in social structure, changing the balance of social forces or dramatically affecting human emotion, events may bring a new regime of signification to prominence. This regime then forms the ideological target in opposition to which new discourses are produced and disseminated in the social environment. Since *target* is the key factor in this model, an event is crucial in affecting the process of ideological production insofar as it generates new targets and/or causes a shift in the position of culture producers in the sociopolitical space, opening up a new angle from which the target is viewed, interpreted, and criticized, and leading to new ideological resolutions.

Islamic modernism in India was thus produced within the pluralistic discursive context that was shaped by the reorganization of social forces following the Sepoy Mutiny of 1857–59.[2] Likewise, modern cultural change in Egypt began after the brief interlude of the French occupation of the country (1798–1801), which weakened the Mamluk, exposed Egyptians to a new superior Western power, and proved consequential for the transformation of Egypt in the subsequent decades. Consequential for the emergence of other cultural movements in Egypt were such events as the defeat of the Urabi Rebellion (1879–82) and the British occupation of the country, which set the stage for the rise of territorial nationalism around the turn of the twentieth century, and the economic crisis of the early 1930s that contributed to the cultural shift away from liberal nationalism and toward supraterritorial ideologies from the mid-1930s on. The military coup in 1952 set the stage for the rise of religious extremism in the country.[3]

Likewise, the Iranian Constitutional Revolution of 1905 gave impetus to Shi 'i political modernism, anticlerical secularism, and modern nationalism, which remained the dominant discourse until the U.S.-British-engineered coup in 1953. The breakdown of Reza Shah's authoritarian rule in 1941 as a result of the Allied invasion of the country created a political space favorable for the emergence of liberal nationalism, but the coup of 1953 was another significant event that marked a new episode in the country's contemporary history where the newly empowered Shah undermined the organization of secular oppositional movements, channeling oppositional politics into the religious medium—hence the rise of radical Islamism. Finally, the Iranian Revolution of 1979 and the imposition of a monolithic religious discourse from above by the ruling clerics set the stage for the decline of religious fundamentalism and the rise of Islamic reformism.[4] Other Islamic countries also experienced cultural change following a major event. Syria's crisis of 1860 during which scores of Christians and Jews were massacred by Muslim mobs, Abdülhamid pan Islamic despotism, and the Turkish revolution of 1908 contributed to the rise of liberal Arabism among Syrian intellectuals. The Baathist 1963 coup in Syria that led to the formation of an intrusive secular Arab socialist regime resulted in the decline of secular ideologies and the rise of militant Islamic fundamentalism.[5] Finally, the 1962 Algerian independence was a historical event marking the breakdown of the religion-secular alliance between the ulama (Muslim theologians) and the Western educated elite, which led the liberation movement against the French. The Islamic movement was then developed into a strong protest in 1964 against the socialism of Ben Bella's regime. It was further radicalized in reaction to the leftward shift in the policies of the Boumédienne's regime in the early seventies.[6]

Table 10.1 presents a summary list of these events and the subsequent cultural outcomes. In these cases, an event is a causal factor in historical change, and the change itself is measured in terms of, according to Moaddel (2005), differences in the dominant cultural trends in society before and after the event, using the discourses of intellectual leaders as indicators of these trends. However, the attribution of causality to an event is much more complicated than it first appears. For, not all occurrences are eventful, not every event marks a new cultural episode, and not every rupture in a local structure tears social bonds in the structure of the larger society. A fight in a local bar, Sewell (1996) explains, while breaking the usual routine of sociability, may have no serious consequences.

Table 10.1   Significant events and cultural change in the Islamic world

Episode	*Discourse*
Sepoy mutiny in India (1857–59)	Islamic modernism
Napoleon invasion of Egypt (1798–1801)	The rise of liberal age
Assembly of delegates (1866), economic crisis, Urabi rebellion (1879–82), British occupation of Egypt	Development of liberal nationalist thought
The crisis of 1860 in Syria, Abdülhamid despotism (1876–1908)	Development of liberal Arab nationalism
Iranian Constitutional Revolution (1905–11)	Anticlerical secularism, modern nationalism
Economic crisis of the 1930s, following the economic boom of 1920s	The crisis of orientation (mid–930s): the decline of liberal nationalism, the rise of Arab nationalism, and the Muslim Brothers
Military coups in Egypt (1952), Iran (1953), Syria (1963), and shift in the state's policies in Algeria in 1970.	Decline of secular ideologies and the rise of religious extremism, Islamic fundamentalism
The Iranian Revolution of 1977–79	Decline of Islamic fundamentalism and the rise of reformism

"But if, say, one of the combatants is white and the other black, the initial rupture could be amplified by a rupture in the system of race relations that also structures interactions in the bar, and this could lead to a generalized racial brawl, which could touch off a city-wide riot, which in turn could permanently embitter race relations, discredit the mayor and police chief, and scare off private investments—and, of course, alter the mode of sociability in bars" (44).

To stress further the signification process involved in transcending a local occurrence into a major national event, we may cite the British infliction of a swift and severe punishment on a group of villagers for killing one of their officers in Dinshawai, Egypt, in June 1906. The cruelty with which the sentence was carried out—the condemned men were flogged and hanged in their own village, while their families were looking on—caused indignation among Egyptians. Ali Yusuf wrote 23 articles in *al-Muayyad*, Egyptian nationalist Mustafa Kamil fully exploited the incident in Paris, and hardly a poet kept silent. Qasim Amin recorded that "every one I met had a broken heart and a lump in his throat. There was nervousness in every gesture—in their hands and their voices. Sadness was on every face, but it was a peculiar sort of sadness. It was confused, distracted and visibly subdued by superior force. . . . The spirits of the hanged men seemed to hover over every place in the city" (Ahmed 1960: 63). The intense emotions that the incident aroused and the unity of identity between the villagers experiencing the trauma and the wider Egyptian public, however, signified that something broader was happening in the country's political landscape: the rise of a generalized nationalist consciousness that enabled educated Egyptians to join in common cause with the peasants against the British (Berque 1972: 237–38). The British had been attacked in Egypt before the Dinshawai incident, and they had displayed their unshaken resolve by punishing the perpetrators swiftly. In this case, however, the suffering of the villagers was transcended beyond a national trauma, representing an instance of the ongoing struggle of Egyptians against the British for national liberation (Moaddel 2005).

Thus, events may or may not attain signification attributes, and this apparent indeterminacy has led Sewell (1996: 844) to admit that "the conception of historical events retains significant theoretical and methodological ambiguities." Furthermore, since cultural change is the result of human action, and humans begin to act when events shape their attitudes and emotions, historical materials—for example, books, polemics, documents, and other traces of human actions—are hardly adequate for a systematic assessment of event-induced attitudinal and value changes. Researchers in the field of public opinion, on the other hand, have made considerable advances in understanding the influence of events in shaping mass-level belief systems and attitudes, using a more sophisticated survey research methodology. They, nonetheless, share Sewell's concern.

These researchers have also offered considerable empirical evidence that connects events to attitudinal change, collective memory, and emotion: that a sudden political crisis abroad may increase Americans' support for the president through what is known as the rally-around-the-flag effect (Mueller 1973); that abrupt changes in foreign policy opinions among Americans are connected to specific events, particularly war or political conflict (Page and Shapiro 1992: 332–34); that while some events have historical effects (Converse 1987: 69), the influence of other events is cohort-dependent (Jennings 1987: 77)—that is, "the crucial carrier of collective memories of an event are not all who were alive when the event occurred, but mainly those individuals who experienced the event during their critical ages of adolescence and early adulthood" (Schuman and Rodgers 2004: 250)—that different generational experiences shape the individuals' acceptance of varying politically-significant historical analogies—that is, whether Persian Gulf War was analogous to World War II or to the Vietnam War (Mannheim 1952; Schuman and Reiger 1992: 315–17); and that "broad-based collective events derive much of their potential power by inciting strong emotional feelings and provoking active discussion" (Pennebaker, Paez, and Rimé 1997: viii). Generally, public opinion researchers have coined the terms event-graded (Featherman and Lerner 1985) or episodic (Alwin, Cohen, and Newcomb 1991: 17) in order to capture the magnitude of event-induced changes in individual attitudes.

Yet, as is the case in comparative historical sociology, the problem of the attribution of causality to events is not fully resolved in the public opinion literature, and the reasoning behind this problem is not too different from that of Sewell's. As Page and Shapiro (1992: 335–36) note, there are ambiguities in connecting events to opinion changes; whereas events have some unmediated impact, their influences often work through the interpretive and manipulative processes unleashed by politically powerful individuals and through the control mechanisms these individuals exert. These "mediators," they say, "in turn, may be influenced by various actors in society, including organized interests, corporations, and mass movements" (353). Ambiguities, for these authors, arise because of the difficulties in dissecting the impact of the occurrences from the influence

of "the spin doctors"—the interpretations of the occurrences by politically weighty individuals and groups.

The problem of causality may not be due to the ambiguities of events,
but rather to the way in which events are conceptualized. The primary
question is not whether events cause a change in people's perceptions
and attitudes, but rather under what conditions events cause this change.
Certain occurrences have no notable political or social consequences,
despite their magnitude in affecting human conditions, whereas others
become eventful, having significant impacts on social relationships, attitudes, and emotion. Horrendous "events," says Alexander (2004: 8), "do
not, in and of themselves, create collective trauma. [They] . . . are not
inherently traumatic. Trauma is a socially mediated attribution." We thus
argue that the significance of an occurrence may not be derived from the
thing that happened, but from the kind of meaning the event carries for
social actors. And the meaning itself is not haphazardly produced. It
is structured by the nature of the political and cultural context in which
social actors are embedded as well as by the type of occurrences.

Given that the dynamics of public opinion are tied to the dynamics of
politics (Sniderman 1993: 220), an event may affect public opinion
through its political relevance and ramifications. As a result of insertion
into the political process, events are constituted by and through the
social process of representation. An occurrence becomes eventful in
contributing to change, when it gains socially constituted attributes
that convey meanings for individuals. These attributes give the event a
distinctive identity. In fact, the symbolic significance of an occurrence
and the kind of interpretation that is attached to it by various groups and
influential individuals, while being contested by diverse groups
and revised in different historical episodes, form the key elements from
which an event is constructed. We thus contend that events are consequential in bringing about outcomes—in this case, attitude change—
when they are popped or incorporated into the ongoing cultural debate
and political conflict.[7]

To understand how events contribute to attitudinal changes, therefore, it is necessary to obtain adequate comprehension of the nature of
the historically significant issues being debated in society, the framing
contests, and the individuals and groups that are involved in this contest.
Issues are points of contestations and conflicts among different political
and cultural contenders. Events provide the sense experience or information for different sides of the conflict to articulate their positions on
these issues, to promote their resolutions of the issues, and change the
balance of forces in their favor in order to win over public attitudes to

their side. If historical events initiate and push forward moments of change, historical issues are the pivots around which such changes revolve. Changes in people's attitudes toward issues following an event are indicative of the manner in which people have interpreted the event.

Linking Theory and Data

The event of 9/11 is distinctive not just in terms of the method the terrorists used and the extent of devastation they caused. It is also unique because the terrorists, proclaiming themselves as representative agents of the Islamic world, launched their violence on Americans with the intention to affect the attitudes of the public in Islamic countries. They justified their terrorism based on an image, which they themselves created, of Muslim nations tormented and traumatized by the American-led "Jewish–Crusade alliance" (Sageman 2004: 20). If the image is true and the act is justified, they expected that the Islamic publics would rally to their side. In other words, as the terrorists were aiming to destroy America's symbol of success and greatness, they were also aiming to destroy, metaphorically, the edifice of the secular discourse around which cultural warfare has been intensely waged in Islamic countries, including Egypt and Morocco. Given that the terrorists' agenda was based on the rejection of Western values on such principles of social organization as religion, gender, and politics, a favorable societal impact of their action would have been a shift in the public opinion away from these values.

To be sure, the influence of events is spatialized; *where* events happen is important in influencing collective memory (Griffin 2004, Scott and Zac 1993). And it is reasonable to expect that 9/11 would have a much more dramatic effect on people living in proximity to ground zero than on those who were farther away. Moreover, for the publics of Middle Eastern countries, the event of 9/11 is certainly different from such events as, for example, the military coup of 1952 in Egypt, Algerian independence of 1962, or the Iranian Revolution of 1979, which deeply affected not only people's emotions and values but the structure and rules of social organizations as well. What is more, considering anecdotal evidence, newspaper reports, and commentaries by public officials and opinion leaders in Arab countries, many among the Islamic publics have held the view that 9/11 had nothing to do with Muslims or Islam, even questioning the possibility of a group of terrorists being capable of successfully launching the attacks on the World Trade Center and the Pentagon.[8] How could then one connect 9/11 to changes in people's attitudes in Arab countries?

Nonetheless, the increasingly interconnectedness of different parts of the world through systems of mass communication and transportation as a result of globalization may to some degree overcome the problem of distance as news about events are broadcasted globally and instantaneously. Furthermore, Muslims' disengagements of the terrorists act from their religion or even denial of the possibility that a small group can carry out such a vicious attack may at least indicate that they could not remain indifferent to what transpired on that fateful day. Remoteness and denial notwithstanding, what seems clear is that the Middle Eastern publics have also had close encounters and experiences with the political violence perpetrated by radical Islamic groups in their own societies. Within the context of these encounters and experiences, 9/11 may thus gain meanings and become eventful. We thus argue that the nature and extent of the impact of 9/11 on public attitudes depends on the degree to which the event has relevance for the ongoing conflict between radical Islamism and the secular government and groups in these countries. In the following narrative, we thus first present the state of cultural and political conflict between the followers of radical Islamism and the secular governments in Egypt and Morocco in the decades preceding 9/11. We also discuss the issues being contested. We then develop hypotheses about the effects of 9/11 on people's attitudes toward these issues. Next, we use the values survey data collected before and after 9/11 to assess the impact of this event on the value orientations of the publics toward these issues in the two Islamic countries.

Contests for the Intellectual Control of Society: Egypt and Morocco

In the modern period, Middle Eastern countries have experienced such diverse cultural movements as Islamic modernism, liberal nationalism, Arabism and Arab nationalism, Arab socialism, and monarchy-centered nationalism. Yet, despite this diversity, the issues in relation to which the intellectual leaders of these movements formulated their discourses have remained remarkably invariant. These issues are related to Western culture, the form of government, the role of religion in politics, national identity, and the status of women. These cultural movements represent different resolutions of these issues. In Islamic modernism, for example, Western culture is acknowledged favorably, Islamic political theory and the idea of constitutionalism are reconciled, the construction of the modern state is endorsed, and a feminist exegesis of the Quran is advanced in order to defend women's rights. In Islamic fundamentalism, on the other hand, Western culture is portrayed as decadent, constitutionalism is abandoned in favor of the unity of religion and politics in an Islamic government, and the institutions of male domination and gender segregation are prescribed and rigorously defended (Moaddel 2005).

The degree to which the attitudes of the Islamic publics converge with the fundamentalist positions on these issues may be an indication of the level of support for radical Islamism in society.

Religion and Politics in Egypt

The liberal age in Egypt declined in the mid-1930s before the onslaught of two movements united by their common hostilities to liberal nationalism and parliamentary politics. One was Arab nationalism, which was used by the "free officers" of the Egyptian army to stage the 1952 coup, and the other was the fundamentalism of the Muslim Brothers (Gershoni and Jankowski 1995). Although the Brothers were not an extremist group and in the 1940s opted to participate in parliamentary politics, as pluralism declined and their participation in electoral competitions was blocked, an extremist trend prevailed in their midst. This process was reinforced after the coup, when the Arab nationalist leaders imposed a monolithic regime of signification on Egyptian society. One of the spokespeople for the growing religious extremism was Sayyid Qutb (1906–66), who rejected the Islamicity of the existing order and depicted Egypt as a throwback to the state of the ignorance (*jahiliyya*) that, in Muslim view, had characterized the conditions of pre-Islamic Arabia (Kepel 1984; Mitchell 1969). His disciple, Muhammadd Abd al-Salam Faraj (1954–82), further claimed that the current rulers of Islamic countries were all apostates and should be overthrown in order to establish a truly Islamic state (Akhavi 1992: 94–95).

Several factors are believed to have strengthened radical Islamism in the 1970s through the 1980s: (1) the Arab defeat in the 1967 war with Israel, which eroded the legitimacy of Arab nationalism; (2) President Sadat's courting of the Islamic groups in order to weaken the leftist legacy of his predecessor Nassir; (3) the Iranian revolution, which provided an example of a successful Islamic revolution; and (4) reaction to the Soviet invasion of Afghanistan, which mobilized Muslim activists from all over the Islamic world and brought them together in one place to interact, share ideas, and gain considerable military training. However, in their plans to change society according to their view of a proper Islamic order, a significant portion of Muslim activists failed to utilize the favorable cultural environment in a peaceful and moderate manner. They preferred to use force and violence in order to effectuate change.

The major incidents perpetrated by the adherents of extremism include a failed plot by an Islamic liberation organization to launch a coup by first killing President Sadat and his top officials in 1974; the formation of a puritan group that ran afoul of the law in 1976 and the kidnapping and killing of a former minister in 1977 by this group; the assassination of President Sadat in 1981; the launching of a campaign of terror against Egyptian officials, secular writers, and the Copts in the 1980s; an attempt on President Mubarak's life in Addis Ababa in 1995; and the killing of more than 60 tourists in Luxor in 1997. These campaigns of terror not only failed to produce an Islamic state but also resulted in the perpetrators taking heavy losses. Nearly, all the leaders of the radical Islamic groups were either killed or captured by security forces. The leadership of one of the two major terrorist groups, Islamic jihad, fled Egypt to escape from persecution and joined forces with Osama bin Laden's al-Qaeda. The leadership of the other group, Jama'a Islamiyya, and a large number of its followers were captured and imprisoned (Sageman 2004: 25–51). If these groups had any success, it was to force the government to take an Islamic posture on the public stage, the secularist writers to engage in self-censorship to avoid becoming the target of attack by the extremists, and the women to wear headscarfs to prevent harassment by Muslim activists.

Heavy losses and the general failure to Islamize society naturally forced the imprisoned leadership of the Islamic group to reflect on the correctness and effectiveness of their tactics. As early as July 1997, the leaders of Jama'a Islamiyya announced from prison a unilateral ceasefire, reasoning that the terrorist campaign in Egypt had been a failure and the strategy of mobilizing the public to overthrow the government had backfired, turning Egyptians against them. Instead, they insisted on using peaceful means in the pursuit of their religious objectives. They also condemned the Luxor massacre (Sageman 2004: 47). After 9/11, they even criticized Osama bin Laden for his obsession with jihad, the destruction of the World Trade Center, and the killing of innocent people, a terrorist act that did not serve Muslims (Ahmed 2002).

Religion and Politics in Morocco

Unlike Egypt, which has been dominated by secular politics since the time of Muhammad Ali in the early nineteenth century, the Moroccan regime has been based on the Islamic identity of the monarch. The king is portrayed as a defender of Islam, a descendant of the Prophet, a bearer of the Sufi virtues, a holy man, and a dispenser of God's blessing in the world (Lapidus 1992: 19). Morocco under King Hassan II (r. 1961–99) experienced considerable transformation, however (Sabagh 1993). The king modified religious tradition and promoted a liberal economy and multiparty politics. He described his political strategy as "homeopathic democracy," a process of controlled and well-managed change that maintains social peace while promoting economic development and general welfare (Combs-Schilling 1989; Maddy-Weitzman 1997; Zartman 1987).

The first major threat to the kingdom, since independence from France in 1956, came from the socialist and leftist forces in the 1960s. In addition to the use of force and propaganda (Munson 1993: 149), the king also courted Islamic groups to curb the influence of the left. This policy was similar to that of Egyptian President Sadat, which also contributed to a similar outcome—the rise of Islamic extremism in the 1970s. Represented by a Muslim Youth Association (formed in 1969 and legally accredited in 1972), the extremist trend considered itself the vanguard of an authentic Islamic revolution and launched a violent campaign against secular groups by assassinating a left–wing leader and two of his supporters. Other major Islamic trends, predominantly nonviolent, were nonetheless socially aggressive in promoting what they considered the moral standards of a virtuous society. Led by a mosque preacher in Tangier, Fqih al-Zamzami, this movement focused on matters of individual piety and righteousness, criticizing corruption and the concentration of wealth. Another and more radical trend was that of Abdl al-Salam Yasin, a former education ministry school inspector, who organized the outlawed *al-Adl wal-Ihsan* (Justice and Charity) movement (Munson 1993: 153–58, 162–73).

With the upsurge of Islamic fundamentalism (Barber 1994; *The Economist* 1995: 44), Moroccan university campuses became the scene of conflict between Islamic and leftist groups. In 1994, violent confrontations between these groups left seven people dead (Kokan 1994: 11). In 1997, the security forces put down strikes by students at the University of Casablanca and the University of Marrakesh in order to curb the rising tide of the radical Islamization of the students (*The Economist* 1997: 45). Even when King Hassan embarked on a policy of change and reform, the chief beneficiaries were such fundamentalist politicians as Abdelilah Ben Kirane, a member of Morocco's Islamic youth movement who in the 1970s was elected to parliament and promised that Morocco would apply its constitution as a true Islamist state (*The Economist* 1999: 46). Emboldened Islamic activists even forced the king to shelve the pro-women reform program even though, in 1994, women's groups collected one million signatures petitioning for the revision of the personal status law (Fernea 2000; Maddy-Weitzman 1997). The new king, Mohammed VI, however, was more committed to reform, but when he launched a "national action plan" to give more rights to women, the Islamic groups mobilized their supporters in opposition. In 2000, the Moroccan government and the Islamic groups staged rival rallies for and against, respectively, the plan. In these rallies, the fundamentalists outnumbered the government's supporters by ten to one (*The Economist* 2000: 44, 46). Pressure from them and some of the ulama forced the government to turn the proposals over to a committee for revision.

In addition, Islamic activists began a vociferous campaign to express discontent with what they considered "the prevalence of nudity and semi-nudity on the country's beaches . . . They claimed that hundreds of [their] . . . members, both men and women, flocked to the country's beaches, holding congregational prayers, rebuking and enjoining less modest Moroccans to do good and forsake evil deeds, and jumping into the water fully clothed" (Crescent International 2001). Some extremists went as far as kidnapping and killing the individuals who allegedly engaged in drinking alcohol, going to bars, or dancing (Irvine 2002).

September 11 and Changes in the Balances of Cultural Forces in Egypt and Morocco

While al-Qaeda presented itself as the vanguard of the Islamic movement to free Muslim nations allegedly subjugated by the agents of the far enemy, the legacy of radical Islamism in Egypt and Morocco portrays a different picture. For well over the two decades preceding 9/11, Islamic extremists were involved in extensive acts of violence, assassinations and kidnappings, and harassments of religious minorities, of secular intellectuals, and of people whose lifestyle in their view was un-Islamic. Decades of radical Islamism, however, not only failed to produce a successful Islamic revolution but also contributed to public indignation against the religious extremists.[9] We thus propose that when the news of 9/11 had reached Egyptians and Moroccans, in all likelihood this background played a key role in their assessments of the event and its meanings. For them, the horrific violence on the U.S. soil represented another instance of the violent activities committed by the religious extremists. Consequently, it changed the balance of cultural forces in the two countries in favor of the proponents of modern values—democracy, gender equality, and secularism.

We thus propose that far from winning them over, the terrorism of 9/11 further alienated the Islamic publics, contributing to changes in their attitudes in a direction away from the ideology of Islamic extremism.

Before and After 9/11 Surveys in

Egypt and Morocco

The pre-9/11 survey in Egypt was carried out in August–September 2001, and the post-9/11 about six months later, in January–February 2002.[10] Of the national representative sample of 3,000 Egyptian adults (16 or older) randomly selected to be interviewed, 2,230 cases were completed just before 9/11. These cases covered the governorates of Cairo, Alex, Menofia, Bani Suef, Sohaq, and Aswan. The other 770 cases covering the governorates of Sohag, Aswan, and South Sinai were completed after 9/11. The post-9/11 survey was based on a sample of 1,000 adults randomly selected from the six governorates that were covered by the survey before 9/11. Table 10.2 summarizes the distribution of the pre- and post-9/11 samples by governorates.

In Morocco, the pre-9/11 survey of a national representative sample of 1,251 adults (18 or older) was completed in August 2001. The post-9/11 survey of a representative sample of 1,013 adults was carried out in February 2002, about six months after the completion of the first survey. All the surveys were based on face-to-face interviews.

Table 10.2 Distribution of samples before and after 9/11 by governorates of Egypt. The data in brackets [ ] were collected between September 11 and October 30

Governorate	Sample size before 9/11	Sample size after 9/11
1. Cairo	400	180
2. Alex	200	90
3. Ismailia	[170]	
4. Menofia	630	285
5. Kafr el-Sheikh	[500]	
6. Bani Suef	320	140
7. Sohag	500	225
8. Aswan	180	80
9. South Sinai	[100]	
Total	2230 [3000]	1000

Indicators of Sociopolitical and Cultural Attitudes

Table 10.3 reports the questions and coding that are used to measure the Egyptians' and Moroccans' attitudes toward historically significant sociopolitical and cultural issues. These questions measure the respondents' attitudes toward (1) Western cultural invasion, (2) religious authorities, (3) the shari 'a, (4) religion and politics, (5) women, (6) democracy, (7) strong leader, and (8) whose interests the country's economy serves. Except for a few items, the survey questionnaires in Egypt and Morocco were identical.

For a more effective analysis and better comprehension, composite measures of the variables that were fairly to highly correlated and reflected a common concept were constructed. The first composite measure is based on attitudes toward religious authorities: indicators 2a–2d. For both countries, zero-order correlation coefficients among these indicators ranged from .40 to .72. The average of these variables is used as a composite index of attitudes toward religious authorities (religious authorities).[11] The second composite measure is based on attitudes toward democracy: questions 6a–6d. Among these four questions, 6d displayed little variation across the surveys. Before 9/11, 97 precent of Egyptians *agreed strongly* or *agreed* that democracy is the best system of government, compared to 99 percent after 9/11. For Morocco before and after 9/11, these figures were 96 percent and 96 percent. Because of the minimal variability, we dropped this indicator from further analysis. Indicators 6a–6c, on the other hand, displayed considerable variability across the surveys. The size of zero-order correlation coefficients among these indicators ranged from 0.39 to 0.54. A composite measure based on these questions (Democracy) was constructed in the same way as the composite variable for attitudes toward Religious authorities.

The means and standard deviations of all the indicators of attitude changes that are used in the analysis and the percentage mean differences before and after 9/11 for Egypt and Morocco are reported in table 10.4. This table summarizes attitudes for the two countries before and after 9/11.

Hypotheses

Between the surveys that were completed just before 9/11 and those completed about six months later, a host of other events also transpired. These events were: (1) the launching of a massive campaign against radical Islamism and the authoritarian governments in the Middle East that were implicated, either directly or otherwise, in the rise of religious

Table 10.3   Indicators of Change in Egyptian and Moroccan Worldviews

---

1. Western cultural invasion: *Do you consider Western cultural invasion to be (5) very important, (4) important, (3) somewhat important, (2) least important, or (1) not important problem?* (not included in pre−9/11 survey in Morocco)

2. Religious authorities: *Do you think—(1) No, (2) Yes—that the religious authorities in this country are giving adequate answers*
   a) *To the moral problems and needs of the individual?*
   b) *To the problems of family life?*
   c) *To people's spiritual needs?*
   d) *To the social problems facing our country today?*

3. The shari 'a: *Do you consider (5) very important, (4) important, (3) somewhat important, (2) least important, or (1) not important for a good government to implement only the shari 'a?* (not included in pre−9/11 survey in Morocco)

4. Religion and Politics: *Could you please tell me if you (5) agree strongly, (4) agree, (3) neither agree or disagree, (2) disagree, or (1) disagree strongly, with the following:*
   a) *Politicians who do not believe in God are unfit for public office*
   b) *It would be better for your country if more people with strong religious beliefs hold public office (religious people in public office)*
   c) *Religious leaders should not influence the government* (not included in the Egyptian surveys)

5. Women: *Do you (4) agree strongly, (3) agree, (2) disagree, or (1) disagree strongly with:*
   a) *On the whole, men make better political leaders than women do?*
   b) *A university education is more important for a boy than for a girl*
   c) *Do you (3) agree, (2) neither agree nor disagree, or (1) disagree with men should have more right to a job than women*

6. Democracy: *Do you (1) agree strongly, (2) agree, (3) disagree, or (4) disagree strongly, with*
   a) *In democracy, the economy runs badly?*
   b) *Democracies are indecisive?*
   c) *Democracies aren't good at maintaining order?*
   d) *Democracy may have problems but it's better than any other form of government?*

7. Strong leader: *Is it (4) a very good, (3) fairly good, (2) fairly bad or (1) very bad to have a strong head of government who does not have to bother with parliament and elections?*

8. The Economy Serves whose interests: *Generally speaking, would you say that this country's economy is run (1) for the benefit of all the people or (2) by a few big interests looking out for themselves?*

Table 10.4 The means and standard deviations of indicators of attitudes change and percentage mean differences for Egypt and Morocco between before and after 9/11

Variable	Egypt				Morocco				Egypt	Morocco
	Before 9/1		After 9/1		Before 9/1		After 9/1		%Mean Change	%Mean Change
	Mean	SD	Mean	SD	Mean	SD	Mean	SD		
1. Western cultural invasion	4.50	0.87	4.62	0.69	—	—	4.55	0.84	2.53	—
2. Men make better political leaders	3.41	0.80	3.01	0.90	3.20	1.01	3.02	1.04	−11.86	−5.46
3. University education more important for boys	2.18	1.08	1.80	0.93	2.71	1.21	1.94	0.98	−17.36	−28.37
4. Men have more rights to a job	2.88	0.34	2.92	0.27	2.79	0.57	2.61	0.75	1.41	−6.50
5. Strong leader	1.57	0.73	1.26	0.50	1.55	1.01	1.55	0.96	−19.32	−0.19
6. Democracy	2.99	0.63	3.12	0.48	2.27	0.78	2.70	0.70	4.09	19.32
7. Satisfaction with religious authorities	1.87	0.24	1.69	0.37	1.97	0.14	1.94	0.19	−9.59	−1.44
8. Atheist politicians unfit for public office	4.43	1.08	4.45	1.07	4.61	0.85	4.24	1.21	0.27	−7.99
9. Religious people in public office	4.39	0.84	4.16	0.95	3.58	1.41	3.64	1.25	−5.24	1.63
10. Religious leaders should not influence politics	—	—	—	1.19	3.53	1.45	3.93	1.20	—	11.36
11. Good govt. implements only the shari 'a	4.21	1.00	3.92	1.19	—	—	—	—	−6.94	—
12. Economy serves big interests	1.68	0.47	1.77	0.42	1.74	0.44	1.79	0.41	5.66	2.90

extremism; (2) the U.S. military invasion of Afghanistan, overthrow of the Taliban, and stepped-up efforts at regime change and nation-building; and (3) sharpened U.S. rhetoric against Iran and Iraq as part of the axis of evil, and against Saudi Arabia as a conniving ally. In assessing the impact of 9/11 on the worldviews of Egyptians and Moroccans, as we have argued, the event cannot be detached from the interpretations of it by diverse actors. The massive campaign against religious extremism has been certainly an important factor in shaping public opinion against Islamic fundamentalism. To counter that, al-Qaeda and other Muslim extremists also continued their campaign against the United States and its values.

However, given the legacy of Islamic extremism in Egypt and Morocco, we argue that the terrorist attack would not be likely to promote favorable attitudes toward the ideology of radical Islamism. We have formulated several explicit hypotheses suggesting that, contrary to the terrorists' expectations, the violence of 9/11 would produce a shift in public attitudes toward:

1. democracy
2. gender equality
3. secularism

We do not believe that this change in public opinion is a result of the U.S. military intervention in Afghanistan and the shift in its policy toward regime change. It is hard to sustain that the military intervention, which unavoidably entailed the destruction of Muslim lives and property, would prompt the Egyptian and Moroccan publics to develop more favorable attitudes toward Western values. To connect 9/11 to changes in attitudes, we propose, following Blumer (1969), that people formulate orientations toward events in terms of the meaning these events have for them, and that this meaning is shaped by their past experiences. If, for example, a group of Palestinians danced at the refugee camp after hearing the news of the terrorist attack on the World Trade Center in New York, while some Iranians held candlelight vigil to express their sympathy with the U.S. public, it was because these two groups of people have different political experiences—the former facing the U.S. unwavering support for Israel and the latter having to live under an autocratic anti-American Islamic fundamentalist regime.

There is, however, one way to assess a possible effect of the U.S. intervention on the attitudes of Egyptians and Moroccans. We argue that if the U.S. intervention and military presence in the Middle East would have promoted Western values, then there must be less concern among the publics with Western cultural invasion after 9/11 than before. That is, *the Islamic publics would become less concerned with Western cultural invasion.*

Support for democracy is measured in terms of the respondent's score on the composite measure of democracy and attitude toward a strong leader; for gender equality in terms of attitudes toward the three gender-related variables—"men make better political leaders," "boys have more rights to university education," and "men have more rights to a job"; for secularism in terms of the respondent's score on the composite measure of satisfaction with religious authorities, and attitudes toward "politicians who do not believe in God are unfit for public office," "having people with strong religious views hold public office," "religious leaders should not influence the government," and "a good government implements only the shari 'a." Only one variable measures concern with Western cultural invasion. We propose that the Egyptian and Moroccan publics would become more supportive of democracy and less supportive of a strong leader; more in favor of gender equality in political leadership, in gaining access to university education, and in the job market; less satisfied with religious authorities, less supportive of the shari 'a, less supportive of having religious people hold public office, less unfavorable toward atheist politicians, and more in favor of religious leaders not interfering in politics; and less concern with Western cultural invasion after 9/11 than they did before.

Furthermore, given the authoritarian nature of Egyptian and Moroccan governments and lack of transparency in their conduct, the shift in attitudes toward democracy and secularism and away from religious fundamentalism may not be associated with an increase in support for the secular government. Because of political sensitivity, researchers were not allowed to ask questions about people's satisfaction with the current ruler or his government's economic performance. Instead, the respondents were asked whether their country's economy runs for the benefits of a special few or for the benefits of all the people. This question is then used as a proxy measure of the degree of support for the political system. We propose that:

After 9/11, a higher percentage of Egyptians and Moroccans would believe that the economy runs for the interests of a special few than they did before 9/11.

Moderators: Education, Gender, and Age

Events do not uniformly affect all members of society. The influence of event often interacts with age, education, and gender. Mannheim (1952) was among the first to recognize the significance of common cohort experiences in shaping attitudes. Following his lead, researchers further uncovered the vulnerability of younger cohorts to the influences of social and political events (Alwin, Cohen, and Newcomb 1991; Sear 1981; Schuman and Rieger 1992; Schuman and Rodgers 2004). Schuman and Scott (1989) found that when people of varying ages were asked what historical events seemed especially important to them, they disproportionately refer to events that occurred in their late teens and early twenties. Pennebaker and Banasik (1997: 14) report that "research dealing with autobiographical memories suggests that people tend to spontaneously recall memories that were formed between the ages of 12 and 25."

To assess the age-differential impact of 9/11, we created a dichotomous variable, where respondents aged below 26 are treated as the impressionable group and coded "1" and respondents aged 26 and above are coded "0," and propose that:

The event of 9/11 would result in more extensive changes in the attitudes of the younger cohort than it would in the attitudes of the older cohort.

Researchers have also established that attitude change may depend on the likelihood of comprehending the meaning of an event and on the ability to learn from it. These factors, in turn, depend on one's level of political awareness and preexisting knowledge of political affairs (Delli Carpini and Ketter 1989: 216; Price and Zaller 1993: 157; Zaller 1992: 148). It has been argued that the well-informed are more likely to express opinions, to use ideological terminology correctly, to possess stable opinions, to make use of facts in political discussion, to take an active part in politics, and to pick up new information easily and retain it readily (Kinder 1998: 176). One of the key determinants of political awareness and knowledge of politics is formal education, as "higher education clearly promotes political engagement and learning about politics" (Delli Carpini and Ketter 1989: 278). Education is also an indicator of cognitive ability (Stimson 1975), which strengthens the information processing efficiency of citizens and encourages certain values among individuals, including "openness of mind, a respect for science and empirical knowledge, an awareness of complexity and possibilities for change, and tolerance, not only of people but of points of view" (Sniderman et al. 1991: 9).

Considering these propositions and to assess the effects of the interaction of 9/11 and education on attitude change, we constructed a dichtomous variable based on high and low educational level (0 = low, and 1 = high), and propose that:[12]

The event of 9/11 would result in more extensive changes in the attitudes of the high education group than in the attitudes of the low education group.

Finally, studies have shown persistent gender differences in attitudes and value orientations (Delli Carpini and Keeter 1989; Inglehart and

Welzel 2005; Moaddel 2006; Page and Shapiro 1992; Zaller 1992). Moreover, given that gender is one of the most important organizing principles of Islamic societies and that some of the key issues in the cultural debates in contemporary Egypt and Morocco are related to the status of women, we explore the effect of the interaction between gender and 9/11 on attitude change. Gender is coded as a dichotomous variable (male = 0, female = 1). We propose that:

The impact of 9/11 on the attitudes of Egyptians and Moroccans would be moderated by gender.

Effects of 9/11

The independent variable based on pre- and post-9/11 surveys was created as a dichotomous variable (0 = before 9/11, 1 = after 9/11). Analyses were applied separately to Egyptian and Moroccan samples. We begin by presenting zero-order correlations among the variables. We then use multivariate analysis of variance to determine both the impact of 9/11 and the moderating effects of age, education, and gender.

Taken all together, 11 variable indicators are used in pre- and post-9/11 Egyptian data. Table 10.5 presents the zero-order correlation matrix among these indicators.[13] As this table shows, except for one indicator— "atheist politicians are unfit for public office"—9/11 is significantly associated with attitudinal changes in all the other variables. It increased the respondents' concerns about "Western cultural invasion." On attitudes toward gender relations, 9/11 had a negative effect on attitudes toward "men make better political leaders" and "university education is more important for boys," but a positive effect on attitudes toward "men have more right to a job." On political attitudes, it negatively affected attitudes toward "strong leader," and positively affected attitudes toward democracy. It also had negative effects on all the religion-related variables (except for the indicator mentioned). Finally, 9/11 enhanced the respondents' view that the country runs for the benefits of a special few. While the direction of change in two of the indicators—attitudes toward "Western cultural invasion" and "men have more rights to a job"—were contrary to our prediction, all other changes were in the expected direction in Egypt.

For Morocco, questions related to Western cultural invasion and the shari 'a were not included in the first survey, but the surveys contained an additional question "religious leaders should not influence the government." As a result, 10 indicators were included in the analysis. Table 10.6 presents the zero-order correlations among these indicators.

272

Table 10.5 Zero-order correlation coefficients between September 11 and the dependent variables for Egypt

	September 11	Western cultural invasion	Men make better political leaders	Univ. ed more important for boys	Men have more rights to a job	Strong leader	Democracy	Satisfaction with religious authorities	Atheist politicians unfit for public office	Religious people in public office	Good govt. implements only the shari'a	Economy serves big interests
September 11	1.000											
Western cultural invasion	0.055**	1.000										
Men make better political leaders	−0.225***	0.094***	1.000									
Univ. ed more important for boys	−0.128***	0.040*	0.198***	1.000								
Men have more rights to a job	0.060**	0.026	0.114***	0.082***	1.000							
Strong leader	−0.191***	−0.101***	0.042*	0.101***	−0.037	1.000						
Democracy	0.088***	0.063**	0.007	−0.118***	0.021	−0.161***	1.000					
Satisfaction with religious authorities	−0.299***	0.004	0.125***	0.012	−0.061**	0.075***	0.004	1.000				
Atheist politicians unfit for public office	−0.003	−0.009	−0.015	−0.005	−0.003	0.009	0.007	0.026	1.000			
Religious people in public office	−0.125***	0.011	0.138***	0.090***	0.035	0.055***	0.110***	0.005	−0.036	1.000		
Good govt. implements only the shari'a	−0.118***	0.063***	0.151***	0.028	0.014	0.051**	0.019	0.048*	−0.029	0.230***	1.000	
Economy serves big interests	0.076***	0.036	−0.049*	0.015	0.059**	−0.030	−0.034	−0.098***	−0.019	−0.006	−0.026	1.000

Listwise N = 2580

Note: *p < .05, **p < .01, ***p < .001 (two-tailed tests).

Table 10.6 Zero-order correlation coefficients between September 11 and the dependent variables for Morocco

September 11	1.000										
Men make better political leaders	−0.094*	1.000									
Univ. ed more important for boys	−0.245***	0.320***	1.000								
Men have more rights to a job	−0.090*	0.146**	0.155***	1.000							
Strong leader	−0.034	−0.072	0.074	0.075	1.000						
Democracy	0.311***	−0.028	−0.096*	−0.069	−0.100*	1.000					
Atheist politicians unfit for public office	−0.178***	0.125**	0.193***	0.140**	−0.006	−0.205***	1.000				
Religious person in public office	−0.092	0.194***	0.227***	0.152***	0.013	−0.127**	0.341***	1.000			
Religious leaders not influence govt	0.182***	0.033	0.001	0.081	0.119**	−0.102*	0.106*	−0.095*	1.000		
Satisfaction with religious authorities	−0.099*	0.083	0.096*	0.131**	0.053	−0.086*	0.337***	0.272***	0.027	1.000	
Economy serves big interests	0.024	0.040	−0.008	−0.039	−0.103*	0.001	0.067	−0.043	−0.007	0.082	1.000
Listwise N = 528											

Note: *p < .05, **p < .01, ***p < .001 (two-tailed tests).

The event of 9/11 had no significant effect on three of the indicators—"strong leader," "religious people in public office," and "the economy serves a few big interests." It had negative effects on all three gender-related questions—"men make better political leaders," "university education is more important for boys," and men have more right to a job. It had a positive effect on attitudes toward democracy. On the religion indicators, 9/11 enhanced unfavorable attitudes toward the involvement of religion in politics and lowered satisfaction with religious authorities. That is, it had negative effects on attitudes that "atheist politicians are unfit for public office," on "people with strong religious beliefs hold public office," and on satisfaction with "religious authorities," but a positive effect on attitudes toward "religious leaders should not influence the government."

In sum, after 9/11 it appears that a shift occurred in the attitudes of Egyptians and Moroccans in favor of gender equality, democracy, and secularism.[14] In Egypt, the largest changes occurred in attitudes toward religious authorities ($r = -.299$) and attitudes in favor of gender equality in political leadership ($r = -.225$) and university education ($r = -.128$). The increase in concern about the Western cultural invasion was the lowest among the significant attitudinal changes ($r = .055$). In Morocco, the largest changes were in attitudes toward democracy ($r = .311$), gender equality in university education ($r = -.245$), and "religious leaders should not influence the government" ($r = .182$). The change in attitudes toward "men have more right to a job" was the lowest ($r = -090$) among the statistically significant changes.

Multivariate Analyses

Taking all the dependent variables together as a vector (a set of variables), and taking into consideration that they are all correlated, a 2 (pre-and post-9/11) $\times$ 2(young versus old cohort) $\times$ 2 (low versus high education) $\times$ 2 (male versus female) multivariate analysis of variance was used to tests for overall differences between pre- and post-9/11 samples, overall differences for young and old age groups, overall differences between low and high educational groups, overall differences between male and female, and the interaction effects of 9/11 with age, education, and gender. This was followed by univariate analyses of variance that tested the statistical significance of each variable separately. Since we are interested in the effects of 9/11 and the effects of the interaction of 9/11 with age, education, and gender on the dependent variables, we discuss findings that pertain to these relationships only (table 10. 7).[15]

Table 10.7 Education, gender, age, September 11 and value change in Egypt and Morocco

Egypt: N = 1592 (before 9/11), 931 (after 9/11), 1866 (low education) 657 (high education), 1355 (male), 1168 (female), 623 (aged 16–25), 1899 (aged 26+)

Morocco: N = 349 (before 9/11), 241 (after 9/11), 489 (low education), 101 (high education), 392 (male), 198 (female), 182 (aged 18–25), 408 (aged 26+)

	(1) Sept. 11		(2) Age		(3) Education		(4) Gender		(5) Interaction of Age and 9/11		(6) Interaction of Education & 9/11		(7) Interaction of Gender& 9/11		(8) R^2	
	Egypt	Morocco	Egypt	Morocco	Egypt	Morocco	Egypt	Morocco	Egypt	Morocco	Egypt	Morocco	Egypt	Morocco	Egypt	Morocco
Western cultural invasion	6.71*	—	5.36*	—	2.58	—	7.28**	—	<1	—	<1	—	<1	—	0.015	—
Men make better political leaders	53.61***	1.93	6.69*	<1	11.40***	4.75*	113.8***	26.64***	4.08*	<1	<1	<1	<1	<1	0.107	0.070
Univ. ed more important for boys	12.40***	10.85***	<1	<1	32.87***	9.76**	77.28***	8.02**	4.94*	<1	1.18	<1	1.34	<1	0.072	0.124
Men have more right to jobs	7.31**	8.19**	5.42*	<1	<1	14.34***	15.87***	22.36***	1.16	1.57	2.26	<1	6.85**	3.73+	0.024	0.091
Strong leader	70.31***	<1	1.93	<1	1.09	2.08	<1	<1	1.04	2.20	<1	1.57	<1	<1	0.038	0.020
Democracy	33.23***	8.76**	<1	<1	2.33	7.18**	2.87	<1	1.48	1.47	13.34***	10.63***	<1	<1	0.019	0.133
Satisfaction with religious author	204.5***	7.54**	<1	<1	47.26***	10.10**	17.72***	1.32	10.20***	<1	42.4***	1.38	1.00	<1	0.131	0.041
Atheist politicians unfit for office	<1	7.10**	<1	<1	<1	1.99	<1	<1	1.12	3.48+	<1	<1	<1	<1	0.003	0.069
Religious people in public office	7.64**	1.78	<1	5.80**	26.12***	2.32	<1	<1	2.79+	<1	2.78*	<1	14.40***	<1	0.043	0.069
Religion leaders not influence pol.	—	14.33***	—	3.45+	—	—	—	<1	—	1.82	—	<1	—	<1	—	0.041
Good govt. implements shari'a	16.04***	—	<1	—	23.96***	—	<1	—	<1	—	<1	—	4.80*	—	0.028	—
Economy serves big interest	9.94**	<1	<1	3.99*	15.88***	<1	<1	1.47	<1	1.00	<1	2.09	<1	1.55	0.014	0.022
F-value	34.39***	5.80***	1.95*	1.32	13.62***	3.99***	19.70***	5.08***	2.27*	1.30	5.92***	1.79+	2.29**	0.80		
DF (hypothesis, error)	11.2502	10, 571	11.2502	10, 571	11.2502	10, 571	11.2502	10, 571	11.2502	10, 571	11.2502	10, 571	11.2502	10, 571		

Note: $^+$ p < .10, *p < .05, **p < .01, ***p < .001.

September 11 and Attitude Change

For Egypt, the main effect of the difference between pre- and post-9/11 samples is significant (9/11-main effect: F_{mult} [11, 2502] = 34.39, $p < .001$). All the interaction effects are also significant (9/11*Age: F_{mult} [11, 2502] = 2.27, $p < .05$; 9/11*Education: F_{mult} [11, 2502] = 5.92, $p < .001$; and 9/11*Gender: F_{mult} [11, 2502] = 2.29, $p < .01$). Likewise, for Morocco, the main effect of the difference between pre- and post-9/11 samples is significant (9/11-main effect: F_{mult} [10, 571] = 5.80, $p < .001$), but only the interaction between 9/11 and education is significant (9/11*Education: F_{mult} [10, 571] = 1.79, $p < .1$).[16]

Assessing the effect of 9/11 on each of the variables individually, for Egypt, our analysis also shows that each of the dependent variables has significantly changed, except for attitudes toward atheist politicians. After 9/11, Egyptians expressed less favorable attitudes toward "men make better political leaders," "university education is more important for boys," "having a strong leader as a characteristic of a good government," "religious authorities," "having people with strong religious beliefs hold public office," and "the implementation of the shari 'a as a characteristic of a good government" than they did before 9/11. They also developed a more favorable attitude toward democracy, but grew more critical of the government as more Egyptians believed that their "economy serves a few big interests" before and after 9/11. Before and after comparison of the sample data thus shows that the attitudes of Egyptians changed in favor of democracy, gender equality, and secular politics, all in a direction consistent with Western values and different from the values of radical Islamism.[17] There are, however, two exceptions to this pattern. One is that more Egyptians believed that "men should have more rights to a job" after 9/11 than they did before. The other is that they grew more concerned with "Western cultural invasion" after 9/11 than they did before. The increase in favorable attitudes toward "men have more rights to a job than women do" might be associated with the deteriorating economic conditions in Egypt, a result of the terrorism-induced decline in tourism. In a society where men are expected to be the breadwinner of the family, there would be a growing support for priority accorded to men over women in a tight job market. The heightened concerns with Western cultural invasion after 9/11, on the other hand, may be related to the American-led invasion of Afghanistan and the increase in rhetoric both by the U.S. government and in the media against Iran and Iraq as parts of the axis of evil and against religious establishment in Saudi Arabia as supportive of terrorism and promoters of religious intolerance. An examination of the R^2 values for Egypt demonstrates that the three variables that the model explained the most variations are attitudes toward "religious authorities," toward "men make better political leaders," and toward "university education is more important for boys," explaining 13 percent, almost 11 percent, and 7 percent of the total variations in these variables, respectively.

In Morocco, taking the effect of 9/11 on each of the variables individually, the multivariate analysis also shows that there is no significant difference in the respondents' attitudes for four of the indicators—attitudes toward "men make better political leaders," "having a strong leader as the characteristics of a good government," "having people with strong religious beliefs hold public office," and "economy serves a few big interests." On all other indicators, Moroccans, after 9/11, expressed less favorable attitudes toward "university education is more important for boys," toward "men have more rights to a job," toward "atheist politicians are unfit for public office," and toward "religious authorities" than they did before 9/11. At the same time, they grew more supportive of democracy and of the view that "religious leaders should not influence the government" after 9/11 than they did before. In general, Moroccans, like Egyptians, thus developed more favorable attitudes toward democracy, gender equality, and secularism between the two samples. An examination of the R^2 values for Morocco shows that the three variables that the model explained the most variations are attitudes toward democracy, "university education is more important for boys," and "having people with strong religious beliefs hold public office," explaining 13percent, 12.5percent, and 7percent of the total variations in these variables, respectively.

Age, Education, Gender, September 11, and

Attitude Change

Table 10.7 also summarizes the effects of 9/11-age interaction, 9/11-education interaction, and 9/11-gender interaction on attitude change in Egypt and Morocco. In Egypt, 9/11-age interaction has significant effects on attitudes toward "men make better political leaders," "university education is more important for boys," "religious authorities," and "having people with strong religious beliefs hold public office." In all these cases, it appears that the changes in attitudes were more dramatic for the older cohort than for the younger cohort. That is, before and after 9/11, there was a larger decline among those in the older cohort than among respondents in the younger cohort in attitudes toward "men make better political leaders" and "university education is more important for boys," "religious authorities," and "having people with strong religious beliefs hold public office." These interactions are presented graphically in figures 10.1–10.4. These findings are contrary to the impressionable-years hypothesis presented in the literature.

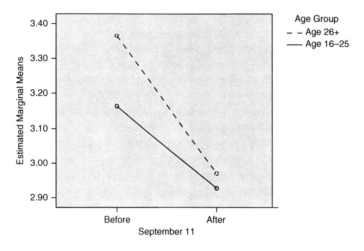

Figure 10.1 Mean differences in the support of the statement "Men make better political leaders" (1 = low support . . . , 4 = high support) between pre- and post-9/11 samples within each age group for Egypt

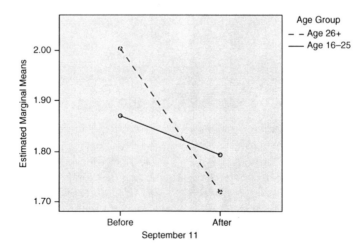

Figure 10.2 Mean differences in the support of the statement "Education is more important for boys" (1 = low support . . . , 4 = high support) between pre- and post-9/11 samples within each age group for Egypt

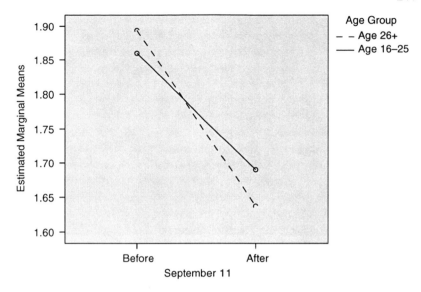

Figure 10.3 Mean differences in satisfaction with religious authorities (1 = not satisfied, 2 = satisfied) between pre- and post-9/11 samples within each age group for Egypt

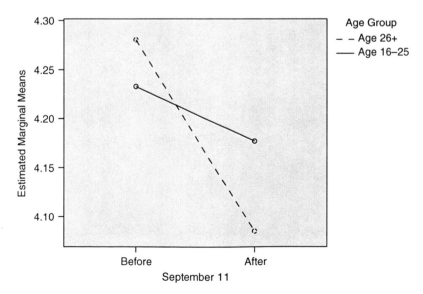

Figure 10.4 Mean differences in the support of people with strong religious beliefs holding public office (1 = low support . . . , 5 = high support) between pre- and post-9/11 samples within each age group for Egypt

There was also a significant interaction of 9/11 and education for the Egyptian sample on attitudes toward "democracy," "religious authorities," and a marginal effect for "having people with strong religious beliefs hold public office." These interactions are presented graphically in figures 10.5 through 10.7. According to figures 10.5 and 10.6, people with higher education grew more favorable toward democracy and less satisfied with religious authorities after 9/11 than did those with lower education. These changes are especially noteworthy considering that the differences in attitudes toward democracy and satisfaction with religious authorities between low and high educational groups were negligible before 9/11. However, on "having people with strong religious beliefs hold public office," the less educated changed their attitudes more dramatically than the more educated (figure 10.7). On this measure, people with low education became more secular after 9/11 than those with more education.

There are also significant interaction effects between gender and 9/11 on attitudes toward "men have more rights to a job," "having people with strong religious beliefs hold public office," and "the implementation of the shari 'a as a characteristic of a good government" among Egyptians. Post 9/11, women's favorable attitudes toward "men have more rights to a job" increased and converged with men's, a factor that

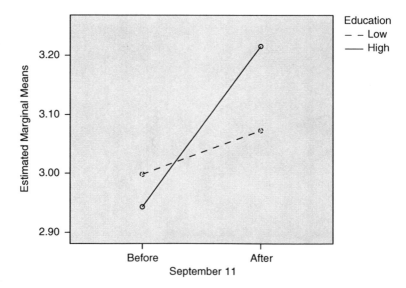

Figure 10.5 Mean differences in support for democracy (1 = low support . . . , 4 = high support) between pre- and post-9/11 samples within each education group for Egypt

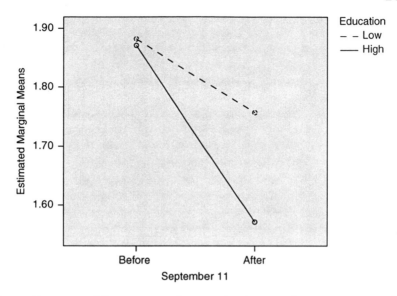

Figure 10.6 Mean differences in satisfaction with religious authorities (1 = not satisfied, 2 = satisfied) between pre- and post-9/11 samples within each education group for Egypt

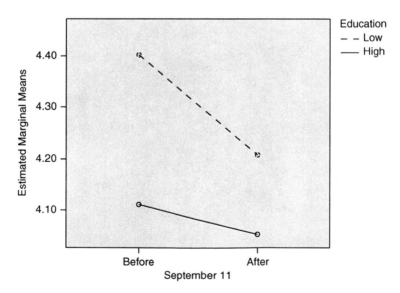

Figure 10.7 Mean differences in support of people with strong religious beliefs holding public office (1 = low support . . . , 5 = high support) between pre- and post-9/11 samples within each education group for Egypt

is contrary to our expectation. However, there was a dramatic decline in men's support for "having people with strong religious beliefs hold public office," and "the implementation of the shari 'a as a characteristic of a good government" before and after 9/11. On the last two measures, men became more secular after 9/11 than women, as shown in figures 10.8–10.10.

For Morocco, there are only three significant interaction effects. These are the interaction of 9/11 and age on attitudes toward "politicians who do not believe in God are unfit for public office," the interaction of 9/11 and education on attitudes toward democracy, and the interaction of 9/11 and gender on attitudes toward "men have more rights to a job." According to figure 10.11, before and after 9/11, there was a larger decline among the older cohort than among the younger cohort in attitudes favorable toward "men have more right to a job." As was true in Egypt, the members of the older cohort seemed to be more amenable to change than the members of the younger cohort.

Similar to Egypt, the interaction between education and 9/11 significantly enhanced attitudes toward democracy in Morocco. Unlike Egypt, however, 9/11 appeared to have affected the attitudes in favor of democracy among low educational groups much more dramatically than

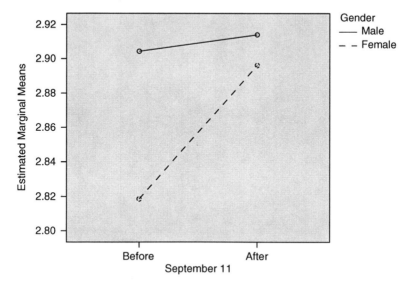

Figure 10.8 Mean differences in support of the statement "When jobs are scarce, men should have more right to a job than women" (1 = low support . . . , 4 = high support) between pre- and post-9/11 samples for men and women in Egypt

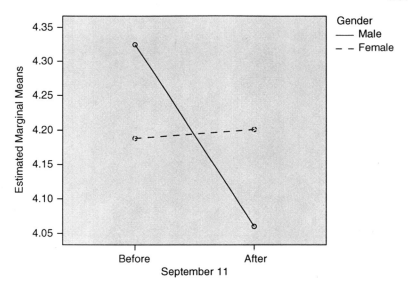

Figure 10.9 Mean differences in support of people with strong religious beliefs holding public office (1 = low support . . . , 5 = high support) between pre- and post-9/11 samples for men and women in Egypt

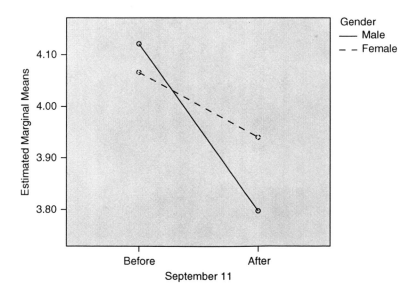

Figure 10.10 Mean differences in support for the shari 'a (1 = low support . . . , 5 = high support) between pre- and post-9/11 samples for men and women in Egypt

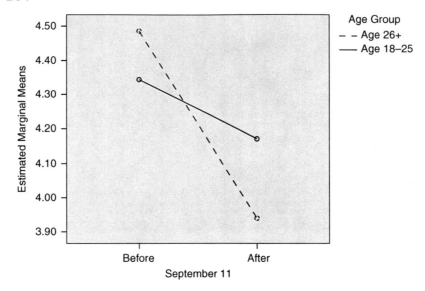

Figure 10.11 Mean differences in support of the statement "Politicians who don't believe in God are unfit for public office" (1 = low support . . . , 5 = high support) between pre- and post-9/11 samples within each age group in Morocco

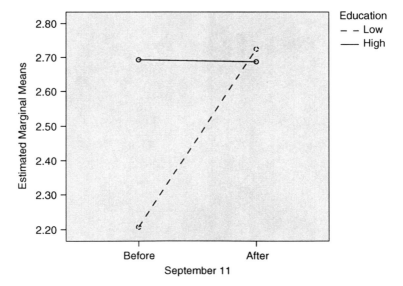

Figure 10.12 Mean differences in support for democracy (1 = low support . . ., 4 = high support) between pre- and post-9/11 samples within each education group for Morocco

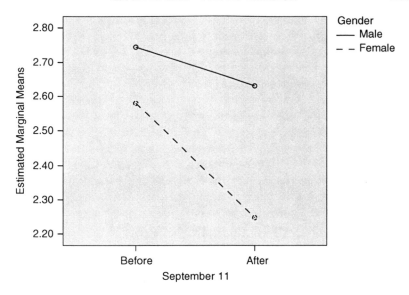

Figure 10.13 Mean differences in support of the statement "When jobs are scarce, men should have more right to a job than women" (1 = low support . . ., 4 = high support) between pre- and post-9/11 samples for men and women in Morocco

it did among high educational groups, where there was no change. As a result, in Morocco, there was a convergence of attitudes between these two groups toward democracy (figure 10.12). The interaction between gender and 9/11 also had significant effects on attitudes toward "men have more rights to a job." Women's attitudes in favor of gender equality in the job market changed dramatically after 9/11, while men's attitudes toward this issue remained about the same (figure 10.13).

Conclusions

Al-Qaeda justified its violence against the United States on September 11, 2001 for the trauma that it believed "the Jewish-Crusade alliance" had inflicted on Muslim nations. The gruesome act was also intended to rally the Muslim publics behind their banner for the construction of a virtuous Islamic order. We assessed the impact of this event on the Egyptian and Moroccan publics in order to determine whether the tactic drove them toward the ideology of radical Islamism or misfired, having just the opposite effects. We argued that above and beyond Muslims' condemnation of the mass taking of innocent lives, for the event to have a broader impact in causing attitudinal change, it must be relevant in a meaningful way to the ongoing political conflict and cultural warfare in their society. Using this proposition, we first analyzed the state of radical Islamism in Egypt and Morocco, the only two countries where almost identical national values survey data were available for before and after 9/11. We proposed that a record of extremist activities in both countries portrayed an image of Islamic fundamentalism that was far removed from the one that al-Qaeda projected as the agent of "Muslim collectivity" to justify its discourse and action. For the Islamic publics, a legacy of kidnappings, assassinations, and the harassment of secular intellectuals and women by radical Islamic groups appeared to have been a better representation of radical Islamism than al-Qaeda's self-depicted portrayal of a religious avant-garde.[18] Thus, the Egyptian and Moroccan publics, although quite far away from the shores where the terrorists wreaked the greatest havoc, were affected by the cultural shock waves the event had generated. This effect, however, was different from what the terrorists intended, as they turned away from the ideology of religious extremism and toward Western values of democracy, gender equality, and secularism.

Recent social-scientific studies of event-triggered changes have focused on topics like nationalist feelings, foreign policy opinion options, collective and flashbulb memories, and emotions (Converse 1987; Jennings 1987; Mueller 1973; Pennebaker, Paez, and Rimé 1997; Page and Shapiro 1992; Schuman and Reiger 1992; Schuman and Rodgers 2004;). In this study, we focused on the impact of an event on people's attitudes toward significant issues. Issues are important because cultural change involves resolution of the issues being contested. In the contemporary Islamic countries, such issues as those related to the form of government, the relationship between religion and politics, the status of women, and Western culture have been the concerns of diverse intellectual leaders and political activists. Thus, understanding how the value orientations of ordinary people toward these issues are affected by an event provides insights into an important mechanism of change that may contribute to a larger cultural transformation and the emergence of a new cultural pattern.

Furthermore, the impact of events is not uniform for all members of society and can be moderated by age, education, and gender. In our analysis, however, these variables had significant moderating effects on only some of the 9/11-induced attitudinal changes, and these effects were not quite consistent with extant sociological generalizations. For example, considering the attitudes that were significantly affected by 9/11-cohort interactions, the older cohort displayed more dramatic attitudinal changes than the younger cohort in both countries. This departure from the impressionable-years hypothesis may be an outcome of the different political socializations experienced by the older and younger generations in the national and historical context of Egypt and Morocco. The older generations in both countries had come of age during the period characterized by the popularity of such secular ideologies as Arab nationalism or Arab socialism as well as state feminism, while the younger generation was socialized during the period of the decline of secularism and the rise of Islamic fundamentalism. This is perhaps the reason why the older generation that was raised in a more secular cultural environment had a stronger predisposition to turn away from the ideology of radical Islamism than the younger generation. This interpretation is plausible because 9/11-cohort interaction significantly affected attitudes toward some of the religious or gender issues, over which the Islamic fundamentalists and Arab nationalists were sharply divided. On such other issues as those related to the desirability of having a strong leader or to democracy, where both groups had in the past maintained similar attitudes (Gershoni and Jankowski 1995; Moaddel 2005), there were no significant moderation effects of cohort on the attitudinal impact of 9/11. Overall, on the measures that there were significant 9/11-age interaction effects for both countries (figures 10.1–10.4, and 10.11), there was no significant cohort difference, except in attitudes toward "men make better political leaders," where the younger cohort were significantly less supportive of this view than the older cohort in the Egyptian sample (table 10.7, column 2). We may thus argue that 9/11 had a convergence effect, narrowing the gap between the attitudes of the older and younger cohorts.

The 9/11-education interaction had inconsistent effects across Egypt and Morocco. In Egypt, where the high educational group displayed more dramatic changes in attitudes favorable toward democracy and unfavorable toward religious authorities than the low educational group (figures 10.5–10.6), these effects are consistent with the view that education contributes to democratic and secular thought. In attitudes toward "having people with strong religious beliefs hold public office," on the other hand, the less educated Egyptians grew less supportive of this attitude than the more educated. Given that the more educated were less supportive of this view (Table 7, column 3), the 9/11-education interaction had a convergence effect, narrowing the gaps between the low and high educational groups (figure 10.7). Likewise, in Morocco, the low educational group grew more supportive of democracy than the high educational group before and after 9/11. Given that the more educated were significantly more supportive of democracy than the less educated Moroccans (table 10.7, column 3), here again 9/11 had a similar convergence effect (figure 10.12).

Finally, the event–gender interaction effects were also inconsistent across the two countries. In Egypt, women grew less supportive of gender equality than men in the job market before and after 9/11 (figure 10.8), while in Morocco it was just the opposite—a significantly higher number of women than men disagreed with "men have more rights to a job" between the two samples (figure 10.13). Although in both countries there were significant gender differences on issues related to women, feminist issues were much more intensely debated in Morocco than in Egypt. We may thus speculate that the varying 9/11-gender interaction effects are related to the difference in the national-historical context between the two countries. In Egypt, on the other hand, issues related to the relationship between religion and politics are much more intensely debated than in Morocco. This is probably why more Egyptian men than women showed a decline in their attitudes toward "having people with strong religious view hold public office" and "a good government implements only the shari 'a" (figures 10.9 and 10.10, respectively) before and after 9/11.

Although the specific categories of people who have displayed more manifestly event-induced attitudinal changes may naturally provide a stronger social support for changes in social institutions and structure than do other groups of people, further attitudinal research in Islamic countries are necessary in order to make a more effectively generalization about the relationship between cohort, education, and gender, and attitude change. However, our study has established that the event of 9/11 significantly affected Egyptian and Moroccan attitudes in a direction favorable to democracy, gender equality, and secularism.

The extent to which such changes cause rupture in social structure, generating a new cultural pattern, is not only contingent on the availability of social resources and the emergence of favorable political space that permits the rise of a new cultural movement, but also on people's collective knowledge about their desires, attention span, and focus on pertinent issues, and articulation of preferences into a program for action by political leaders and activists. Insofar as both the public at large and intellectual leaders focus on the devastation caused by a religiously inspired political violence, they tend not only to distance themselves from its perpetrators but also shy away from the discursive framework that shapes such religious movements.

At the same time, reactions by the state or politically powerful groups to an event may also impact people's attitudes and change their attention span. Far from promoting Western values such other post-9/11 events as the U.S. invasion of Afghanistan, sharpened rhetoric against Iraq and other Islamic countries, and step-up efforts at regime change may induce a different form of attitudinal changes one that could potentially divert the public attention away from the issues of democracy, gender equality, and secularism. If we use concerns with Western culture as a proxy measure of the public attitudes toward the U.S. interventions in the Middle East, and if we take our cue from the fact that Egyptians grew more concerned with Western cultural invasion after 9/11 than they were before, then it would be hard to attribute changes in Egyptian attitudes in favor of democracy, gender equality, and secularism to the U.S. invasion of Afghanistan and step-up rhetoric and efforts at regime change. Given this change, it is a bit more convincing to argue that the changes in Egyptian (and Moroccan) attitudes toward modern values are consequences of 9/11 attacks and the massive anti-Islamic fundamentalist campaign ensued afterward. Should the U.S. military interventions in the Middle East remain unabated in the foreseeable future and Muslim causalities as a consequence continue to increase, we may speculate that the public would divert its attention away from the issues of democracy, gender equality, and secularism, and increasingly focus on the destruction caused by the highhandedness of the U.S. government, all giving rise to a representation of Muslim trauma that would in turn feed the ideology of radical Islamism.[19] On the other hand, the success of the U.S.-led coalition forces in Afghanistan and Iraq in establishing security and promoting economic development may prompt the Islamic publics to focus on the domestic sources of their social problems and the extremist forces in their midst.

These considerations underscore that events matter in the process of attitude formation, as they affect people's attention span, change the balance of cultural forces, and introduce new factors into the social process that may significantly alter the existing cultural pattern. Events affect people's attitudes when they provide additional information that is relevant to the cultural debates over significant issues. The role of events in this process can be explained and even predicted provided that the knowledge of the contending issues is available. If the event of 9/11 had considerably enhanced Moroccan and Egyptian orientations in favor of gender equality and democracy and lessened their satisfactions with religious authorities, it was because they were reacting to their authoritarian rulers, who have failed to improve their socioeconomic conditions and establish an inclusive transparent government, and to the dominant religious opposition groups whose extremism exacerbated social problems. It can be postulated that for reflective Muslims who have seen the failure of Islamic government in Iran, the extremism of the Taliban in Afghanistan, and the destruction of life and property caused by radical Islamic organizations, 9/11 became a moment of reckoning. The event forced them to choose, and they chose democracy, gender equality, and less involvement of religion in politics more extensively after 9/11 than they did before.

Notes

Direct all correspondence to Mansoor Moaddel, Population Studies Center, Institute for Social Research, The University of Michigan, 426 Thompson Street, Ann Arbor, MI 48106-1248; e-mail: mmoaddel@umich.edu. This chapter is supported by two grants from the National Science Foundation (SES-0097282, SES-0139908) and a grant from the Ford Foundation. The pre-9/11 survey in Morocco was supported by a grant from Spain's Telefónica Foundation in Morocco, and was carried out under the supervision of Dr. Juan Diez-Nicolas at Complutense University, Madrid, Spain. We would like to thank Lary Griffin, Stuart Karabenick, Robert Robinson, and Howard Schuman for their invaluable comments. Editorial assistance of Julie de Jong is also gratefully appreciated. An earlier version of this chapter was presented at a Congressional Briefing on June 16, 2002. This chapter originally appeared in the *Interdisciplinary Journal of Research and Religion* Volume 2, and is reprinted here with permission from the journal's editor.

1. These remarks aired on Qatar's Al-Jazeera television station and were translated from Arabic. This text was reported by *USA Today* on Sunday, October 7, 2001.
2. For the impact of the Mutiny in contributing to the rise of Islamic modernism, see Hali (1979), Malik (1980), Troll (1978), Richter (1908), and Russell (1957).
3. For information about events and cultural change in different periods in nineteenth- and twentieth-century Egypt, see Hourani (1991, 1983), Vatikiotis (1980), Marsot (1968a and b, and 1984), Baer (1962), Hunter (1984), Heyworth-Dunne (1968), Wendell (1972), Ahmed (1960), Gershoni and Jankowski (1995), Issawi (1954), Kepel (1984), Mitchell (1969), Lia (1998), and Moaddel (2002).
4. For analyses of sociocultural and political changes in Iran in the nineteenth and twentieth centuries, see Abrahamian (1982), Afary (1996), Kashani-Sabet (1999), Moaddel (1993, 2002), Arjomand (1984), Dabashi (1993), Akhavi (1980).
5. For the rise of Arabism, pan-Arab nationalism, and Islamic fundamentalism in Syria, see Antonius (1938), Salibi (1968), Dawn (1973), Zeine (1973), Haim (1962), Cleveland (1971), Hourani (1983), Khoury (1983, 1987), Khalidi (1991), Dawisha (2003), Batatu (1982), Hinnebusch (1982, 1990), Keilany (1973), Olson (1982), Rabinovich (1972), Seale (1965), Torrey (1964), and Moaddel (1996).
6. For analyses of social change in Algeria, see Robert (1988), Ruedy (1990), Christelow (1991), Ottaway and Ottaway (1970), Vallin (1973), Burgat and Dowell (1997).
7. Our contention is in fact born out by the findings of the extant research on the role of political events in shaping collective memory and emotions. That is, the emotional impact of an event depends not simply on the event itself, but rather on such other factors as, for example, the emotional nature of the narration of the event (e.g., the kidnapped former Belgian prime minister telling his audience about his ordeal in captivity), feeding collective memory (Rimé and Christophe 1997); on the nature of the political environment—whether open discussions are encouraged or repressed—that creates positive or negative emotional climate induced by sharing past unfavorable political events (Paez, Basabe, and Gonzales 1997: 147); and on people's group belonging and social identity that decide the degree to which "emotional experiences tied to specific political events can result in vivid flashbulb memories"—for

example, British upper class members have a higher level of emotional experiences and flash-bulb memories of the fall of Thatcherism than others (Gaskell and Wright 1997: 187). And events themselves do not produce flashbulb memories; the creation of such memories rather depends on the emotionality with which people react to the announcement of an unexpected political event (Finkenauer, Gisle, and Luminet 1997: 206).

8. For example, the Saudi interior minister, in an interview with the Kuwaiti newspaper, *Al Siyasa*, on November 29, 2003 blamed the "Zionists" for the attacks. See International Crisis Group, "Can Saudi Arabia Reform Itself?" Middle East Report No 28, Cairo, Egypt (July 14, 2004), 8, note 21.

9. According to the BBC correspondent Stephanie Irvine (2002, 1), "the trial in Morocco of three Saudis and seven Moroccans accused of being part of an al-Qaeda plot has shaken the image many Moroccans hold of their country as a peaceful, tolerant Muslim state. Many here now fear their country is under threat from the import of radical, fundamentalist ideas from abroad."

10. Systematic comparative values surveys of Middle Eastern countries began as an NSF-sponsored collaborative pilot project between Mansoor Moaddel, Eastern Michigan University (SBR-9820062), Ronald Inglehart, the University of Michigan (SBR-9820060), and overseas collaborators: Saad ed-Din Ibrahim, Ibn Khaldun Center for Development Study, Cairo, Egypt; Abdul Hamid Safwat, Suez Canal University, Egypt; Taghi Azadarmaki, the University of Tehran, Tehran, Iran; and Mustafa Hamarneh and Tony Sabbagh, the University of Jordan, Amman, Jordan. Collectively, the investigators designed and pretested a questionnaire focusing on the attitudes Egyptians, Jordanians, and Iranians toward a variety of gender, religious, socioeconomic, cultural, and political issues. The questionnaire also replicated key items from the WVS questionnaire in order to permit comparisons between these countries and the data from more than seventy societies covered by those surveys. Following the completion of the pilot study in 1999 and in collaboration with overseas colleagues—Abdul Hamid Abdul Latif, Ain Shams University, Cairo, Egypt; Taghi Azadarmaki, the University of Tehran, Tehran, Iran; and Mustafa Hamarneh, Tony Sabbagh, and Fares al-Braizat, the University of Jordan, Amman, Jordan—and financial support from the National Science Foundation (SES-0097282), the Ford Foundation, and Bank of Sweden Tercentenary Foundation full-scale surveys of the national representative samples of 3000 Egyptians, 1200 Jordanians, and 2500 Iranians were carried out in 2000–01. Using a similar questionnaire, a national value survey was carried out in Morocco under the supervision of Juan Diez-Nicolas, Complutense University, Madrid, Spain. The post-9/11 surveys in Egypt were carried under the supervision of Abdul Hamid Abdul Latif of Ain Shams University. In Morocco, both pre- and post-9/11 surveys were carried out by SEREC, a marketing research firm in Casablanca, Morocco.

11. That is, Religion $= (2a + 2b + 2c + 2d)/4$. Factor analytic technique yielded the same results.

12. Low education group included people with
    1. No formal education,
    2. Incomplete primary school,
    3. Complete primary school,
    4. Incomplete secondary school: technical/vocational type,
    5. Complete secondary school: technical/vocational type,
    6. Incomplete secondary: university-preparatory type, or
    7. Complete secondary: university-preparatory type.
    High education group consisted of people with
    1. Some university-level education, without degree, or
    2. University-level education, with degree.

13. Coding on attitudes toward Western culture, men make better political leaders, boys have more right to university education, men have more right to a job, strong leader, religious authorities, religious in public office, religion and politics, shari 'a, and country operates in whose interests were reversed so that positive correlation with 9/11 indicates increase support for the value in question.

14. To be sure, the two surveys showed little change in certain crucial aspects of religious beliefs and practices among Egyptians and Moroccans before and after 9/11. In both periods, almost 100 % of the respondents in the samples expressed belief in God, life after death, soul, hell, and heaven; and indicated that they would get comfort from religion. There was also little change in the high percentage of the respondents who considered religiosity to be a favorable quality for women to have (more than 96 % in all the samples), or in the percentage of the respondents describing self as a religious person (98 % or more in all the samples). On two indicators, there are differences between Egyptian and Moroccan samples. While Egyptian data showed no significant difference in participation in religious services or in the percentage of the respondents who considered religiosity as an important trait for children to have before and after 9/11, a significantly lower percentage of Moroccans reported participating in religious services or considered religiosity to be an important trait for their child after 9/11 than they did before 9/11. This difference indicates that while there has been a decline in people's orientation toward religion in both countries, the nature of this decline was different between Egypt and Morocco.
15. Since changes in people's attitudes may be affected by differences in marital status and subjective social class identification between the two samples, these variables are included in the model as control variables.
16. The main effects of education and gender differences are significant in both countries. The main effect of age differences is significant only for Egypt.
17. The multivariate analysis assesses the significance of the difference between the two samples. We determine the direction of the change in terms of the sign of the correlation coefficients presented in the correlation matrices for both countries.
18. Our argument here is parallel to what Sniderman (1993: 221) defines as "likeability" heuristic; ordinary citizens using "a rule of thumb that yields approximately accurate predictions of where politically salient groups stand on major issues."
19. If the violence of 9/11 contributed to attitudinal change toward Western values, the U.S. invasion of Afghanistan and Iraq and failure to establish a stable democratic government (thus far) in these countries and the innocent lives in Afghanistan and Iraq who were killed as a result of the U.S. military actions against the insurgents and terrorists groups have created a favorable context for religious activists to advance the view that the United States, under the pretext of fighting terrorism, intends to control and subjugate Muslim nations and undermine their religion. In fact, contributing to the insurgent movement in Iraq were such factors as aerial bombardments of the suspected rebel hideouts, which increased the number of civilian deaths, the U.S. ignorance of Iraqi/Islamic culture, mistreatments of Iraqi detainees, and the general failure of the government to improve the economic and security conditions in the country. The success of the Egyptian Muslim Brothers in recent parliamentary elections and other Islamic fundamentalist groups in the Persian Gulf countries may thus be partly attributed to the resurgence of anti-American feelings in Arab countries.

References

Afary, Janet. 1996. *The Iranian Constitutional Revolution, 1906–1911.* New York: Columbia University Press.

Ahmed, Jamal Mohammed. 1960. *The Intellectual Origins of Egyptian Nationalism.* London: Oxford University.

Ahmed, Makram Muhammad. 2002. *al-Mussawar.* 4054–55.

Akhavi, Shahrough. 1980. *Religion and Politics in Contemporary Iran.* Albany, NY: University of New York Press.

———. 1992. "The Clergy's Concepts of Rule in Egypt and Iran." *The Annals of the American Academy of Political and Social Sciences* 524 (November): 92–119.

Alexander, Jeffrey C. 2004. "Toward a Theory of Cultural Trauma." In *Cultural Trauma and Collective Identity*, edited by Jeffrey C. Alexander, Ron Eyerman, Bernhard Giesen, Neil J. Smelser, and Piotr Sztompka, pp. 1–30. Berkeley: University of California Press.

Antonius, George. 1961. *The Arab Awakening: The Story on the Arab National Movement.* London: Hamish Hamilton.

Arjomand, Said A. 1984. *From Nationalism to Revolutionary Islam.* Albany, NY: State University of New York Press.

Barber, Ben. 1994. "Tide of Religious Fervor Could Submerge Morocco." *Insight* (July 11): 15–16.

Batatu, Hanna. 1982. "Syria's Muslim Brethren." *Merip Reports* 110: 12–20, 34, 36.

Blumer, Herbert. 1969. *Symbolic Interactionism: Perspective and Method.* Englewood Cliffs, NJ: Prentice-Hall.

Burgat, Francois and William Dowell. 1997. *The Islamic Movement in North Africa.* Austin: Center for Middle Eastern Studies, University of Texas at Austin.

Christelow, Allan. 1987. "Ritual, Culture and Politics of Islamic Reformism in Algeria." *Middle Eastern Studies* 23(3): 255–73.

Cleveland, William L. 1971. *The Making of An Arab Nationalist: Ottomanism and Arabism in the Life and Thought of Sati' al-Husri.* Princeton: Princeton University Press.

Collins, Randall. 1998. *The Sociology of Philosophies: A Global Theory of Intellectual Change.* Cambridge: Harvard University Press.

Combs-Schilling, Elaine. 1989. *Sacred Performances: Islam, Sexuality and Sacrifice.* New York: Columbia University Press.

Converse, Philip E. 1964 "The Nature of Belief Systems in Mass Publics." In *Ideology and Discontent*, edited by David E. Apter. New York: Free Press, pp. 206–61.

———. 1987. "The Enduring Impact of the Vietnam War on American Public Opinion." In *After the Storm: American Society a Decade After the Vietnam War*, pp. 53–75. Taipei: Republic of China: Institute of American Culture.

Crescent International. 2001. "Morocco's Moderate Islamic Movement Puts Pressure on Monarchy over Palestine." http://www.muslimedia.com/archives/oaw01/moroc-pal.htm, internet edition (January 1–15, 2001) accessed September 26, 2006.

Dabashi, Hamid. 1993. *Theology of Discontent.* New York: New York University Press.

Dawisha, Adeed. 2003. *Arab Nationalism in the Twentieth Century: From Triumph to Despair.* Princeton: Princeton University Press.

Dawn, C. Ernest. 1973. *From Ottomanism to Arabism: Essay on the Origins of Arab Nationalism.* Chicago: University of Illinois Press.

Delli Carpini, Michael X. and Scott Keeter. 1989. *What Americans Know about Politics and Why It Matters.* New Haven: Yale University Press.

Entman, Robert M. 2003. *Projections of Power: Framing News, Public Opinion, and U.S. Foreign Policy.* Chicago: University of Chicago Press.

Featherman, David L. and Richard M. Lerner. 1985. "Ontogenesis and Sociogenesis: Problematic for Theory and Research about Development and Socialization across the Lifespan." *American Sociological Review* 50(5): 659–76.

Fernea, Elizabeth. 2000. "The Challenges for Middle Eastern Women in the 21st Century." *Middle East Journal* 54(2) (April): 185–93.

Finkenauer, Catrin, Lydia Gisle, and Olivier Luminet. 1997. "When Individual Memories Are Socially Shaped: Flashbulb Memories of Sociopolitical Events." In *Collective Memory of Political*

Events: Social Psychological Perspectives, edited by James W. Pennebaker, Dario Paez, and Bernard Rimé, pp. 191–208. Mahwah, NJ: Lawrence Erlbaum Associates.

Gaskell, George D. and Daniel Wright. 1997. "Group Difference in Memory for a Political Event." In *Collective Memory of Political Events: Social Psychological Perspectives* Pennebaker, James W., Dario Paez, and Bernard Rimé, pp. 175–90. Mahwah, NJ: Lawrence Erlbaum Associates.

Gergen, Kenneth J. 1973. "Social Psychology as History." *Journal of Personality and Social Psychology* 26(2): 309–20.

Gershoni, Israel and James P. Jankowski. 1995. *Redefining the Egyptian Nation, 1930–1945.* Cambridge: Cambridge University Press.

Griffin, Larry J. 2004. "Generations and Collective Memory" Revisited: Race, Region, and Memory of Civil Rights." *American Sociological Review* 69(4) (August): 544–57.

Gunaratna, Rohan. 2002. *Inside Al Qaeda Global Network of Terror.* New York: Columbia University Press.

Haim, Sylvia G. (ed.). 1962. *Arab Nationalism: An Anthology.* Berkeley: University of California Press.

Hali, Altaf Husain. 1979 [1901]. *Hayat-i-Javed.* Translated by K. H. Qadiri and David J. Matthews. Delhi, India: Idarah-i Adabiyat-i Delli.

Hinnebusch, Raymond A. 1982. "The Islamic Movement in Syria: Sectarian Conflict and Urban Rebellion in an Authoritarian Populist Regime." In *Islamic Resurgence*, edited by Ali E. Hillal Dessouki, pp. 138–69. New York: Praeger Publishers.

———. 1990. *Authoritarian Power and State Formation in the Ba'thist Syria: Army, Party, and Peasant.* San Francisco: Westview.

Hourani, Albert, 1991. *The History of the Arab People.* New York: Warner Books.

Hyman, Herbert H. 1959. *Political Socialization.* Glencoe, IL: The Free Press.

Irvine, Stephanie. 2002. "Morocco's Crackdown on Islamists." BBC, http://news.bbc.co.uk/2/hi/africa/2559777.stm (December 10, 2002) accessed December 10, 2002.

Issawi, Charles. 1954. *Egypt at Mid-century: An Economic Survey.* London: Oxford University Press.

Jackman, Mary R. 1973. "Education and Prejudice or Education and Response-Set?" *American Sociological Review* 38(3) (June): 327–39.

———. 1978. "General and Applied Tolerance: Does Education Increase Commitment to Racial Integration?" *American Journal of Political Science* 22(2) (May): 302–24.

Jackman, Mary R. and Michael J. Muha. 1984. "Education and Intergroup Attitudes: Moral Enlightenment, Superficial Democratic Commitment, or Ideological Refinement?" *American Sociological Review* 49(6) (December): 751–69.

Jennings, M. Kent. 1987. "Comments." In *After the Storm: American Society a Decade After the Vietnam War*, pp. 77–79. Taipei, Republic of China: Institute of American Culture.

Kashani-Sabet, Firoozeh. 1999. *Frontier Fictions: Shaping the Iranian Nation, 1804–1946.* Princeton: Princeton University Press.

Keilany, Ziad. 1973. "Socialism and Economic Change in Syria." *Middle Eastern Studies* 9(1): 61–72.

Kepel, Gilles. 1984. *Muslim Extremism in Egypt: The Prophet and Pharao.* Berkeley: University of California Press.

Khalidi, Rashid, Lisa Anderson, Muhammad Muslih, and Reeva S. Simon (eds.). 1991. *The Origins of Arab Nationalism.* New York: Columbia University Press.

Khoury, Philip S. 1983. *Urban Notable and Arab Nationalism.* Cambridge: Cambridge University Press.

———. 1987. *Syria and the French Mandate: The Politics of Arab Nationalism, 1920–1945.* Princeton: Princeton University Press.

Kinder, Donald R. 1998. "Communication and Opinion." *Annual Review of Political Science.* 1: 167–97.

Kokan, Jane 1994. "Letter from Rabat (Islamic Fundamentalism in Morocco)." *New Statesman & Society* 7(294) (March 18): 11.

Lapidus, Ira M. 1992. "The Golden Age: The Political Concepts of Islam," *The Annals of the American Academy of Political and Social Sciences* 524 (November): 13–25.

Lia, Brynjar. 1998. *The Society of the Muslim Brothers in Egypt: The Rise of an Islamic Mass Movement 1928–42*. Reading, UK: Ithaca Press.

Maddy-Weitzman, Bruce. 1997. "The Islamic Challenge in North Africa." *MERIA Journal* 1(2).

Malik, Hafeez. 1980. *Sir Sayyid Ahmad Khan and Muslim Modernization in India and Pakistan.* New York: Columbia University Press.

Mannheim, Karl. (1928) 1952. "The Problem of Generations." In *Essays on the Sociology of Knowledge*, edited by Paul Kecskemeti, pp. 276–320. New York: Oxford University Press.

Marsot, Afaf Lutfi. 1968a. "The Role of the Ulama in Egypt During the Early 19th Century." In *Political and Social Change in Modern Egypt*, edited by P.M. Holt, pp. 264–80. London: Oxford University Press.

————. 1968b. *Egypt and Cromer: A Study in Anglo-Egyptian Relations.* New York: Praeger.

————. 1977. *Egypt's Liberal Experiment: 1922–1936.* Los Angeles: University of California Press.

————. 1984. *Egypt in the Reign of Muhammad Ali.* Cambridge: Cambridge University Press.

Mitchell, Richard P. 1969. *The Society of the Muslim Brothers.* London: Oxford University Press.

Moaddel, Mansoor. 2001. "Conditions for Ideological Production: The Origins of Islamic Modernism in India, Egypt, and Iran." *Theory and Society* 30(5): 669–731.

————. 2002. *Jordanian Exceptionalism: An Analysis of State-Religion Relationships in Egypt, Iran, Jordan, and Syria.* New York: Palgrave.

————. 2005. *Islamic Modernism, Nationalism, and Fundamentalism: Episode and Discourse.* Chicago: University of Chicago Press.

————. 2006. "The Saudi Public Speaks: Religion, Gender, and Politics." *International Journal of Middle East Studies* 38(1): 79–108.

Moore, Barrington, Jr. 1966. *Social Origins of Dictatorship and Democracy: Lord and Peasant in the Making of the Modern World.* Boston: Beacon Press.

Mueller, John. E. 1973. *War, Presidential and Public Opinion.* New York: Wiley.

Munson, Henry. 1993. *Religion and Power in Morocco.* New Haven: Yale University Press.

Olson, Robert W. 1982. *The Ba'th and Syria, 1947–1982: The Evolution of ideology, Party, and State.* Princeton: Princeton University Press.

Ottaway, David and Marina Ottaway. 1970. *Algeria: The Politics of A Socialist Revolution.* Berkeley: University of California Press.

Paez, Dario, Nekane Basabe, and Jose Luis Gonzalez. 1997. "Social Processes and Collective Memory: A Cross-Cultural Approach to Remembering Political Events." In *Collective Memory of Political Events: Social Psychological Perspectives*, edited by James W. Pennebaker, Dario Paez, and Bernard Rimé, pp. 147–74. Mahwah, NJ: Lawrence Erlbaum Associates.

Pennebaker, James W., and Becky L. Banasik. 1997. "On the Creation and Maintenance of Collective Memories." In *Collective Memory of Political Events: Social Psychological Perspectives*, edited by James W. Pennabaker, Dario Paez, and Bernard Rimé, pp. 3–19. Mahwah, NJ: Lawrence Earlbaum Associates.

Pennebaker, James W., Dario Paez, and Bernard Rime. 1997. *Collective Memory of Political Events: Social Psychological Perspectives.* Mahwah, NJ: Lawrence Erlbaum Associates.

Price, Vincent and John Zaller. 1993. "Who Gets the News?" *Public Opinion Quarterly* 57(2): 133–164.

Rabinovich, Itamar. 1972. *Syria Under the Ba'th: 1963–66.* Jerusalem: Israel Universities Press.

Richter, Julius, D.D. 1908. *A History of Missions in India.* Translated by Sydney H. Moore. London: Oliphant Anderson & Ferrier.

Rimé, Bernard and Véronique Christope. 1997. "How Individual Emotional Episodes Feed Collective Memory." In *Collective Memory of Political Events: Social Psychological Perspectives*, edited by James W. Pennebaker, Dario Paez, and Bernard Rimé, pp. 131–46 . Mahwah, NJ: Lawrence Erlbaum Associates.

Roberts, Hugh. 1988. "Radical Islamism and the Dilemma of Algerian Nationalism: The Embattled Arians of Algiers." *Third World Quarterly* 10(2): 556–89.

Rubin, D.C., S.E. Wetzler, and R.D. Nebes. 1986. "Autobiographical Memory across the Life Span." In *Autobiographical Memory*, edited by D.C. Rubin, pp. 202–21. Cambridge, England: Cambridge University Press.

Ruedy, John. 1992. *Modern Algeria: The Origins and Development of A Nation*. Bloomington: Indiana University Press.

Russell, William Howard. 1957 [1860]. *My Indian Diary*. London: Cassell & Company.

Sabagh, George. 1993. "The Challenge of Population Growth in Morocco." *Middle East Report* 181 (March–April): 30–35.

Safran, Nadav. 1961. *Egypt in Search of Political Community*. Cambridge: Harvard University Press.

Sageman, Marc. 2004. *Understanding Terror Networks*. Philadelphia: University of Pennsylvania Press.

Salibi, Kamal S. 1968. "The 1860 Upheaval in Damascus as Seen by al-Sayyid Muhammad Abu'l-Su'ud al-Hasibi, Notable and Later *Naqib al-Ashraf* of the City." In *Beginnings of Modernization in the Middle East*, edited by William R. Polk and Richard L. Chambers. Chicago: The University of Chicago Press.

Schuman, Howard and Cheryl Reiger. 1992. "Historical Analogies, Generational Effects, and attitudes toward War." *American Sociological Review* 57(3) (June): 315–26.

Schuman, Howard and Willard L. Rodgers. 2004. "Cohorts, Chronology, and Collective Memories." *Public Opinion Quarterly* 68(2): 217–54.

Schuman, Howard, Robert F. Belli, and Katherine Bischoping. 1997. "The Generational Basis of Historical Knowledge." In *Collective Memory of Political Events: Social Psychological Perspectives*, edited by James W. Pennebaker, Dario Paez, and Bernard Rime, pp. 47–77. Mahwah, NJ: Lawrence Erlbaum Associates.

Schwartz, Stephen. 2002. *The Two Faces of Islam: the Houses of Sa'ud from Tradition to Terror*. New York: Doubleday.

Scott, Jacqueline and Lilian Zac. 1993. "Collective Memories in Britain and the United States." *Public Opinion Quarterly* 57(3): 315–31.

Seale, Patrick. 1965. *The Struggle for Syria: A Study of Post War Arab Politics*. London: Oxford University Press.

Sears, David O. 1981. "Life-Stage Effects on Attitude Change, Especially Among the Elderly." In *Aging: Social Change*, edited by Sara B. Kiesler, James N. Morgan, and Valarie K, pp. 183–204. Oppenheimer. New York: Academic Press.

Sewell, William H., Jr. 1996. "Historical Events as Transformations of Structures: Inventing Revolution at the Bastille." *Theory and Society* 25(6): 841–81.

Smith, Charles D. 1973. "The 'Crisis of Orientation': The Shift of Egyptian Intellectuals to Islamic Subjects in the 1930's." *International Journal of Middle East Studies* 4(4): 382–410.

Sniderman, Paul M. 1993. "The New Look in Public Opinion Research." In *Political Science: The State of the Discipline II*, edited by Ada W. Finifter, pp. 219–45. Washington, DC: The American Political Science Association.

Sniderman, Paul M., Richard A. Brody, and Philip E. Tetlock. 1991. *Reasoning and Choice: Exploration in Political Psychology*. Cambridge: Cambridge University Press.

Stimson, James A. 1975. "Belief Systems: Constraint, Complexity, and the 1972 Election." In *Controversies in American Voting Behavior*, edited by Richard D. Niemi and Herbert F.F. Weisberg, pp. 138–59. San Francisco: Freeman.

Tetlock, Philip E. 1986. "A Value Pluralism Model of Ideological Reasoning." *Journal of Personality and Social Psychology* 50(4): 819–27.

The Economist. 1995. "Disillusion in Morocco: Young Turn to Islam for Economic and Social Reasons." v. 334 (March 25).

———. 1997. "Avoiding the Algerian Precedent," vol. 342 (February 1).

———. 1999. "A Fight for the Faithful: Islamic Fundamentalism Enters Moroccan Politics," v. 351 (May 8).

———. 2000. "Islamist Revival: Protest For and Against Extending the Rights of Women," v. 354 (March 18).

Torrey, Gordon H. 1964. *Syrian Politics and the Military: 1945–1958.* Columbus: Ohio State University Press. Troll, Christian W. 1978. *Sayyid Ahmad Khan: A Reinterpretation of Muslim Theology.* New Delhi: Vikas.

Vallin, Raymond. 1973. "Muslim Socialism in Algeria." In *Man, State, and Society in the Contemporary Maghirb,* edited by I. William Zartman, pp. 50–64. New York: Praeger.

Vatikiotis, Panayiotis J. 1980. *The History of Egypt.* Baltimore, MD: The Johns Hopkins University Press.

Wendell, Charles. 1972. *The Evolution of the Egyptian National Image: From Its Origins to Ahmad Lutfi al-Sayyid.* Berkeley: University of California Press.

Wuthnow, Robert. 1989. *Communities of Discourse: Ideology and Social Structure in the Reformation, the Enlightenment, and European Socialism.* Cambridage: Harvard University Press.

Zaller, John. R. 1992. *The Nature and Origins of Mass Opinion.* Cambridge: Cambridge University Press.

Zartman, I. William. 1987. "King Hassan's New Morocco." In *The Political Economy of Morocco,* edited by I.W. Zartman, pp. 1–33. New York: Praeger Publishers..

Zeine, N. Zeine. 1973. *The Emergence of Arab Nationalism.* Delmar, NY: Caravan Books.

CHAPTER 11

Xenophobia and In-Group Solidarity in Iraq: A Natural Experiment on the Impact of Insecurity

RONALD INGLEHART, MANSOOR MOADDEL, AND MARK TESSLER

Introduction

Through a series of tragic events, contemporary Iraq has become an ideal place in which to test the thesis that severe insecurity leads to xenophobia. Building on a long research tradition to which political scientists, psychologists, and historians have contributed, Inglehart (1997) and Inglehart and Welzel (2005) argue that "existential security"—the feeling that survival can be taken for granted—is conducive to interpersonal trust, tolerance of foreigners and other out-groups, openness to social change, and a prodemocratic political culture. Conversely, they argue, existential insecurity is conducive to (1) xenophobia and (2) strong in-group solidarity. The fact that insecurity is linked with intolerance of out-groups has been demonstrated repeatedly in history, when demagogues have manipulated mass fears to build strong in-group feeling and rejection of out-groups.

In recent decades, the people of Iraq have experienced exceptional levels of insecurity. After taking power in 1968, Saddam Hussein launched a reign of terror designed to eliminate all potential rivals. He then invaded neighboring countries: Iraq was at war with Iran from

1980 to 1988, and then invaded Kuwait, leading to the first Gulf War in 1991 and the second Gulf War in 2003. The result was massive casualties, severe economic disruption, and eventually, international economic sanctions. A low standard of living was exacerbated by the unpredictability and fear of living under a harshly repressive government. In 2003 foreign military intervention ended Saddam's regime but brought disorder, widespread unemployment, chronic shortages of electric power and clean water, and almost daily terrorist attacks.

In recent years, the Iraqi public has experienced a severe sense of existential insecurity. Though Iraqi life expectancy is by no means the lowest in the world, there seems to be a widespread feeling that life has become unpredictable and society is falling apart. In recent years, Iraq has been the target of more terrorist activity than any other country in the world. During the three years after September 11, 2001, thousands of people were killed in terrorist attacks around the world. Over half the number of these deaths occurred in Iraq.[1] Terrorist attacks are designed to produce a sense of terror and insecurity; consequently, they are designed to get widespread coverage in the mass media—and they get it.

Deaths from terrorist attacks are far more salient than those from other causes. The September 2001 attacks in the United States caused almost 3,000 deaths. They brought an enormous amount of media coverage and widespread anxiety, and led to major changes in how American society operates, from security procedures at airports, to the suspension of long-standing legal norms concerning search and imprisonment, to the invasion of Afghanistan and Iraq. At the same time, the 38,000 deaths per year in automobile accidents and 350,000 annual premature deaths from smoking passed almost unnoticed, though they killed larger numbers of people. Terrorism is designed to cause anxiety and it has been uniquely successful.

Terrorism is not the only factor that has contributed to a pervasive sense of insecurity and xenophobia in Iraq, but it has played a major role. Regional differences in the prevalence of xenophobia within Iraq provide one indicator of this fact. The terrorist attacks in post-Saddam Iraq have been overwhelmingly concentrated in the Arab regions, and the Kurd region has been relatively free from them. Nevertheless, the Kurds suffered almost genocidal persecution under Saddam, and—as we see—they show one of the world's highest levels of xenophobia. But the Arab regions of Iraq show levels of xenophobia that are almost twice as high as those found in the Kurdish region, and far higher than in any other country for which data are available. Thus, insecurity in Iraq seems to reflect both long-term factors linked with the reign of Saddam, and short-term factors linked with the disorder and terrorism that have prevailed since his fall. Since we do not have time series data, it is impossible to measure their relative impact in a conclusive fashion, but the Kurd-Arab comparison suggests that both types of factors are important.

Data from the WVS support the hypothesis that xenophobia and insecurity are linked. One of the major dimensions of cross-cultural variation found in these surveys reflects the polarization between survival values (which tend to be emphasized by those for whom survival is relatively insecure) and self-expression values (emphasized by those who take survival for granted).[2] Across the more than 80 societies from which data are available, among those who rank in the lowest quartile (emphasizing survival values), 20 percent say that they would not like to have foreigners as neighbors; among the top quartile, only 8 percent do so. Thus, Iraq seems to be a strategic case in which to test the hypothesis that existential insecurity leads to high levels of xenophobia and other forms of rejection of out-groups—coupled with intense feelings of in-group solidarity.

This chapter tests these hypotheses. As we see, evidence from a recent representative national survey of the Iraqi public, carried out in connection with the WVS, strongly supports these expectations.[3] The Iraqi public shows higher levels of intolerance of foreigners than any other of the more than 80 societies that have been covered in the WVS. The Iraqi public also shows an exceptionally strong tendency to reject other out-groups, such as women and homosexuals. But, as our hypothesis implies, the Iraqis also show strong feelings of in-group solidarity, as manifested by high levels of national pride and extremely high levels of solidarity with one's own ethnic group within Iraq (i.e., Sunni Kurds, Sunni Arabs, or Shi 'i Arabs).

Although we do not have evidence from earlier surveys that would make it possible to compare these findings with Iraqi society at earlier times, it seems highly unlikely that these characteristics have been a permanent feature of Iraqi society. Prior to Saddam's regime, Iraq was economically one of the more developed Islamic countries, with a relatively highly educated population and with women playing a more active role in economic and social life than in many other Islamic societies. We strongly suspect that the high levels of xenophobia and out-group rejection found today reflect, in large part, the extreme insecurity experienced in recent years. The empirical evidence makes it clear that *today* Iraq is characterized by the highest level of xenophobia found in any of the more than 80 societies that have been investigated by the WVS.

Theoretical Background

Inglehart and Welzel (2005) argue that there is a pervasive tendency for existential insecurity to produce intolerance and xenophobia. When resources are so scarce that it is a question of one group or the other surviving, discrimination against outsiders, strong in-group solidarity and insider-favoritism become increasingly prevalent. Xenophobia becomes widespread when threats to survival dominate people's lives. Survival values are functional under these conditions, but they force people to focus on the well-being of one's in-group, viewing outsiders with suspicion and distrust. At the same time, these conditions induce people to close ranks against dangerous outsiders, producing rejection of outsiders and in-group solidarity. This syndrome of rejection of outsiders, combined with rigid conformity to in-group norms and established traditions, bears some resemblance to the cluster of traits described in the *Authoritarian Personality* literature (Adorno et al. 1950; Christie and Jahoda 1954; Duckitt 1989; Feldman and Stenner 1997; Whitley 1999); but while the Authoritarianism thesis attributed these traits to rigid child-rearing practices, our interpretation attributes them to existential insecurity.

From an historical perspective, the Iraqi worldview has been shaped by a series of military coups in 1958, 1963, and 1968, which made military seizure of power the principal means of regime change (Hopwood et al. 1993). Political instability was compounded by sharp internal ethnic divisions, based on both ethnicity, pitting Kurds against Arabs, and religion, with Sunni confronting Shi 'i. Until recently, the Sunni Arab minority monopolized political power. Initially, their rule rested on Sunni domination of the army, but they extended their power through nationalization of the banks, insurance companies, and large industrial firms. Massive oil revenues enabled the regime to develop a powerful modern repressive apparatus. All of these factors may have contributed to a sense of insecurity and intolerance of outsiders.

From another perspective, Gibson (1996, 1998, 2002), Rohrschneider (1999), Sniderman et al. (2000), and Sniderman and Carmines (1997) have explored the ways in which economic and physical insecurity lead to intolerance of out-groups. Their analyses fit the Iraqi case rather well. Moreover political scientists have often noted the tendency for publics to close ranks behind their nation's leader in time of international conflict—the most recent case being the sharp rise in support for President George W. Bush after the terrorists attacks of September 11, 2001 (See Baum 2002; Bowen 1989; Brody 1991; Callaghan and Virtanen 1993; Edwards and Swenson 1997; Hetherington and Nelson 2003; Krosnick and Brannon 1993; MacKuen 1983; Oneal and Bryan 1995; Parker 1995; Sigelman and Conover 1981). In the beleaguered Iraqi society of today, one would expect to find a similar closing of ranks against outsiders. As the noted historian William McNeill concluded in his analysis of the impact of war on history, "An evident outside threat was, as always, the most powerful social cement known to humankind" (McNeill 1982: 382).

Out-group rejection is not necessarily based on *fear* of the specific out-group: under conditions of insecurity, people tend to cling to the old familiar rules and reject social change—with relatively powerless excluded groups, such as women, ethnic minorities, or homosexuals, being excluded all the more intensely when a society experiences severe existential insecurity.

Findings

As table 11.1 suggests, the Iraqi public currently displays exceptionally high levels of xenophobia. Repeated waves of the WVS have asked representative national samples of the publics of more than 80 societies the question, "On this list are various groups of people. Could you please sort out any that you would not like to have as neighbors?" One of the options on the list was "immigrants/foreign workers." Table 11.1 shows the percentage of the public that indicated they would not want to have foreigners as neighbors, in countries on all six inhabited continents. A more specific version of this question was asked in Iraq: the public was asked about various specific groups of foreigners, ranging from Westerners (the Americans, the British, and French) to neighboring Islamic publics (Iranians, Turks, Kuwaitis, and Jordanians) and also including various groups within Iraqi society.

Perhaps not surprisingly under current conditions, the nationalities of the two main occupying powers were highly unpopular: Americans and British were both rejected as neighbors by overwhelming majorities of 87 percent among the Iraqi public as a whole. But the French—although their government had strongly resisted the invasion of Iraq—were only slightly less unpopular: fully 85 percent of the Iraqi public said it would not like to have French people as neighbors. As hypothesized, under current conditions the Kurds are substantially less likely to reject foreigners than their Arab compatriots, but both groups show extremely high levels of xenophobia in international perspective. Moreover they also reject the publics of nearby, predominantly Islamic countries to a remarkable

Table 11.1   Percentage saying they would not like to have foreigners as neighbors

Iceland	4	China	17
Argentina	4	Belgium	18
Brazil	4	Zimbabwe	18
Canada	5	Philippines	18
Australia	5	Tanzania	18
Sweden	5	Dom. Rep	18
Switzerland	6	Mexico	19
Spain	7	S Africa	19
Japan	7	Latvia	19
Portugal	7	Estonia	19
Uruguay	7	Venezuela	20
Ireland	8	Azerbaijan	20
Finland	8	Kyrgyzstan	20
Colombia	8	Macedonia	21
United States	9	Lithuania	22
Luxembourg	9	Armenia	22
France	10	Bosnia	22
Netherlands	10	Poland	23
Puerto Rico	10	Slovakia	23
Denmark	11	Algeria	23
Peru	11	Bulgaria	24
Britain	12	Nigeria	25
Italy	12	Czech Rep	25
Norway	12	Slovenia	25
Chile	12	Taiwan	25
Belarus	12	Singapore	26
Russia	12	Romania	28
Croatia	12	Pakistan	29
Iran	12	Saudi Arabia	33
W Germany	13	Vietnam	33
Ukraine	13	Turkey	34
Georgia	13	India	36
Uganda	13	Hungary	38
Greece	14	S Korea	38
Albania	14	Indonesia	40
N Ireland	15	Egypt	42
E Germany	15	Jordan	42
Austria	16	Bangladesh	48
Moldova	16	*Iraq: Kurds ("French")*	*51*
Serbia	16	*Iraq: Arabs ("French")*	*90*
Morocco	16		

Source: Latest available data from the World Values Surveys and European Values Survey.

degree. While the percentages who rejected "foreigners" in other countries ranged from as little as 4 or 5 percent to a high of 48 percent in Bangladesh (another society with high levels of existential insecurity), 61 percent of the Iraqi public said that they would not want Turks as neighbors; and 55 percent said they would not want Iranian neighbors (the Kurds being somewhat more tolerant of foreigners than their Arab compatriots, in every case). The only foreign nationality that was *not* rejected by a majority of the Iraqis public was the Jordanians, an ethnically similar nationality that has maintained close supportive ties with the Iraqis. But even here, 44 percent of the Iraqi public said that they would not want to have Jordanians as neighbors—an extremely high level of rejection by global standards.

In keeping with our expectation that insecurity leads to in-group solidarity, the Iraq public does not reject most groups *within* Iraqi society as neighbors—but they reject foreigners to a degree that is virtually unknown in other societies throughout the world, including more than a dozen predominantly Islamic countries. Figure 11.1 illustrates the contrast between the levels of xenophobia found in Iraq—highlighting the fact that the Iraqi Kurds rank only slightly higher than the next highest public, while the Iraqi Arabs are an outlier with far higher levels of xenophobia than are found in any other of the 80 societies.

In non-Islamic societies, respondents were asked whether they would prefer not to have Islamic neighbors. Although the question about

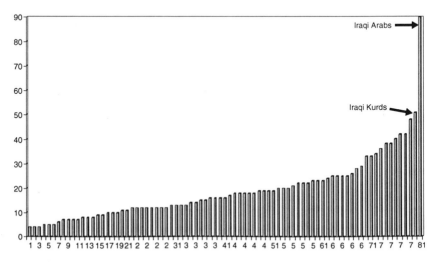

Figure 11.1   Percentage saying they would not want to have foreigners as neighbors, in 80 societies
Source: Data from WVS.

immigrants or foreign workers refers to a relatively broad, general group, this one has a specific target, like the questions asked in Iraq. The responses range from 6 percent in Argentina to a high of 59 percent in Hungary, with a median level of 17 percent saying they would not like to have Muslim neighbors. Most publics are somewhat more likely to reject the idea of having Muslims as neighbors than foreigners in general, but nowhere does the level of rejection begin to approach the 85 percent level of rejection that the Iraqi public expressed for the French, or the 87 percent rejection for the British and Americans. In only two non-Islamic societies does a majority say that they would not like to have Muslims as neighbors, and even there the level of rejection is lower than the level that the Iraqis expressed toward the Turks, a neighboring Islamic people.

Foreigners are not the only out-group that the Iraqi public currently tends to reject. Although they constitute a majority of the population in most societies, women have historically been an out-group, viewed as second-class citizens and excluded from power. In this case, rejection of out-groups is not so much based on fear of that specific group, as on fear of social change: under conditions of insecurity, people tend to cling to the old familiar rules, whatever they are. Respondents to the WVS surveys were asked whether they agreed with the statement that "On the whole, men make better political leaders than women do." In the median society, 52 percent of the public agreed that men make better political leaders than women. But here again the Iraqi public took an extreme position—with 93 percent of the Iraqi Arabs agreeing that men make better political leaders than women, a higher proportion than is found in any other society for which data are available. Again, the Iraqi Kurds are significantly less likely to have a patriarchal outlook than their Arab peers (72 percent agreed), but both groups rank high in international perspective.

This outlook does not seem to be a permanent feature of Iraqi society. Historically, Iraqi women have had more opportunity to pursue higher education and careers than women from many other Islamic societies (Helms 1984; Omar 1994). But in recent years, Iraq has experienced what might be regarded as a tragic field experiment on what happens when people experience severe existential insecurity—and one result is the highest level of support for gender inequality on record.

Facing severe existential insecurity, people tend to close ranks against outsiders. Closing ranks brings obedience to authority and rigid adherence to group norms. Individual autonomy is minimized; loyalty and conformity are stressed. Another battery in the WVS provides a useful indicator of group norms. The respondents were asked: "Here is a list of qualities that children can be encouraged to learn at home. Which, if any, do you consider to be especially important?" The respondent was shown a list of ten goals, from which he or she might select upto five. One of the themes in this battery involved the respondent's relative emphasis on individual autonomy versus group conformity. For example, one of the qualities a child might be encouraged to learn was "independence." Iraqi Arabs were unlikely to emphasize independence: only six publics ranked lower than them in emphasizing it. The Iraqi Kurds, on the other hand, ranked slightly above the international median in emphasizing independence.

But the Iraqi Arabs are more likely to emphasize "obedience" than the publics of any of the 80 other societies for which data are available—and the Kurds also emphasize obedience very strongly. Furthermore, Iraqi Arabs were more likely to emphasize "religious faith" than any other public for which data are available; here again, although the Kurds rank significantly lower than the Arabs, they rank high in international comparison. Overall, if we subtract the percentage emphasizing "independence" from the percentage emphasizing "obedience" and "religious faith," the Iraqi Arabs emphasize conformity to authority and group norms, rather than individual autonomy, more heavily than any other public in the world. As expected, the Iraqi Kurds emphasize conformity less strongly than their Arab compatriots, but they rank relatively high in global perspective. Once again, let us emphasize that we do *not* view the extreme emphasis on obedience and conformity currently found among Iraqi Arabs as a permanent characteristic of that group: it is almost certainly influenced by their recent experience of extreme existential insecurity.

Severe existential insecurity leads to rigid adherence to traditional social norms—and the most central social norms are the ones codified in the religion of a society. Accordingly—although most observers would agree that, prior to Saddam's seizure of power, Iraq was one of the more secular Arab societies; and although Saddam's Baath Socialist Party advocated secularism (Amin 1989; Khadduri 1969)—we would expect the Iraqi public today to place relatively strong emphasis on religion. The evidence supports this expectation. The WVS asked, "For each of the following, indicate how important it is in your life. Would you say it is 'Very important,' 'Rather important,' 'Not very important,' or 'Not at all important'?" They were shown a list that included Family, Friends, Leisure time, Politics, Work, and Religion.

Across the 80 societies for which we have data, the percentage saying that religion is "very important" in their lives ranges from a low of 3 percent to a high of 98 percent. In this context, fully 97 percent of the Arab

Iraqis say that religion is very important in their lives. Only Indonesia ranks higher, and only by an insignificant margin. In a pattern that is by now familiar, the Iraqi Kurds fall well short of the extreme position of their Arab peers, but still rank among the world's most religious publics. Needless to say, a society's emphasis on religion does not simply reflect the extent to which it is currently under stress; religious belief also reflects deep-rooted cultural traditions that change only slowly. While some societies place relatively little emphasis on religion, Islamic societies in general and Arab societies in particular tend to emphasize religion strongly. There is a wide gap between the relatively secular Islamic societies that experienced communist rule (such as Albania, Azerbaijan, and Kyrgystan), and the other Islamic societies, which include eight of the ten most religious societies for which we have data. The emphasis on religion currently found among the Iraqi public seems to reflect Iraq's heritage as an Islamic, largely Arab, society. The extreme position currently taken by the Iraqi Arabs on many variables almost certainly reflects the influence of long-term cultural influences to some extent—but the evidence strongly suggests that it *also* reflects the impact of the intense existential insecurity they have experienced in recent years. Formerly viewed as relatively secular, the Iraqi Arabs *today* seem to emphasize on religion more strongly than virtually any other people in the world.

Each country's respondents were asked whether they agreed with the proposition that "atheists are unfit for public office." Here again, the Iraqi Arabs rank near the top: only the Pakistanis outrank them in emphasis on religion as a prerequisite for public office. Following a familiar pattern, the Iraqi Kurds rank significantly below the Arabs, but nevertheless are among the highest-ranking publics on this variable. As suggested earlier, we attribute this difference, at least in part, to the political autonomy and less extreme insecurity that the Kurds have experienced since 1991.

As hypothesized, the Iraqi public currently shows a strong tendency to reject outsiders and adhere to traditional values. Now let us examine another aspect of this syndrome: in-group solidarity. Each public was asked, "How proud are you to be [YOUR NATIONALITY]?" We find that—despite severe internal divisions that have led many Kurds to want to leave Iraq altogether—the Iraqi public as a whole expresses relatively strong feelings of national pride. Moreover, when we filter out the Kurdish minority (only 34 percent of whom express strong national pride), we find that fully 86 percent of the Arab Iraqis say they are "very proud" to be Iraqi. Only 5 of the 86 publics for which we have data ranked higher (and each of them was besieged in one way or another).

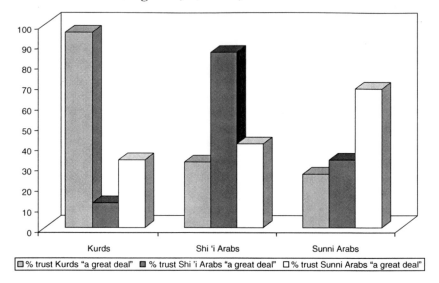

Figure 11.2

Figure 11.2   Interethnic trust in Iraq

The strong national pride expressed by the Iraqi public can hardly be interpreted as an expression of satisfaction with how well their country was doing: when this survey was carried out, conditions could hardly have been worse. It seems to be a defiant expression of solidarity against outsiders.

The Iraqis also show extremely high levels of solidarity with their specific ethnic group (i.e., the Sunni Kurds, Sunni Arabs, or Shi 'i Arabs). As figure 11.2 indicates, 86 percent of the Shi 'is say that they trust other Shi 'is "a great deal"; the corresponding figures are 68 percent among the Sunni Arabs and 96 percent among the Kurds. These figures are exceptionally high in international perspective. Among the publics of the European Union countries, for example, the percentage expressing strong trust in their own nationality ranges from 20 among the Italians to a high of 58 among the Irish[4] (see Euro-Barometer Survey 41). By this standard of comparison, in-group solidarity is extremely high in Iraq.

The Iraqis have a strong sense of in-group solidarity, but they differentiate sharply between their own ethnic group and other groups within Iraqi society, as figure 11.2 also illustrates. The median percentage of Iraqis that strongly trusts the *other* Iraqi ethnic groups is 33; the median percentage of Iraqis that strongly trusts its *own* ethnic group is 86. By comparison, the median percentage of European Union publics who consider their own nationality to be "very" trustworthy is 48 percent;[5] and the median percentage of European Union publics that considers the other EU nationalities to be "very" trustworthy is only 17. Again, by this standard of comparison, in-group solidarity in Iraq is remarkably strong.

Implications

The Iraqi public currently shows intense rejection of out-groups and intense in-group solidarity. What is the outlook for the successful establishment of democracy?

Let us start with the good news. At this point in history, solid majorities of publics throughout the world see democracy as the best form of government. This has not always been the case. During most of the twentieth century, alternatives to democracy such as fascism and communism had massive support. And today, in Islamic societies, theocratic government has widespread appeal. But in the contemporary world, in every country for which we have data, most people aspire to have democracy. Our respondents were asked a series of questions about the problems of democracy, whether democracies were ineffective at running the economy or in keeping order; immediately after these problems were reviewed, they were asked whether they agreed or disagreed with the statement that "Democracy may have problems, but it is better than any other form of government." Solid majorities of the public in every country agreed with this statement, as table 11.2 demonstrates. The 14 Islamic societies included in our surveys rank anywhere from near the top to near the bottom, but in every one of them, a solid majority says that democracy is the best form of government. In beleaguered Iraq, in face of violent opposition, and despite antagonism toward the Western democracies, 85 percent of the public said that democracy was the best form of government, and there is no significant difference between Iraqi Kurds and Arabs on this point. This is an important and encouraging fact. See figure 11.3.

But the situation is more complex than this might seem to indicate. Support for democracy is not incompatible with support for absolute rule by the religious authorities: logically, the two might seem incompatible, but a large part of the Iraqi public has positive feelings toward *both* kinds of government. The Iraqis were asked, "I am going to describe various types of political systems and ask what you think about each of them as a way of governing this country. For each one, would you say it is a very

310

Table 11.2 "Democracy may have problems but it is better than any other form of government." (Percentage agreeing or strongly agreeing)

Country	%	Country	%
Denmark	99	Venezuela	89
Bangladesh	98	Serbia	89
Egypt	98	Finland	88
Iceland	97	Peru	88
Austria	97	Tanzania	88
Greece	97	Algeria	88
W Germany	96	Canada	87
Netherlands	96	S Africa	87
Uruguay	96	Australia	87
Azerbaijan	96	El Salvador	87
Albania	96	Zimbabwe	87
Morocco	96	New Zealand	87
Norway	95	Latvia	86
Croatia	95	Georgia	86
Luxembourg	95	Guatemala	85
Italy	94	Iraq	85
N Ireland	94	Hungary	84
Sweden	94	Taiwan	84
Malta	94	Brazil	83
France	93	Belarus	83
Spain	93	Romania	83
Ireland	93	Chile	82
E Germany	93	Czech Rep	82
Domin. Rep	93	Bulgaria	82
Uganda	93	Pakistan	82
Belgium	92	Slovakia	82
Japan	92	Colombia	81
Montenegro	92	Mexico	79
Argentina	91	Ukraine	79
S Korea	91	Britain	78
Switzerland	91	Philippines	78
India	91	Macedonia	78
Bosnia	91	Kyrgyzstan	78
United States	90	Moldova	75
Puerto Rico	90	Saudi Arabia	74
China	90	Armenia	73
Turkey	90	Vietnam	72
Lithuania	90	Indonesia	71
Estonia	90	Iran	70
Jordan	90	Nigeria	66
Poland	89	Russia	61
Slovenia	89		

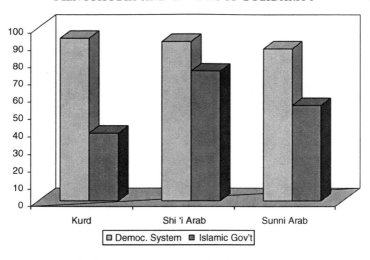

Figure 11.3   Support for democracy versus support for Islamic government

good, fairly good, fairly bad, or very bad way of governing this country?" Among five alternatives, the two leading choices were "Having a democratic system" and "Having an Islamic government, where religious authorities have absolute power." Although support for democracy is widespread, there is also substantial support for rule by religious authorities. Among the Kurds, for example, 92 percent said that a democratic system would be "very good" or "somewhat good"; but 36 percent gave similar positive ratings to "an Islamic government where religious authorities have absolute power." Among Sunni Arabs, the balance was closer: 85 percent gave positive ratings to a democratic system, but more than half also gave positive ratings to an Islamic theocracy. The Shi 'i Arabs were even more closely divided: almost 90 percent had positive feelings toward a democratic system—but more than 70 percent thought that an Islamic theocracy would be good. Even among the Shi 'i Arabs democracy has more support than Islamic theocracy, but democracy is definitely *not* "the only game in town," in Linz and Stepan's (1978) terms.

Democracy in Iraq is also threatened on another front. Our respondents were asked "On the whole, would you say that Iraq would have been better off if Saddam had stayed in power, or is Iraq better off without him?" The vast majority of the Kurds—95 percent—said that Iraq was better off without Saddam (as figure 11.4 indicates). And an overwhelming majority (87 percent) of the Shi 'i Arabs also felt that Iraq was better off without Saddam: only 4 percent thought Iraq would have been better

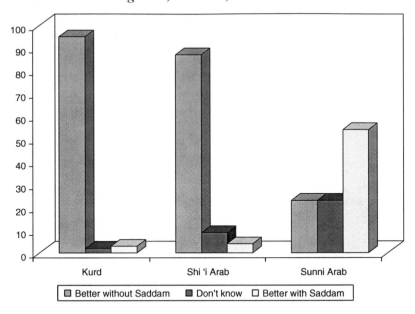

Figure 11.4   Is Iraq better off without Saddam?

off if he had stayed in power, while 9 percent was uncertain. But among the Sunni Arabs, a narrow majority (53 percent) said that Iraq would have been better off if Saddam had stayed in power; the rest were evenly divided between thinking that Iraq was better off without Saddam, and being uncertain. If one wished to put a positive spin on this, one might point out that, even among the Sunni Arab minority (constituting roughly one fifth of the population), only half could be described as Saddam loyalists. But this is a large enough group to cause massive disruption, making stable democracy difficult to attain.

Democracy in Iraq is threatened by support for Islamic rule among the Shi ʻi Arabs, and by nostalgia for Saddam among the Sunni Arabs. But the fact that support for each of these alternatives is limited to one segment of the population limits its potential. Iraq's natural pluralism creates difficulties but it also provides checks and balances.

Alternative Explanations: Economic Development, Islam, and Existential Insecurity

The facts are clear. The Iraqi public in general, and the Iraqi Arabs in particular, currently show the highest levels of xenophobia found among the 80 societies for which data are available. They also show the most sexist outlook and the most intense emphasis on religion among these 80 countries, together with extremely high levels of in-group solidarity. The reasons *for* this outlook can be debated. We attribute it to the exceptionally high levels of existential insecurity that the Iraqis have experienced from the time Saddam came to power in 1968 to the present. But it might be argued that exceptionally high levels of xenophobia, sexism, and intense religiosity have *always* characterized Iraqi society—that they are somehow part of the Iraqi national character. We do not have the time series survey data that would be needed to refute this claim, but historical evidence provides no support for it. Prior to 1968, Iraq was one of the most prosperous Islamic countries with a relatively well educated and socially integrated female population. Iraqi society was relatively tolerant of its Jewish minority and had a relatively relaxed brand of Islam— and from the time he took power, Saddam's regime advocated secularism. None of this would lead one to expect the intense xenophobia, sexism, and religiosity that we find today. We suggest that contemporary Iraq constitutes a natural experiment on the impact of extreme existential insecurity.

Inglehart and Welzel (2005) argue that because economic scarcity is an important source of existential insecurity, low levels of economic development tend to be linked with xenophobia and rejection of outsiders; conversely, high levels of economic development are conducive to tolerance, support for gender equality, and generalized interpersonal trust. To test this hypothesis, we carried out multiple regression analyses using each country's percentage who would not like to have foreigners as neighbors, as the dependent variable—and treating the Iraqi Kurds and Iraqi Arabs as two separate societies. Our independent variables included each society's GNP/capita; a dummy variable for Islamic heritage; and a dummy variable for Iraq.

The results indicate that economic development *is* linked with levels of xenophobia; a society's per capita GNP by itself explains 15 percent of the variation in rejection of foreigners among 80 societies. When we add a dummy variable for Iraq, the adjusted R-squared rises to 49 percent, explaining an additional 34 percent of the variance. On the other hand, when we add a dummy variable that reflects whether a given society is Islamic or non-Islamic, it explains only an additional 6 percent of the variance. A society's level of economic development and the presence of an Islamic heritage both have significant effects on its level of xenophobia— but by far the strongest explanatory variable is whether the society is Iraq or not.

Let us illustrate this in concrete terms. In "low income societies" (as defined by the World Bank) the average percentage rejecting foreigners as neighbors is 23 percent; in "lower middle income societies" the figure is 25 percent; among "upper middle income societies" the figure is 19 percent; and in "high income societies" it is only 11 percent—less than half the level in low income societies. As expected, xenophobia is linked with economic development.

Iraq falls into the lower middle income category, but among Iraqi Kurds, 51 percent rejects foreigners—double the mean figure for lower middle income societies; and among Iraqi Arabs, 90 percent rejects foreigners—almost four times the mean figure for lower middle income societies. The Iraqis are far more xenophobic than their economic level would predict.

On the other hand, an Islamic cultural heritage has only a modest impact on xenophobia. Among Islamic societies other than Iraq, 28 percent rejects foreigners—only slightly above the overall mean for lower middle income societies. But among the Iraqi public as a whole, 82 percent rejects foreigners—almost three times as many as among other Islamic societies.

In short, economic insecurity apparently does contribute to xenophobia—but the Iraqi public shows much higher levels of xenophobia than their economic level (or Islamic heritage) would predict. Some nation-specific factor is making the Iraqi public far more xenophobic than any of the 80 other nations for which we have data. The most obvious factor seems to be the extreme insecurity that the Iraqi public has been experiencing now and for many years. Saddam's reign of terror and repeated wars, followed by military occupation and daily terrorist attacks have all probably contributed to an extreme sense of insecurity and it is impossible to isolate the effects of each of these factors with any precision. Nevertheless, the contrasting patterns found in the Kurdish and Arab regions of Iraq hint at the relative weight of long-term and current conditions. For the Kurdish region suffered more heavily under Saddam than the Arab region, but more recently their roles have been reversed. With this in mind, the 26 point margin by which Iraqi Kurds exceed the mean for middle income societies might be attributed to the impact of the long-term insecurity linked with the terror and wars of the Saddam regime; while the 39 point margin by which Iraqi Arabs exceed the Kurdish level might be attributed to the conditions of the post-Saddam era (including invasion, foreign occupation, and almost daily terrorist bombings).

Conclusion

Evidence from Iraq supports the hypothesis that severe existential insecurity gives rise to xenophobia and rejection of out-groups, on the one hand; and to strong in-group solidarity. The high levels of xenophobia and rejection of out-groups that currently exist in Iraq may hinder the emergence of stable democracy, for there is strong evidence that tolerance, trust, and an egalitarian outlook are conducive to democracy (Inglehart and Welzel 2005). On the other hand, the restoration of public order and a reasonable measure of economic security should bring increasing tolerance and trust of out-groups—and a gradual decline of the intense in-group solidarity that now characterizes Iraqi society. As the psychological gulf between groups decreases, the prospect for stable democracy will improve. But because xenophobia is currently so intense, any government that is seen as dependent on foreign military support is likely to have little legitimacy. Conversely, a new government, elected by a majority of the Iraqi public and no longer dependent on foreigners, should have a much better chance to attain legitimacy. Violent protest against the current government can be presented as resistance to foreign rule; but violence against a democratically elected Iraqi government will be far less acceptable to the great majority of the Iraqi public.

Despite threats that anyone who took part in the elections would be killed, and in the face of suicide bombers attempting to infiltrate the polling places, on election day in January 2005, millions of Iraqis turned out to vote. Although 300 terrorist attacks took place that day, 58 percent of those eligible to vote polled—a higher rate of turnout than in most U.S. Presidential elections. In our survey, 85 percent of the Iraqi public said that "Democracy may have problems, but it is better than any other form of government." Their commitment to democracy seems genuine. They were willing to risk their lives for it.

Postscript: Updated Findings from 2006

The authors of this chapter carried out another survey in Iraq in April 2006, interviewing a representative national sample of 2701 Iraqi adults, with support from the National Science Foundation. The results update the findings presented above, and strengthen their interpretation. The basic thesis of the chapter is that insecurity is conducive to xenophobia.

The new findings show that from 2004 to 2006, a sense of insecurity increased among the Iraq public—and feelings of xenophobia rose with it. A comparison of findings from the two surveys reveals that

- The percentage of Iraqis who strongly agreed that "in Iraq these days life is unpredictable and dangerous" rose from 46 percent in 2004 to 59 percent in 2006. This change varied by ethnicity but there was increasing sense of insecurity among all major ethnic groups.
- During the same period, feelings of xenophobia rose among the Iraqis. The percentage of Iraqis who would not want to have Americans as neighbors went up from 87 percent in 2004 to 90 percent in 2006. The comparable figures were 87 percent and 90 percent for the British, and 84 percent and 90 percent for the French, respectively. People from other Islamic countries also became increasingly unwelcome as neighbors: the percentage of Iraqis who did not wish to have Iranians as neighbors increased from 55 percent to 61 percent between the two surveys, and the comparable figures were 50 percent and 59 percent for Kuwaitis, 59 percent and 71 percent for the Turks, and 43 percent and 61 percent for Jordanians.

Appendix: Fieldwork in Iraq

Face-to-face interviews were conducted with 2,325 Iraqis in November–December, 2004. A total of 2,700 Iraqis were selected for interviews, of whom 2,325 or 89 percent of the total, actually participated in the study. Table A shows the distribution of the sample by area and the response rate. This survey replicated key items from the WVS, supplemented with a battery of questions developed for use in Islamic countries and with additional items that address the specific issues related to current social conditions of Iraq. This questionnaire was discussed with our Iraqi colleagues, and then translated and back-translated from Arabic to English by a person who had not seen the original English version. The result was compared with the original English version, resulting in some modifications. It was then pre-tested with a small sample of Iraqi respondents. The authors then formulated the final version of the questionnaire in light of suggestions received from our Iraqi colleagues.

Table A: The distribution of sample size by area and the response rate

Area	Sample distribution	Completed interviews	Response rate
Baghdad	600	484	0.81
Basrah	180	149	0.83
Tekrit	200	155	0.78
Nasirria	120	101	0.84
Umara	120	111	0.93
Hilla	120	107	0.89
Najaf	120	107	0.89
Diwania	120	103	0.86
Kut	120	102	0.85
Karbala	120	104	0.87
Ramadi	140	118	0.84
Samawa	120	114	0.95
Baquba	140	120	0.86
Kirkuk	120	114	0.95
Sulaimania	200	185	0.93
Erbil	160	151	0.94
Total	2,700	2,325	0.86

Notes

1. These figures are from a September 2, 2004 NBC News report.
2. For a detailed description of this dimension and how it is measured, see Inglehart and Welzel 2005: Chapter 2.
3. This chapter is based on a representative national survey of the Iraqi adult public carried out in November/December, 2004 (N = 2,325). Fieldwork was supported by the NSF and carried out by the Independent Institute for Administration and Civil Society Studies, Baghdad, directed by Munqith M. Daghir. The overall response rate was 89%. For additional details on Iraqi fieldwork, see the Appendix to this chapter. The Iraqi data are compared with the latest available wave of data from the WVS and the EVS, most of which were carried out in 1999–2001. For details concerning these surveys, see Inglehart et al. 2004 and http://www.worldvaluessurvey.org, accessed September 27, 2006.
4. These data are from Euro-Barometer 41.
5. The 1990 WVS asked the publics of 41 societies around the world to what extent they trusted people of their own nationality. The median proportion saying they "trusted them completely" was 20%. This figure is not comparable with those cited earlier because it is based on five response categories (including a mid-point indicating "I neither trust nor distrust them") rather than the four categories used. But the evidence from these surveys does nothing to undermine the conclusion that the Iraqis currently have reasonably high levels of trust in their own nationality. The highest levels of "complete trust" in one's own nationality are found in Turkey and India, with 50 and 55%, respectively: these levels are twice as high as those found in any West European country.

318   *Inglehart, Moaddel, and Tessler*

References

Adorno, Theodor W., Else Frenkel-Brunswik, and Daniel J. Levinson. 1950. *The Authoritarian Personality*. New York: Harper and Row.

Amin, S.H. 1989. *The Legal System of Iraq*. Glasgow, Scotland: Royston Publishers.

Baum, Matthew A. 2002. "The Constituent Foundations of the Rally-Round-the-Flag Phenomenon." *International Studies Quarterly* 46(2): 263–98.

Bowen, Gordon L. 1989. "Presidential Action and Public Opinion about US Nicaraguan Policy." *PS: Political Science and Politics* 22: 793–800.

Brody, Richard A. 1991. *Assessing the President: The Media, Elite Opinion and Public Support.* Stanford: Stanford University Press.

Callaghan, Karen J. and Simon Virtanen. 1993. "Revised Models of the 'Rally Phenomenon': The Case of the Carter Presidency." *Journal of Politics* 55: 756–64.

Christie, Richard and Marie Jahoda. (eds.). 1954. *Studies in the Scope and Method of The Authoritarian Personality*. Glencoe: Free Press.

Duckitt, John. 1989. "Authoritarianism and Group Identification: A New View of an Old Construct." *Political Psychology* 10: 63–84.

Edwards, George C. and Tami Swenson. 1997. "Who Rallies? The Anatomy of a Rally Event." *Journal of Politics* 59: 200–212.

Feldman, Stanley and Karen Stenner. 1997. "Perceived Threat and Authoritarianism." *Political Psychology* 18(4): 741–61.

Gibson, James L. 1996. " 'A Mile Wide but an Inch Deep'? The Structure of Democratic Commitments in the Former USSR." *American Journal of Political Science* 40(2): 396–420.

———. 1998. "A Sober Second Thought: An Experiment in Persuading Russians to Tolerate." *American Journal of Political Science* 42(3): 819–50.

Gibson, James L. 2002. "Becoming Tolerant? Short-term Changes in Russian Political Culture." *British Journal of Political Science* 32: 309–34.

Helms, Christine Moss. 1984. *Iraq: Eastern Flank of the Arab World*. Washington: Brookings Institution.

Hetherington, Marc J. and Michael Nelson. 2003. "Anatomy of a Rally Effect: George W. Bush and the War on Terrorism." *PS: Political Science and Politics* 26: 37–42.

Hopwood, Derek, Habib Ishow, and Thomas Koszinowski. (eds.). 1993. *Iraq: Power and Society*. Reading, UK: Ithaca Press.

Inglehart, Ronald. 1997. *Modernization and Postmodernization: Cultural, Economic and Political Change in 43 Societies*. Princeton: Princeton University Press.

Inglehart, Ronald and Christian Welzel. 2005. *Modernization, Cultural Change and Democracy*. New York: Cambridge University Press.

Inglehart, Ronald, Miguel Basáñez, Jaime Díez-Medrano, Loek Halman, and Ruud Luijkx. (eds.). 2004. *Human Beliefs and Values: A Cross-Cultural Sourcebook Based on the 1999–2001 Values Surveys*. Mexico City: Siglo XXI.

Khadduri, Majid. 1969. *Republican Iraq: A Study of Iraqi Politics since the Revolution of 1958*. London: Oxford University Press.

Krosnick, Jon A. and Laura A. Brannon. 1993. "The Impact of the Gulf War on the Ingredients of Presidential Evaluations: Multidimensional Effects of Political Involvement." *American Political Science Review* 87(4): 963–975.

Linz, Juan and Alfred Stepan. 1978. *Problems of Democratic Transition and Consolidation*. Baltimore: Johns Hopkins University Press.

MacKuen, Michael B. 1983. "Political Drama, Economic Conditions and the Dynamics of Presidential Popularity." *American Journal of Political Science* 27: 165–92.

McNeill, William. 1982. *The Pursuit of Power.* Chicago: University of Chicago Press.

Omar, Suha. 1994. "Women: Honour, Shame, and Dictatorship." In *Iraq since the Gulf War: Prospects for Democracy,* edited by Fran Hazelton, pp. 60–71. London: Zed Books.

Oneal, John R. and Anna L. Bryan. 1995. "The Rally 'Round the Flag Effect in US Foreign Policy Crises, 1950–1985." *Political Behavior* 17(4): 379–401.

Parker, Suzanne L. 1995. "Toward an Understanding of 'Rally' Effects: Public Opinion in the Persian Gulf War." *Public Opinion Quarterly* 59: 526–46.

Rohrschneider, Robert. 1999. *Learning Democracy: Democratic and Economic Values in Unified Germany.* New York: Oxford University Press.

Sigelman, Lee and Patricia Johnston Conover. 1981. "The Dynamics of Presidential Support During International Conflict Situations." *Political Behavior* 3: 303–18.

Sniderman, Paul M. and Edward G. Carmines. 1997. *Reaching Beyond Race.* Cambridge, MA: Harvard University Press.

Sniderman, Paul M., Pierangelo Peri, Rui de Figuerido, and Thomas Piazza. 2000. *The Outsider: Prejudice and Politics in Italy.* Princeton: Princeton University Press.

Whitley, Bernard E. 1999. "Right-Wing Authoritarianism, Social Dominance Orientation, and Prejudice." *Journal of Personality and Social Psychology* 77(1): 126–34.

PART 5

Methodology

CHAPTER 12

Probability Sampling and the Scientific Survey Method for Population Studies: Application to Survey Research in Islamic Countries

STEVEN G. HEERINGA

Introduction

Scientific research on social science topics such as economics, demography, health, and education has entered a period of rapid expansion throughout the Islamic world. Much of this expanded research activity involves the survey method as a source of data. The growth in survey research activity in the Islamic world has occurred on a number of fronts. Many national statistical offices of country governments have independently taken steps to expand research on labor force participation, education and public health. These same national statistical offices have also collaborated with external funders or international organizations to expand and improve existing survey programs or to conduct new studies. Since 2000, government statistical offices in Egypt, Indonesia, Jordan, Morocco, Nigeria, Uzbekistan, and Morocco have collaborated in the Demographic and Health Surveys that are sponsored by the U.S. Agency for International Development (USAID). The United Nations survey division, the World Health Organization (WHO), and other international organizations are also actively working with government and university-based researchers in Islamic countries to design and conduct surveys on social and health-related topics. Bosnia, Kazakhstan, Morocco, Pakistan, Tunisia, Turkey, and the United Arab Emirates are participating in the current WHO World Health Surveys program. Psychiatrists and mental health professionals from Turkey, Pakistan, Indonesia and Lebanon are conducting extensive surveys of their countries' population as part of the WHO World Mental Health Initiative. The World Bank's *Living Standards Measurement Study* (LSMS) focuses on improving the type and quality of household economic and living standards data that are collected by government statistical offices. To date, Albania, Azerbaijan, Morocco, Pakistan, Tunisia, Kyrgzstan, Tajikistan, Kazakhstan, and Uzbekistan have completed one or more LSMS surveys.

Researchers in Islamic countries have been somewhat slower to embrace programs of survey research in the disciplines outside of demography, health, education and economics—specifically in sociology, political science, and public policy. However, a number of Islamic republics and countries with majority Islamic populations are now beginning to participate in international programs of comparative social research such as the World Values Survey (Inglehart et al. 2004). The readers are referred to the substantive chapters of this volume for a discussion of the results from the initial series of WVS in Islamic countries.

The purpose of this chapter is to provide a methodological review focusing on the important aspects of probability sampling and associated scientific survey methods as a robust scientific tool for making statistical inference to national, regional, and local populations. The chapter is not an analysis of a survey data set but a guide to judging the precision and accuracy of survey data. Sections in this chapter address the importance of probability sampling designs for multipurpose surveys and the sources of variance and bias in survey data collections.

The clause in the title, "Application to Research in Islamic Countries," could suggest to the reader that there is a theory or approach to probability sampling method that is unique to studies of Islamic populations. This interpretation is in large part incorrect. Probability sampling design and inference for populations must certainly be adapted to the geographic, demographic, socioeconomic, religious, and culture features of individual societies, but the fundamental elements of the theory and practice of probability sample surveys are universal—as applicable in Egypt, Turkey, and Indonesia as they are in Canada, the United States, or Mexico.

Probability Sampling

Sample surveys such as those described in other chapters of this volume use data collected from a sample of population members to estimate characteristics (means, proportions, rates, percentiles) or to draw inferences concerning relationships among variables (associations, correlation, regressions) in the population as a whole. To extrapolate descriptive or relational findings from a small set of observation to a population requires a statistical mechanism for this process of inference.

The strongest statistical mechanism for inferring from a sample to a population is through a statistical model. An example would be a model in which the researcher assumes that the conditional distribution of household income is a lognormal distribution and that the parameters of this distribution depend only on the age and education of the household head. When the objectives of the survey are highly focused and the statistical model for the variables of interest is well established, the optimal procedure for choosing the sample to observe can be based on the model (Valliant et al. 2000). In such model-based sample designs, the role of the sample observations is for estimation of the model parameters.

Most social scientific problems addressed by surveys are not of this type. The objectives of the survey are not tightly focused, but are multipurpose (Kish 1988) and even in the case of a particular dependent variable of interest, very little is known about the true distributional model for that variable. For these types of survey research inquiries, probability sampling design and inference provide an alternative approach that requires at most very weak assumptions concerning the distributional models for the underlying data (Cochran 1977; Kish 1965). For reasons outlined shortly, statisticians may refer to inferences based on probability samples as "distribution free" or "design-based."

The theory of probability sampling is a relatively recent entry to the broader theories of mathematics and statistics. The groundwork for today's theory of probability sampling inference was laid in statistical arguments (what is a representative sampling method?) and developments (the role of randomization in classical experimental inference) of the early 1900s. Prior to the mid-1930s, many university and government statisticians were using sampling techniques that we today recognize as probability sampling methods. However, it was in 1934, in a paper read before the Royal Statistical Society that Neyman (1934) first outlined the fundamental elements of the theory for making probability sample-based inferences to *target populations*.

Probability samples assume that there is a finite target population from which a sample will be selected. The purpose of the sample data is to draw inferences about the true values of statistics in this population. The population statistic of interest could be as simple as the percentage of the adult population that has completed a primary school education or as complex as a multiple regression coefficient in the population regression of log (household income) on the education and age of the household head. The definition of a probability sample has two key components. The probability of selection for each element in the target population must be known or calculable and the sample design must not exclude any element by assigning it a zero chance of being selected. Probability sampling does not require that each element have an equal probability of selection so long as the probability assigned to each element is known and nonzero.

Probability sampling for surveys yields two positive statistical benefits. Unbiased estimates of the population statistics of interest can be computed from the sample alone if the selection probability for each sample elements is known. Furthermore, robust estimates of the variability (uncertainty) in the sample-based estimate of the population statistic can be computed directly from the sample itself. Neither the computation of the population estimate nor the estimate of sampling error require distributional model assumptions other than the general statistical results for the Law of Large Numbers and the Central Limit Theorem.

Alternative to Probability Sample Surveys

In practice, the seemingly simple requirements of a probability sample survey design—known, nonzero selection probability for each sample element—are not fulfilled without effort or cost. The construction of a comprehensive frame for the survey population and the rigorous adherence to procedures for selection of survey households or individuals require technical training and appear to add costs to already costly survey data collections. Due to lack of statistical or technical expertise or as an attempt to cut costs in the survey process, many commercial and even scientific research organizations will use *non-probability sampling* methods to choose the collection of households or individuals that will be interviewed for the survey. Nonprobability sampling techniques used in practice include *quota samples* and other forms of *convenience samples*.

In quota sampling, specific sample size quotas or target sample sizes are set for subclasses of the target population. Generally the sample quotas are based on simple demographic characteristics, for example quotas for gender, age groups, and geographic region subclasses. A researcher conducting a quota sample survey of 2500 individuals from Lebanon's household population may require that n = 25 men age 45–60 be interviewed in the Mt. Lebanon region. Interviewers may be directed to specific neighborhoods or villages to begin their search for interviewees but are free to select any individual they choose so long the quota for that person's demographic group has not already been filled. The target sample sizes for the demographic and geographic quotas are often based on census data or other sources of population estimates. By matching the marginal proportion of sample cases in each quota cell to the corresponding population proportions, the quota sampler hopes to achieve a *"representative sample,"* that is, a sample for which the survey data will yield unbiased estimates of population characteristics. However, this is only a hope, the data obtained from the quota sample provide no statistical basis for determining that the goal of a representative sample was actually achieved. Individual probabilities of selection for population elements are unknown since the selection of respondents is arbitrary and does not employ true randomization. Interviewers may choose any convenient individual who meets an open quota.

Quick topical surveys or opinion polls commonly use convenience samples of individuals as respondents. Intercepting and interviewing respondents in high traffic areas such as shopping centers, transit locations, athletic events, and so on constitutes a sampling of "convenient," easily accessible persons. Likewise, open solicitations to respond to a survey in a newspaper or magazine, on the Internet or via a broadcast e-mail constitute a convenience sample. Such samples are highly vulnerable to sample selection biases and in fact are often used by advocacy organizations to collect "survey data" that support their position on public issues or policy actions.

In the strictest sense, these and other forms of nonprobability sampling lack a statistical basis for making inference from the chosen sample to the population that sample is designed to represent. The common analytical approach that is often used with non-probability sample data is to compute population estimates, standard errors, and confidence intervals just as though a probability sample of the population had been drawn. This "substitution" of a nonprobability sample for a probability sample in estimation and inference assumes unbiasedness of the arbitrary procedure used to identify the sample. Now in fact, all nonprobability samples are not necessarily seriously biased. The problem is that given the arbitrary nature of respondent choice, biases are highly likely and are impossible to measure. The true error of the sample estimates generated from non–probability samples cannot be estimated.

Total Survey Error

Probability sampling provides a robust, theoretical basis for unbiased estimation of population statistics and the associated sampling variance.

Table 12.1   Taxonomy of survey errors

Variable Errors	Biases
Sampling variance	Sample selection bias
Interviewer variance	Frame coverage bias
Response variance	Measurement bias
Coding variance	Nonresponse bias

However, a successful scientific survey depends not only on control of sampling variances but also other sources of error. The collection of all sources of error that can influence the precision and accuracy of survey estimates of population statistics is termed *total survey error* (Groves 1989; Lessler and Kalsbeek 1992). Total Survey Error for a survey estimate is defined as:

$$Total\ Survey\ Error\ =\ Variance\ +\ Bias^2,$$

the variance of the estimate plus the square of the bias in the sample estimate. Table 12.1 provides a typical taxonomy of survey errors.

Variable Errors

The sources of error that cause sample estimates to disperse randomly about the true and unknown population value of interest are termed variable errors. *Sampling variances* derive from the statistical fact only a subset of the full target population observed. As samples sizes increase, the sampling variance decreases and disappears entirely if a complete census of the target population is conducted. Probability sampling theory provides well-defined guidance for estimating sampling variances for survey estimates. When the sample is selected using simple random sampling (SRS) methods, exact analytical formulae are available for most statistics important to survey analysts (Cochran 1977). For example, the sample variance of a survey estimate of the population proportion for a binary variable, y, is estimated as:

$$\mathrm{var}(\hat{p})_{srs} = (1 - n/N) \cdot \hat{\sigma}^2/n; \text{ where } \hat{\sigma}^2 = \hat{p} \times (1 - \hat{p})$$
and, n = sample size, N = population size.

In practice, most probability sample surveys do not employ simple random sampling techniques but use more complex design features such as stratification and clustering to improve statistical efficiency or reduce costs. Complex sample designs that include stratification, clustering, or unequal selection probabilities for elements require more sophisticated statistical procedures to estimate sample variances of survey statistics. Special software for estimating sampling variances for complex sample survey estimates are readily available in major data analysis software packages or as stand-alone programs (Heeringa and Liu 1997).

Sampling variance for survey estimates is partially controlled by the sample designer. Referring to the preceding formula, σ^2, the variance of random variable y is a property of the population being surveyed—the sample designer cannot change it. For survey estimates that are proportions (or equivalently percentages), σ^2 is a function of the proportion, p. For an SRS sample of n = 1000 cases, figure 12.1 illustrates how the standard error (square root of the sampling variance) of a sample estimate of this proportion varies with the mean value, p, for the population characteristic of interest.

From figure 12.1, if the mean proportion for a population characteristic is p = .2, an SRS sample of n = 1000 cases will estimate this population proportion with a standard error of approximately se(p)≅.012. If instead the mean proportion for the population characteristic is p = .5, the same SRS sample of n = 1000 cases would estimate that proportion with a standard error of se(p)≅.016.

The two questions that survey statisticians are asked most frequently are, "How large a sample do I need?" and "What response rate must I have for the results of my survey to be valid?" Neither question has a simple

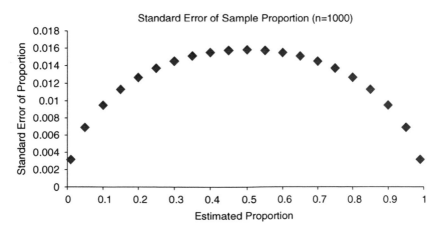

Figure 12.1 Illustration of the relationship between survey estimates of proportions and the SRS estimates of standard errors (Assumes n = 1000)

answer. In each case, the answer is specific to the particular analysis—the variables, statistics, and sample subclasses—that the researcher has in mind and the level of precision and accuracy that they require. The sample designer cannot control the natural variability of a characteristic in the population, however, they do have control over the survey sample size, n. By varying n, they can determine the amount of sampling variability for a survey estimate. This is illustrated in figure 12.2. This figure shows the relationship of the standard error (square root of sampling variance) of an estimated proportion, p = .5, to the size of the simple random sample. If an SRS of n = 300 is chosen for the survey, the standard error of the estimated proportion near .5 will be slightly less than .03 and an approximate 95% confidence interval for the estimated proportion will be :

$\hat{p} \pm 1.96 \times se(\hat{p})$
$.5 \pm 1.96 \times .03\ (.44, .56)$

If a larger sample size of n = 1500 were used instead, the standard error of estimated proportions near .5 would be approximately .013 and the corresponding 95 percent confidence interval for a survey estimate of this proportion would be:

$.5 \pm 1.96 \times .013\ (.475, .525)$.

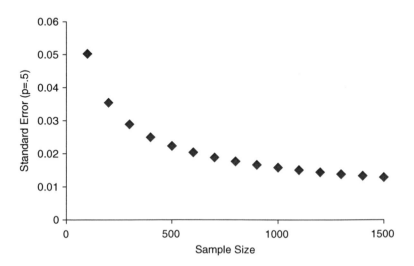

Figure 12.2 Relationship of standard error of a proportion to sample size Illustration for a simple random sample and p = .5

Probability samples that employ complex features such as stratification, clustering, and weighting require adjustments to this basic sample size versus sample precision relationship for simple random sampling (see Kish 1965). In addition to sampling variability, survey estimates are also subject to random sources of error. *Interviewer variance and measurement variance* (Fuller 1987; Groves 1989) enter the data during the actual interview and may be attributed to random inaccuracies in the way interviewers ask survey questions, record the survey answer, or the way that the respondent reports the response. In scientific surveys, researchers aim to minimize measurement variance by carefully training interviewers and designing and pretesting questions so that they are clearly worded and have comprehensive, easy-to-interpret response categories. To minimize these sources of variability in the survey data, social scientists and public health researchers who contract with a survey firm or organization to conduct a survey should inquire carefully about interviewer training and monitoring procedures as well as the firm's experience in designing and pretesting survey questionnaires. Readers interested in an in-depth treatment of interviewer variance and other measurement errors are referred to in Biemer et al. (1991).

Coding variance is primarily a technical source of random error in the data set. Research staff responsible for coding the survey data and transcribing the information to a computer file for analysis may make random errors. If coders must translate a respondents' verbatim answer to a survey question to a categorical code for the variable there may be errors in the assigned code categories. Data entry staff responsible for transcribing recorded responses from paper questionnaires to computer readable files may make random keystroke errors. Here again, researchers should ensure that the staff responsible for coding and data entry is properly trained and supervised and that established quality control procedures are in place to identify and correct random errors in these processes. On the surface, this appears to be a relatively easy thing to do. However, easy as it may seem, many important survey programs have had to seriously delay the analysis of the survey data or in extreme cases had to completely recode and reenter data due to poor quality control in the initial efforts.

Biases

The English word bias has many meanings but in the statistical context it refers to the tendency of a statistical estimate to deviate systematically

332 *Steven G. Heeringa*

from the true value it is intended to estimate. Students of statistics, including survey researchers, have long been taught that "unbiasedness" —the absence of bias—is one of the most desirable properties of a statistical estimator or procedure. In survey practice, bias should certainly be avoided; however, elimination of all sources of bias in survey data is probably neither practical nor even efficient when both the costs and benefits of reducing bias are considered.

While in theory perfect execution of a probability sample survey will result in data that permit unbiased estimates of population statistics, in practice even the most carefully designed surveys may be subject to small biases. This is not cause to reject probability sampling as failing to deliver in practice what it promises in theory. Total survey error is always minimized by starting with a robust probability sample design and working carefully to control where possible and measure the sources of bias that can enter the survey data as that design is implemented and the survey data are collected.

Survey biases listed in the survey error taxonomy given table 12.1 above may be grouped into two major types, *sampling bias* and *nonsampling bias* (Kish 1965). In order to discuss sampling bias it is necessary to introduce several important definitions and concepts. As described earlier, sample surveys are conducted in order to estimate characteristics and relationships among variables in a larger population. The population that the survey is intended to describe is termed the *target population*. For example, the target population for a government-sponsored employment study in Indonesia might be defined as adult members of the Indonesian population age 16–65 that are not disabled or otherwise unable to perform work. The research team assigned to design and conduct this survey would be quick to point out that the target population includes individuals on remote islands in the archipelago that would be very costly and impractical to sample and interview successfully. Furthermore, there is highly restricted access to target population members who are in prisons, institutions, or in the military. After careful consideration of these arguments, the agency sponsoring the survey agrees that the survey sample may be restricted to noninstitutional, nonmilitary population members who reside on the 10 most populous islands. The formal agreement to restrict the target population to household populations on 10 islands results in a new population of inference termed the *survey population*. The probability sample for the survey will be designed to produce unbiased estimates for the survey population. To the extent that the employment characteristics of the smaller survey population differ from that of the full target population, inferences from the sample data to the target population may be systematically biased.

It is common in survey practice for researchers to opt for survey population definitions that exclude small segments of the target population that are extremely costly or difficult to survey. Sparsely distributed or inaccessible populations, geographic regions involved in civil strife or border conflicts are often excluded from survey populations for national surveys. For example, a national survey in Uzbekistan may exclude sparsely settled regions in the west bordering on the Aral Sea. In Egypt, the cost of interviewing remote desert-dwelling households might lead to excluding these difficult-to-reach households from the survey populations. Regions on the southern border of Lebanon may be excluded from a national survey for security reasons. In the United States, sparsely populated areas in the wilderness of Alaska or on small islands in Hawaii may be excluded from the survey population for cost reasons. In such cases, the total proportion of the national population actually excluded from the survey population is small, typically less than 2–3 percent of the total population. Consequently, there is little potential for large systematic bias as a result of the small differences between the target population and survey population definitions.

In probability samples, the greatest potential for sampling bias can be attributed to noncoverage of survey population elements. Recall that probability samples require that each element in the population have a known, nonzero probability of being selected. At a minimum, this requires a means to identify each population element. The *sample frame* is the list or equivalent enumeration device by which all population members are identified and assigned a nonzero selection probability. For surveys of households and individuals, the sample frame may be a population registry for households or individual population members. In countries where up-to-date registries are not maintained, area probability sample frames (Kish 1965) are the standard method for sampling households and individuals.

Sample frame noncoverage occurs when population elements are systematically excluded from the population registry or the data sources (maps and census counts) used to develop area probability frames. While working on a national sample design for Egypt in 1993, the research team I was part of encountered the following coverage problem. An area probability sample frame was being developed based on data from the 1988 Egyptian census and map materials supplied by the Egyptian government. Within the municipal boundaries of Cairo, a large population (hundreds of thousands) of unofficial residents had "settled" in an area that the census reported as uninhabited due to a policy of only recording census data for permanent or legal residents of the city. This large population of unofficial residents could only be represented in the survey population by using special procedures to enumerate and select a sample of households from the illegal settlement areas. The extent to which omission of population elements from the sampling frame will bias survey results depends of course on the size of the noncoverage and how covered and noncovered populations may differ in regard to the survey variables of interest. Many survey populations include nomads or populations that migrate on a seasonal basis. Special procedures must also be employed if these mobile populations are to be represented by the survey data.

Sample noncoverage bias may also occur in the process of screening selected dwelling units to identify and select eligible survey respondents. In surveys of individuals such as opinion surveys or labor force participation surveys, a common procedure is to make contact with the occupants of sample dwelling units and prepare a complete roster of all persons living in the sample unit. A single respondent is then selected from the household roster. If the household roster is not completed carefully for each sample household, omitted individuals will have no chance to be selected for the survey. Methodological studies have shown that young adult men and older persons are most likely to be omitted from household rosters.

Nonsampling Bias

Survey data is vulnerable to nonsampling bias from two primary sources, *measurement bias*—systematic bias in the way respondents interpret and respond to questions—and *survey nonresponse*. Measurement bias may be deliberate on the part of the respondent. Survey respondents who are asked to report their household income may underreport or fail to mention sources of income such as the sale of a parcel of land. Survey questions that ask about participation in elections, educational activities, or religious observances may be subject to over-reporting of participation, a phenomenon termed "social desirability" bias. Poorly worded or "leading" questions or questionnaires that place questions out of context may yield biased measures for the constructs the research investigator is truly interested in. In recent years, a number of programs of international, comparative survey research have been launched. The WVS program described elsewhere in this volume is one example. Measurement bias is a particular concern for cross-national research programs. Not only are there problems of accuracy for the translations of standardized instruments, but also some constructs may not transfer smoothly among nations and cultures. An example from an international survey program on mental health is a standardized screening question for symptoms of major depression. In English the question reads, "Have you ever in your life had periods of a week or more when you felt sad and blue?" Translated literally into many languages, the "sad and blue" description leaves many respondents thinking about unusual changes in their complexion. This is not to say that international comparative research is not feasible. It does emphasize that researchers from the different nations and cultures that will participate in the study should review the question wording, even for questions that appear simple.

Survey nonresponse is another potential source of bias in sample-based estimates of population characteristics. The failure to obtain any data on a sample household or individual is termed *unit nonresponse*. A missing response to one or more individual variable items in an otherwise complete interview questionnaire is termed "item nonresponse" (Little and Rubin 2002). Nonresponse to voluntary surveys including those conducted by universities and other scientific research organizations has become a major problem in countries in Western Europe and North America. Response rates to commercial surveys conducted by market research and political polling organizations are at all-time lows. Fortunately, the trend toward lower survey response rates has not affected research in Islamic countries and populations to the same extent as it has in Europe and the Americas.

Survey methodologists (Groves and Couper 1998) who study the underlying reasons for nonresponse in household population surveys stress the finding that unit nonresponse includes two components: *refusals* or *noninterviews* in which the respondent is identified but actively refuses to complete the survey interview; and noncontact—failure to contact or speak to the sample household. The active refusal component of survey nonresponse can be addressed by training interviewers in effective introductions to the survey and refusal aversion methods. A common practice when a household refuses the interview is to mail a special letter explaining the importance of the survey and the protections employed to prevent disclosure of individual unit identities in the survey data and reports. A second interviewer who specializes in refusal conversion then revisits the household and attempts a second time to obtain the interview. If the practice is culturally acceptable, financial incentives or small gifts are also used to reduce nonresponse to the survey interview. The noncontact component of survey nonresponse is minimized through careful scheduling of contact attempts with the household or individual respondent. Contact attempts with sample units should be spread out over time and include different times of the days, days of the week, and also weekends being careful to avoid days and times of special events or religious observances.

Increasing nonresponse rates in European and North American surveys have generated a large amount of new research activities on methods to prevent nonresponse and also investigations into the nature of nonresponse bias itself. Nonresponse bias in survey estimates of simple statistics such as population means or proportions is a function of the response rate and the difference in the values of the statistic for responding and nonresponding members of the sample. For estimates of a population proportion, the nonresponse bias can be expressed using the following formula:

$$Bias_{(NR)}\ (p) = (1 - RRate) \times (p_R - p_{NR})$$

where *RRate* is the expected value of the population response rate, p_r is the proportion for respondents and p_{nr} is the proportion for nonrespondents. The absolute value of the expected nonresponse bias increases with the product of nonresponse rate and the difference in mean values of p for respondents and nonrespondents. If the response rate is high or proportions for respondents and nonrespondents do not differ, the nonresponse bias will be very small. Unlike sampling variance that decreases as sample size increases, nonresponse bias is persistent—its expected value is not a function of sample size and remains unchanged regardless of how large or small the size of the survey sample.

The potential impact of nonresponse bias on the analysis of survey data may be best illustrated through a simple example. Assume a researcher is interested in studying parents' views on the need for increased government spending (hence potential increases in taxes) for elementary science education. Among parents who agree to participate in the survey, the expected proportion that support increased spending on elementary science education is $P_r = .6$ while for noncooperating parents $P_{nr} = .5$—a major difference between respondents and nonrespondents. If 42 percent of the original random sample of n = 1000 parents agreed to participate, the expected nonresponse bias for the proportion of interest would be:

$$Bias_{NR}(\hat{p}) = (1 - RR) \times (P_r - P_{nr})$$
$$= (1 - .42) \times (.6 - .5) = 0.058.$$

If we assume for simplicity that the original sample of parents was selected using SRS, the researcher would develop the following 95 percent confidence interval for this estimate:

$$\hat{p}_r \pm 1.96 \star [\hat{p} \star (1 - \hat{p})/(n)]^{1/2} \cong \hat{p}r \pm 1.96 \star [.6 \star (1 - .6)/(1000)]^{1/2}$$
$$= \hat{p}r \pm 0.16$$

In this case, the size of the expected nonresponse bias is relatively large in comparison to the size of the 95% confidence interval half width—a result of the low response rate and the major difference in expected proportions for respondent and nonrespondent cases.

The purpose of this example is not to magnify the potential seriousness of nonresponse bias in survey estimation—high response rates and/or smaller differences in the expected statistics for respondents and nonrespondents would decrease the size of the expected bias. Some recent research has suggested that we may be overly concerned about the seriousness of nonresponse bias for certain types of survey measures—especially measures of respondent attitudes and expectations (Curtin et al. 2000; Keeter et al. 2000). However, the example makes the point that we cannot be complacent and ignore the potential for nonresponse bias in the survey estimation process.

Summary

The aim of this chapter has been to review the importance of probability sampling and related scientific survey methods for social scientific as well as important policy research on household populations. For multipurpose surveys with broad and important implications for our understanding of societies, their attitudes, behaviors, and characteristics, careful, robust approaches in the design and collection of the survey data are no less essential than they are to the physical scientist who works in a laboratory. Social scientists and other researchers who employ survey methods as a scientific tool must of course consider total cost and effort in the design of a study. In the words of Professor Leslie Kish in his 1977 presidential address to the American Statistical Association: "To err is human, to forgive divine, but to include errors in your design is statistical." Sources of error in survey data are fact—they cannot be assumed away or ignored. Statistical survey designs and procedures must therefore be balanced in regard to total cost and the sources of error. Probability sample designs provide a robust approach to measurement of the variance in survey data and a best basis from which to try to measure the impact of both sampling and nonsampling bias on the estimates derived from the sample. Shoddy methods purported to be "representative" or even established methods with no basis in theory for unbiased ness of full sample estimates or measurability of variance should not be accepted as a substitute for important social scientific and policy research.

References

Biemer, Paul P, Robert M. Groves, Lars E. Lyberg, Nancy A. Mathiowetz, and Seymour Sudman. (eds.). 1991. *Measurement Errors in Surveys*. New York: John Wiley and Sons.

Cochran, William G. 1977. *Sampling Techniques, 3rd Edition*. New York: John Wiley and Sons.

Curtin, Richard, Stanley Presser, and Eleanor Singer. 2000. "The Effects of Response Rate on Changes in the Index of Consumer Sentiment." *Public Opinion Quarterly* 64: 413–28.

Fuller, Wayne A. 1987. *Measurement Error Models*. New York: John Wiley and Sons.

Groves, Robert M. 1989. *Survey Errors and Survey Costs*. New York: John Wiley and Sons.

Groves, Robert M. and Mick P. Couper. 1998. *Nonresponse in Household Interview Surveys*. New York: John Wiley and Sons.

Heeringa, Steven G. and Jinyun Liu. 1997. "Complex Sample Design Effects and Inference for Mental Health Survey Data." *International Journal of Methods in Psychiatric Research* 7(1): 221–30.

Inglehart, Ronald, Miguel Basáñez, Jaime Díez-Medrano, Loek Halman, and Ruud Luijkx (eds.). 2004. *Human Beliefs and Values: A Cross-Cultural Sourcebook based on the 1999–2001 Values Surveys*. Mexico City: Siglo XXI.

Keeter, Scott, Carolyn Miller, Andrew Kohut, Robert M. Groves, and Stanley Presser. 2000. "Consequences of Reducing Nonresponse in a National Telephone Survey." *Public Opinion Quarterly* 64: 125–48.

Kish, Leslie. 1965. *Survey Sampling*. New York: John Wiley and Sons.

———. 1988. "Multi-Purpose Sample Designs." *Survey Methodology* 14(1): 19–32.

Lessler, Judith T. and William D. Kalsbeek. 1992. *Nonsampling Errors in Surveys* New York: John Wiley and Sons.

Little, Roderick J.A. and Donald B. Rubin. 2002. *Statistical Analysis with Missing Data, 2nd Edition*. New York: John Wiley and Sons.

Neyman, Jerzy. 1934. "On Two Different Aspects of the Representative Method." *Journal of the Royal Statistical Society* 97: 558–625.

Valliant, Richard, Alan H. Dorfman, and Richard M. Royall. 2000. *Finite Population Sampling and Inference: A Prediction Approach*. New York: John Wiley and Sons.

INDEX

traditional/secular-rational values, 52,
54
Economic attitudes
in Algeria, 141–2, 143, 145
in Bangladesh, 141–2, 143, 145
association with democracy attitudes,
113
determinants of, 144–51
in Egypt, 141–2, 143, 145, 267, 271–2,
274, 275–7
in Indonesia, 141–2, 143, 145
in Islam, 127–8, 152
association with Islamic law attitudes,
139, 140–2, 152
in Jordan, 141–2, 143, 146
laissez-faire individualism, 128, 130,
132, 133, 152
modernists, 127–8, 133, 152–3
moral cosmology's impact, 129, 152
in Morocco, 267, 271–2, 274, 275,
277
orthodoxy, 127–8, 133, 152–3
in Pakistan, 141–2, 143, 145
in Saudi Arabia, 141–2, 143, 146
standard of living, 135–6
survey questions, 266–7, 111, 140
see also under moral cosmology; see also
under communitarianism
Economic communitarianism, see under
communitarianism
Economic development
interaction with cultural heritage,
30–2
in a democracy, 40, 50, 107
in Jordan, 203
migration, 72
modernization theory, 30
population growth, 188
in Saudi Arabia, 211–12
differences between societies, 25, 33–4,
45, 59
traditional/secular-rational values, 29
value change, 7–9
xenophobia attitudes, 313–14

Economic egalitarianism, see under moral
cosmology; see also under
communitarianism
Economic hardships, and xenophobia, 20
Economic inequality, see Gini coefficient
Economic justice, see under moral
cosmology; see also under
communitarianism
Economic morality, see socioeconomic
morality
Economic security
as a survival/self-expression values, 28,
40
xenophobia, 301–2, 313–14, 315
Economies, and Islam, 126–7
see also under rentier states
Education levels
as an indicator of cognitive ability, 13,
270
association with communitarianism,
137, 144–6, 148–9
association with control, 184–5, 198
association with democracy attitudes,
19, 121, 237–8, 240
association with democracy
development, 162
association with effects of events, 270,
287–8
as a determinant of political awareness,
13, 270
association with gender, 19, 38–9, 243,
305
association with happiness, 195–6, 202
association with health, 183, 184, 187,
193, 201
association with polygamy attitudes,
229–30
association with religiosity, 19
association with religious behavior,
227–8, 240
association with value differences, 13
interaction with 9/11 and attitude
change, 270, 276, 277–8, 280–2,
284–5, 287–8

Health ratings
determinants of, 18–19, 181–2, 204
association with education levels (see
also specific countries, e.g., Iran:
and health), 201
equality among sub-groups, 183
generational differences, 200
association with levels of happiness,
185–7, 199–200, 204–5
association with perceived control,
199–200, 204–5
association with religiosity, 186–7
self-reporting, 182–3
survey questions, 189–90
Heuristics in reasoning, 10
Hijaz, Saudi Arabia, 210–11
Homeopathic democracy, 262
Homosexuality attitudes
association with moral cosmology, 152
points of caution in studies, 14, 233
as survival/self-expression values, 28–9,
39
tolerance of among different societies,
37–8
see also under xenophobia attitudes
Human Development Index (HDI)
ratings, 52, 138, 140–1
Human development, process of, 51
Hunter, James D., 129, 156
Huntington, Samuel P., 30, 52, 105
Hussein, Saddam, 311–12

Ibadat (acts of worship), 132
Identity incorporation, definition of, 74
Ideological production, 252–3
Ijtihad (independent reasoning), 132, 133,
156
Ikhwan tribal warriors, 210–11
Immigrants
attitudes towards, 61
Muslim ethnic enclave, 72, 81
Europeanized Muslims, 72
illegal and underground Muslims, 73
living in Europe, 71, 72
Muslim professionals and
intellectuals, 73

religious values, 75
resulting communities, 73
in Spain, 65
value differences, 17, 65
Immigration, 72–3
asylum, 72
policies, 72
underground migration, 72
value change, 78–9
Income levels
association with communitarianism
attitudes, 151
association with democracy attitudes,
121, 239–40, 243
determinants of, 15, 161, 240
differing values across societies, 29–30,
32–4, 314
association with gender role attitudes,
230
association with happiness ratings, 193,
195–6, 202–3
association with health ratings, 193,
195–6
inequality, 243
association with perceived control,
193, 195, 198, 202–3
association with polygamy attitudes,
230
association with religious behavior,
226–8, 241
association with xenophobia attitudes,
314
see also under rentier states; *see also under*
economic development; *see also*
communitarianism
Index of dissimilarity, *see* dissimilarity
index
India
colonization, 72
Islamic modernism, 253
Muslim immigrants, 84
Indonesia
colonization, 72
communitarianism attitudes, 142–7
economic statistics, 164
fuel exports, 164

Breinigsville, PA USA
12 December 2009
229105BV00001B/2/P